Also by Colman Andrews

Flavors of the Riviera
Everything on the Table
Best Restaurants/Los Angeles

CATALAN CUISINE

CATALAN CUISINE

VIVID FLAVORS FROM SPAIN'S MEDITERRANEAN COAST

COLMAN ANDREWS

The Harvard Common Press
Boston, Massachusetts

For Leslie,
malgrat tot

The Harvard Common Press
535 Albany Street
Boston, Massachusetts 02118
www.harvardcommonpress.com

First Harvard Common Press edition 1999

Printed in the United States of America
Printed on acid-free paper

The Library of Congress has cataloged the earlier printing as follows:

Library of Congress Cataloging-in-Publication Data
Andrews, Colman.
    Catalan cuisine : Europe's last great culinary secret / Colman Andrews.
        p. cm.
    Originally published: New York: Macmillan, 1988.
    Includes bibliographical references and index.
    ISBN 1-55832-154-3 (pbk.)
        1. Cookery, Spanish—Catalonian style. 1. Title.
TX723.5.S7A62 1999   99-17178
641.5946'7—dc21   CIP

ISBN-13: 978-1-55832-329-2
ISBN-10: 1-55832-329-5

Special bulk-order discounts are available on this and other Harvard Common Press books.
Companies and organizations may purchase books for premiums or resale, or may arrange a custom
edition, by contacting the Marketing Director at the address above.

10 9 8 7 6 5 4 3 2

CONTENTS

CONTENTS

PREFACE TO THE 1999 EDITION

Between 1984 and 1987, I spent more than a year's worth of months in the region of Catalonia, in northeastern Spain, and in the culturally related *països catalans,* or Catalan lands—the Valencia region, the Balearic Islands, Andorra, the region of Roussillon in southern France, and the town of Alghero in Sardinia. Most of my research and recipe-gathering for this book was done during that period. Since that time, there have been many changes in the Catalan gastronomic landscape. Barcelona, Catalonia's enchanting capital, was dramatically transformed both physically and in spirit by the large-scale urban redesign projects that preceded the 1992 Olympic Games there. In the process, the city opened itself up for the first time in recent memory to the waterfront and the sea beyond, becoming more noticeably "Mediterranean" as a result, and also losing some of its best and most definitively Catalan (but inland-style) restaurants, including several that were essential to the preparation of this book. Other noteworthy restaurants elsewhere in the Catalan-speaking world have closed, or changed ownership or philosophy, in the past decade, and several important chefs and food writers have died. Because the contributions of these people and places remains vital—and to avoid turning the following pages into a kind of gastronomic necrology—I have left their names intact in this edition and the book remains a record of their signal contributions.

When *Catalan Cuisine* was first published, the region it covers and the dishes it describes were all but unknown in the United States. (More than one reviewer wrote that the book was about a place called "Catalan," perhaps thinking "Cataland.") Today, there are more than a dozen restaurants in the U.S. that claim to be Catalan; at least two, a contemporary Mediterranean restaurant in New York City and an elegant hotel dining room in Arizona, seem to have been directly inspired by this book. In addition, basic elements of the Catalan repertoire, such as allioli (garlic sauce), romesco (a sauce based on chiles and ground nuts), calçots (grilled giant spring onions, served with a kind of romesco), pa amb tomàquet (which might be called the Catalan bruschetta), and various preparations of salt cod, now turn up with some frequency on menus at non-Catalan restaurants around this country and have added interesting new accents to the American culinary vocabulary.

As gratifying as these developments are, and as pleased as I am to bear, perhaps, some small responsibility for them, I don't think the unique and immensely varied cooking of Catalonia and its neighbors has yet been fully understood here. I think there's a lot of this "undiscovered" cuisine still to be discovered, and I continue to believe that it's very much worth discovering. I hope that this new edition of *Catalan Cuisine* will continue to play a part in introducing this wonderful food, along with the people who cook it and the places from which it comes, to all those who love the real flavors of the Mediterranean.

ACKNOWLEDGMENTS

A book of this kind—a mix of history, anecdote, observation, and culinary formulas—is by definition not so much written as it is compiled, and I must sincerely thank all those who have helped me so generously and enthusiastically in my job of compilation—inviting me into their homes (and kitchens), sharing recipes and lore with me, answering my many questions (and sometimes posing better ones on my behalf), and in general making my work both easier and more happily complex.

Most of all, I must express my gratitude to Jean Leon, of Beverly Hills and Pla del Penedès, restaurateur and winegrower, who gave me summer quarters in the middle of his vineyards and whose introductions seemed to open Barcelona to me—and certainly brought me many good new friends and able teachers; to Agustí and Lluïsa Jausàs, serious connoisseurs and perfect hosts, who became nothing less than my guardian angels in Barcelona (and whose splendid little private library of food and wine books, incidentally, gave me access to many treasures I might not otherwise have found); to Luís Tellechea, another gracious host and guardian, who was my first guide to the Costa Brava and the Vall d'Aran and my best guide, over many a bottle and many a meal, to the wines of Catalonia; to Luís Bettónica, who patiently explained the basics to me and pointed me in all the right directions; to Jaume Subirós of the Hotel Ampurdán in Figueres, who gave me his time and his best recipes (and those of his illustrious father-in-law, the late Josep Mercader) without demur, and who helped me get so many details right; and to Linda Zimmerman in Los Angeles, who went to great lengths to find out how the Catalans cook and why, and then not just to *test* most of the recipes herein but to question, adapt, improve, and sometimes all but reinvent them, and to give them coherent form.

Others whose help was indispensable to me include Llorenç Torrado (the Baedeker of La Boqueria), Anna Solé (who taught me more Catalan than she realizes), Pascual Iranzo, Manuel Pagès, Nèstor and Tin Luján, Climent Maynés and Gloria Blanco, Lluís and Lola Cruanyas, and the late Ramon Cabau, all in Barcelona; Carles Camós, Joaquim Vich, José R. Gispert, and Rossend Colomé and Pau Carbó (the bakers of Pla del Penedès), in various other corners of Catalonia; Bernard and Sabine Dauré and Eliane Thibaut-Comelade in the Roussillon; Llorenç and Fusca Millo in Valencia; Pablo Llull, Bartolomé Esteva, and Jaime Mesquida on the island of Majorca; Ugo Saccardi and Moreno Cecchini in Alghe-

ACKNOWLEDGMENTS

ro; Alan Davidson of World's End, London; and especially Paula Wolfert in New York, who offered much wise counsel and confided some of her best kitchen secrets, and Charles Perry in Los Angeles, who granted me constant access, at the ring of a telephone, to his encyclopedic knowledge of both language and food history.

My thanks are due as well, for both recipes and advice, to scores of chefs and restaurateurs in Catalonia, the Roussillon, Valencia and its region, and the Balearic Islands (besides those mentioned above)—among them Josep Julià, Rosa Grau and Javier García-Ruano, Reynaldo and Juli Serrat, Antonio Ferrer, Josep Esteve, Ramon Parellada, Joan Figueres, Francina Magrané, Jaume and Josep Font, Josep Maria and Maria-Dolores Boix, Carles Llavià, Joaquim Sanals Pi, Paquita and Lolita Reixach, Josep Maria Morell, Maria-Teresa Cornet and Ramon Lluís, Angela Aunos Paba and Rosa Paba Jacquet, Emilio Sanllehy Meya, Antonio and Josep Borrás, Antonio and Simón Tomás, Pascual Campos, Ely Buxeda and Jean-Marie Patrouix, and M. Arnaudies and Pierre Gironès.

And my thanks to Jordi Marquet, Pierre Torrès, Loretta Cervi, Darrell Corti, Montse Guillén, Marimar Torres, Emilio Nuñez, and Antoni Artigau, all of them invaluable sources of information and assistance . . .

to Manuel Raventós, Maria-Dolores Sanvisens, Isabel Monteagudo, Dorothy Faltín, Joan and Rosa-María Villanueva, Francesc Ribo and Angela Azpiroz, Ronald and Lori Calnan, Joan Domènech, "Charlie" Ristol, Gaspi and Tere Aznar, Emil Teixidor, Roberto Mazzella, Mario Consorte, Santiago Costa and María-Luisa Albacar of the Barcelona Tourist Board, Alvaro Renedo and Aurora Nuñez of the Tourist Office of Spain in Los Angeles and José-Luís Estevez of the New York branch, Michael Roberts, Juan José Alvarez, Roberto Hernandez, Pedro de Oleza, Jon Sheppod, Claude Segal, Mary Lyons, Stan Cox, Sr., John Stachowiak, the Tarragona Rotary Club, and the management and staff of the Hotel Colón in Barcelona (especially Elisio Gretz and Joan Domingo), for their many kindnesses great and small . . .

to Lluís Llach and Maria del Mar Bonet, whom I know only through their music, for having helped to set the scene so often . . .

to Joanna Krotz and Dorothy Kalins for letting me write about Catalan cuisine in the first place in *Metropolitan Home;* to Barbara Lowenstein and Susan Ginsburg for making it possible for me to expand that first article into the book at hand; to Judy Kern for the fine-tuning; and to Ann Finlayson for the very smart and thorough copy-editing . . .

and to Alice Waters, Jonathan Waxman, Bradley Ogden, Mark Miller, Lydia Shire, Ruth Reichl, and (again) Charles Perry, for that week in Barcelona.

Finally, I must thank the late Jaume Ciurana and his wife, Maria-Dolores, who were my first friends in Catalonia. Ciurana, who knew Catalan gastronomy—Catalan *everything*—immensely well, and who literally wrote the book on the region's wines and olive oils, was kind enough to take an interest in my project and to help me in every way he could. I hope that he would not have been disappointed in the result.

Any errors, misinterpretations, mistranslations, or indefensible oversimplifications in the pages that follow are my own, of course, and occur despite the best efforts of those named above.

A NOTE ON SPELLING AND USAGE

Many personal and place names in Catalan-speaking regions have both Catalan and Castilian (i.e., "Spanish") forms—or, in the Roussillon, Catalan and *French* ones. Sometimes the differences between the two are minor. In Catalan, for instance, one might visit the resort town of Roses in the province of Girona, while in Castilian it would be Rosas in the province of Gerona; the Castilian "Luís" merely picks up an extra "l" to become "Lluís" in Catalan, "Juan" softens into "Joan" (pronounced *zhwan*), and "Miguel"—a typesetter's nightmare—shifts subtly to "Miquel." In other cases, though, the Castilian and the Catalan diverge rather more substantially. The island of Ibiza, for example, is known in the latter language as "Eivissa" (pronounced about the same, but very different to the eye), "Pedro" turns into "Pere," and "Pablo" becomes "Pau" (which, nicely enough, also means "peace").

Matters are further complicated by the fact that maps and regional road signs might be in either language, or in both, and that many Catalan speakers use the two forms of their first name more or less interchangeably, depending on the circumstance—and, of course, on the language in which they're speaking or writing at the time. The Lluís Cruanyas mentioned in the preceding acknowledgments, for instance, is sometimes just plain Luís (though Lluís Llach is always Lluís Llach).

I've tried to solve the problem with personal names by using, insofar as possible, whichever form seems to be favored by the owner of said name—though, frankly, I'm not sure I've always got it right. With geographical names in Spain, I have employed the Catalan form over the Castilian in most cases, both out of what I suppose might be called cultural courtesy (the public use of Catalan, forbidden here for so long, is today something of a point of pride among the local citizenry) and simply because that's the form in which I came to know most of these names in the first place and thus the form in which I automatically think of them. In France, on the other hand, I have left names in French ("Perpignan" rather than the Catalan "Perpinyà," for instance), because Catalan forms are little honored on the Gallic side of the border. And in speaking of places well-known outside the area—Ibiza, say, or for that matter Catalonia (which the Catalans call "Catalunya") itself—I have used the accepted English spelling of the name, or what I believe to be the most universally recognizable version of it. When I think that this admittedly inconsistent system might cause confusion, I have noted an alternative form in parenthesis.

Personal names present a further complication. In both Catalan and Castilian, a man formally bears two last names, his father's and his mother's (in that order), either joined together by a conjunction—*i* in the former language, *y* in the latter—or simply following one another; women take the last names of *their* father and mother in the same way, and traditionally do not adopt their husband's last name(s) upon marriage. For simplicity's sake, I have taken the liberty of rendering most of the names herein in the usual Anglo-Saxon fashion, dropping the maternal name—unless patronymic and matronymic are hyphenated or the bearer is widely known by both as in the case, for instance, of author/politician Manuel Vázquez Montalbán)—and giving wives their husband's (father's) name. When married women use a name other than their spouse's professionally, I have abided by that usage.

In my bibliography, of course, I have recorded each name exactly as it appears in the cited book itself—despite the plurality of forms this practice has occasionally yielded.

Names of dishes are given in Catalan or in the appropriate local dialect of same, with an English translation provided—when there *is* an English translation. (All translations in this volume are my own, incidentally, unless otherwise noted.) Catalan spelling has only recently been standardized, and in quoting from older sources and mentioning older book titles, I have let archaic or idiosyncratic spellings stand. In other cases, I have taken as my ultimate authority Pompeu Fabra's classic *Diccionari general de la llengua catalana*.

I have used the admittedly inexact terms "Moor" and "Arab" frequently herein— "Moor" (and "Moorish") to refer to the eighth century Islamic conquerers of Spain and their direct descendants, and "Arab" (and "Arabic") to refer, more or less, to preconquest cultural and linguistic matters. (The Moorish conquerers, thus, brought Arab influences into Catalan kitchens.) And I have used the term "Catalan" to refer to persons, places, and things that are culturally and/or linguistically Catalan, and the term "Catalonian" to pertain specifically to the region of Catalonia itself.

AUTHOR'S NOTE

I first ate something approximating Catalan cuisine in the early 1970s. The late Jock Livingston and his wife Micaela, who were then co-owners of the Studio Grill in Hollywood (with current sole proprietor Ardison Phillips) and who had traveled in Catalonia, used to offer, at their establishment, a delicious, complicated fish stew which they called *zarzuela a la Port Lligat.* Now, based on what I have since learned, I doubt sincerely that *zarzuela* (*sarsuela* in Catalan)—which literally means a kind of light opera or variety show and which in the food sense is an elaborate, touristy sort of neobouillabaisse found mostly in pricey restaurants—has ever, in fact, been served in the tiny Costa Brava cove of Portlligat (current home of the great Catalan surrealist Dalí, incidentally). But it *is* a genuine Catalan invention, and the vivid flavors of the dish as it was made in Hollywood back then, introduced by some of the Grill's roasted red peppers with anchovies and followed by one of Micaela's perfect flans, gave me—long before I realized it—what turned out to be a surprisingly accurate idea of what the food of Catalonia is really like.

I first *went* to Catalonia—which, in the narrowest sense, is the northeasternmost administrative region of contemporary Spain,

abutting the French border on the Mediterranean coast—in 1985. One of the books I consulted in preparation for my trip was British author Jan Read's tiny *Simon & Schuster Pocket Guide to Spanish Wines*—which includes brief notes on Spain's regional gastronomy. In his chapter on Catalonia, Read recommends, among other eating places, the dining room of the Motel (now Hotel) Ampurdán in Figueres, describing it as a "highly sophisticated restaurant started by Josep Mercader, founder of the new Catalan cuisine." These few words were, in a sense, directly responsible for the existence of the volume at hand.

My interest in other Mediterranean cuisines had by this time taught me, inter alia, that the cuisine of Catalonia had ancient roots and was still full of undisguised references to the cooking of medieval times and even to that of the Romans, who had once occupied this part of Spain—and thus the notion that there might be a *new* Catalan culinary idiom, presumably inspired at least in part by the traditions of the distant past, fascinated me. I thought it might make a very good story, in fact, and knowing nothing more about it than what Read had so offhandedly betrayed, I talked myself into an assignment on the subject for the magazine called *Metropolitan Home.* The resulting article, based on that first brief trip of mine to the region, led to a book proposal on Catalan cuisine in general, to the better part of two years spent back in Catalonia and vicinity, and finally to this book itself.

"Catalunya, com té una llengua, un dret, uns costums, una història pròpia i un ideal politic, té una cuina. Hi ha regions, nacionalitats, pobles que tenen un plat especial, caracteristic, però no una cuina. Catalunya la té, i té més encara: té un gran poder d'assimilació de plats d'altres cuines com la francesa i la italiana: fa seus els plats d'aquelles cuines i els modifica segons el seu estil i el seu gust. . . . La cuina catalana és, essencialment, senzilla; no és cara i és fàcil."

"Catalonia, just as it has a language, law, customs, its own history, and a political ideal, has a cuisine. There are regions, nationalities, peoples which have a special, characteristic dish without having a cuisine. Catalonia does have one, and it has something else besides: a great power to assimilate the dishes of other cuisines, like the French and the Italian, making them its own and modifying them according to its own style and taste. . . . Catalan cuisine is essentially natural; it is not expensive, and it is easy."

—Ferran Agulló
Llibre de la cuina catalana

"A la taula i al llit, al primer crit."

"To the table and to bed at first cry."
　　　　　　　　　　—Catalan proverb

CATALAN CUISINE

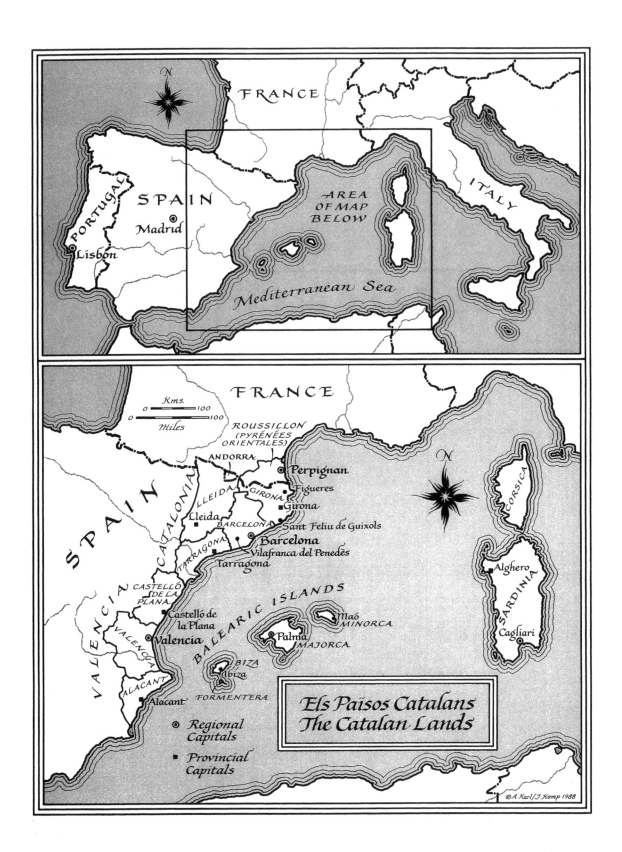

Els Països Catalans
The Catalan Lands

Regional Capitals
Provincial Capitals

INTRODUCTION

I. WHAT IS CATALAN CUISINE?

Catalan cuisine is a caldron full of prawns and monkfish simmering in rich broth on a butane stove in the galley of a fishing boat off the Costa Brava port of Palamós; it's a brace of rabbits roasting on an open fire beside a slate-roofed fieldstone farmhouse in the eastern Pyrénées while a silent grandmother with a strong right arm beats olive oil and garlic into a thick, emphatic sauce; it's an elegant salad of white beans, celery leaves, and marinated salt cod posed on a cool black plate in a restaurant dining room in Barcelona. It's also anchovies, foie gras, pigs' feet, and snails, grilled green onions dipped in spicy nut sauce, pigeon breast infused with vinegar and herbs, eggplant and peppers baked in ashes, veal braised with mushrooms, duck stewed with pears, paella, potato omelets, custard glazed with burnt sugar, fresh green figs drizzled with anisette, toasted hazelnuts still warm from the oven. . . .

It is, to put it another way, the cooking (and the simple, uncooked food) of the region

of Catalonia in northeastern Spain—and, by extension, of the historically and linguistically related *"països catalans"* or "Catalan lands" that more or less surround it: Valencia and its provinces to the south; the mountain suzerainty of Andorra and the French region of the Roussillon to the north; the Balearic Islands of Formentera, Ibiza, Minorca, and Majorca to the east; and even, anachronistically, the city of Alghero (l'Alguer in Catalan), still further east on the Italian island of Sardinia. (It should be noted that the idea of grouping all these places together as *"els països catalans"* is a specifically Catalonian and/or Catalanist conceit, and is not universally honored in the regions in question. Valencia and the Balearics tend to object particularly vociferously to being called "Catalan," both pointing out quite correctly that they have plenty of non-Catalan history and culture of their own. But the "Catalan lands" do all *speak* Catalan, or a dialect of it, and—more to the point for present purposes— they do all share a common culinary heritage and many present-day dishes and cooking methods, whether they like it or not, or are even aware of it.)

In one sense, Catalan cuisine is Spanish, being prepared and consumed today primarily in Spain. (The Catalan cooking of Andorra, the Roussillon, and Alghero, alas, is rather rare.) In philosophy and origin, though, it has relatively little to do with the predominately Castilian culture that has given Spain its popular identity for the past 400 years or so. Like Catalonia itself, Catalan cuisine looks outward, toward Europe and the Mediterranean, rather than back into the Iberian interior. Anyway, it's a real cuisine, distinct and elaborate in a way that the cooking of, say, Castile, Andalusia, and Extremadura are not. It's more than just a collection of regional dishes or a culinary dialect, that is. It's a complex and sophisticated system of recipes and techniques, first codified as early as the fourteenth century. It was born out of the cooking of the Romans, who occupied the area for almost 700 years (until A.D. 476), and was enriched in later centuries by invading Visigoths and, more importantly, Moors, and still later by French and Italian merchants and immigrant restaurateurs.

Despite its ancient origins, however, and despite the fact that it remains probably closer to its medieval roots than any other modern Western European culinary idiom, Catalan cuisine is based on ingredients that are for the most part familiar and well-liked in America today: onions, peppers, eggplant, tomatoes, garlic, olive oil, and fresh herbs (especially parsley, which goes by the pretty name of *julivert* in Catalan); fresh fish and shellfish of many kinds; rice, eggs, pasta, wild mushrooms, wild game, duck and goose, chicken, veal and pork (including a wide variety of sausages); apples and pears; almonds, hazelnuts, and pine nuts; chick-peas, favas, lentils, red and white beans, and black-eyed peas; cinnamon and chocolate; bread and wine. . . .

What Catalan cuisine does with such materials, on the other hand, is sometimes not what we'd expect at all. Those nuts, for instance, are often pulverized and used to flavor and thicken sauces; cinnamon and chocolate appear in savory dishes as well as sweet ones; poultry might be cooked with fruit, and both meat and vegetables can function as dessert—pork sausage with lemon juice and sugar, say, or deep-fried eggplant pieces dipped in honey. Unusual matings of ingredients abound: rabbit with snails, salt cod with raisins, chicken with shrimp, squid stuffed with pork, and so on. Some dishes are as ingenuous as *Pa amb Tomà-quet*—dry bread or toast rubbed with fresh tomato and seasoned with olive oil and salt; others, like the Empordà (Ampurdán) region's legendary *es niu* ("the nest"), a casserole of game birds, unlikely seafood, meatballs, and potatoes, moistened with garlic sauce, verge positively on the baroque.

I came to Catalan cuisine as a novice, an outsider—and immediately fell in love with it. I was taken by its freshness and vitality, haunted by its resonances of the past, thrilled by its forthright, vivid flavors. But I think what fascinated me most of all about it, and what seemed to define it best, was precisely its unexpectedness, its surprising way of doing unfamiliar things with familiar raw materials—its tricks and twists, its top spin. It's an accessible cuisine to us, I think, but at the same time an exotic and mysterious one. We can enjoy it almost intuitively, but we don't *know* it—and that, to me at least, gives it great appeal. It's like a delicious secret in a language we almost understand—a secret begging to be told. It is also, I think, Europe's last great undiscovered cuisine.

II. SOME NOTES OF A PRACTICAL NATURE

The people of the *països catalans* are intensely chauvinistic about their culinary raw materials. "Our fish is obviously the best in the Medi-terranean," a resident of the Costa Brava will announce. "You probably can't make this dish anywhere but here," a Minorcan restaurateur will warn, "because where else will you find eggplant like this?" Even the water is special. It

is well-known, for instance, that true paella can be made only in and around Valencia—because only there does the H$_2$O have exactly the right mineral content. These matters are not open to debate; they are local gospel.

We can't exactly reproduce the raw materials of this far-off region in America, of course—but we can and should pay special attention, in cooking Catalan cuisine, to the quality of the products we start with. Whenever possible, we should seek out the most perfect garden tomatoes, the ripest and most flavorful pears, the freshest shrimp and monkfish, the youngest and most tender veal. Catalan dishes are often very simple, unelaborated, without a lot of seasoning—and if they're made with mediocre products, they just won't taste like very much. If they're made with the best you can obtain, on the other hand—and if you put off trying certain dishes until the raw materials they require are at their seasonal peak—they can be stunningly good.

Individual chapters to follow will discuss specific products—fish, sausages, wild mushrooms, etc.—and recommend substitutions when appropriate. In the meantime, though, here are some notes on a few basics:

Salt and pepper. Authentic Catalan food (like the food of most of Spain) is salty, period, and if your aim in cooking any of the specialties described in the present volume is to give some houseguest from the *països catalans* a taste of home, don't wield that saltshaker timidly. But for most of the rest of us, a less-than-authentic dose will probably suffice. Anyway, because salt tolerance is a highly subjective matter, I have usually, in the recipes that follow, simply recommended that you add salt to taste. I prefer coarse-grained salt (sea salt

or coarse kosher salt, for instance) to the granulated variety because the latter usually contains additives (to prevent caking) that can lend a bitter taste to dishes—and also, though this might just be my imagination, because it seems "saltier," and thus can be applied with a lighter hand.

In some recipes, I have specified black or white pepper. Where I have not, either may be used. Color aside, however, I think it's *very* important for the pepper to be freshly ground, always. The preground, powdery kind is about as exciting as canned peas in comparison.

Olive Oil. Spanish olive oil is good, and Catalan olive oil is *very* good—and even the best of it costs less than its French or Italian counterparts. I recommend it highly. But I further recommend that, wherever it might come from, you use a mild extra-virgin oil (not a dark green, pungent one) whenever possible in these recipes—not just for dressings and the like, but for frying and sautéing too. Extra-virgin oil tastes better, to begin with. More important, though, it has fewer impurities than the lower grades and thus doesn't smoke or burn as quickly—and it leaves food tasting "cleaner" as a result. It needn't be prohibitively expensive, either. The excellent Catalonian Verge de Borges brand, for instance, costs around $10 a liter in this country, and some non-Catalonian extra-virgins (Ybarra and Goya are among the best) are as little as half that. (See pages 115–118 for more on Catalonian olive oil.)

Lard. In that brief list, a few pages back, of culinary raw materials basic to the *països catalans*, I deliberately left one out—a material not only common but in fact essential to Catalan cooking. That material is rendered pork fat—lard. I left it out, I guess, because I didn't want to scare anyone away too soon. I know full well that few food words are so immediately unappetizing to the contemporary American cook (or diner). But one unique feature of Catalan cuisine is precisely its use of lard and olive oil, together, in the same dish—a practice I have not encountered in any other cooking idiom. And lard adds its own flavor to the mix—a *good* flavor—that olive oil and butter cannot imitate.

Author Nèstor Luján has written that "to think of Catalan cuisine solely as a cuisine of olive oil is [and I don't think this part needs translating] *una inexactitud i una ingratitud imperdonables.*" I agree—and thus, though I have reduced the quantity of lard (of all cooking fats, for that matter) traditionally called for in the following recipes, I have left *some* lard in wherever it's appropriate. It really does add an important dimension to this food, and I hope that you will not omit it.

Anyway, if it's any consolation, Paula Wolfert has pointed out in *The Cooking of South-West France* that lard actually contains far less cholesterol than butter—10 percent versus 22 percent. And lard, according to the U.S. Department of Agriculture's *Composition of Food* handbook, is only slightly higher in calories than olive oil, with 902 per 100 grams compared with oil's 884.

A Trick with Tomatoes. Apart from salads, almost every Catalan dish that includes tomatoes calls for them to be peeled, seeded, and chopped. There is a very easy way to minimize the labor this process usually involves—a method recommended by well-known Barcelona (and ex-New York) restaurateur Montse Guillén. Her method is simply to slice a whole unpeeled tomato in half horizontally,

squeeze out the seeds, and then grate the fruit on the large holes of a four-sided grater, flattening it out with the palm of your hand as you go—and of course stopping when the peel is about to reach the holes. The result is a sort of instant coarse puree, perfect for cooking.

Ingredients for Baking. Unless otherwise specified, the *flour* recommended for use in the following recipes is unbleached and presifted; the *instant flour* is Wondra brand. The *butter* is sweet (unsalted). The *eggs* are large (not extra large), and are always used at room temperature. And the *yeast* is Fleischmann's active dry yeast (in .6-ounce packages) or the equivalent.

Two Cooking Vessels. Some of the most famous dishes in Catalan cuisine are named after the pots or pans in which they're cooked—among them *tupí, caldereta, greixonera, olla,* and, best-known of all, paella. The paella (from the Latin word *patella,* a shallow pan—as in the "pan" of the kneecap) is a wide, flat metal dish with two ear-shaped handles. It is generally considered all but a necessity for the proper preparation of the great rice specialty that bears its name, and indeed its shape is perfect for making the dish—allowing for even evaporation of the cooking liquid and exposing a large quantity of rice to the surface of the pan, where it can form the so-called *socarrat,* a lightly burnt bottom crust much prized by paella aficionados. A pan 14 or 15 inches in diameter, the size most often found in the United States, is sufficient to make a paella for four to six people. (See pages 207–210 for more on paella.)

A paella (the pan) might be useful if you want to make a paella (the dish)—but another Catalan cooking vessel is so protean in its uses and abilities as to be almost essential to anyone who wants to develop a Catalan culinary repertoire. This is the cassola (*cazuela* in Castilian, both words deriving from the Arabic *qaṣʿah*, a kind of bowl). Deeper than a paella, with straighter, higher sides, the cassola is usually made of earthenware, with a glazed interior. In fact, such vessels have been well-known in America for years, but they usually end up as fruit bowls or mere decoration, which is a pity considering their culinary possibilities. The cassola distributes heat evenly and retains it well. Its glaze is the original nonstick surface (and cleans easily if something does adhere). It can be used both in the oven and on top of the stove, and it can travel straight from the kitchen to the table as a serving dish. In Catalan cooking, the cassola is widely used for rice dishes and fish stews (you can even make a perfectly good paella in it), but it also works well for soups, for almost any kind of meat, seafood, or poultry dish cooked in a sauce, and, in smaller sizes, for some desserts.

A cassola must be cured before using, though—which not all vendors of the item bother to tell you. There are several ways to go about this, but the method I was taught in Catalonia is this: Soak the cassola in water overnight, dry it thoroughly, then rub the unglazed portion of the *outside* with a peeled clove of raw garlic. Next, fill the vessel almost to the top with water (some add a half cup or so of vinegar) and bring it to a boil slowly over a gas flame—don't use a cassola on an electric burner—cooking it until the liquid is almost gone. Pour out what remains and dry the cassola again. It is now ready for use.

But never put hot liquids into a cold cassola or vice versa, and turn the flame up gradually when you use it on a burner. It will crack eventually—it *is* only earthenware, after all—but it will last for at least two or three years if handled properly. Both the paella and and cassola are sold at cookware stores and some Spanish and Hispanic markets. They cost a mere $10–$15 each. (A paella makes a good, if not very tight, cover for a cassola, by the way.)

Mortar and Pestle. The *morter* (mortar) and its inevitable companion the *mà de morter* ("hand of the mortar" or pestle) are also very useful in Catalan cooking. Whether or not you master the art of making *allioli* with them (see pages 29–31), they are virtually indispensable for obtaining the proper consistency for a *picada* (see pages 40–41)—that all-important paste that is the soul of so much Catalan cuisine. I recommend a mortar and pestle made of marble or heavy porcelain, with a bowl at least 6 inches in diameter.

III. THE BROWN FOOD PROBLEM

Catalan cuisine isn't very pretty sometimes. Like much traditional cooking around the world, it tends to be monochromatic, murky-looking *brown*. It is food made to be eaten, not admired from a few steps back. Its aim is not to seduce the jaded but to fill and please the hungry—and sometimes the very act of concentrating flavors to this end demands a smudging of the palette.

There are exceptions, of course. A paella can be beautifully arranged, accented handsomely with the greens and reds of its constituent vegetables; a *Truita de Pagès* (mixed-vegetable omelet, page 123) or a *Coca amb Recapte* (a pizzalike tart "with everything," page 193) can be riotously colorful; certain dishes at top Barcelona or Costa Brava restaurants—Eldorado Petit or Florián, say—can be as elegantly presented as any specialty of the nouvelle cuisine. But all those carmelized onions, melted-down tomatoes, and ground almonds, all that toasted saffron, sautéed parsley, and strong red wine that go into so many other Catalan dishes, separately or in combination, can make for pretty heavy going visually—however much they might add gastronomically.

I'm not quite sure what to do about this problem, other than to warn you about it in advance—and to note that Catalan cuisine is *not,* after all, Japanese or Californian or contemporary French, and shouldn't be expected to look like it. I might add, however, that—depending on the dish—a little thinly sliced tomato or hard-boiled egg, some strips of raw or lightly cooked bell pepper, or a sprinkling of chopped parsley can provide bright garnish without compromising Catalan identity.

IV. ABOUT THE RECIPES

Author Nèstor Luján has observed that the proverbial individualism of the Catalans is manifested even in their cooking, and that thus, "The same dishes admit an infinity of variations, not just locally but even from family to family." In choosing which dishes to include here in the first place, and then which variations of them to offer, I have been guided above all simply by my own tastes—having been unable to think of another standard, offhand, to whose imperatives I would be willing to sign my name. At the same time, though, I've tried hard to keep my choices "authentic," and have not intentionally employed unorthodox (or un-Catalan) ingredients or techniques in my representations of the great Catalan classics. On the other hand, some of the recipes herein are strictly contemporary—modernizations of old dishes or new inventions altogether—recipes that traditionalists might not recognize but that are no less Catalan, I would argue, just because they belong to our own age. (French cuisine didn't stop with Fernand Point, and Catalan cuisine doesn't stop with Ferran Agulló.) And I have included a small number of dishes that I must admit aren't really Catalan at all—but that are popular in the region nonetheless. For my purposes, ultimately (and to paraphrase Pete Seeger), if Catalans eat it, it must be Catalan cuisine—not exactly true, of course, but a useful convention on occasion.

The recipes themselves come from several different sources. Some are borrowed from earlier (often Catalan-language) books on the subject—beginning with the fifteenth-century *Libre del coch.* Others have been generously supplied, at my request, by some of the better restaurants of the *països catalans;* still others are of mixed parentage—reconstructions or syntheses, based on my own recollections of dishes, with help from assorted chefs and various published sources. And a very few of the recipes I've included are my own ideas—improvisations on a Catalan theme, if you will—

turned into workable formulas by recipe-tester Linda Zimmerman. I have, of course, assigned proper credit to the recipes I've used whenever possible—and have identified my own improvisations.

V. HOW THIS BOOK IS ORGANIZED

Most cookbooks, reasonably enough, group recipes according to their ingredients or place in the meal—appetizers, salads, fish dishes, and so on. The present volume is set up rather differently, in a manner that might seem somewhat capricious at first but that has its own logic (in there somewhere).

The first section is background—brief sketches of the *països catalans* themselves and a consideration of the people who inhabit them, the language they speak, and the food they cook (and have cooked over the centuries). The second section presents Catalan cuisine's four basic sauces—which are not exactly sauces at all, as will be seen. The third section is devoted to some of the most important raw materials (or classes of same) used in the cuisine—from *albergínies* (eggplant) to *"el porc"* (the pig, vital to this cooking)—and to some dishes, both essential and peripheral, that are made from them. (A few raw materials—onions, tomatoes, and garlic, for instance—are so ubiquitous in Catalan cuisine that they have been incorporated into the book as a whole instead of being confined to a single chapter.) The next section is concerned with specific dishes or genres of dishes (salads, *fideus* noodles, beef stews, etc.), arranged (at last) in more or less the familiar soup-to-nuts order, and concluding with recipes for a few alcoholic concoctions, a catchall miscellany of additional recipes, and a chapter of "Legends and Curiosities"—dishes which, for reasons that will become apparent, probably can't or won't be reproduced in the average American kitchen (but which bear describing anyway). Finally, there are a few pages on the wines of the *països catalans* and on restaurants in these parts, followed by several other appendices—including a note on food sources, a glossary, and a bibliography.

I hope this sort of apparent randomness of organization might actually help the reader get a better picture, faster, of what this food is all about—an impressionistic one rather than a scientific one, maybe, but no less accurate for that. This is a book to browse in, in other words. For those who want to use these pages simply to cook from, however, each chapter is cross-referenced to other dishes using the same basic ingredients, and there is a special index in which the usual cookbook groupings are observed.

PART ONE: WHERE, WHO, AND WHAT

I. CATALONIA AND ELS PAÏSOS CATALANS

Food is of and from a place; it needs a context to give it authenticity. A dish that comes from nowhere lacks weight, lacks resonance. Catalan cuisine comes from somewhere, to be sure: Catalonia and the related *països catalans*. But not everybody, I realize, knows exactly where (or what) those regions are—and thus a brief tour of the Catalan lands might be in order here.

Officially, then, Catalonia is the northeasternmost administrative region of Spain—just under 12,500 square miles of farmland, seacoast, and mountains extending from the Pyrénées and the French border in the north to the Cape of Tortosa in the south, and from Aragon in the west to the Mediterranean in the east. The region encompasses four provinces, Barcelona, Girona (Gerona), Lleida (Lérida), and Tarragona, each of them divided into a number of *comarques* (singular: *comarca*)—thirty-seven of them in all. A wide variety of terrain and climate (from alpine to continental) may be found here, and there are few European crops that are not grown, at least in token quantities.

In 1977, after the death of Franco, Catalonia was granted regional autonomy. It now has its own local government, the Generalitat—a descendant of the body of the same name established in the thirteenth century by the Corts Catalans or Catalan parliament (which, incidentally, predated England's by roughly a century). Catalonia has a population of over six million today, and is a wealthy region by Spanish standards, accounting for about 20 percent of the country's gross national product.

Barcelona, Catalonia's capital, is the largest city in Spain, and an important industrial center. It is also one of the most beautiful, elegant, and immediately engaging cities in Europe—offering visitors an embarrassment of attractions, including a well-preserved Gothic quarter, a wealth of turn-of-the-century Moderniste architecture (most notably that of native Catalonian Antoni Gaudí), a number of fine museums (among them one dedicated to Catalan artist Joan Miró and another to one-time Barcelona resident Pablo Picasso), the famous Ramblas (the tree-lined promenade leading down to the sea that is the main artery of

13

the city's highly animated street life), and a large population of very good restaurants. (The local restaurant association claims 1455 as its founding date!)

The province of Barcelona fans outward from the city, reaching up into the Pyrénées and down into Catalonia's best vineyard land (in the *comarques* of the Alt Penedès and Anoia, where most of Spain's *cava* or "champagne," among other good wines, is made).

Northeast of Barcelona province, abutting the French border, is the province of Girona—stretching to the edges of Andorra in the Pyrénées but best-known to the world for its Mediterranean Costa Brava or "Wild Coast." It is tempting to suggest that the only thing still feral about this overbuilt strip of shoreline is the traffic on its little highways on a summer evening, but in truth, its thickets of high-rise apartment buildings and hotels and its annual inundation by half-naked northern Europeans notwithstanding, the Costa Brava's great, wild, natural beauty somehow seems to keep shining through. Beyond the inevitable take-out chicken stands and burger bars, the area is also home to a high percentage of Catalonia's best and most serious restaurants.

Lleida is the only one of Catalonia's provinces without a seacoast. The *city* of Lleida is primarily an industrial center, but it is surrounded by flattish plains filled with prolific market gardens, and is near important orchard country and olive groves.

The pleasant city of Tarragona, in the province of the same name, was long the capital of Roman Spain, and is rich in ruins of the period. To the south, rice paddies and lagoons alternate with pretty resort towns along the province's Costa Dorada—which ends in the citrus groves of the plain of Alcanar. Inland is the Priorat, famous for its severe mountain landscapes, its attractive hill towns and monasteries, and its good, strong wines; and the Alt Camp, home of the remarkable culinary celebration called the *calçotada* (see pages 164–167).

Beyond these four provinces, in three directions, extend the rest of the *països catalans*. The usual formula for defining their boundaries is, "From Salses to Guardamar and from Fraga to l'Alguer." Salses is about ten miles north of Perpignan, well into France. Guardamar de Segura is south of Valencia, south even of Alicante (Alacant in Catalan), in the heart of the Spanish Levant. Fraga is in Aragon, just across the border from Lleida. L'Alguer (Alghero) is 300 miles or so from the Catalonian mainland, past the Balearics, on the northwest coast of Sardinia—an isolated reminder of the one-time breadth of Catalan power in the Mediterranean.

Most of French Catalonia today is in the *département* of the Pyrénées-Orientales—but the area is widely known under its old provincial name, the Roussillon (El Rosselló in Catalan). The region's capital is the handsome metropolis of Perpignan, considered to be the "second city" of Catalonia (after Barcelona). The Roussillon in general is an important agricultural area, with nearly 40,000 acres of orchards and vegetable farms, mostly in the Pyrenean foothills. It also produces good wines, constantly improving, both on the coast and in its haunting upland valleys, watched over by the remains of ancient Cathar castles.

The "suzerainty" (for want of a better term) of Andorra has been accessible by surfaced road from Spain only since 1913 and from France only since 1931—though it is administered jointly, and has been since 1278, by the bishopric of Urgell (in Spain) and the head of the French state. It has no taxes, no military service, and no constitution, and shares the postal services of both Spain and France. Andorra has long been famous, as both its legal and its geographical situation might suggest, as a smuggler's paradise. Today, it is also a major market for tax-free cigarettes, alcohol, perfume, and cameras. Little food is produced here, with tobacco being the main farm crop.

The *països valencià* or region of Valencia begins where official Catalonia leaves off in the south, and hugs the coastline down through the provinces of Castelló (Castillón) de la Plana, Valencia itself, and Alicante. This is the region, above all, of the *huertas* (*hortes* in Catalan), the intensely cultivated citrus orchards and flower and vegetable gardens that flood the countryside with thick waves of rich, dark green. Further inland, in drier zones, olives, carob, wine grapes, and the region's superb almonds are grown. (Xixona [Jijona], in the dramatic interior mountainscape of Alicante province, is the center of Spain's *turrón* or nougat industry.) Valencia itself is the second largest port in Spain and the third largest city. I find it a strange place, hard to get to know—but it has an undeniable and not at all unpleasant baroque flamboyance overall. South of Valencia, along the coast, is a vast marsh, full of rice fields, called La Albufera (from the Arabic *al-buhaira*, "the lake")—and it is thus not surprising that Valencia is noted for its rice dishes, one of which, paella, is certainly the most famous (if most frequently debased) representative of Spain's cooking in the world.

The Balearic Islands—Ibiza, Minorca, and Majorca being the main ones—are clustered close together roughly fifty miles off the Spanish coast. The three are so different from one another, though, that they might just as well be scattered all over the Mediterranean. Ibiza, a Phoenician port 3,000 years ago, is today best-known as a sort of bacchanalian summertime fantasyland, full of nude sunbathers, wealthy Euro-trash, and what are still referred to locally as "hippys"—all the usual colorful flotsam, that is, that traditionally rides the fair-weather currents of Mare Nostrum. But the island against which the bacchanalia is set is very pretty by itself, with its jagged, rocky coastline, its serious little mountains wooded in juniper and pine, its blindingly white houses with their tiny windows and flat roofs (always with a cistern on top to catch badly needed rainwater)—and there are some very good local culinary specialties, though they are rarely served in the island's restaurants.

Minorca was under British rule for most of the eighteenth century, and bears many traces of the occupation. It is said to be the only place in Spain with sash windows, for instance, and the only place with rocking chairs. The British also brought dairy herds to the island, and Minorca is famous today for its ice cream and cheese. It's a peculiar-looking island, rather claustrophobic somehow, with few vast open spaces and with low fieldstone walls everywhere, like veins pushed up through the skin of the land. Maybe partly for this reason, it remains relatively unspoiled, and is a popular resort for Spaniards—and of course for the British.

Majorca is the largest of the Balearics, nearly 2,000 square miles in area, with considerable variation in physical features—from

sandy coves to flat vineyard and orchard land to pine-covered hills and real mountains 5,000 feet or so above sea level. The capital, Palma de Mallorca, is a handsome, cosmopolitan city, facing a wide bay and watched over by a magnificent buttressed cathedral (partially restored by Gaudí) on a hill above the port. Majorca was an important wine-producing center in the eighteenth and early nineteenth centuries, and there are limited efforts now to revive the industry. Majorcan almonds are famous, as are the island's figs and tomatoes. Majorcan gastronomy, which has a long and fascinating history and boasts many extraordinary dishes, is, alas, today, as a Majorcan winemaker of my acquaintance puts it, "mostly a family matter."

The last little bit of *els països catalans* is the city of Alghero (l'Alguer in Catalan) on the Italian island of Sardinia—sometimes called Sardinia's "little Barcelona." Alghero was first occupied by Catalan-Aragonese forces in the mid-fourteenth century, and remained part of the Catalan-speaking empire for nearly 400 years. As a result, the city is full of Catalan-style houses, religious edifices, and fortifications, and some Catalan street names—Carrer del Forn, Plaça del Portal, etc.—are still used. The local citizenry even continued to speak Catalan (albeit in an archaic and somewhat Italian-flavored form) until recent years—though it is seldom heard on the streets today. Catalan culinary influence was strong throughout Sardinia, to the point that one expert on the island's customs has written that "Sardinian gastronomy in general is specifically Catalan." Recipes for several Algherese Catalan dishes appear in the pages that follow.

II. THE CATALANS AND THEIR LANGUAGE

If food is of and from a place, it is even more so of and from—and by—a people. And it is axiomatic, I think, that the more complex and colorful a people's history—and the more other races it has come into contact with—the richer and more varied its cuisine will be. (The English, a cynic might point out, are something of an anomaly in this regard.) And the history of the Catalans, needless to say, is nothing if not complex and colorful.

Not much is known about the Iberian tribes that originally inhabited the region, but it *is* known that there were Phocaean Greek settlements on the Catalan coast as early as the sixth century B.C., and that Carthaginians followed in the late fourth or early third century B.C. The first full-scale foreign occupation of the area began in 218 B.C., when Roman armies landed on the Catalan coast at the start of the bloody Second Punic War—whence, in time, they conquered the entire Iberian Peninsula, remaining in power there until A.D. 476.

In a sense, Rome made Catalonia; it *certainly* helped make Catalan gastronomy. Romans introduced the first large-scale plantings of olive trees and grapevines to the region, for instance, as well as techniques for the production of oil and wine—subsequently so important to the local table. They also brought leavened bread to Catalonia for the first time, as well as favas, chick-peas, lentils, and other such legumes—and quite possibly taught locals the art of curing ham. (Catalan ham, whatever its origins, enjoyed a high reputation in Rome itself.)

The Moors, who arrived in Spain in A.D. 711, had even greater influence on Catalan cuisine—even though they remained in Catalonia for a comparatively short time. To begin with, they brought with them or popularized such raw materials as rice, eggplant, almonds and hazelnuts, spinach, oranges, cane sugar, and saffron—all of them now essential to the region's cookery. They also installed (or greatly improved) systems of irrigation throughout the area (creating the lush *huertas* of Valencia, for instance), established basic local pastry styles, and left Catalonia and the Balearics with a taste for sweet-and-sour flavor combinations.

In the ninth century, a Cerdanyan nobleman with the unfortunate name of Guifré el Pilós or Wilfred the Shaggy founded the long-lived House of Barcelona, subsequently so important in Mediterranean affairs, and became the first to unite most of the surrounding territory under a single rule. Legend has it that he also spontaneously created Catalonia's heraldic symbol, the *senyera*—four red bars on a field of yellow—by drawing his bloody fingers across the golden shield of his ally, Charles the Bald, during a set-to with the Moors. It is at about this time, too, that the name "Catalonia" (in one form or another) first appeared. Its origins are uncertain, but it is sometimes said to have been a corruption of the term "Gothalaunia," "Land of the Goths"—a reference to the 250-year occupation of the region by Visigothic tribes before the coming of the Arabs.

One of Wilfred's descendants, Ramón Ber-

enguer IV, brought Catalonia and the neighboring kingdom of Aragon together by marrying Petronilla, the Aragonese queen—and from that time until both were subsumed into Castile in the fifteenth century, Aragon and Catalonia enjoyed a complicated, on-again off-again alliance that made them joint masters, at the height of their power, of most of the European Mediterranean—not just of Spain down through the Levant and part of France (including much of Provence), but also of Corsica, Sardinia, Sicily, a full half of the Italian boot, and even, for a time, a large chunk of Greece.

The thirteenth, fourteenth, and fifteenth centuries were Catalonia's Golden Age. It helped rule the Mediterranean not only politically but economically, and the port of Barcelona was said to have berthed a thousand ships at a time. Catalan literature flourished. The acclaimed Majorcan poet/philosopher (and pioneering novelist) Ramon Llull was active during this period, as was the great Catalan physician and author Arnau de Vilanova (Arnaud de Villeneuve)—who has been called "the first European nutritionist and dietician," and who is sometimes credited with having introduced the process of distilling alcohol into Europe from the Arab world.

It was in the midst of this literary flowering that the first Catalan gastronomic manuscripts appeared. In 1384, for instance, the Gironan priest Francesc Eiximenis discussed table manners, food service, and wine in one volume of his projected thirteen-part opus *Lo Crestià* ("The Christian"). Earlier, in 1331, the anonymous *Llibre del coc de la canonja de Tarragona* ("Cookbook of the Canon of Tarragona") had set down dietary rules and recommendations for ecclesiastics in the See of Tarragona and described common food products and dishes of the time. Earliest and most important of all, however, was the *Libre de Sent Soví* (or *Sensoví*), usually dated at 1324—one of the very first European cooking manuals, and one of the most influential, even outside Spain. Some of its recipes were reproduced almost exactly in the popular fifteenth-century Italian cookbooks *Libro di arte coquinaria* (whose author called Catalan chefs the world's best) and *Platina de honesta voluptate et valetudine*—and from there entered the European culinary mainstream. The meaning of the term "Sent Soví" is something of a mystery, as is the identity of the work's author (though evidence suggests that he might have been a Catalan chef to the English court), but the work is a fascinating one, demonstrating the extent of Moorish contributions to the region's kitchens, prescribing the use of numerous cooking utensils and techniques still commonly employed in Catalonia, and offering instructions for concocting dishes that with little adaptation could be—and sometimes are—produced and happily consumed today.

The other great Catalan culinary text of the Middle Ages—and the first that was a real printed book rather than a manuscript—was the *Libre del coch* ("Book of the Cook") ascribed to one Mestre Robert, sometimes also known as Robert or Rupert de Nola. (Again, the author's identity is something of a mystery.) The earliest known edition of the book was published in Barcelona in 1520, although some of its recipes refer to Lenten dietary restrictions that were abandoned in 1491—suggesting that it dates at least from that year. The *Libre del coch* is a much more "international" collection than the *Sent Soví*, and includes some dishes that are clearly Provençal or Italian, and even a few that apparently come from Istria or Dalmatia. Like its illustrious predecessor, however, it anticipates the spirit, and often the specific flavors, of more recent Catalan cuisine. Both volumes, incidentally, are much discussed in Catalan culinary circles today and have been extremely important to the contemporary revival of traditional cooking in the region.

Not much is known about Catalan cuisine in the seventeenth and eighteenth centuries (cookbooks from the period are virtually nonexistent), but its quality and complexity were quite probably curtailed. We do know, however, that, despite a dramatic decline in Catalan economic and political power during this era, trade between Barcelona and Italy continued, and that as early as the eighteenth century Italian restaurants began appearing in the Catalan capital (and Italian dishes in Catalan cuisine). Between 1640 and 1813, too, Catalonia was repeatedly annexed or invaded by the French, and there is bound to have been some culinary give-and-take as a result. Most important, however, it was during these years that the food products of the New World that were to revolutionize Mediterranean cooking so dramatically, including such sweet fruits of Columbus's explorations as squash, potatoes, peppers, and above all tomatoes—found a home in Catalonia and a conduit from there into much of the rest of Europe.

Catalonia was integrated into Spain once and for all in 1716 by the Spanish king, Philip V, who abolished most local laws and governmental functions and, in effect, dissolved what remained of a Catalan state. Ironically, though, in its death Catalonia was in a sense reborn.

Joined unequivocally to greater Spain for the first time in its history and forced by circumstance to produce and sell its wares as part of that nation, it suddenly found itself with access to a host of previously untapped world markets. Fledgling industry flourished, and there was a major agricultural revival. In the nineteenth century there was even a *"Renaixença"* or Renaissance of Catalan literature, sparked by the publication of Bonaventura Carles Aribau's poem *"La Pàtria"* in the periodical *El Vapor* in 1833—and the first more-or-less modern-day Catalan cookbook, the anonymous *La Cuynera catalana,* appeared in Barcelona as a part of this reflorescence in 1835.

Catalonia's history has been far from calmly rosy since that time, of course. Among other things, it backed the wrong (or at least the losing) side in the nineteenth-century Carlist Wars of succession and supported the Republican cause during the tragic Spanish Civil War—in both cases suffering further repression in the aftermath. But much has gone well for the region, too, and it has turned out to be a proud, exciting, successful part of modern Spain—still plagued by conflicts with the central government, to be sure, but also surprisingly independent of it, not only in its new regional autonomy but also in its spirit and its sense of cultural tradition.

One of the things that has kept Catalonia alive over the centuries, and *the* thing that most firmly links the *països catalans* together, is the Catalan language. Catalan is not, as it has often been described, a dialect of Spanish, nor is it, as one American travel writer suggested recently, "sort of a cross between Spanish and French." Its closest relatives are the *langue d'oc* tongues of southern France—Provençal, Gascon, and Occitan, among others—but it is a language of its own, as different from Castilian Spanish as Italian or Portuguese are.

Catalan is spoken today by roughly six million people in Spain, France, Andorra, and Alghero, and since 1975 has been one of Spain's four recognized national languages (the others being Castilian, Basque, and Galician). It is, as British author Basil Collier described it earlier in this century, "a language suited to vigorous and concise expression, possessing a rich vocabulary and well-endowed with racy turns of speech." During the Franco era, the public use of Catalan was at first forbidden altogether and later severely limited. Today, however, Catalan is everywhere in the region: on billboards, storefronts, and menus; on television and the radio; in all manner of public discourse. This gives Catalonia an unfamiliar, vaguely exotic air, almost as if it were some whole new country speaking an idiom previously unknown. This fact can confuse the traveler, it must be noted. He might well be in Spain, that is, but no measure of fluency in "Spanish" will prepare him for the fact that, here, *tancat* means "closed," *diumenge* means "Sunday," and *si us plau* means "please"—or that that *amanida* he just ordered is nothing but an *ensalada* in disguise.

Still, Catalan is not a particularly difficult language to become informally acquainted with, especially for anybody with a smattering of French or Italian (or, better yet, both), or even with some memory of high-school Latin. It is relatively easy to pronounce, too. For one thing, it lacks the sibilance and wealth of dental fricatives that can make Castilian speech sound like a blur of lisps and hisses. Contrary to popular opinion, for instance, the Catalan-speaking resident of Barcelona does *not* call the city "*Barth*-uh-lona"; instead, he pronounces it more or less as we would in English, with a soft *c*. (See pages 306–308 for notes on the pronunciation of Catalan names for specific food products and dishes.)

To avoid confusion in the pages that follow, incidentally, it should be noted that Catalan nouns often change form in the plural. Nouns ending in *a*, for instance, take the plural endings *es* or *ques* (*paella, paelles, comarca, comarques*); masculine nouns ending in certain consonants add *os* (*marisc, mariscos*), with those ending in *s* doubling that letter (*pastis, pastissos*); some nouns ending in vowels add *ns* (*vi, vins; canaló, canalons*). Occasionally, where I think a plural form might be particularly unrecognizable, I have indicated the singular form in parentheses.

III. HOW THE CATALANS EAT

It occurred to me one evening, after I had been in Catalonia for a couple of months, that not once in the region had I yet eaten any *tapas* (*tapes* in Catalan)—those little snacks and nibbles and tiny portions of grander dishes that are such a rage in America right now and that have for so long been such an integral part of Spanish life. I had seen *tapas* bars by the score, of course, especially in Barcelona—but I had

never seemed to have the time or the opportunity or even the impulse to visit one. Here in the very country of their birth (and subsequent elaboration), I realized, I had almost forgotten that *tapas* even existed—a curious state of affairs, to be sure. And then it dawned on me why: As a novice to Catalonia, I had asked locals to show me the gastronomic ropes, letting the diverse collection of Catalans I had met (and dined with) help shape my perceptions—not unreasonably, I think—of Catalan eating habits as a whole. And not once had any of these Catalans—regardless of age, profession, or income bracket—so much as mentioned *tapas*. It was as if the *tapas* bars I'd seen had been installed for someone else—for tourists, maybe, or for transplants from other parts of Spain. It was as if *tapas* had no relationship whatsoever to the Catalan diet.

Was this true? I asked a food-loving friend of mine, a Barcelona attorney. He smiled. "I'll tell you a story," he said. "Once I was in Málaga with some business associates—one from Madrid, two Andalusians, and another Catalan. We met in a bar one night and drank some beer and ate some *tapas* for about three hours. Then I said, 'Well, where shall we have dinner?' The non-Catalans were shocked. 'But we just *had* dinner,' they said. The other Catalan and I looked at one another and said, 'Well, *we* didn't.' And we went to a restaurant and ate something in the normal fashion. Our friends thought that was very funny. But that's the way we Catalans are. If we don't sit down at a real table for real food, we don't think we've been properly fed."

Tapas, in other words, aren't much more than a culinary footnote in Catalonia—an attractive gloss, maybe, but nothing very meaty in themselves. For that reason, though a number of the appetizers for which I offer recipes in the following pages can certainly function as *tapas*, I will devote no further space herein to the thing itself.

Catalans are serious about food. Their appetite—in gastronomy as in other matters—is built-in, as a couple of popular local proverbs or *refranys* suggest: *"Pecat de gola Déu el perdona"* goes the first, meaning "God pardons the sin of gluttony." The second counsels, *"Val més que faci mal que no pas que en quedi"*— "It's better that it makes you sick than that you don't eat it all." (Consider yourself warned by a third *refrany*, though: *"Mata més gent la taula que la guerra,"* or "The table kills more people than war does.") Accounts of the way people ate in Catalonia earlier in this century betray a trencherman mentality as well. Ferran Agulló noted in his *Llibre de la cuina catalana* ("Book of Catalan Cuisine"), published in 1933, that most Catalan city dwellers ate four meals a day—beginning with an *esmorzar* or breakfast of hot chocolate or coffee with milk, toast, assorted pastries, bread soup, leftover vegetables fried in oil, farmer's cheese, sardines (grilled or marinated), grilled herring with muscat grapes, and a variety of omelets. Even wine was frequently included in the morning meal, though Agulló doesn't mention it. Manuel Pagès, director of the Raïmat winery, has described to me the typical country breakfast of his own childhood in the Penedès, in approximately the same era of which Agulló wrote: "People started work in the fields at 5 A.M. or so, and between about 9 and 10:30 they would stop to eat. They had more or less the same thing every day: lamb cutlets, fried potatoes, fried eggs, fried beans, bread with tomato and oil or with honey or

marmalade, coffee with milk, and plenty of wine." He adds, "We didn't have much money, but we ate a lot."

As much as Catalans love to eat, however, they're serious about food in another way too. At least since the time of Francesc Eiximenis and Arnau de Vilanova, they have been concerned with the salutary effects of what they consume. Since the eighteenth century, cookbooks of the region have regularly included specific dishes for the ill and convalescent (borage soup and stewed peas with oil and pepper were among the restoratives prescribed by Fra Sever d'Olot, for instance, in his 1787 Gironan manuscript *Llibre de l'art de quynar*, "Book of the Art of Cooking"), and have even offered recipes for purely medicinal preparations—for example, a solution of white wine, olive oil, and powdered gold (!) to treat burns and hemorrhoids, found in a Majorcan work of the late nineteenth century. Another Majorcan cookbook, the anonymous *La Cuyna mallorquina* ("The Majorcan Kitchen"), published in 1886, approaches a contemporary sensibility with some of its advice on food and its consumption—noting, among other things, that roasted or boiled meat was much healthier than fried meat, that it was good to dine at the same hours every day to promote regularity, and that "If you sit down at the table without hunger and with a full stomach, you're asking for a colic." And one Joseph Cunill de Bosch (whose last name means "wild rabbit," incidentally) went so far, in his 1907-vintage *La Cuyna catalana* ("The Catalan Kitchen"), as to propose a formula in which good food, good health, and national achievement were inextricably associated. "Good cooks make good dishes," he wrote in part. "Good dishes are eaten with pleasure. Food eaten with pleasure . . . keeps you healthy . . . [which] means that your bodily functions are regular. Regular bodily functions make nations strong. Strong nations lead the pack, and eventually become masters of the world." A bad cook, by Cunill de Bosch's reasoning, then, is practically a traitor to his people—an idea, I must say, with which I have more than a little sympathy.

Catalonia has a long restaurant tradition. The first public eating places in the region of which we have any record are the *hostals* or inns of medieval times—particularly those of Barcelona, a city whose maritime importance gave it a large transient population. By the turn

of the seventeenth century, the city was full of wine and pastry shops as well, and even had its first real restaurants, the *fondes* (singular: *fonda*), complete with table settings and multicourse menus.

By the eighteenth century, at least two typical Barcelona dishes that remain extremely popular today were being served in these establishments—*Bacallà a la Llauna* (see page 80), which is salt cod cooked on a "tin" *(llauna)* with garlic and paprika, and *popets saltejats amb all i julivert*, or baby octopus sautéed with garlic and parsley. From this century, too, dates the oldest Barcelona restaurant still in operation, Can Culleretes, opened in 1786 as a café. Another ancient eating place still going strong is the Siete Puertas (Set Portes in Catalan), the "Seven Doors"—founded in 1840 and today more or less the La Coupole of Barcelona. Also in 1840 the first hotel/restaurant guide to the city appeared. As Barcelona restaurant critic Luís Bettónica has pointed out, by that time the metropolis had become "one of the capitals best supplied with public tables in all of Europe."

The most famous restaurants of the nineteenth century were the so-called *fondes de sisos* or "inns of the sixes"—named that because for six *quartos* (a *quarto* being three-hundredths of a peseta), one could eat one's fill of some hearty dish like *Cap i Pota* (stewed calf's head and foot; see page 113) or the *pot-au-feu*-like *Escudella i Carn d'Olla* (see page 231), with bread and wine included. Grander places—often run by French or Italian immigrants—began appearing a bit later, offering the more refined (and expensive) *sopar de duro* ("dinner of the *duro*," a five-peseta coin), typically consisting of a rice dish, a sauced dish of some kind, a fish course and then one of fowl, dessert, wine, coffee, and a good cigar—all presented, as another Barcelona restaurant critic, Carmen Casas, has put it, "with *ad hoc* service in surroundings that approached the luxurious." A number of dishes that are now considered the definitive classics of Catalan cuisine date from this era—among them *Sarsuela* (an elaborate fish stew, see page 221), *Canalons* (i.e., *Cannelloni*) *a la Barcelonesa* (see page 204), *Botifarra amb Mongetes* (Pork Sausage with White Beans, see page 110), *Fricandó* (Braised Veal with Wild Mushrooms, see page 243), *Faves a la Catalana* (Favas with Blood Sausage and Bacon, see page 105), *Samfaina* (the Catalan *ratatouille,* see page 42), and *Gall Dindi Farcit Nadelenc* (Stuffed Christmas Turkey, with nuts and dried fruit, see page 75).

In 1903, in his delightful *The Gourmet's Guide to Europe,* gentleman restaurant critic Lieutenant-Colonel Newnham-Davis called Barcelona "better off in the matter of restaurants than any town in Spain, the capital [i.e., Madrid] included." The establishments he went on to recommend, however—such legendary Barcelona "greats" as La Rabasada, Justin's, the Restaurant Colón (in the hotel of the same name), the Restaurant Français, the Maison Dorée, and so on—served few Catalan dishes, specializing instead in high-class traditional French fare along the lines of turbot with *sauce hollandaise* and *carré d'agneau Maintenon.*

Few of the grand old Barcelona restaurants survived the Civil War and the world war that followed it. The Colón, for instance, had become a "people's canteen" when the hotel that housed it was requisitioned as Communist Party headquarters in May of 1937—and, with

the hotel, was subsequently bombed and partially destroyed by *franquista* forces, and eventually torn down. (The Hotel Colón that stands today across the street from Barcelona's Gothic cathedral, comfortable and old-style though it may be, dates from the 1950s, and is related to the original in name only.) Other establishments lost their proprietors through reemigration, or simply fell victim to the depressed postwar economy. In more recent years, the most famous restaurant in the city, at least among visitors, was the informal, inexpensive Los Caracoles—a far cry from the continental elegance of old. (It is still in business, incidentally, but has lost its famous proprietor and much of its quality.)

The first real bright spot in contemporary Barcelona dining was an establishment called Agut d'Avignon, opened in 1962 by the late Ramon Cabau. (The Avignon in question, incidentally, wasn't the French city of the same name, but rather Barcelona's own nearby carrer Avinyó or Avignon Street—the same thoroughfare that lent its name to Picasso's landmark painting, *Les Demoiselles d'Avignon.*) Cabau knew and respected Catalan culinary tradition, and his food was often old-fashioned in appearance—but his sensibility was modern and his standards were extremely high, and his example inspired countless other restaurant professionals to use better ingredients and take more care with their cooking.

An ultimately even more influential revivification of Catalan cuisine, though, began not in Barcelona at all, but in the town of Figueres, near the French border—in the restaurant portion of a functional roadside hostelry called the Motel Ampurdán. The late Jaume Ciurana once told me that he thought the "new" Catalan cuisine was built on three elements, like the three legs of a stool: traditional Catalan country cooking, bourgeois Barcelona home cooking, and "creation"—the imagination of the region's younger chefs. (I suspect that the stool might in fact be of the four-legged variety, the added appendage being the strong influence of France's nouvelle cuisine, which crossed international borders in the 1970s faster than a jet-set smuggler—but that's another story.) In any case, the owner of the Motel (now *Hotel*) Ampurdán, a chef named Josep Mercader, was able significantly and successfully to integrate the old and the new, the urban and the rural, in Catalan cuisine in a way that brought it not only into the twentieth century, but also into a class of serious restaurants that had previously considered the only *real* cuisine to be French, or maybe Italian.

Josep Mercader i Brugués was born in Cadaqués, a pretty fishing-village-turned-resort-town on the Costa Brava, in 1926. The men in his family had traditionally been fishermen, but Mercader apparently decided at an early age to investigate the restaurant trade, and as a young man he began apprenticeships with several prominent local chefs—most notably Alfons Roger at the Hotel Miramar in Llança (Lansa), Joan Suner at the Hotel França in Portbou, and the legendary Pere Granollers, who had been head chef at the Hotel de Paris in Monte Carlo for twenty years and was now semiretired to Portbou's railway station restaurant. When Mercader felt it was time to strike out on his own, in 1961, he opened what he called a "motel"—in fact a three-story *hotel*— on the old pre-autoroute national road to France. He preferred the more modest name he said, because he saw his establishment primarily as a rest stop for automobile-borne travelers. And stop and rest and eat the travelers did. The

Motel Ampurdán was a success—and in 1969, Mercader opened a second place, a much more elaborate resort hotel on a cliff outside the seaside town of Roses (Rosas), called the Almadraba Park.

It was at about this time that Mercader started experimenting seriously in his Ampurdán kitchen. Until then, his food had been mostly French-influenced or "Spanish" in style, with some traditional Catalan dishes added. Now, however, he began to tinker with the latter, stripping them down a bit and then dressing them up. The result wasn't just some facile imitation of nouvelle cuisine; this was the real thing, sensible and highly professional—and based on clever small transformations rather than on jarring big juxtapositions. Two examples illustrate the basic idea: *Escalivada* (see page 169) is a Catalan classic, a simple dish of eggplant and red peppers (and sometimes onions and/or tomatoes) roasted over a wood fire or in a bed of hot embers, peeled, cut into strips, and then dressed with olive oil and sometimes minced garlic; Mercader prepared the vegetables in the usual way—and then turned them into a rich, smooth, rosy-pink mousse. *Crema Catalana* (see page 247) is the Catalan version of *crème brulée,* a creamy custard topped with a glassy sheet of carmelized sugar; again, Mercader made the dish in the conventional manner to begin with—but instead of serving it as it was, he fed it into an ice-cream maker and froze its flavors into new intensity. Both these dishes have since been widely copied throughout Catalonia, and even sometimes improved upon, as have scores of other Motel Ampurdán creations—Fava Salad with Fresh Mint (see page 106), Stuffed Eggplant with Anchovies (see page 48), cold shrimp mousse with cucumber *coulis*, grilled sole with tomato mousse-line, etc., etc. But Mercader would hardly have minded. He was a culinary pioneer, but he was also a deliberate inspiration to other chefs. He might genuinely be called the father of contemporary Catalan cuisine—and his sudden death in 1979, of heart failure, robbed Catalonia (and for that matter Spain) of one of its most important and productive citizens. Happily, Mercader's son-in-law, Jaume Subirós, carries on ably in his place—and the Hotel Ampurdán is still a must on any food-lover's Catalonian itinerary.

In tracing the recent history of Catalan cuisine, I have concentrated on restaurants and said very little about the survival and development of Catalan culinary traditions in the home. That's for two reasons: First of all because home cooking, by its very nature, is a private matter, hard to get at—and usually so idiosyncratic, so personal, as to be virtually useless as a source of generalization; and second because, well . . .

No living cuisine, however thoroughly codified, is frozen in time. Cuisines, like languages, must borrow, accommodate, change accents, lose and gain valuable vocabulary. And, though traditionalists in the matter might disagree, I believe that—in the absence of old-style court patronage—cuisines today are most likely to undergo these processes in restaurants. This is certainly the case with Catalan cuisine, I would argue. Home cooking in the *països catalans* might remain relatively authentic and well-made in some areas (mostly in the Balearics and the Empordà, I think), but it is also limited, compartmentalized, even xeno-phobic. The farmer in the Cerdanya (Cerdaña) has no idea what his counterpart near Castelló de la Plana eats for lunch and doesn't much care; the fisherman in Majorca and the one on the Roussillon's Côte Vermeille might cook up fish stews that are almost identical, yet each believes his own to be some purely local wonderwork.

In restaurants, though, Catalan cuisine becomes, perforce, both cosmopolitan and vital. Styles overlap, specialties of different regions stand side by side, and non-Catalan influences appear—to be assimilated, as Ferran Agulló once put it, with "great power," strengthening the cuisine and giving it international credibility. I'm glad there are strict constructionists safeguarding the traditions of true, old-fashioned Catalan cuisine, because I think it's important to preserve and study any historical system so rich and influential (and also because a lot of the old dishes, made in the old way, are delicious). But I'm also convinced that Catalan cuisine, like any other, has got to make itself comfortable in the modern world if it is to survive and flourish. And I suspect that a Hotel Ampurdán, or a Sa Punta, a Hispania, a Petit París, a Florian, or an Eldorado Petit (to name a few of Catalonia's other best contemporary-style restaurants), however much they might sometimes deviate from the doctrines of de Nola, et al., do more toward this end than any hundred culinary sentimentalists remembering with fondness the *escudella* their grandparents ate six times a week, or complaining about the admittedly indefensible quality of the modern-day mass-market chicken.

But now to the recipes—and may God pardon our sins of gluttony. . . .

PART TWO: SAUCES

Catalan cuisine is built around four basic sauces: *allioli, sofregit, picada,* and *samfaina.* It must be pointed out, however, that these aren't really sauces in the conventional French or Italian sense: *Allioli*—an emulsion of garlic, olive oil, and (inauthentically but very commonly) eggs—is sometimes stirred into a dish for added emphasis, but it is primarily a condiment, to be dabbed or slathered onto this or that at table; *sofregit,* which is made by cooking onions and usually tomatoes (and occasionally herbs and/or other vegetables) down almost to melting, is a *base* for sauces rather than a sauce itself; *picada,* a dense paste usually composed of garlic, almonds, fried bread, and olive oil, with such other possible additions as parsley, hazelnuts, pine nuts, chocolate, and saffron (among other things), is a thickening and flavoring agent—a sort of glorified roux; and *samfaina* is a ratatouillelike vegetable mixture, which can be made *into* a sauce by puréeing (with or without cream or some other dilution), but which is also eaten as a side dish or used as a coarsely textured cloak (hardly a sauce) for meat, fish, and fowl.

If these four basic sauces aren't really sauces, however, they certainly *are* basic—especially *sofregit* and *picada,* which are almost always used in tandem (one to start the preparation of a dish and the other to finish it), and which seem to appear in almost every traditional Catalan soup, sauce, or stew recipe. And if you learn how to make all four of them in their simplest forms, you will have understood the very foundations of Catalan cuisine.

ALLIOLI

Allioli might be called the Catalan catsup—though of course it is better and far more reputable gastronomically than catsup. It's the all-purpose tabletop relish, the diner's friend, the enhancer of good food and disguiser of bad. In one form or another, it can go on or into almost anything—seafood, noodle and rice dishes, soups, stews, vegetables, snails. It is all but obligatory with grilled meats, especially pork, rabbit, and chicken. It even gets spread plain on bread. For all I know, folks take baths in it.

Strictly speaking, the name is the recipe: *all* (garlic), *i* (and), *oli* (oil). The oil, of course, is olive oil; that's a given in the *països catalans.* Salt, of course, is added, another given. Anything else, claim purists, is just (shall we say) gilding the lily. Well, *maybe* a few drops of lemon juice or vinegar or a combination of the two, if you insist upon a tingle of acidity. ("Heaven and hell are both full of people who eat *allioli* with lemon juice and without, with vinegar and without," suggests author Manuel Vázquez Montalbán.) But a little crustless white bread to thicken it, as some sources recommend? No. And *eggs?* Never. "*Allioli* made with eggs," an old-school Catalan bartender announced to me one evening as we were discussing the subject, "isn't *allioli* at all. It's just fancy mayonnaise." The fact that *allioli*'s closest relatives, the *aïoli* of Provence and the lesser-known *aïllade* of the Languedoc, always do include eggs—and thus really *are* "fancy mayonnaise"—is taken by some Catalans simply as further proof of what they have long suspected: that the French don't know very much about food after all. Big talk aside, however, the plain truth is that the vast majority of the *allioli* served in Catalonia and vicinity today *is* made with eggs, especially in restaurants—and purism be damned. The eggless variety is just too difficult to whip up, and too fragile—capable of instantaneous and capricious breakdown.

Where *allioli* came from in the first place is hard to say. "As in the case of Homer," notes Valencian gastronome Llorenç Millo, "dozens of cities dispute the honor of having been its birthplace." Millo does reveal, however, that Pliny the Elder (A.D. 23–79), who served as *procurator* in Roman Tarragona for a year, gives what is apparently the first written recipe for the sauce in one of his manuscripts: "When garlic is beaten with oil and vinegar," he observes (approximately), "it is wondrous how the foam increases." Wherever it might come

from, though, *allioli* has been popular in the *països catalans* for hundreds of years (it's even mentioned in the *Libre del coch*), and is indeed a thing, as Joseph Cunill de Bosch has said, "*purament catalana*"—purely Catalan.

Here are some recipes for *allioli* both with and without eggs, a recipe for mayonnaise, and several variations on the theme.

Allioli Autèntic
(AUTHENTIC *ALLIOLI*)

Allioli in its purest form is white and shiny, rather like lemon sorbet in appearance. It is very strong in garlic flavor, and a little goes a long way—except among the garlic-mad, of course. It is, as noted, practically de rigueur in Catalan cooking to accompany grilled meat and fowl (especially chicken, rabbit, and pork), and is traditional as well with snails and with many kinds of fish and shellfish. Fishermen are famous for their mastery of its manufacture, in fact, as are rural mothers and grandmothers—while some of the region's most famous chefs openly admit that they can't always get the damned thing to work. The tricky part is coaxing an emulsion to form without eggs or other thickeners, and this takes a lot of practice. In answer to the obvious question, no, you cannot make *Allioli Autèntic* in a food processor, at least in my experience; the very thought is sacrilege to a good Catalan (that's part of his *heritage* you're threatening to throw into that machine, for heaven's sake). More to the point, though, the oil and garlic get too homogenized in a processor, and the emulsion doesn't hold. If all this doesn't discourage you, and you'd still like to, er, try your hand at making the real thing, this is how it's done:

TO MAKE 1–1¼ CUPS

6 cloves garlic (or more to taste),
    peeled
½ teaspoon salt
1 cup mild extra-virgin olive oil
(see note)

Cut each clove of garlic in half lengthwise and discard any green pieces, then mince the garlic finely.

Scatter salt in the bowl of a large mortar and add the garlic. Mash the garlic gently with a pestle, mixing it with the salt until it takes on the consistency of a thick paste.

Add the olive oil very slowly, a few drops at a time, while stirring the mixture with the pestle, using slow, even motions and always stirring in the same direction. Continue adding oil until an emulsion forms. Less than a full cup might be sufficient to obtain this result, in which case do not use the rest, as it will "break" the emulsion.

Serve immediately.

Note: It is very important for the success of the emulsion that all the ingredients be at room temperature—even the garlic.

Allioli amb Ous

(*ALLIOLI* WITH EGGS)

This, as noted, is by far the most common kind of *allioli* in the *països catalans* today—and, tradition aside, the fact is that there's nothing wrong with it at all. Some Catalans even prefer it to the original version, because it's subtler and adds garlic character to dishes without overpowering them. *Allioli* with eggs *can* be made in a food processor quite easily, though it's not particularly difficult by hand either. The following recipe, a plain and simple formula based on the preceding one, will work equally well (with minor variation) for either method. I haven't included lemon juice or vinegar in the recipe, incidentally, because I like my *allioli* without their added bite; but a few drops of either (or both) stirred in at the last minute won't affect the emulsion and will cut the sauce's richness a bit.

TO MAKE 1–1¼ CUPS

6 cloves garlic (or more to taste),
    peeled
½ teaspoon salt
2 egg yolks (or 1 egg yolk and 1
    whole egg; see below)
1 cup mild extra-virgin olive oil

BY HAND:

Prepare a garlic paste as in the previous recipe.

Add the egg yolks to the mortar, mix with the garlic paste, and then proceed as in previous recipe, adding the oil slowly until an emulsion forms.

BY FOOD PROCESSOR:

Again, prepare a garlic paste as in the previous recipe.

Put the paste into the work bowl of a food processor, and then add 1 egg yolk and 1 whole egg (instead of 2 egg yolks).

Process for several seconds, then, with the machine still running, pour a slow, steady stream of oil through the feed tube, until an emulsion forms.

Serve immediately (although, unlike the eggless version, this *allioli* will hold its emulsion for several days at least if refrigerated).

Allioli Negat

("DROWNED" *ALLIOLI*)

"Allioli negat, dòna'l al gat," says the proverb—"Give 'drowned' *allioli* to the cat." Disregard this advice. Drowned *allioli*, a specialty of the Costa Brava, is broken *allioli*, *allioli* with its molecules unclasped, *allioli* that has turned from a creamy emulsion into a bath of liquid oil swamping (drowning) the minced, crushed garlic it contains. It is an intentional mistake, in other words—regular *allioli*, with or without eggs, deliberately pushed too far, made to shatter. The result is delicious, and somehow even more unctuous than its emulsified forebear. *Allioli Negat* is always stirred *into* something—most often *fideus* noodles and fish soups or stews—and it adds much character to them. The cat has character enough already.

TO MAKE 1¼–1½ CUPS

6 cloves garlic (or more to taste), peeled
½ teaspoon salt
2 egg yolks or 1 egg yolk and 1 whole egg (optional)
1–1¼ cups mild extra-virgin olive oil (see note)

Follow the instructions in one of the two preceding recipes, for *allioli* with or without eggs, but continue adding oil after an emulsion forms, until it breaks again, and the sauce thins. The amount of oil necessary to achieve this effect will vary. Watch the *allioli* carefully, and don't add more than you need to get it to break. The finished *Allioli Negat* should look curdled.

Note: Again, make sure that all the ingredients are at room temperature before beginning.

Allioli amb Fruita

(*ALLIOLI* WITH FRUIT)

Allioli admits of more possibilities than might be apparent at first. It can be simultaneously thickened and flavored, for instance, with honey (see page 276); in Majorca and some parts of Catalonia, boiled potatoes or tomatoes are stirred into it (see page 102); in France, under the guise of *aïllade à la toulousaine*, it includes blanched, pulverized walnuts. And in the Catalonian Pyrénées and Pyrenean foothills, it is sometimes elaborated with puréed fruit—most notably quince (a specialty of the *comarques* of the Pallars Sobirà and Pallars Jussà), apples, and pears. These fruit *allio-lis* make superb and unusual accompaniments to grilled and roasted meats—again, above all, to rabbit, chicken, and pork. They can be made with eggs if you wish, but there's really no reason to do so, since the fruit and oil alone will form a very nice emulsion. This recipe is eggless, then.

TO MAKE 1½–1¾ CUPS

1 large ripe quince or 2 small ripe
    apples or pears
3–4 cloves garlic, peeled
½ teaspoon salt
3–4 ounces mild extra-virgin olive oil

Peel and core the fruit and cut it into large cubes, then cook in water to cover in a covered pot for about 5 minutes, or until the fruit is soft but not mushy. Drain and cool.

Prepare a garlic paste as for *Allioli Autèntic* (see page 30), then stir the fruit into the mortar and work with the pestle until smooth.

Add the oil slowly, as for *Allioli Autèntic* until an emulsion forms.

Correct the salt if necessary, and serve immediately, or refrigerate until ready.

Mussolina d'All

(GARLIC MOUSSELINE)

Mussolina d'All, refined if not invented by Josep Mercader at the Hotel Ampurdán, is in effect an *allioli* made with roasted garlic—which makes it milder and sweeter than the conventional version. "It has the flavor of gar-

lic, but is easier on the stomach," notes Mercader's son-in-law and successor, Jaume Subirós. (Author Josep Pla: "Garlic is the Genghis Khan of Catalan cuisine.") The Hotel Ampurdán, in fact, usually makes this sauce with *all tendre*, green garlic (i.e., the scallionlike shoots of the young garlic plant)—which is available in some specialty markets, and can of course be grown in the home garden—but ordinary garlic works just as well. *Mussolina d'All* is called for specifically in three of the recipes in this book (see pages 35, 108, and 127); in general, though, it is a wonderful addition to almost any kind of simply cooked fish or vegetables, especially when applied lightly and browned a bit under a broiler or salamander, which will cause it to puff up slightly like a half-hearted soufflé.

TO MAKE 1–1¼ CUPS

12 cloves garlic or bulbs from 24
    shoots green garlic
½ teaspoon salt
2 egg yolks (or 1 egg yolk and 1
    whole egg; see below)
1 cup mild extra-virgin olive oil

Roast the garlic, unpeeled, in a preheated 350° oven for 30 minutes or until soft.

Let the garlic cool, then cut the root end off each clove or bulb and squeeze the cooked garlic out into a bowl.

Using the cooked garlic in place of raw minced garlic, proceed according to the recipe for *Allioli amb Ous* (see page 31), either by hand or with a food processor—again using 1 egg yolk and 1 whole egg instead of 2 egg yolks for the latter method.

Maionesa

(MAYONNAISE)

The French sometimes claim that mayonnaise, that most ubiquitous of condiments, was invented in—or at least named for—the city of Mayenne, northwest of Le Mans, in Normandy. Catalans know better. Mayonnaise, they are certain, was invented on the island of Minorca, and named after the island's capital, Maó (Mahón in Castilian). And why not? It is, after all, just *allioli* with eggs—minus the garlic.

There are many stories about its discovery, of course. One holds that, after he had expelled the English from the island in 1756, Maréchal Richelieu (grandnephew of the notorious cardinal) was out walking in the Minorcan countryside one day and suddenly grew hungry. Stopping at the nearest shack, he asked a local peasant woman to make him something to eat. Realizing that he must be an important person, she improvised a sauce for him out of a few precious eggs she had been hoarding. He loved it, and honored it with the name of the nearest city.

According to another story, King Carlos III of Spain stopped in Maó on his way from Barcelona to Naples in 1760, and was feted by the local governor. (A proverb: *"Si vols tenir molts amics, fes molts convits"*; i.e., "If you want to have lots of friends, give lots of parties.") The centerpiece of the royal banquet was a magnificent *llagosta* (spiny lobster), a crustacean for which Minorca is particularly famous, simply grilled. But the king took one look at the beast and decided he wasn't hungry. The governor sent to the kitchen and ordered his chef to create a sauce, in an instant, that would make the *llagosta* more appetizing. He whipped up some you-know-what—which the king of course loved, and later introduced to his court in Madrid.

A much more likely explanation of the invention of mayonnaise, however, is simply that some French chef or other on the island (the French held Minorca, it should be noted, for roughly twenty-five years off and on) decided to soften the pungency of *allioli* by leaving out its strongest ingredient. (Josep Pla again: *"Allioli* is to mayonnaise as a lion is to a house cat.")

TO MAKE 1½–2 CUPS

1 teaspoon salt
2 egg yolks (or 1 egg yolk and 1
    whole egg; see below)
1 teaspoon lemon juice
1 teaspoon good white wine vinegar
¼ teaspoon freshly ground white
    pepper
1¼ cups mild extra-virgin olive oil
    (or, for lighter mayonnaise, ¾
    cup olive oil and ½ cup light
    salad oil)

Following the procedure described above for *Allioli amb Ous* (see pages 31–32), either by hand or in a food processor, mix all ingredients except the olive oil together, then add olive oil slowly as for *allioli*—again substituting 1 egg yolk and 1 whole egg for 2 egg yolks if you use the food processor.

Note: Fresh homemade mayonnaise goes superbly well with cold grilled lobster or chicken, as well as fulfilling the more usual functions.

Musclos Gratinats, Estil Antonio Ferrer

(ANTONIO FERRER'S GRATINÉED MUSSELS)

Other recipes calling for *allioli* and its relations are scattered throughout this book (see page 36), but to begin with, here is one example of how one of them can be used—a sort of Catalan version of oysters Rockefeller, if you will. Antonio Ferrer, who created this dish, is the owner-chef of the imaginative Barcelona restaurant La Odisea.

TO SERVE 4 (AS APPETIZER)

6 tablespoons butter
Salt
2 dozen mussels, cleaned (see note)
2 cups dry white wine
2 cups fresh spinach, blanched and
    finely chopped, or one 10-ounce
    package frozen spinach, thawed
    and finely chopped
¾ cup heavy cream
1 tablespoon flour
Salt and pepper
1 cup Mussolina d'All (see page 33)

Melt half the butter in a large pot, and add salt to taste, then add the mussels. Cover the pot tightly, and cook on medium heat for about 2 minutes, shaking the pot constantly but lightly.

Add the wine, raise the heat, recover the pot, and cook 3–4 minutes more on high heat.

When the mussels have opened, remove from heat at once, drain, and allow to cool. Remove and discard one shell from each mussel, then set the remaining shells (with mussel meat) aside.

Melt the remaining butter in a saucepan, add the spinach, and toss over medium-high heat, stirring and cooking until all moisture evaporates.

In a small pan, heat the cream almost to the boiling point (but do not boil). Meanwhile, in another saucepan, lightly brown the flour (approximately 1 minute), then slowly add the hot cream to it, stirring well. Salt and pepper to taste, and cook until smooth and thick.

Add the spinach to the cream and cook briefly, stirring well, until a thick spinach cream has formed.

Place about 1 teaspoon of the creamed spinach on top of each mussel, and top with enough Mussolina d'All to cover lightly. (Do not use too much; you may have some left over.)

Brown the mussolina briefly under a salamander or broiler until it is slightly puffed up and golden-brown in color.

_____

Note· To clean mussels, rinse them under running water, brushing if necessary with a small stiff brush, then pull off the "beards" and discard. Place the mussels in a large bowl with cold water to cover. Stir them around briefly with your hands, letting them knock together, then let them soak for about 10 minutes. Remove mussels from the bowl. If there is sand at the bottom of the bowl, repeat the process, continuing until no sand remains.

See Also:

Cigrons amb Mussolina d'All (Chick-peas with Garlic Mousseline), page 108
Pastís Calent de Rap amb Mussolina d'All (Warm Monkfish Terrine with Garlic Mousseline), page 127
Fideus a Banda (Catalan Pasta and Rascasse, in Two Courses), page 197
Arròs a Banda (Rice and Rascasse, in Two Courses), page 199
Conill Farcit amb Allioli de Poma i Mel (Stuffed Rabbit with Apple and Honey Allioli), page 276
Patates amb Allioli (Scalloped Potatoes with Allioli), page 276

SOFREGIT

"First, make a *sofregit*. . . ." Thus begin literally hundreds of Catalan recipes; it's the "Once upon a time" of Catalan cuisine, the ritual opening, the jumping-off point. *Sofregit* is present in almost every sauced and stewed dish the idiom admits, at least traditionally, and helps define the idiom itself. The Castilian *sofrito* and the Italian *soffritto* (or *battuto*) are related, certainly; but *sofregit* is simpler than its cousins, more fundamental—and more widely used by far. If you're going to cook Catalan, you must learn how to make a good *sofregit,* period. Luckily, there's nothing to it. As noted earlier, it's simply onions and (usually) tomatoes, sometimes with herbs and/or other vegetables added, cooked down into a sort of mush (or *confiture,* to be a bit more elegant about it). It's the first thing into the pot, laying the foundation for what's to come. Everything else is built upon it and draws flavor from it. It's a real *fond de cuisine.*

Sofregit is mentioned in the *Libre de Sent Soví* (c. 1324), and thus has obviously been a part of Catalan cuisine since medieval times. At first, of course, it never contained tomatoes, since that fruit reached Spain from the Americas only in the sixteenth century. Instead, it was usually made of onions and leeks, with bacon or salt pork sometimes added. Onions remain its most important element, and it is perfectly possible to make a *sofregit* from them (and oil) alone. Mild, sweet onions are best for *sofregit,* and Maui, Vidalia, or Walla-Walla onions are best of all (though considering their price, these are undeniably an extravagance, and aren't really necessary).

The word *sofregit* itself derives from the Catalan verb *sofregir,* meaning to "underfry" or fry lightly. *Sofregit* is lightly fried, though, only in the sense that it is fried slowly, gently, on a "light" flame. In fact, this process properly continues for a long time. (Chef Josep Lladonosa: "The authentic Catalan *sofregit* requires a technique of patience and calm.") A usable *sofregit* may be made in 15 or 20 minutes, but a really good one takes much longer. At the excellent home-style Cypsele restaurant in Palafrugell, for instance, the onions are cooked for at least an hour—"Until they're black but not burned." At Big Rock in nearby Platja d'Aro, the onions soften and darken exquisitely in big pots on the back of a warm griddle for as long as two days.

Author Nèstor Luján grows almost rhapsodic over the onion question, writing that they should ideally reach "the strange and mysterious color that, in the School of Venice, the brushstrokes of the great master Titian obtain." Good luck. Me, I'm happy if I can get them to a Turneresque pale golden-brown. To do this, I let them simmer in plenty of olive oil on the lowest flame my stove will hold and in the biggest pan I have, stirring them occasionally and pouring off the excess oil when they are done—saving it, of course, for other cooking (for instance, frying bread for a *picada;* see page 40). I often use a *sofregit,* incidentally, as the starting point for soups and stocks that aren't Catalan at all.

Whenever a *sofregit* is called for in the recipes that follow (which is often), specific quantities and ingredients are mentioned. Here, though, is a basic recipe and the basic technique.

Sofregit

TO MAKE 1–1½ CUPS

Olive oil
3 onions, chopped (but not minced)
6 tomatoes, seeded and grated (see
page 7) or peeled, seeded, and
chopped

Cover the bottom of a cassola, Dutch oven, or large skillet with at least ½ inch of oil, heat for several minutes, then add the onions. Reduce the heat and cook uncovered until the onions are wilted, stirring occasionally. Continue cooking in this manner until the onions have turned golden-brown and are beginning to carmelize, adding and cooking off a bit of water if desired. For a darker *sofregit,* the process may be continued until the onions reach the desired color—but do not let them burn.

Add the tomatoes and mix well, then continue cooking until all liquid has evaporated, and the tomatoes have begun to "melt" into the onions. (At this point, add herbs if called for in specific recipe.)

Note: If a specific *sofregit* recipe calls for garlic or other vegetables (leeks, bell peppers, etc.), add them after the onions have wilted, adding more oil if necessary. *Sofregit,* with or without tomatoes, may be made in larger quantities and stored in the refrigerator, covered with a thin layer of oil, in an airtight container, for two or three weeks at least. (It will last longer with tomatoes added, due to greater acidity.)

PICADA

The *picada* is, with *sofregit,* one of the bookends of Catalan cuisine, helping to hold dishes together and give them form. It has been called the idiom's single most important sauce—though, as we have seen, it isn't really a sauce at all—and has been used in Catalonia and vicinity at least since the thirteenth or fourteenth century, and probably much longer. No other European cuisine has anything quite like the *picada*—which, as noted, is a thickening and flavoring agent made up of such ingredients as garlic, fried bread, olive oil (or some other liquid), and various nuts, herbs, and/or spices, all pounded together with a mortar and pestle. (The word *picada* itself, which is modern, derives from the verb *picar*—one of whose many meanings is "to crush.") The *picada*'s closest relatives are probably Italy's *pesto* (which likewise involves garlic, nuts, and herbs crushed in a mortar) and *gremolada* (the Milanese herb-and-garlic mixture traditionally added to *osso buco*)—but *pesto* clearly *is* a sauce, and both substances, unlike the *picada,* have limited and highly specialized uses, and a more or less regularized composition. Another stylistic analogue to the *picada* is the blend of pulverized spices, nuts, seeds, etc. on which the *moles* of Mexico are based—but these blends, too, are used only for a single class of dishes, lacking the *picada*'s versatility and range. (Anyway, though I'm not for a moment suggesting that *moles* as we know them might be partly Catalan in origin, it is interesting to note that the most famous of them, *mole poblano,* is said to have been invented in a Spanish convent in Pueblo—and that the most popular cookbook by far in the Spain of the *conquistadores* was the Catalan *Libre del coch,* in which the idea of the *picada,* if not its name, figures prominently.)

When Paula Wolfert discovered the *picada* while collecting Catalan recipes for her book *My World of Food,* she thought it was the best thing since sliced bread (which, after all, is one of its ingredients)—and pointed out that it might well have applications far beyond Catalan cuisine. "The *picada* is the future of cooking," she went so far as to enthuse at one point. That might be something of an exaggeration, but the concept of the *picada* is undeniably a fascinating—and adaptable—one. Some pages back, I called the *picada* "sort of a glorified roux"—but in fact it doesn't swell up as dramatically as roux does, or thicken quite as relentlessly. It adds more heart than heft. It is also more complex in flavor than roux, containing many more elements, and is said to be much more easily digestible—simply because the flour it contains has already been baked into bread (and bread, of course, is easier on the stomach than unbaked flour). The *picada* is usually stirred into the pot a mere five or ten minutes before cooking is completed, at which time—as anyone who has ever tasted a dish before and after its addition will testify—it seems to fill in all the holes, plug all the gaps in flavor. It's a kind of secret ingredient. If it's made (and applied) correctly, you can't even really taste it—but you'd notice its absence in an instant. You could indeed, I think (*pace* Paula Wolfert), add some version of the *picada* to non-Catalan dishes quite successfully. (Chili con carne, beef stew, spaghetti sauce, and various kinds of gravy come immediately to mind.)

There are innumerable variations on the *picada.* The Big Rock restaurant in Platja d'Aro, for instance, uses a bare-bones simple formula of garlic, almonds, fried bread, and olive oil. Ignasi Domènech's classic cooking text *La Teca* (which might be translated simply as "Food" or even "Grub"), on the other hand, prescribes a busy blend of oil, garlic, saffron, almonds, hazelnuts, cinnamon, parsley, and cookies soaked in sherrylike *vi ranci.* Other possible ingredients include chocolate, walnuts, pine nuts (common in some regions), marjoram and other herbs, nutmeg and other spices, black peppercorns, even fish livers, sea urchin roe, or well-pulverized baby crabs (these last three in the Empordà region almost exclusively). Here are notes on some of the ingredients most often used:

Almonds. Buy almonds preblanched and skinless, or blanch them by covering them with boiling water and letting them sit, off the heat, for two or three minutes, then skin by draining them, immersing them in cold water, and rubbing the skins off gently with your hands. (Some bits of almond skin may remain, but won't adversely affect the *picada.*) Before use, almonds should be roasted in a 350°–400° oven until lightly browned. (Watch them closely so that they don't burn, and shake the pan periodically to help them roast evenly. Dry almonds thoroughly with a clean towel before roasting if you have just blanched them.) Roasted almonds will keep for at least three or four weeks in the freezer, in a sealed plastic bag or other airtight container, and need not be thawed before use.

Hazelnuts. These needn't be blanched, but should be roasted as above. If they still have their skins, rub them gently in a clean towel or between your palms after roasting, first allowing them to cool for 10 or 15 minutes. Hazelnuts, too, may be frozen and used unthawed.

Pine Nuts. These should always be bought already shelled and skinned (they are virtually impossible to shell and skin at home) and, again, roasted as above. (They will take less time to brown than almonds or hazelnuts, so watch them particularly carefully.) I don't recommend freezing pine nuts, as it seems to affect their texture.

Fried Bread. Use any good French- or Italian-style bread, preferably "country-style" and not sourdough. The "slice" called for in the recipes that follow is from a standard French-style loaf, about 3 to 4 inches in diameter; if you are using larger country-style loafs, use half a slice instead. To prepare bread for a *picada*, remove the crusts, slice it about half an inch thick, and brown it in plenty of hot olive oil. (The hotter the oil—up to a reasonable point, of course—the less of it the bread will absorb.) Drain the bread on paper towels, and allow it to cool and dry a bit before using.

Chocolate. The chocolate used in savory dishes in Catalonia, in the *picada* and otherwise, is usually a variety called *xocolata a la pedra*—chocolate "on the stone," named for the curved stone cradles on which it was traditionally rolled out. Commercial brands of *xocolata a la pedra* usually contain rice flour and cinnamon in addition to cacao and some sugar. The closest equivalent I've been able to find in the United States is the Spanish (but not Catalan) Ybarra brand of cooking chocolate, which contains cacao, sugar, cinnamon, and almond powder (in place of rice flour), and adds lecithin. Some Catalan chefs prefer con-ventional confectioner's chocolate to *xocolata a la pedra,* the former being somewhat sweeter, and this works well, too. I don't recommend bitter or unsweetened chocolate, though.

Saffron. Though saffron is famously expensive, a little goes a long way—and I recommend that you use the best grade possible. To the spice trade, that grade is usually designated as Mancha Superior—though you'll seldom find that name on a package. Mancha Superior has a deep red color, almost blood-red, with comparatively little yellow showing. (Always buy saffron in thread form, in any case; powder invariably conceals lower quality.) Saffron should be toasted very lightly before use, preferably in a dry skillet on top of the stove. Shake the saffron constantly and be very careful not to let it burn. (Saffron makes an excellent, light, easy-to-carry souvenir of Spain, by the way, and is much cheaper there than here. I always bring back a quarter pound or so, for my own use and for much-appreciated gifts.)

Parsley. Although any fresh parsley will do for the *picada* (and for other uses herein), Italian parsley is closer to the variety found in the *països catalans* and lends dishes a much better flavor.

Picada

(CATALAN "ROUX")

The exact composition of the *picada* called for in the following recipes will vary from one to the next, sometimes rather substantially. Here, though, is a basic, all-purpose version.

TO MAKE ½ CUP

2 cloves garlic, minced
15 almonds, blanched and roasted (see
    page 39)
15 hazelnuts, blanched and roasted
    (see page 39)
1 slice fried bread (see page 40)
¼ teaspoon salt
2 sprigs parsley, minced
Olive oil

Crush or grind all ingredients, except the parsley and oil, together with a mortar and pestle or in a spice mill. (See note.)

Add the parsley, and mash it into the mixture.

Add enough oil to barely cover the picada, then work it into the mixture slowly and thoroughly to form a thick paste.

Note: The *picada* may be finished in a food processor or blender if you wish, but it *must* be started in a mortar or spice mill (preferably the former) so that the nuts and bread are indeed pulverized together and not just finely ground. Remember: The constituent elements of a good *picada* should not be recognizable in the finished dish; if the grainy texture of ground nuts or breadcrumbs is discernible, the *picada* has not been properly made.

SAMFAINA

Nèstor Luján has called *samfaina* "a kind of baroque *sofregit*." (It too is based on onions, after all, and is often cooked down to a marmaladelike consistency.) He has also said that it is, to the Catalan mind, "the most important, unique and incorruptible dish which Catalan cuisine has brought to gastronomy." That *samfaina* (also sometimes known as *xamfaina*, *sanfaina*, and *chanfaina*) is, for all practical purposes, virtually identical to the ratatouille of the Côte d'Azur doesn't necessarily gainsay the Catalan opinion. As noted earlier, the Catalans once held sway in that part of France— and, in the absence of extant Provençal or Niçoise cookbooks from medieval and Renaissance times, who is to say that the Catalans didn't bring the dish to French shores in the first place? (Especially considering the early popularity of the eggplant in the *països catalans* and the fact that the Catalans were using tomatoes, peppers, and zucchini widely before their French neighbors were.) *Samfaina* is, in any case, a quintessentially (post-Columbian) Mediterranean specialty—and one that invariably brightens any table at which it appears.

Samfaina

TO MAKE 6–8 CUPS

⅔ cup extra-virgin olive oil
4 cloves garlic, minced
2½ pounds onions, halved and thinly sliced

1½ pounds Japanese eggplant, skin on, cut into 1-inch cubes
1 pound zucchini, skin on, cut into ½–1-inch cubes
8 medium tomatoes, seeded and grated (see page 7) or peeled, seeded, and chopped
1½ pounds red (if possible) or green bell peppers, roasted, peeled, and cut into strips as for Escalivada *(see page 170)*
Salt and pepper

Heat the oil in a cassola or Dutch oven and add the garlic, onions, eggplant, and zucchini. Stir well so that all vegetables are coated with oil.

Cover the pan and cook for 10 minutes on low heat. Uncover and turn heat up slightly, cooking until the liquid has evaporated. Stir occasionally.

Add the tomatoes and peppers, reduce heat, and simmer uncovered until the liquid has again evaporated and the vegetables are very soft.

Season to taste.

Note: If you are preparing *samfaina* for use as a sauce, cook longer, adding water if necessary, until the mixture has attained a marmaladelike consistency, and the vegetables have lost their form.

Petits Pastisos de Samfaina amb Anxoves

(*SAMFAINA* TARTLETS WITH ANCHOVIES)

This is a variation on a dish served as an appetizer at the pleasant, turn-of-the-century-style El Gran Café in Barcelona. It also makes an unusual side dish, or, with a small salad, an agreeable light lunch.

TO MAKE 6 TARTLETS

Six 4-inch tart pastry (pâte brisée) *shells, baked and cooled (see note)*
3 cups samfaina *(see page 42)*
12 anchovy filets, soaked in water for 1 hour and patted dry

Preheat the oven to 375°, then heat the tart shells through (about 2 minutes).

Meanwhile, warm the *samfaina* on medium-low heat.

Remove the tart shells from the oven, and spoon about ½ cup of *samfaina* into each, smoothing it gently with the back of a spoon. Crisscross 2 anchovy filets across each tartlet.

Pass briefly under a broiler or salamander and serve immediately.

Note: I recommend Julia Child's tart pastry dough recipe, as published in *From Julia Child's Kitchen* (New York: Alfred A. Knopf, Inc., 1970), if you want to make pastry shells from scratch. Storebought shells may of course be used, but with some inevitable sacrifice of flavor and texture.

"Filet" de Vedella amb Crema de Samfaina

(ROAST VEAL FILET WITH SAMFAINA CREAM)

This is a recipe created by Josep Mercader at the Hotel Ampurdán in Figueres. The *comarques* of l'Alt Empordà (where Figueres is located) and neighboring El Gironès (Girona) are famous for the quality of their veal. This recipe, however, works equally well with beef.

TO SERVE 4 (AS MAIN COURSE)

1 tablespoon goose fat or lard
Olive oil
2 pounds veal or beef tenderloin (center cut), trimmed of fat if necessary
1½ cups veal or beef stock
2 cups heavy cream
1 cup samfaina *(see page 42), made without zucchini and with the eggplant peeled*

Heat goose fat or lard with a bit of olive oil in a cast-iron skillet or other heavy pan, then sear the meat quickly on all sides, using tongs to turn it.

Remove the meat from the skillet, and let it rest on a wire rack for about ½ hour.

Pour off the excess fat from the skillet, then deglaze with veal stock, cooking until the liquid is reduced to about ½ cup.

Roast the meat in a preheated oven—about 1 hour at 325° for pink veal (meat thermometer should read about 170°) or 20 minutes at 450° for rare beef (meat thermometer should read about 140°), or longer (or even shorter) to taste.

Meanwhile, stir the cream into the reduced veal stock, bring to a boil, and simmer until the liquid is reduced by half.

Purée the *samfaina* in a food processor or blender or pass it through a food mill, then add to the cream mixture, and stir well until the sauce is an even, rosy color.

Slice the meat into quarter-inch slices, and pour hot *samfaina* sauce over it.

Note The Hotel Ampurdán serves this dish with more *samfaina,* not puréed, on the side. If this seems a bit repetitious to you, another good accompaniment would be simple roasted potatoes—or, if you feel like living dangerously, potatoes fried in more of that goose fat or lard.

See Also:

Pollastre Rostit amb Samfaina (Roast Chicken with *Samfaina*), page 71

Bacallà amb Samfaina (Salt Cod with *Samfaina*), page 81

Cap i Pota amb Samfaina (Stewed Calf's Head and Foot with *Samfaina*), page 113

Truita de Samfaina (*Samfaina* Omelet), page 123

PART THREE: THE RAW MATERIALS

What is the single most important food-stuff in Catalan cuisine, the single ingredient that most saliently defines it (and I don't mean salt)? I don't know. Garlic, maybe. The tomato, perhaps. Rice? Salt cod? Pork?

What I do know is that some culinary raw materials are very obviously more important to the cuisine than others: that garlic (and onions), for instance, are vital to it, while shallots and leeks (though they're certainly used) are not; that tomatoes are honored more than zucchini, rice more than potatoes (though potatoes are much-loved), salt cod and pork more than, say, lobster and lamb.

I've picked out some fifteen such raw materials (or classes of same) to write about here in some detail—items without which I simply cannot imagine Catalan cuisine as I have come to know it. As noted earlier, I exempt from this list the *really* important ones—garlic, onions, and tomatoes above all—because there's hardly a dish in this whole idiom (it sometimes seems) that doesn't include them. They don't get chapters of their own, that is, because *every* chapter (almost) is about them. Those other fifteen, though, are a bit more specialized, and deserve some separate attention. They are eggplant, almonds and other nuts, anchovies, rice, poultry, salt cod,

wild mushrooms, wild game, snails, legumes (or pulses), organ meats, olives and olive oil, eggs, fresh fish and shellfish, and pork. What follow are notes on (and recipes involving) each, arranged alphabetically according to their Catalan names.

ALBERGÍNIES
(EGGPLANT)

The eggplant or aubergine *(Solanum melongena),* a relative of the potato, apparently comes originally from Southeast Asia. It was known in India and in the Arabic-speaking world at least by the ninth century A.D., and it is the Arabs who brought it to Spain. There are recipes for eggplant in the first known Catalan cookbook, the fourteenth-century *Libre de Sent Soví,* and the word *aubergine*—although ultimately derived from the Arabic word *al-badhinjan* (as were such other European names for the thing as the Italian *melanzana* and the Castilian *berenjena*)—apparently reached French and English directly from the Catalan word *albergínia.* Eggplant, in any case, remains extremely popular in the *països catalans* today, especially in northeastern Catalonia and the Balearic Islands—and has been so strongly associated with the region's cooking that the *Larousse Gastronomique* defines a garnish *à la catalane* as diced eggplant sautéed in oil.

The best eggplant I've ever tasted, whether simply fried or included in some more complex dish, has been on the islands of Minorca and Majorca. The vegetables of the Balearics in general are superb, in fact—a function, claims Majorcan journalist Pablo Llull, not only of the islands' rich soil and hospitable climate but also of the simple fact that cold stores are virtually unknown in the Balearics, and that most vegetables are thus consumed within a day or so of their harvest. Whatever the reasons, the eggplant of these two places

is superb—small, firm, usually dark purple in color, either pear-shaped or elongated, sweet. The closest equivalents in the United States are probably the Long Purple and Barbentane varieties, both commonly sold as "Japanese eggplant"—and, in fact, I prefer such varieties for all Catalan recipes. If you buy eggplant of more conventional design, try to find dense little ones, palm-of-the-hand-sized or less—and avoid at all costs the huge, light, spongy kind.

In honor of the eggplant of Minorca and Majorca, I've included a recipe from each island in this chapter, plus a third inspired by a dish from the latter place.

Albergínies Farcides amb Anxoves
(STUFFED EGGPLANT WITH ANCHOVIES)

This is another creation of the late Josep Mercader, father of contemporary Catalan cooking. Like so many of his dishes, it is closely related to a traditional Catalan specialty—but is finished with a twist. When I first encountered this dish, incidentally, I knew little enough Catalan to think it was going to be eggplant stuffed with anchovies—an idea which, frankly, appealed to me greatly, since most days I'd rather eat anchovies than filet mignon, but one which I suspected most American diners might find rather daunting. In fact, however, the eggplant is stuffed with eggplant itself, tomatoes, and a breadcrumb mixture, and then merely garnished with anchovies.

48

My own mild disappointment aside, I find this to be a wonderful conceit—a deliciously assertive marriage of two primal Mediterranean flavors (or *five*, if you count the olive oil, tomatoes, and garlic). When the American chef Jonathan Waxman first tasted this dish at the Hotel Ampurdán, I might add, he noted that it reminded him of something New Orleans master chef Paul Prudhomme might have concocted—and indeed it does have something of a Prudhomme-style intensity and complexity to it. *Alberginies Farcides amb Anxoves* can be served, incidentally, either as an appetizer or as a side dish, perhaps alongside some simply grilled fish or chicken.

TO SERVE 6 (AS APPETIZER OR SIDE DISH)

6 firm Japanese eggplants or small
*   conventional eggplants (about 6–8*
*   ounces apiece)*
Olive oil
2 cloves garlic, peeled
½ pound tomatoes, seeded and grated
*   (see page 7) or peeled, seeded, and*
*   finely chopped*
1 sprig fresh thyme, removed from
*   stem (or ¼ teaspoon dried)*
¼ teaspoon sugar
Salt and pepper
1 sprig parsley
¼ cup breadcrumbs
24 anchovy filets, soaked in water for
*   1 hour and patted dry*

Cut the eggplants in half lengthwise and make a small furrow in the flesh of each with the tip of a spoon, setting aside the pulp.

Cover the bottom of a pan lightly with oil, then sauté the garlic until light golden-brown. Remove the garlic, and set aside.

Add the tomatoes, reserved eggplant pulp, thyme, sugar, and salt and pepper to taste to the pan, stir well, and cook over low heat for about 45 minutes or until a thick tomato sauce forms.

Meanwhile, in another pan, fry the eggplant on all sides in oil until lightly browned, then drain and arrange cut side up in a lightly oiled broilerproof baking dish.

Mince the sautéed garlic together with the parsley, and mix with breadcrumbs.

Spoon tomato sauce onto each eggplant half, distributing it evenly among them; then set 2 anchovy filets into the sauce on top of each.

Sprinkle the breadcrumb mixture over the anchovies and tomato sauce, and drizzle a few drops of oil over each eggplant.

Brown under the broiler for about 5 minutes.

Alberginies d'Anfós

(EGGPLANT "SANDWICHES" WITH GROUPER MOUSSE)

This Minorcan dish bears some obvious kinship to the preceding Empordanese one—there are many similarities between the cooking styles of the Empordà and the Balearics—though the two are very different in final form. Both regions prepare eggplant stuffed with its own pulp and with breadcrumbs, onions, garlic, and fresh herbs. A Minorcan variation on the theme, formerly available only to the wealthier inhabitants of the island (or to successful fisherman, I suppose), added a forcemeat of fish to the stuffing. The present recipe is a further refinement still, created by opera singer/restaurateur Antonio Borrás and his brother and chef Josep at their delightful Rocamar restaurant, on a little inlet next to the port of Maó (Mahón), Minorca's capital. *Anfós* is grouper *(Epinephelus guaza)*, called *mero* in Castilian and a justly popular fish in the Spanish Mediterranean. Grouper is often available in Florida and other southeastern states, and is worth looking for. In its absence, sea bass or halibut make a good substitute.

TO SERVE 4 (AS APPETIZER)

*¾ pound grouper, sea bass or halibut,
    or other firm-fleshed ocean
    whitefish
Fish stock*

50

*2 teaspoons fresh fines herbes (a
mixture of parsley, tarragon,
chervil, and chives, finely minced
and mixed together) or ½
teaspoon dried*
½ small onion, minced
2 cloves garlic, minced
Olive oil
Flour
Heavy Cream
Salt and pepper
*4 small Japanese eggplants, cut into
½ inch slices*
1 egg, lightly beaten

Place the fish in a saucepan, and cover with fish stock. Add fines herbes, and bring the stock to a boil. Lower the heat, and simmer covered for about 15 minutes. Remove the fish from the stock, and set the stock aside. Allow the fish to cool; then remove and discard skin and bones if any, and flake the flesh with a fork.

Sauté the onions and garlic in a small amount of oil until the onions are wilted but not browned.

In a food processor or blender, with a food mill, or by hand with a fork or whisk, mix the fish, onions and garlic, and 2 tablespoons flour together, blending well; then add equal amounts of cream and reserved fish stock to form a thick paste. (Do not overprocess; the mixture should not be too smooth.) Salt and pepper to taste and set aside.

Dust the eggplant slices with flour, and salt lightly; then sauté lightly in oil and drain.

When the eggplant cools, make "sandwiches" by spreading about 1 tablespoon of fish mixture onto half the sautéed eggplant slices, then topping each one with another slice, continuing until the eggplant is used up.

Dip the sandwiches into egg, then dust with flour, and fry quickly in hot oil.

Drain and serve immediately.

Note: Rocamar often serves this dish with a small salad of chopped raw tomatoes drizzled with olive oil, which I find to be a perfect counterpoint. The "sandwiches" might also be presented on a bed of shredded lettuce—or, if they seem too plain to you as they are, topped with a small quantity of tomato sauce (as for *Pebrots Farcits amb Porc i Calamars*, page 180).

Flam d'Albergínies
(EGGPLANT FLAN)

This delicate and unusual eggplant dish is sometimes served as an appetizer special at the highly sophisticated Reno restaurant in Barcelona, widely considered to be one of Catalonia's best eating places.

TO SERVE 6 (AS APPETIZER)

*4 Japanese eggplants, roasted, peeled,
and cut into strips as for
Escalivada (see page 170)*
4 eggs
14 ounces heavy cream
Salt and white pepper
Butter
*4 medium red peppers, roasted, peeled,
and cut into strips as for
Escalivada*

Preheat the oven to 350°.

Chop the eggplant coarsely.

Beat the eggs and half the cream together; then add the eggplant, and season to taste, stirring well with a whisk or blending until smooth in a blender or food processor.

Butter six ½-cup soufflé molds or custard cups; then pour some of the eggplant mixture into each, distributing it evenly.

Bake, uncovered, in a *bain-marie* in the center of the preheated oven for 25–30 minutes, or until a knife inserted into center of a mold comes out clean.

Remove the molds from the oven, and cool slightly.

Meanwhile, purée the peppers in a food processor, blender, or food mill.

Bring the remaining cream to a boil; then immediately lower the heat, and stir in enough pepper purée to obtain a rich, red color. (The sauce should be creamy, but not too thin.)

Invert the molds onto individual serving plates, and cover with sauce, or cover the bottoms of the plates with sauce, and invert the molds on top.

Cassola d'Albergínies

(EGGPLANT "OMELET" WITH RAISINS AND PINE NUTS)

This dish was an accident. I had found several recipes in older Majorcan cookbooks for a dish of this name—literally eggplant cooked in a cassola or glazed earthenware dish. In these recipes, the eggplant was invariably mixed with eggs and milk, and baked into what I imagined must turn out to be a sort of chunky

soufflé. When recipe-tester Linda Zimmerman and I tried to re-create the dish for the first time, though, we did something wrong—I'm still not sure what—and instead of a soufflé, we got a kind of omelet with a dark golden-brown bottom crust. It looked a bit strange but tasted wonderful—and for some reason I thought it might taste even better with raisins and pine nuts (both common Catalan ingredients) mixed in.

We tried again and came up with the following dish—which is emphatically not authentically Catalan (or Majorcan), but which uses ingredients common to Catalan (and Majorcan) cuisine, and which, I must humbly admit, isn't bad at all.

I highly recommend that you try making this dish in a cassola (see page 8), incidentally, both to remain true to its name and to obtain that attractive golden-brown color we got.

TO SERVE 4–6 (AS APPETIZER OR LIGHT MAIN COURSE)

3 cups olive oil (see note)
8 Japanese eggplants, skin on, cut into 3 × ½-inch strips
2 cloves garlic, peeled
2 tablespoons breadcrumbs
⅓ cup milk
¼ cup golden raisins or sultanas, plumped in warm water for 10 minutes
¼ cup pine nuts, lightly toasted
4 eggs, beaten
Salt

Preheat the oven to 350°.

Heat the oil in a cassola to about 375°;

then fry the eggplant pieces very quickly in batches. Remove, and drain.

In a mortar, crush garlic and breadcrumbs together; then add just enough milk to form a thick paste.

Pour off the cooking oil from the cassola, leaving a light film on the bottom; then distribute the eggplant evenly on the bottom of the vessel.

Add the garlic mixture, raisins, and pine nuts to the eggs; add a dash of salt; then pour over the eggplant.

Bake about 15 minutes, or until the eggs are set and somewhat dry.

Flip the omelet out very carefully, upside down, onto a large serving platter, cut into pie-like wedges, and serve hot or at room temperature.

Note: Don't skimp on the quantity of oil called for. Ironically, eggplant absorbs *less* oil when fried in an ample amount than when fried in too little. Also, handle the cassola carefully when pouring off the oil, as it gets very hot and retains its heat for a long time.

Albergínies Dolçes

(FRIED EGGPLANT WITH SUGAR OR HONEY)

The idea for this recipe comes from a delightful little Majorcan cookbook called *Cocina selecta mallorquina* by the late Coloma Abrinas Vidal—a work which has gone through at least fifteen editions since it was first published in 1961. Vidal's recipes are old-fashioned, and represent Majorcan bourgeois cooking of the late nineteenth and early twen-

tieth century, but they are simple and often turn out very well, even in a modern American kitchen. If the idea of eating eggplant as a dessert seems strange to you, remember that it *is* a fruit; the Greeks even make a kind of sugary preserve out of it, to be eaten by the spoonful. Anyway, the sugar or honey counteracts the slight bitterness eggplant betrays.

TO SERVE 4–6 (AS SNACK OR DESSERT)

⅔ cup flour or instant flour
1 cup water
½ teaspoon salt
¼ teaspoon baking soda
Olive oil
4–6 Japanese eggplants, skin on, cut into 3 × ½-inch strips
Superfine sugar or honey (preferably Spanish or Provençal)

Make a batter of the flour and water; then add the salt and baking soda, and whisk briskly. Allow to rest for 5–10 minutes.

Fill a cassola or other deep pan with at least ¾-inch of oil (or use deep-fryer), and heat the oil to about 375°.

Dip the eggplant pieces into the batter and fry until golden-brown, turning once if you are using a cassola or other pan that is not a deep-fryer.

Drain, sprinkle with sugar or drizzle with honey, and serve immediately.

See Also:

SAMFAINA, page 42
ESCALIVADA, pages 169–170
Tumbet (Majorcan Vegetable Casserole), page 274

AMETLLES, AVELLANES, I PINYONS

(ALMONDS, HAZELNUTS, AND PINE NUTS)

The first time I had Catalan almonds was at the venerable wine firm of De Muller in Tarragona. A bowl of them came out with samples of the company's lovely *vi ranci*. I didn't pay much attention to them at first since I was concentrating on the wine, but I happened to be watching as one of the directors of the firm casually picked one of them up, rubbed it quickly between his fingers (thereby crinkling off its skin), and popped it into his mouth—and I idly followed suit. The almond was delicious—a crunchy concatenation of smoky, salty, earthy flavors. It got my attention right away, and I suppose I must have promptly inhaled half the bowl. They were the best almonds I had ever tasted.

A close second must be the almonds I ate one afternoon at a little wine estate and farm on the island of Ibiza, called Can del Mulo. Ibiza is a salty island, short on water, and what water there is tends to be salty itself. (Ibizencos brag that they bake their bread—and very good bread it is—without salt. They mean without *added* salt; the water they use brings plenty of its own.) Somehow, though, the proprietors of Can del Mulo—European-based American businessman Ronald Calnan and his Italian-born wife Lori—manage to keep their estate magnificently green, to fill a swimming pool, and to grow excellent wine grapes, vegetables, and . . . almonds.

And it was alongside that pool one August afternoon that I first tasted those almonds—still hot from a light roasting and accompanied by Can del Mulo's own sparkling wine and by a plate of little grape-sized home-grown cherry tomatoes, sprinkled with coarse sea salt. "Put a tomato and an almond in your mouth at the same time," Lori said. I did and was instantly transported to some corner of gastronomic paradise. The sweetness and acidity of the tomatoes, the sting of the salt, and the warm intensity of the almonds knit together perfectly; I could not, at that moment, have imagined anything—any mere truffle or spoonful of caviar or forkful of some new creation by Troisgros or Guérard—tasting better.

Unfortunately, Spanish almonds—Tarragonan, Ibizenco, or otherwise—are all but unavailable in the United States. California is the world's largest producer of the nuts, and it owns the domestic market. Spanish almonds in the United States would be bulls to New Castile. There's nothing wrong with California almonds, of course. They can be very good. But they are almonds on a different level, almonds which just simply aren't quite the same thing at all. Spanish almonds are usually larger than their California counterparts, flatter, and more, well, almond-shaped—more graceful-looking, if you will. Their skin is dark brown and loose, relatively easy to rub off, and they have a rich, deep almond flavor. California almonds, which are different varieties altogether in most cases, tend to be plump and squat, with lighter, striated skin that is difficult to remove. They often have a moist, slightly chewy texture, and are

rarely as intense in flavor as the Spanish ones. Still, of course, they're better than nothing—and they work passably well in the Catalan dishes that call for almonds.

I have fond memories of Catalan hazelnuts, too—especially some small, very round ones, roasted to blackness and still hot enough to burn the fingers, which I encountered one day at a big communal luncheon near Tarragona. (There's something about those Tarragona nut trees. . . .) But I find American-grown hazelnuts (also called filberts) to be more successful than American-grown almonds in general—more vividly "Spanish" in

flavor—and perhaps for that reason I don't romanticize the Catalan ones as much.

Almonds and hazelnuts are sometimes said to have been introduced into Catalonia by the Moors, but linguistic evidence suggests that the Romans may have imported them first. (The Catalan words for both—*ametlla* and *avellana* respectively—derive from Latin, not Arabic.) Pine nuts, the edible seeds of certain pine trees, probably predated almost everybody—but it seems reasonable to suppose that it was the Moors, who used them amply in their own cooking, who first popularized their culinary use in the region. In any case, like almonds and hazelnuts, they are very highly regarded in the *països catalans* (author Josep M. Espinàs calls them "the caviar of the forest"), and very widely used—especially in pastries and of course in the all-important *picada* (see page 38).

Walnuts, which the Catalans think go particularly well with wine (as do I), are also widely grown in the region today—there's even a *comarca* in the province of Lleida called La Noguera, "The Walnut Tree"—as are chestnuts, which are commonly associated with the dead in Catalan tradition and thus served mostly at wakes (famous in Catalonia for their gastronomic sophistication) and on holidays commemorating the departed.

Pit d'Indiot amb Salsa d'Ametlles

(TURKEY BREAST WITH ALMOND SAUCE)

Turkey—*indiot* or *gall dindi* ("Indian rooster") in Catalan—has been known in the *països catalans* at least since the early seventeenth century, and has long been a popular holiday treat. In fact, it is as much a part of the traditional Christmas dinner in Catalonia today as it is in the United States (see page 75). Here is another use for turkey, though—inspired by, though different from, a dish described by Coloma Abrinas Vidal in her charming book *Cocina selecta mallorquina*.

TO SERVE 4 (AS MAIN COURSE)

5 cloves garlic
Olive oil
1 tablespoon lard
1½ pounds turkey breast, sliced
1 onion, coarsely chopped
2 tomatoes, seeded and grated (see page 7) or peeled, seeded, and chopped
2 ounces sobrassada *or* chorizo *sausage, skin removed (see page 147)*
¾–1 cup chicken or turkey stock
12 almonds, blanched and roasted (see page 39)

Roast the garlic in a preheated 350° oven for about 30 minutes.

Meanwhile, lightly cover the bottom of a cassola or other wide cooking vessel with olive oil, add the lard, and heat; then brown the turkey slices quickly on both sides. Remove the turkey, and set aside on a large plate (to catch the juices).

In the same cassola with the same fat, make a *sofregit* (see page 38) of the onion and tomatoes, plus the roasted garlic, squeezed from its skin and finely minced.

When the *sofregit* is well-cooked, add the sausage, and stir into the mixture until dissolved and heated through.

Purée contents of the cassola in food processor, blender, or food mill, then return to the pan and stir in ¾ cup of stock plus any juices that have seeped from the turkey.

Pulverize almonds in a food mill, or crush them fine with a mortar and pestle; then add them to the liquid.

Stir well and bring the liquid to a boil, adding more stock if necessary. Reduce the heat, return the turkey slices to the pan, and simmer until the turkey is just reheated.

Note: A typical Majorcan accompaniment to a dish of this sort would be fried potatoes. And, again, be careful of the *cassola* when pouring liquid from it, as it will be very hot.

Panellets
(CATALAN MARZIPAN COOKIES)

Panellets, which are traditionally served on the holiday of Tots Sants or All Saints, November 1, are perhaps the most popular single confection in Catalonia. There are countless versions of this specialty, which invariably has a marzipan or almond paste base, but the most common one is made with pine nuts. Crushed hazelnuts also work very nicely, so I have split this recipe into two parts, one for each of the two kinds of nuts. If you want to use all one variety or the other, of course, you may do so.

TO MAKE 24 COOKIES

*½ pound Idaho or other baking
    potatoes, peeled and quartered
2¼ cups almonds, blanched and
    roasted (see page 39)
2 cups sugar
2 egg yolks
¼ teaspoon vanilla
1 tablespoon grated lemon rind
⅓–½ cup flour*

*2 egg whites, lightly beaten
1½ cups pine nuts (not toasted)
1½ cups hazelnuts (not roasted),
    coarsely crushed
Butter or shortening*

Boil the potatoes until soft; then drain, and put through a ricer.

Preheat the oven to 475°.

Pulverize the almonds in a food mill, or crush them fine with a mortar and pestle.

In a large bowl, mix the potatoes, almonds, sugar, egg yolks, vanilla, and lemon rind.

Sprinkle ⅓ cup flour on a pastry board, and transfer the potato mixture to it; then knead flour and potato mixture together well. (The finished dough should have the consistency of marzipan; depending upon the moisture content of the potatoes, it might be necessary to add more flour.)

Shape the dough into balls 1–1½ inches in diameter, flattening the bottoms slightly.

Dip the balls into beaten egg whites, roll half of them in pine nuts and half in hazelnuts; then bake on a lightly buttered cookie sheet for about 20 minutes or until the nuts have turned golden-brown.

Cool before serving.

Note: Panellets are traditionally served with *vi ranci*, a specialty of the Tarragona region. The term literally means "rancid wine," but, applied to wine, *ranci* also has the sense of "aged" or "mellow"—and *vi ranci* is in fact a sherrylike fortified wine capable, at its best, of great complexity and finesse. A few excellent examples of *vi ranci* are imported into the U.S. by Corti Bros. in Sacramento (see page 304). A reasonable substitute would be good quality dry or medium-dry sherry.

ANXOVES
(ANCHOVIES)

I knew Jaume Subirós was my kind of guy the moment I first climbed into his car, a sleek new dark-gray Citroën BX 19 TRD. It smelled of anchovies. A few days earlier, he explained, as we soared off on a tour of the Empordà countryside, he had been transporting a big jar full of the pungent little fish from his hotel in Roses to his hotel in Figueres, and the jar had toppled over. "I rather like the smell," he confessed sheepishly. I told him I did too.

Subirós was born near Figueres, in the village of Vilamalla. The family home was on the main road, and one day a chef named Josep Mercader stopped to ask if he could put up a sign advertising his new establishment, the Motel Ampurdán, on the side of the house. Subirós senior agreed—on the condition that Mercader give his young son a job. Thus, at the age of eleven, Jaume Subirós became a bellboy at Mercader's place. At fifteen, he was promoted to the hotel dining room—which was to become the single most influential restaurant in modern-day Catalonia—and by the age of twenty-five he had learned the business inside out, married the boss's daughter (Anna-Maria), and become director of a new Mercader venture, the Almadraba Park Hotel in nearby Roses. When Mercader died suddenly in 1979, in the midst of the Catalan culinary revolution he had instigated, Subirós and his wife took over both hotels, complete with the Ampurdán's now-famous restaurant—which remains one of the finest and most innovative in Catalonia.

One of the local traditions whose exercise Subirós inherited from Mercader—one of the local traditions the latter had not been tempted to update—was precisely the thing that had led to that assertive smell in Subirós's Citroën: the old-fashioned curing of anchovies in wooden barrels—in this case in a cool, dark cellar at the Almadraba Park. Now, I must quickly explain that these anchovies—Catalan anchovies in general—have little in common with those sad little dark-brown oil-soaked filets we buy in oval-shaped cans. Catalan anchovies are plump and light in color, and roughly twice the size of the canned variety—and they are packed whole, if not in wood then in glass, with only the heads removed, and not in oil at all but in coarse salt.

The anchovies in the cellar at the Almadraba Park come from Cadaqués—whence are landed, it has been said, "the best anchovies in the Mediterranean" (though such other anchovy-catching Costa Brava ports as Sant Feliu de Guixols, Palamós, and L'Escala might demur). In any case, the fish are only hours old when Subirós gets them. He then soaks them for several days in water of approximately the same salinity as the sea—a process said to leach out much of their own natural salt. Next, the heads are severed and the anchovies are packed in small barrels between layers of salt seasoned with sprigs of fresh thyme and a few black peppercorns. This packing is generally done in May, and the anchovies can be eaten as early as September or October of the same year— though they will last for at least eighteen months. (One local expert on the subject once stated categorically, in fact, that an anchovy less than one year old "cannot be decently served.") Whatever their age, before the anchovies are eaten, they are rinsed, gutted, pulled apart into two filets (with the spines usually discarded but occasionally saved; see page 60), then soaked and/or rinsed again and patted dry. The results are near-miraculous. The anchovies come out sweet, subtle, slightly tart, pleasantly pasty in consistency, and thoroughly delicious—and, believe it or not, much less salty than their oil-packed counterparts. Though they are sometimes used in cooking (as the recipes that follow will demonstrate), in fact, such anchovies are good—and mild—enough to be eaten straight, usually with *Pa amb Tomàquet* (see page 187) or just with bread (or toast) and butter.

As I've indicated, I love anchovies, period—but the ones Subirós prepares at the Almadraba Park (and ferries to the Hotel Ampurdán in the back of his car) are among the best I've ever tasted. Unfortunately, they're not exported—nor, to the best of my knowledge, are any other Catalan anchovies, even of commercial grade. In their stead, I recommend the Arlequin brand from Santoña (in Cantabria, on the Atlantic coast of Spain) or the Minasso Serafino brand from the Italian Riviera—both packed whole and in salt—or the oil-packed filets sold under the Duet or A. Viadero labels, both from Spain. (Spanish and Italian anchovies are better, in general, than the Portuguese variety.) Whatever kind of anchovies you use, though, whether for cooking or plain eating, I recommend that you soak them in water for an hour or so first, Catalan-style, to desalt them.

Anxoves Fregides

(DEEP-FRIED ANCHOVIES)

Deep-fried anchovies are a surprising but delightful hors d'oeuvre served on the Costa Brava. This particular recipe comes from Manuel Vázquez Montalbán's wonderful celebration of Catalan cuisine, *L'Art de menjar a Catalunya* ("The Art of Eating in Catalonia").

TO SERVE 4–6 (AS APPETIZER)

½ cup flour
1 cup light white wine
Olive oil
48 anchovy filets, soaked in water for
    1 hour and patted dry

Make a batter of the flour and white wine, mixing well until very smooth.

Fill a cassola or other deep pan with at least ¾-inch of oil (or use a deep-fryer), and heat the oil to about 375°.

Dip the anchovy filets in the batter, and fry until golden-brown on both sides.

Drain, and serve immediately.

Espinas d'Anxoves Fregides

(DEEP-FRIED ANCHOVY SPINES)

Eating deep-fried anchovy spines at the Hotel Ampurdán for the first time one evening, I suddenly understood quite vividly the difference between fancy French contemporary cooking and the straightforward Catalan variety. A practitioner of the former, challenged to do something different with anchovies, would probably stuff ravioli with anchovy mousse and toss it with caviar butter, or maybe push slivers of the fish into snow-pea pods and arrange them in a salad with sweetbreads and oyster mushrooms, or else use *goujonettes* of anchovy to garnish sautéed foie gras—or some damned thing like that. A Catalan, on the other hand—forever practical—might simply fasten onto a part of the anchovy anyone else would have thrown away (the *spines*, for heaven's sake), and with nothing more than a little flour, milk, and hot oil, turn this residuum into smart, simple little hors d'oeuvre of almost addictive savor—which of course is exactly what Josep Mercader did.

I realize of course that deep-fried anchovy spines sound like a joke and that anchovy spines are not an item you can pick up handily at your local Safeway—but they really do taste very good (the bones, of course, dissolve in the mouth), and if you have both access to the spine-in anchovies mentioned earlier (see page 59) and a sense of fun, I recommend highly that you try them. To obtain the spines, hold the spine-in anchovies under lightly running water, one at a time, and carefully open the belly of each with your thumb. Pull the filets apart, then lift the spine gently from whichever side it has clung to. This is obviously time-consuming labor, but if you've got the room, do it the way the Catalans do—with a friend or two to share the work and a glass or two of wine.

TO SERVE 4–6 (AS APPETIZER)

*40–50 anchovy spines, well-rinsed and
  patted dry*
1 cup milk
Olive oil
¾ cup flour

Soak the spines in the milk for ½ hour.

Fill a cassola or other deep pan with at least ¾-inch of oil (or use a deep-fryer), and heat the oil to about 375°.

Dust the spines lightly with flour, and fry until golden-brown.

Drain, and serve immediately.

Petits Fullats de Cotlliure

(ANCHOVY-BUTTER CANAPÉS)

The French Catalan town of Collioure (Cotlliure in Catalan)—which Josep Pla once rather cryptically called "the egg yolk of the French Catalan coast"—is also famous for its anchovies, which are traditionally cured not just with salt and pepper but with juniper, bay leaves, and a touch of saltpeter. I don't like them as much as those of the Costa Brava myself. They're usually even bigger and can be as rich and oily as herring (which is *too* rich and oily for anchovies in my book). Pla didn't much like them either, and once claimed that they didn't come from local waters at all but were fished off the coast of North Africa—obviously inferior anchovy territory, he assumed. Anyway, they are eaten frequently in French Catalonia, often just with roasted peppers and hard-boiled eggs, but sometimes in the form of a tart-sized anchovy-butter pastry called a *fullat* (which just means *feuilleté*). In working out a recipe for this Collioure specialty, though, I felt that turning the dish into bite-sized canapés might make it a little more palatable to the American eater. The following recipe is authentic in ingredients, then, but not in size.

TO SERVE 4–6 (AS APPETIZER)

1 pound puff pastry dough (see note)
1 egg yolk, beaten with 1 teaspoon
*   water*
1 cup butter, softened
10 anchovy filets, soaked in water for
*   1 hour and patted dry, then*
*   mashed with a fork or a mortar*
*   and pestle*
Lemon juice
½ hard-boiled egg, finely chopped
*   (optional)*
½ tomato, unpeeled and finely
*   chopped (optional)*
2–3 additional anchovy filets, cut into
*   1-inch lengths (optional)*

Roll the puff pastry dough out to ¼-inch thickness and cut out canapé shells with a 2-inch fluted pastry cutter.

Place the shells on a baking sheet that has been lightly sprayed with water or lined with baker's parchment paper; then make an indent no more than ⅛-inch deep in each one with a 1-inch pastry cutter.

Chill the shells, on their baking sheet, in the freezer or refrigerator for ½ hour.

Meanwhile, preheat the oven to 450°.

Remove the shells from the freezer or refrigerator, glaze with the egg yolk and water mixture, and bake for 12–15 minutes or until puffed up and golden-brown. (Cover the shells with another sheet of baker's parchment paper if you wish, to insure more even rising.)

Cool the shells for several minutes; then very carefully pull out the 1-inch pastry centers and set aside. Remove any raw pastry from the interior.

Cream the butter until very fluffy, then gradually whip in the mashed anchovies. Add several drops of lemon juice and mix well.

Spoon the anchovy butter into the shells, decorating the top of each one with chopped egg, chopped tomato, or anchovy pieces, or replacing the pastry lid.

Note: I recommend Julia Child's puff pastry dough recipe, as published in *Julia Child and Company* (Alfred A. Knopf, Inc., 1978), or that offered by Bernard Clayton, Jr., in his *The Complete Book of Pastry* (Simon & Schuster, 1981). Packaged puff pastry dough may of course be used, but with some inevitable sacrifice of flavor and texture.

See Also:

Petits Pastisos de Samfaina amb Anxoves (*Samfaina* Tartlets with Anchovies), page 43
Alberginies Farcides amb Anxoves (Stuffed Eggplants with Anchovies), page 48
"Garum" (Anchovy-Olive *Pâté*), page 118
Pa amb Tomàquet (Catalan Tomato Bread), page 187

ARRÒS
(RICE)

"If you explain the composition of a dish like rice with fish and chicken to a French chef," Josep Pla once wrote, "you'll hear from him a forceful and decisive 'Get thee behind me!'" Pla thought that the French, that is, would find the whole idea of such a dish almost satanically subversive—and he was probably right. Catalans (and Valencians), on the other hand, love dishes of this kind—love both their conceptual simplicity and their baroque adjunction of ingredients—and have for centuries.

Like so much else, rice was apparently first cultivated in the *països catalans* by the Moors. By later medieval times, it had become a staple of the Catalan diet, and rice recipes appear in both the *Libre de Sent Soví* and the *Libre del coch*. Today, rice cooking is one of the region's greatest culinary glories, celebrated not only by Valencia's world-famous paella but also by a considerable repertoire of rice specialties from Barcelona (both city and province), the Costa Brava, Andorra, and the Balearic Islands.

In cooking any of these specialties—recipes for many of which appear in the following pages—it's important to use only short- or round-grain rice, not the long-grain variety called for in so many American paella and "Spanish rice" recipes. Valencian rice is some-

times available in the United States, from Spanish or Hispanic markets; if you can't find it, substitute Italian *aborio* (as for risotto), California Blue Rose, or Japanese short-grain.

It should be noted that most Catalan rice dishes, paella most definitely included, are usually served at room temperature, or at least warm rather than hot—and that, for whatever reasons, they really do taste better that way. Thus, for most of the rice recipes in this book, I have advised a brief "rest period" for the dish after it is cooked—which not only allows the flavors to marry somewhat, but lets you prepare the dish at least a little bit ahead of time if you wish. Most rice dishes are served in small portions as a first course in the *països catalans*, although more complex ones (*Arròs amb Crosta, Arròs Negre,* and various *paelles,* for instance) make perfect main courses or one-dish meals.

Arròs amb Capetes de Torero

(RICE WITH SALT COD, CHICK-PEAS, AND SWEET RED PEPPERS)

Capetes de torero are bullfighters' capes. This delicious rice specialty bears the name because sections of roasted, peeled red pepper are arranged, capelike, on its surface. I first encountered the dish in Valencia, at a restaurant called Gargantúa—said to offer cooking *"de la tradición y de la imaginación."* This, I suppose, might be said to represent both. The following recipe is my own re-creation of the dish.

TO SERVE 4–6 (AS MAIN COURSE)

2 cups chick-peas, cooked (about ⅔ cup dry)
½ teaspoon saffron, lightly toasted
Salt
6 ounces salt cod, not desalted
½ cup olive oil
2–3 tomatoes, seeded and grated (see page 7) or peeled, seeded, and chopped
1 head garlic, separated into cloves, peeled, and chopped
1¾ cups short-grain rice (see page 63)
Salt and pepper
1 large red bell pepper, roasted and peeled as for Escalivada *(see page 170) and cut into four pieces of equal size*

If you are using dried chick-peas, soak them overnight; then cook in about 2½ cups cold water (or follow package directions), adding saffron and a pinch of salt when the peas are almost done. If you are using canned chick-peas, heat through in a saucepan on low heat, and stir in saffron and salt.

Cook unsoaked salt cod in enough water to cover, bringing to a boil, then simmering about 8 minutes. Drain, and cool, then remove bones and skin, and crumble salt cod into small pieces.

Heat the oil in a cassola or large saucepan; then sauté the tomatoes and garlic until the tomatoes have dissolved.

Add the salt cod to the tomato mixture, and stir well; then add the rice, stirring to coat each grain. Salt and pepper to taste.

Add 4½ cups water, bring to a boil; then reduce the heat and simmer uncovered on medium heat for about 10 minutes.

Stir the chick-peas into the rice, and arrange red pepper *"capetes"* on top; then continue cooking for about 10 minutes more, or until the rice is cooked and the water is absorbed.

When the dish is finished, let it stand 5–10 minutes off the heat before serving.

Arròs amb Crosta

(RICE WITH AN EGG CRUST)

The town of Elx (Elche in Castilian), just southwest of Alicante in the *país valencià*, is famous for three things: an immense grove of date palms, 100,000 of them or more (the largest such grove in Europe by far); the stunningly beautiful *Dama de Elche*, a prehistoric polychrome bust of a woman—elegant, proud, elaborately accoutered, mysterious—discovered in the nearby ruins of La Alcudia in 1897 (and now on display at the Museo Arqueológico Nacional in Madrid); and *Arròs amb Crosta.*

Unlike most rice dishes in Catalonia and the region of Valencia, *Arròs amb Crosta* is finished in the oven. It is a real home-style dish, but it is also prepared superbly in such restaurants as Els Capellans and the Parque Municipal in Elx, and Casa Corro in Orihuela. The recipe that follows is an amalgam of several versions I've encountered.

TO SERVE 4–6 (AS MAIN COURSE)

2½ quarts water
½ pound lean pork, cut into large
    cubes
½ pound boneless and skinless
    chicken meat
½ pound ground veal, rolled into
    1-inch meatballs
¼ pound thick-cut bacon, cut into
    ½-inch cubes
2 onions, 1 whole and 1 chopped
1 carrot
1 small turnip
4 tomatoes, seeded and grated (see
    page 7) or peeled, seeded, and
    chopped
2 sprigs parsley, finely minced
Olive oil
1½ cups short-grain rice (see page 63)
6 eggs, beaten
Salt and pepper

Place the water, pork, chicken, meatballs, and bacon in a large pot, and bring to a boil, skimming off the foam.

Add the whole onion, the carrot, and turnip and a dash of salt, and return to a boil (again skimming off the foam); then lower the heat, and simmer, covered, for 2 hours.

Remove, and discard the vegetables; then remove the meat, and set it aside to cool.

Reduce the cooking liquid on medium-high heat to about 4 cups, and reserve.

When the meats have cooled, chop coarsely, and mix together. Salt and pepper to taste.

In a cassola or Dutch oven, make a *sofregit* (see page 38) with the chopped onion, the tomatoes, parsley, and oil.

Meanwhile, preheat the oven to 350°.

Add the rice to the cassola, stirring to coat each grain with *sofregit;* then add about 3½ cups of the reserved cooking liquid, and stir well.

Bake 15 minutes; then remove from the oven. If any liquid remains, cook on low heat on top of the stove until it evaporates.

Mix the beaten eggs with the chopped meats, pour the mixture over the rice, and return to the oven. Bake until golden-brown, about 5–7 minutes.

Serve directly from the cassola.

Arròs Negre

(BLACK RICE)

This is Catalonia's greatest rice dish—a dark, rich, briny seafood specialty, blackened (and transported to a higher plane of flavor) with the ink of cuttlefish. It is a dramatic dish to look at and a wonderful one to taste. It takes a bit of hard work to fashion, but the results are worth it.

Arròs Negre is a specialty of the Costa Brava, and I must have tasted it in a dozen private homes and restaurants in the region—most notably (among the restaurants) at Cypsele in Palafrugell, Can Toni and Eldorado Petit in Sant Feliu de Guixols, and Big Rock in Platja d'Aro. The best I've ever had, though, was in Barcelona, at a superb little place called Els Perols de l'Empordà ("The Cooking Pots of the Ampurdán"). Proprietors Reynaldo and Juli Serrat (she is the chef) have been kind enough to offer me their recipe, which I hereby pass along. The great success of the dish at their restaurant, of course, depends largely on the hours-old fish and shellfish they obtain from the fish markets of the Costa Brava, and on the use of fresh cuttlefish, both for its flesh and for its ink. This is a recipe, then, for which you should splurge on the best and the freshest possible seafood. Even fresh cuttlefish is available in some parts of the United States, though it is hard to find. It is not the same thing as squid, exactly. Its flesh is thicker and sweeter, and its ink is richer in flavor. Nonetheless, fresh squid (and squid ink) may be substituted—or you could use a combination of canned Spanish cuttlefish (sold in some Spanish and Hispanic markets), for its ink, and fresh squid.

TO SERVE 6 (AS MAIN COURSE)

*1 medium-sized cuttlefish (about ½
    pound) or 2–3 large squid, cleaned
    and cut into small pieces, with
    ink sac(s) set aside (see note)*

*Olive oil
2 onions, chopped
2 tomatoes, seeded and grated (see
    page 7) or peeled, seeded, and
    chopped
1 pound monkfish, cut into 6 pieces
12 mussels, cleaned
6 large shrimp, shells on
3 cups short-grain rice (see page 63)
5–6 cups fish stock
2 cloves garlic, minced
2 sprigs parsley, minced
Salt*

Cook the cuttlefish or squid in a cassola, Dutch oven, or large skillet in a small amount of olive oil until just done (about 2–3 minutes).

Add the onion, with more oil if necessary, and cook until soft; then add the tomato and cook, stirring well, until it has almost dissolved.

Add the remaining fish and shellfish to the cassola, and mix in well.

Place the ink sac(s) in a sieve, hold it over the cassola, and crush sac(s) with the back of a spoon. Pour a few tablespoons of water through the sieve to extract more ink.

Bring the fish stock to a boil; then reduce to a simmer.

Meanwhile, add the rice to the cassola, and stir well so that all grains are coated with oil and ink.

Slowly add the fish stock, stir well, and bring to a boil. Add the garlic, parsley, and salt to taste; then reduce the heat, and cook on very low heat, uncovered, for 15–20 minutes or until all the liquid is absorbed but the rice is still creamy. (Do not stir.)

When the dish is finished, let it stand 5–10 minutes off the heat before serving.

Note: The ink sac in both cuttlefish and squid is a little silver-gray pouch located beneath the tentacles. It is easy to find, but treat it gently so that it doesn't break.

With the growing popularity of Italian-style black rice and black pasta, cuttlefish or squid ink has recently become available in small jars or plastic pouches (like soy sauce at Chinese take-out places). The quality of such ink is fine—but why pay for something (and it's generally quite expensive) that comes free with the cuttlefish or squid itself? If you are using such ink, substitute about 2 teaspoons of it for the ink called for in this recipe.

See Also:

Arròs a Banda (Rice and Rascasse, in Two
   Courses), page 199
PAELLA, pages 207–217

AVIRAMS
(POULTRY)

My favorite part of Catalonia, outside of Barcelona anyway, is the *comarca* of the Alt Empordà, in Spain's far northeastern corner—a region born, legend has it, out of the union of a shepherd and a Siren, and thus a child of both land and sea. Both aspects of its supposed heritage, certainly, are magnificently represented in the Alt Empordà—but its interior reaches, especially the countryside around Figueres, seem something very special to me. The topography is perfect, changing constantly from flatlands to rolling hills to steep hills, and then sometimes dropping down suddenly toward the sea—always varied but always in harmony,

never hiding the horizon but never homogenizing into insipidity. The region has its ugly little towns and jarring signs of uneasily assimilated industry, to be sure, but it also has its groves of shaggy pines and stands of red-banded cork oak, its scattering of olive trees with their ghostly gray-green leaves, its old stone churches and walled medieval villages. It has been called a kind of Catalonia in miniature, boasting at least small samples of nearly every kind of physical beauty that the area as a whole can offer.

Its symbolic aspects (and its industry and its inevitable tourism) aside, however, the Alt Empordà remains above all real farm country—the kind of place where roads are sometimes blocked with sheep, horsecarts still haul grapes, goats wander mischievously through vineyards . . . and where some of Europe's most delicious ducks and geese are raised.

The geese are tricky. They are fragile creatures, capable of catching cold and dying overnight—sometimes, perhaps as some vague instinctual revenge, the night before they are scheduled to be slaughtered. Even their eggs don't hatch about half the time, a local farmer told me. But the geese that make it through to eating age—about six months is considered to be optimum hereabouts—have sweet, rich meat in which you'd swear you could almost taste the nuts and grains on which they commonly feed. Ducks—usually of the species called Barbary—are easier, and are put to more uses.

Cured duck breast "ham" is a recent innovation in the region and has become very popular all over Catalonia (the best I've ever had is at the *xampanyería,* or "champagne" bar, called El Cava del Palau in Barcelona); more glamorously, there are now at least three producers of very good duck *foie gras* in this corner of Catalonia, most notably the Cooperativa Coll-Verd in the village of Alfar. But the main use to which ducks and geese are put in the Alt Empordà is as constituents of four closely related dishes that are among the crowning achievements of Catalan cuisine—duck with pears, duck with turnips, goose with pears, and goose with turnips—all of them rich, intensely flavored, complex dishes, perhaps of Roman origin, and all unabashedly brown and heavy-looking—but, if properly made, quite incredible to taste. (Recipes for duck with pears and goose with turnips follow.)

Chicken is also highly regarded in the Alt

Empordà, as indeed it is throughout Catalonia. Until recent years, all Catalan chickens were free-range and raised on small or at least privately owned farms. (Such chickens were sometimes called *gratapallers* or "haystack scratchers" for their foraging habits.) Today, however, mass-produced feed-lot birds are increasingly common—a fact which Catalan food lovers tend to rail against with surprising passion. Guinea hen (the superlative fowl the French call *pintade*) is well-known in Catalonia, too, as is turkey—an early import from the Americas that found favor in the region almost immediately. That noted citizen of the Alt Empordà, Salvador Dalí, in fact, has written that the first recipe for turkey appeared in Catalonia as early as 1617—although I haven't been able to verify this. Dalí also once proposed, in his book *My Secret Life* (and in his famous surrealistic prose style), that the turkey "always awakens in man the flight of the cannibal angels of his cruelty"—citing as an example a recipe appearing in the Neapolitan author Giambattista Della Porta's sixteenth-century *Magia naturalis*, in which a turkey is roasted without first killing it, "so as to achieve that supreme refinement: to make it possible to eat it cooked and living." This recipe, I am happy to say, is not a Catalan one.

Ànec amb Peres

(DUCK WITH PEARS)

There are as many recipes for this Catalan classic as there are chefs who cook it. I particularly like this version, though—a rather refined one, from the Eldorado Petit restaurants in Barcelona and Sant Feliu de Guixols (the latter town in the Alt Empordà).

TO SERVE 4–6 (AS MAIN COURSE)

Two 4-pound ducks
Salt and pepper
Olive oil
2 onions, 1 whole and 1 chopped
2 carrots, 1 whole and 1 chopped
3 sprigs parsley, 2 whole and 1 minced
1 stalk celery
1 bay leaf
1 sprig fresh thyme, minced, or ¼
  teaspoon dried
4 pears, peeled and cored
12 cloves garlic, minced
½ cup vi ranci *(see note page 57) or*
  dry sherry
3 tomatoes, seeded and grated (see page
  7) or peeled, seeded, and chopped
4 tablespoons flour

Preheat the oven to 450°.

Cut the ducks in half, and set aside the necks, giblets, and wing tips (severed at the first joint).

Prick the skin of the ducks with a fork, season with salt and pepper to taste; then roast for 1 hour, or until golden-brown, on a rack in a roasting pan.

Meanwhile, brown the necks, giblets, and wing tips lightly in a small amount of oil; then place them in a stockpot with the whole onion, carrot, and parsley sprigs, the celery, bay leaf, thyme, salt and pepper to taste, and water to cover. Bring to a boil, and simmer uncovered for 1 hour.

Parboil the pears for about 5 minutes; then cool and set aside.

In a cassola or Dutch oven, make a *sofregit* (see page 38) of the garlic, chopped onion, and minced parsley in a small amount of oil mixed with some duck fat skimmed from the roasting pan.

When the ducks have cooked, skim excess fat from the roasting pan, deglaze with *vi ranci* or sherry, and add the pan juices to the cassola.

Add the tomatoes and chopped carrot, and cook on low heat until the tomatoes have disintegrated and the mixture has thickened.

Strain the giblet stock, and add it to the cassola, then stir in the flour. Bring the liquid to a boil, lower the heat, and simmer for 10 minutes, or until the sauce is thick.

Cut the pears into quarters or eighths (depending on size) and cut the duck halves in half again, then add both to the cassola and simmer for 10 minutes or until tender.

Correct the seasoning if necessary.

Oca amb Naps

(GOOSE WITH TURNIPS)

Can Bonay is a "casino" in the medieval walled town of Peratallada, east of Girona—but it is not a casino in the usual sense. A casino in Catalonia is sometimes just a social club, where men congregate—or used to, anyway—to jabber and play cards. Commonly, such places would have a bar on the ground floor and gaming tables upstairs. As the old customs died out, some of these casinos turned their upper portions into restaurants—and Can Bonay is one of them. The food is simple,

hearty, and purely Catalan here—huge bowls of snails with *allioli* on the side, fish baked Costa Brava-style on a bed of thinly sliced potatoes, crisp pork jowls roasted with onions, and such—and, above all, Goose with Turnips.

Turnips were cultivated in the Pyrénées as early as the fourteenth century, and Catalonia's most famous ones, from the mountain village of Talltendre, are long and thin (and sometimes, surprisingly, black-skinned). Our usual globe-shaped variety don't taste quite the same, but will work adequately for this dish. Here is Can Bonay's recipe:

TO SERVE 4–6 (AS MAIN COURSE)

One 10–pound goose
1 tablespoon lard
3 slices French or Italian bread, crusts removed
1 goose liver (regular size, not foie gras)
Olive oil
3 onions, 1 whole and 2 chopped
1 carrot
1 stalk celery
1 bay leaf
2 whole sprigs parsley
Salt and pepper to taste
4 tomatoes, seeded and grated (see page 7) or peeled, seeded, and chopped
24 almonds, blanched and roasted (see page 39)
2 pounds turnips, cut into 3 × *½-inch strips*

Cut the goose into 12 serving pieces, and set aside the neck, giblets, backbone, and wing tips (severed at first joint).

Wash the goose, pat dry; then sauté in the lard until well-browned.

Remove any excess fat from the pan, and set aside. Fry the bread and then the goose liver in the remaining fat, and set them aside.

In a stockpot, brown the necks, giblets, backbone, and wing tips lightly in a small amount of oil. Add the whole onion, the carrot, celery, bay leaf, parsley, salt and pepper to taste, and water to cover. Bring to a boil, and simmer uncovered for 1 hour.

In a cassola or Dutch oven, make a *sofregit* (see page 38) of the chopped onions and tomatoes in oil mixed with about 1 tablespoon of the reserved goose fat.

Add the goose to the cassola, then strain the giblet stock, and add it. If the goose and vegetables aren't completely covered by the liquid, add water until they are. Bring the liquid to a boil, lower the heat, and simmer for 20 minutes.

Meanwhile, make a *picada* (see page 40) of the almonds, fried bread, and goose liver, moistened with a small amount of cooking liquid.

Add the *picada* to the cassola and stir in well, then cover the cassola and simmer for about 1½ hours, or until the goose is very tender.

Meanwhile, parboil the turnips for about 3 minutes, dry thoroughly, then brown in the remaining reserved goose fat until almost caramelized. Drain, and add to the cassola about 15 minutes before cooking is completed.

Pollastre Rostit amb Samfaina

(ROAST CHICKEN WITH *SAMFAINA*)

This is another Catalan classic, a dish I've enjoyed frequently throughout the region. It is very simple.

TO SERVE 4 (AS MAIN COURSE)

One 4–5-pound roasting chicken
Olive oil
Salt and pepper
5 cups samfaina *(see page 42)*

Preheat the oven to 375°.

Cut the chicken into 6 or 8 serving pieces, rub all surfaces well with olive oil, and season with salt and pepper; then roast skin side up for 1–1½ hours, or until the skin is golden-brown, and the juices run clear when a thigh is pierced with a fork.

Remove the chicken from the roasting pan, and set aside, keeping it warm.

Pour off any excess fat, then deglaze the roasting pan with a few tablespoons of water.

Add the *samfaina* to the pan, and stir well; then add chicken, and simmer briefly until heated through.

Note: Roasted or fried potatoes are the classic accompaniment to this dish.

Rostit de Festa Major

(HOLIDAY ROAST CHICKEN)

Every city, town, and village in the *països catalans* has an annual *festa major* or main holiday—a sort of "our town" festival—usually held on the feast day of the local patron saint and *always* a day of serious feasting. The traditional pièce de résistance of the holiday meal in much of Catalonia is some version of this simple, succulent roast chicken. In smaller towns, families still take big terra-cotta or cast-iron baking dishes filled with the makings of the dish to the local bakery and let the *rostit* cook slowly in the radiated heat of the big brick bread ovens. I've seen ovens ten feet deep and a dozen feet across, in fact, filled with whole phalanxes of such pots and casseroles, each one concealing its own brand of homey culinary alchemy—a hundred slightly different flavors in a hundred slightly different vessels, I would wager. This version of the dish is typical of the Empordà region.

TO SERVE 6 (AS MAIN COURSE)

1 large roasting chicken (5–6 pounds)
2 tablespoons lard
Olive oil
6 small white onions, 2–2½ inches in diameter, peeled and halved or quartered
1 large head garlic, separated into cloves and peeled
1 stick cinnamon
1 bay leaf
Salt and pepper
1 cup cognac

Preheat the oven to 375°.

Cut the chicken into 10–12 serving pieces; then brown thoroughly in the lard and a small amount of oil (in batches if necessary) in a cassola, Dutch oven, or roasting pan.

When the chicken is well-browned, add the onions and garlic cloves to the pan, stirring to coat well with lard and oil; then add the cinnamon, bay leaf, and salt and pepper to taste.

Pour the cognac over the chicken pieces, and roast uncovered for 1½ hours, turning the chicken after 45 minutes and basting occasionally with the pan juices while roasting.

Moisten the chicken pieces with a small amount of the pan juices before serving.

Note: Fried or roasted potatoes and/or a simple green salad are the traditional accompaniments to a *Rostit de Festa Major,* and—this being, after all, a dish for festive occasions—*cava* or champagne is considered the appropriate wine.

"Pius Nonos"

(CHICKEN AND POTATO CROQUETTES)

I found this recipe in a recent facsimile reprint of a book called *La Cuyna mallorquina,* first published anonymously in 1886 in Felanitx, southeast of Palma on the island of Majorca. The book is believed to have been written by one Don Pere d'Alcàntara Penya, described by a contemporary as "a highly likable, humane, and cordial personality," and remembered to this day in Felanitx as a great

connoisseur of true local cooking. I like this recipe because it's easy and because it's fried—and because it's a wonderful way to use up leftover chicken (and, for that matter, leftover mashed potatoes).

The name of the dish confused me for some time, though, and none of my culinary advisers, in Catalonia or on Majorca itself, seemed to be able to translate it satisfactorily for me. Then, over lunch on the Costa Brava one day, my friend Lluïsa Jausàs, after puzzling for some moments over the words "Pius Nonos" as I had scrawled them in my notebook, suddenly laughed and said, "I think you'll understand it better if you write it like this. . . ." She took my pen and wrote the following: "Pius IX."

These were croquettes, in other words, named for a Pope. "Pius" is simply a Latin name much favored by Catholic pontiffs (there have been twelve Popes of that name thus far); *nono* is a Castilian word meaning "ninth" but exclusively in the papal sense. This particular Pius, who was born in 1792 and was Pope from 1846 until his death in 1878, has a special

meaning to (shall we say) pious Spaniards: It was he who signed the concordat with Queen Isabella II in 1851 that made Roman Catholicism Spain's sole recognized religion. Just why this or any other action should have earned him the honor of having leftover-chicken croquettes named after him, I still don't know—but perhaps it has something to do with the fact that their conical shape somewhat resembles the shape of the papal tiara.

TO SERVE 4 (AS APPETIZER OR LIGHT MAIN COURSE)

1 onion, minced
2 cloves garlic, minced
1 tablespoon lard
Olive oil
2 ounces European-style ham (prosciutto or Black Forest type), minced
1½ cups leftover chicken, skinned, boned, and minced
2 ounces butter, softened
1 egg yolk and 1 lightly beaten whole egg
1¾ cups mashed potatoes (about 1 pound potatoes, peeled, quartered, and boiled in salted water for 20–25 minutes or until done; then drained and mashed)
Salt and pepper
Breadcrumbs
2–3 sprigs parsley, minced
2 lemons (optional)

In a cassola or large skillet, make a *sofregit* (see page 38) of the onion and garlic in lard and a small amount of oil.

Stir in the ham and chicken, mix well, sauté on low heat for about 5 minutes; then remove pan from heat, and set aside to cool.

Stir the butter and egg yolk into the mashed potatoes, and salt and pepper to taste; then place in the refrigerator for 20–30 minutes or until moldable.

Shape the potato mixture into 12–16 balls about 1½–2 inches in diameter; then form each into a small flat patty between your hands. Place 1 teaspoon of the chicken mixture in the center of each patty, then close the potatoes around it, cupping each croquette in the palm of your hand and forming it into a bell or cone shape.

Gently flatten the bottom of each croquette; dip them in beaten egg; roll in breadcrumbs; then fry in at least 1 inch of oil heated to 375° in a cassola or deep pan (or use deep-fryer), turning them to brown on all sides.

Drain on paper towels as cooked; then sprinkle with parsley. Squeeze a few drops of fresh lemon juice over each croquette if desired.

Pintada a la Catalana

(GUINEA HEN IN LEMON AND GARLIC SAUCE)

Ely Buxeda is a French Catalan entertainer, who once toured Europe with his crooning vocals and syrupy saxophone but who now confines his performances to an occasional turn at the pleasant restaurant he runs in the seaside wine town of Banyuls, a few miles north of the Spanish border. I have a certain affection for his establishment—which is called Le Sardinal, "The Sardine Net"—be-cause it was the first Catalan restaurant I ever visited, a good three years before I first set foot in Spanish Catalonia.

I must admit that I don't remember what I ate my first time at Le Sardinal, other than some rich Collioure anchovies—but when I went back, five years later, in the company of one of the directors of the Templers union of Banyuls wine cooperatives, I tasted this guinea hen dish and immediately begged for the recipe. Le Sardinal's chef, Jean-Marie Patrouix, who isn't Catalan but who knows how to cook as if he were (which I mean as a compliment), promptly scribbled it out for me.

TO SERVE 4 (AS MAIN COURSE)

One 3–4-pound guinea hen or chicken
Olive oil
1 onion, chopped
2–3 heads garlic, separated into cloves
 and peeled
¼ pound European-style ham
 (prosciutto or Black Forest type),
 cut into julienne strips about 2
 inches long
1 lemon rind, grated
Juice of 1 lemon
2½ cups rich chicken or veal stock
Orange extract
1 cup dry white wine
Salt and pepper
8–12 rounds (3 inches in diameter)
 French or Italian bread, lightly
 toasted and allowed to dry to
 crispness
4 paper-thin slices lemon (optional)

Cut the guinea hen or chicken into 8 serving pieces.

Sauté the pieces in olive oil in a cassola or large skillet until golden-brown; then remove, and set aside.

In the same oil, make a *sofregit* (see page 38) of the onion, whole garlic cloves, and ham.

Return the guinea hen or chicken to the cassola and add the lemon rind, lemon juice, stock, a few drops of orange extract, the wine, and salt and pepper to taste.

Simmer partially covered until the chicken is very tender and the liquid is reduced by half (about 1½–2 hours).

Garnish with the dried bread and, if you wish, with lemon slices.

Gall Dindi Farcit Nadelenc

(STUFFED CHRISTMAS TURKEY)

As noted earlier, turkey is associated with Christmas in Catalonia as much as it is in the United States. The context in which it is traditionally presented on that holiday (or that holiday's eve) is, however, somewhat different from the American version. An old-fashioned Catalan Christmas banquet would invariably begin with *Escudella i Carn d'Olla* (see page 231), the Ur-Catalan specialty of assorted meats and vegetables cooked in stock and then served in two courses—broth first, meats later.

Next, in many families, would come *menuts de pollastre*—various chicken organs, chopped up and fried, usually with potatoes. The stuffed turkey (or, in poorer households, capon or rooster) would follow—and then sometimes a whole baked fish of some kind would be offered. *Turróns,* assorted Catalan (or Valencian) nougats, are the essential Christmas dessert, often succeeded by the crisp, thin, rolled cookies called *Neules* (see page 260) and a glass or two of *vi dolç,* sweet wine. The American diner need not attempt to reproduce such an ambitious menu. Anyway, Catalan-style stuffed turkey fits in very well with the usual Yankee accompaniments to such a meal.

TO SERVE 8–10 (AS MAIN COURSE)

One 10–12-pound turkey
Salt and pepper
Cinnamon
Lard
Olive oil
6 ounces botifarra *sausage (see page 147), casing removed, crumbled*
6 ounces European-style ham *(prosciutto or Black Forest type), cut into julienne strips about 2 inches long*
20 prunes, pitted, plumped in warm *water for 10 minutes, and coarsely chopped*
¾ cup golden raisins or sultanas, *plumped in warm water for 10 minutes*
12 chestnuts, boiled, peeled, and *quartered*
1 cup breadcrumbs
3 sprigs parsley, 2 whole and 1 finely *minced*

2½ cups vi ranci *(see note page 57) or dry sherry*
2 bay leaves
2 sprigs fresh oregano or marjoram, or *½ teaspoon dried, wrapped securely in cheesecloth*
1 onion
1 carrot
1 stalk celery

Remove the giblets and neck from the turkey, and set aside.

Preheat the oven to 325°.

Wash, and thoroughly dry the turkey; then dust the interior cavity with salt, pepper, and cinnamon.

Heat about 1 tablespoon of lard with a small amount of oil in a cassola or large skillet; then add the sausage, ham, prunes, raisins, and chestnuts, and sauté until the whole mixture is lightly browned.

Stir in the breadcrumbs, and mix well; then add ¼ teaspoon cinnamon, the minced parsley, and salt and pepper to taste. Mix well again; then add 1½ cups *vi ranci* or sherry and simmer uncovered until the liquid has evaporated.

Let the mixture cool, then stuff the turkey with it.

Truss the turkey; then rub the exterior with lard or oil, season with salt and pepper, and roast on a rack in an uncovered roasting pan for 3½–4½ hours (about 15–20 minutes per pound), breast side down, basting occasionally with the pan juices.

When the turkey is about half-cooked, turn it breast side up, pour the remaining *vi ranci* or sherry over it, and add 1 cup water, 1 bay leaf, and the oregano or marjoram to the roasting pan. (Pour the water directly into the pan bottom, not over the turkey.)

Meanwhile, brown the turkey giblets and neck lightly in a small amount of lard or oil; then place them in a stockpot with the onion, carrot, celery, whole parsley sprigs, the remaining bay leaf, salt and pepper to taste, and water to cover. Bring to a boil and simmer uncovered for 1 hour.

When the turkey is done, let it rest on the roasting rack, out of the oven, for about 20 minutes before serving.

Meanwhile, strain the giblet stock, then remove the oregano and marjoram from the roasting pan, pour off any excess fat and pan juices, and deglaze the pan with the stock. Boil the stock down for about 10 minutes, until it is reduced by about half. Correct the seasoning if necessary.

Remove the stuffing from the turkey, and place it in the center of a large, warm serving platter. Carve the turkey, and arrange the meat on top of the stuffing. Pour some of the gravy over the bird and stuffing, and serve the rest on the side.

See Also:

Pit d'Indiot amb Salsa d'Ametlles (Turkey Breast with Almond Sauce), page 56

Esqueixada de Pollastre (Shredded Chicken Salad), page 175

Escabetx de Gallina, Colomí, o Perdiu (Pickled Chicken, Pigeon, or Partridge), page 177

Coca d'Ànec i Olives (Duck and Olive *Coca*), page 195

Pebrots Farcits amb Ànec (Sweet Red Peppers Stuffed with Duck), page 181

Canalons d'Ànec (*Canalons* with Ground Duck), page 205

Mar i Muntanya I (Chicken and Prawn Ragout), page 226

BACALLÀ
(SALT COD)

I've had the feeling almost from the day I started writing this volume that salt cod was going to be my hardest sell. Some readers will probably believe me when I say that lard is a necessary ingredient in many Catalan dishes; others, I suspect—though certainly fewer—may actually pull the spines out of anchovies and then fry and eat them; I'll bet a few hardy souls will even try that recipe on page 114 for, well, the part of the bull that makes him a bull and not a steer. But salt cod? I just don't know. It's a tough one.

Cod isn't particularly favored in the United States. It suggests frozen fish sticks somehow and, of course, cod liver oil. Add the dreaded word "salt" to it, and I reckon you might as well be talking cat food as far as most Americans are concerned. But I've decided to be bull-headed about the matter, and have included eight different salt cod recipes here—plus another nine scattered through other chapters. Why? Because salt cod is a vital staple of Catalan cuisine. And because the stuff is wonderful.

To begin with, salt cod *isn't* "too salty." Saying that salt cod is too salty is like saying that frozen peas are too cold. Salting (and drying), like freezing, is a means of preservation, and in both cases a certain amount of preparation is required to make the preserved thing fit to eat. With rare exceptions, salt cod is always *desalted* before it's used—and if it's desalted correctly, it ends up retaining no more salt than fresh fish does.

That brings up another argument against salt cod. Why eat fish preserved in this archaic manner when there's so much of the fresh (or almost-fresh-tasting frozen) variety around? The best way I can answer that question is simply to ask, then, Why eat ham, bacon, or sausage when there's so much fresh meat in the marketplace? (Salt cod is, in a sense, the ham of the sea—animal flesh cured at the time of its slaughter to last, and add flavor to dishes, all year round.) Why eat pickles when fresh vegetables are in season? Why, for that matter, drink wine—fermentation is a means of preservation, too, don't forget—while you can still find a bunch or two of actual grapes?

Most methods of preservation change the item being preserved—often for the worse, admittedly, but sometimes for the better. Salting and drying cod preserves the fish, but it also transforms it into a greater creature, turns it ivory-smooth in texture, crystallizes (if you will) its flavor. Fresh cod, if truth be told, is really rather an insipid fish; salt cod can be something of a gastronomic marvel. (Manuel Raventós, director general of the massive Codorníu wine company, once told me that when he serves salt cod to non-European visitors, they sometimes remark on how very fresh it tastes!)

What *is* salt cod, finally? It's simply fresh cod *(Gadus morrhua)*, cured either in tanks of brine or in huge kenches (bins) packed with rock salt, then dried either in the sun and wind (the traditional method, obviously) or in temperature-controlled drying rooms. Its common European names—*bacalao* in Castilian Spanish, *baccalà* in Italian, *bacalhau* in Portuguese, Catalan's *bacallà*, etc.—are of disputed etymology. They apparently do *not* derive, as is frequently suggested, from the Latin word *baculum*, meaning ''staff'' or ''walking stick'' (supposedly for the stick-hard consistency of salt cod's dried, splayed carcasses). The distinguished Catalan etymologist Juan Corominas proposes that the word might be related to the modern French word for fresh cod, *cabillaud*—which in turn might come from a Dutch or Hanseatic corruption of a Gascon version of a (still with me?) Latin augmentative form of a *diminuative* form of the Latin word *caput*, head (because cod was considered to have a big, or a ''big little'' head). The French, you will be happy to hear, call salt cod *morue*, which apparently comes directly (as does cod's Linnaean name) from the Latin word for cod, *morus*.

In any case, salt cod is first mentioned in an eleventh-century Flemish manuscript, and some scholars think it might have existed as much as 200 years earlier. Though it is consumed today primarily in Africa, the Caribbean, and the European Mediterranean, most salt cod is actually processed in Scandinavia and Canada—and the Norwegians, above all, have most likely been selling the stuff to lower Europe for at least 400 years. The first reference to salt cod in Catalonia dates from 1640, and today there are said to be literally hundreds of *bacallà* recipes known to Catalan cuisine.

It might seem strange that this sort of preserved fish should have become so popular in Catalonia and other Mediterranean lands, where fish of the fresh sort is so obviously plentiful—but fresh fish was rarely available inland in earlier times and couldn't always be counted on even on the coast (as in times of bad weather or plain fisherman's bad luck). And during Lent and other fast periods, in these largely Catholic countries, meat and poultry were strictly forbidden—so that it was often *bacallà* or nothing. Catalan author-chef Domènec Moli has even gone so far as to suggest that, "*Bacallà* is, in our society, the only positive result of Lent."

Most salt cod sold in the United States today comes from Canada. Of that, the best is probably from Nova Scotia and Quebec and the poorest from Newfoundland—and the best of the best is the so-called Gaspé variety, which is lightly cured and almost always sun-dried. Catalan chefs seem to favor Norwegian *bacallà*, and this is sometimes available here, too—and is worth looking for. Salt cod is sold in several different forms in the United States: in boneless, skinless strips or filets, usually packed in one-pound wooden boxes or wax-paper cartons; in large loin pieces with some skin and bone still attached; as what the trade calls middles, which are rectangular pieces, partially boned, usually an inch-and-a-half or two inches thick; and as whole fish, spread out winglike and crystallized in salt.

The whole fish, usually found in hard-core Portuguese or Caribbean markets, are a bit much to deal with unless you plan to commit yourself to salt cod seriously. The boxed cod is fine for recipes calling for *bacallà* to be puréed or flaked, and the loin pieces will give you both thin strips of fish (for puréeing or flaking) and thicker ones for recipes that require bigger chunks. Best of all, if you can find them, are

the middles. They're usually cut from larger cod, and thus have better texture than smaller pieces—and they're adaptable to any form, from purées to "steaks."

There can be considerable variation in quality from one piece of salt cod to the next. Unfortunately, there's rarely much choice in this country—and in the case of the prepacked variety, you can't even see the fish in the first place. When you *can* see it, look for a white or grayish-white color (a yellow tinge indicates overdryness, and an amber cast is a sign of kench-curing, which sometimes yields unevenly dried or salted fish); on the other hand, salt cod that's *too* white might have been chemically bleached and will have a faintly bitter taste. In general, buy salt cod cut from the largest pieces possible, and look for a supple texture rather than a firm, pressed one.

Author Alan Davidson quotes a Basque salt cod expert named José Castillo as saying, "I regard *bacalao* as though it were steel. If you do not give it the necessary 'tempering,' it will not be in the right state." That tempering is, of course, the desalting process. There are a number of variations on this process, and the trouble with all of them is that no two pieces of salt cod seem to be salted exactly alike, and thus no two lose their salt in exactly the same amount of time. Manuel Pagès of the Raïmat winery once told me that *bacallà* can be desalted by soaking it for a week or even two in *salted* water—the idea being that the salt in the fish will form crystals with that in the water. I'll take his word for it.

Meanwhile, though, I usually just soak salt cod in plain water, in the refrigerator, for about 48 hours—changing the water three or four times a day. Paula Wolfert suggests adding a cup of milk to the water during the final soak. Jaume Subirós of the Hotel Ampurdán and Barcelona author-chef Llorenç Torrado both counsel soaking *bacallà* for more like three or four days. But both of these experts and Wolfert—and I—agree that the only sure way to tell whether a piece of salt cod is sufficiently desalted is to nibble on a corner of it.

Though salt cod is poached for some recipes, I don't recommend poaching it as a means of desalting—though that method is suggested in some books and on some of those aforementioned wooden or waxed-paper pack-

ages; salt cod has a nasty tendency to disintegrate in too much hot water. Jaume Subirós, incidentally, likes to soak his *bacallà* for some dishes for an extra day, after it's desalted, in olive oil flavored with a few peeled cloves of raw garlic. I think this is a lovely idea.

Bacallà a la Llauna

(SALT COD WITH GARLIC AND PAPRIKA "ON THE TIN")

This dish takes its name from the tin plate or *llauna* on which it was originally baked (though today it is usually made in a conven-

tional metal baking dish or heavy skillet). Created in the *fondes* of eighteenth-century Barcelona (see page 23), *Bacallà a la Llauna* has become one of the most popular preparations of salt cod in all of Catalonia, and one of the best. I first encountered it in Barcelona myself, at a restaurant called Chicoa—which specializes in *bacallà* dishes, and in first-rate Catalan traditional food in general. It's a simple dish, ever so slightly sharp and slightly sweet, and is a delicious reminder that *bacallà* can sometimes look (and be cooked) like a real piece of *fish*. There are several variations on *Bacallà a la Llauna*—some with parsley added, some without the wine, some which even omit the garlic. This is my own interpretation of the version I like best.

TO SERVE 4 (AS MAIN COURSE)

*1 1/2 pounds thick-cut salt cod,
    desalted (see page 79), skinned,
    boned, and cut into small steaks
    about 4 × 2 inches*
Flour
Olive oil
2 cloves garlic, minced
*1 tomato, seeded and grated (see page
    7) or peeled, seeded, and chopped*
1/2 teaspoon sweet paprika
Salt and pepper
2/3 cup dry white wine

Preheat the oven to 400°.

Dust the salt cod with flour, and sauté it in a small amount of oil until lightly browned. Remove from the pan, drain on paper towels, and place in a lightly oiled metal baking dish or heavy skillet.

Scrape the excess flour from pan, add more oil if necessary, and sauté the garlic and tomatoes together. When the tomato has begun to change color, season the mixture with paprika, and salt and pepper to taste.

Add the wine to the pan, and reduce to a thick sauce.

Pour the sauce over the salt cod, making sure all pieces are well-covered.

Bake 10–15 minutes, or until the fish is cooked through.

Bacallà amb Samfaina

(SALT COD WITH *SAMFAINA*)

Carles Camós is a big, friendly, self-taught (and mother-taught) chef who got his start in the restaurant business as coproprietor of a bistro in the Costa Brava port of Palamós with the unlikely name of Big Rock. (The name was a one-upsmanly reference to the Hard Rock Café, which had just opened to rave reviews in London when Camós went into the trade.) Gradually, Big Rock turned into a serious restaurant and even gained a star from the *Guide Michelin*. In 1985, Camós moved from Palamós to another Costa Brava town, Platja d'Aro, and installed his Big Rock in a nineteenth-century Catalan mansion on a hilltop overlooking the sea. The food has gotten even better, and, as I write this, Camós is hoping for a second *Michelin* star. This refined version of a classic Catalan dish is one of his specialties—and because his *samfaina* is slightly different from the standard version, I give his recipe for that as well.

TO SERVE 4–6 (AS MAIN COURSE)

6 tomatoes, seeded and grated (see
    page 7) or peeled, seeded, and
    chopped.
Olive oil
2 red (if possible) or green bell
    peppers, unpeeled, cut into
    ¼-inch dice
4 Japanese eggplants, unpeeled, cut
    into ¼-inch dice
1 medium zucchini, unpeeled, cut into
    ¼-inch dice
1½ pounds thick-cut salt cod,
    desalted (see page 79), skinned,
    boned, and cut into 8–10 pieces
Salt and pepper
Flour (see note)

Cook the tomatoes in a small amount of oil for 20–25 minutes or until they form a thick purée.

In another pan, sauté the peppers, eggplant, and zucchini, added in that order, in a small amount of oil until soft.

Preheat the oven to 375°.

Add the vegetables to the tomato purée, and cook uncovered on low heat for 20 minutes; then add salt and pepper to taste.

Dust the salt cod with flour, and sauté in a small amount of oil until golden-brown. Drain on paper towels, and place in a lightly oiled baking dish.

Cover the salt cod with the vegetable mixture and bake for 10 minutes, or until the fish is cooked through.

Note: Camós suggests a "low-calorie" variation: Instead of dusting the salt cod with flour and sautéing it, steam it and then add it to the baking dish, and proceed as above.

Bacallà a la Manresana

(SALT COD MANRESA-STYLE)

Manresa is an ancient town, built by the Romans on the ruins of a Neolithic settlement, destroyed by the Arabs, and rebuilt during the Christian Reconquest of Spain. Situated in the mountains just north of the fabled monastery of Montserrat, it is famous for such mountain fare as wild game and wild mushrooms, for the classic Cap i Pota amb Samfaina (see page 113), and for not one but two Manresa-style preparations of bacallà—one with quince-enriched all-ioli (see page 32) and one (the more interesting, I think) made approximately as follows:

TO SERVE 4 (AS MAIN COURSE)

1½ pounds thick-cut salt cod,
    desalted (see page 79), skinned,
    boned, and cut into 1½–2-inch
    cubes
Flour
Olive oil
1 cup pine nuts, lightly toasted
8 prunes, pitted, plumped in warm
    water for 10 minutes, and coarsely
    chopped
1 pound spinach or Swiss chard,
    steamed or boiled in plain water,
    well-drained, and coarsely
    chopped
2 sprigs parsley, minced
Salt and pepper

Dust the salt cod with flour, and sauté in about ½ inch of hot oil until golden-brown on all sides. Drain on paper towels, and set aside.

Add the remaining ingredients except salt and pepper to the same pan, and cook on low heat until the spinach or chard turns dark green.

Drain the oil from the spinach mixture, then return the spinach to the pan, and add the salt cod. Heat through, and add salt and pepper to taste.

Bacallà amb Mel

(SALT COD WITH HONEY)

I remember a game I used to play with friends, in younger years, of trying to invent the most unlikely or revolting-sounding food combinations possible—things, I recall, like raw oysters with chocolate sauce and pineapple-clam cake. This dish, I imagine, must sound a bit like one of those to many readers— or at least like some mindless nouvelle (or *nova*) excess. In fact, though, salt cod with honey is neither nouvelle nor revolting. It's an old Catalan mountain dish, first mentioned in print in the seventeenth century and said to have been an invention of necessity—the union of two easily stored, well-preserved ingredients, eaten together simply to provide a kind of calorie-loading, essential for survival in cold climates during the cropless winter months.

As for the way it tastes—well, think of something Moroccan (a honey-flavored chicken *tajine*, for instance) or Chinese (sweet-and-sour fish, say); if sweet and salt are balanced skillfully, the result can be extraordinary. Even in Catalonia I must admit, *Bacallà amb Mel* can be a sort of rough-and-ready dish,

lacking in subtlety. Not so this version, which comes from one of the more imaginative restaurants in Barcelona, Petit París (which is not at all French, incidentally: It's on a street called París, and is indeed *petit*—which is a Catalan word as well as a French one). As ex-architect Climent Maynés, who runs the place with his wife Gloria Blanco, notes, his version of the dish contrasts not only sweet and salt but also the sharpness of vinegar and the fresh green crunch of escarole.

TO SERVE 4 (AS MAIN COURSE) OR 6 (AS APPETIZER)

⅓ cup flour
1 teaspoon dry yeast
Salt
1 egg, lightly beaten
2 tablespoons honey, preferably Provençal or Spanish
Olive oil
1½ pounds thick-cut salt cod, desalted (see page 79), skinned, boned, and cut into 1½-inch cubes
1 head young escarole or 2–3 bunches watercress, finely chopped
Honey vinegar or white wine vinegar

Combine the flour and yeast in a mixing bowl with a pinch of salt.

In another bowl, mix the egg, 1 tablespoon of the honey, and about ¼ cup of water together to form a batter; then stir in the flour mixture and mix together well. (Add more water if the batter seems too thick.)

In another bowl, mix the remaining honey with ¼–½ cup of warm water (depending on the sweetness desired), and set aside.

Fill a cassola or other deep pan with at least 1 inch of oil (or use a deep-fryer), and heat the oil to 375°.

Dip the salt cod cubes into the batter, and fry them in batches until golden-brown; then drain on paper towels.

Divide the chopped escarole or watercress into equal portions on individual plates, and dress with a few drops of vinegar (or more to taste).

Divide the salt cod pieces equally among the plates, and drizzle with honey water.

Bacallà amb Roquefort

(SALT COD WITH ROQUEFORT)

Though it is of course a French cheese, aged in the caves of Roquefort-sur-Soulzon, in the Rouergue, 150 miles or so north of the start of the *països catalans*, I always think of Roquefort as being Catalan. That's partly because it is well-loved in Catalonia and served (or cooked with) frequently. But it's also because I've had the best Roquefort of my life— on more than one occasion—in French Catalonia, in the Roussillon, in and around Perpignan.

The quality of that city's Roquefort, in fact, is well-known to the region's residents. But why should this be so? I posed the question one day to one local Roquefort fancier, Bernard Dauré, proprietor of the superb Château de Jau winery near Estagel. "Nobody knows," he answered. "I even asked somebody at the Roquefort cooperative when I visited the town one day whether they perhaps had some displaced Catalan working for them who was sending us all the best. They denied the possibility." His own theory, he added, is simply that the area of Perpignan consumes so *much* Roquefort that what is found in the stores thereabouts is always fresh and in optimum condition.

Whatever the case, if you ever visit Perpignan, try some Roquefort—even if you have to buy it in a supermarket. Having said all that, I wish I could now tell you that *Bacallà amb Roquefort* is a famous specialty of the Roussillon. Alas, it isn't. It is a famous specialty of Petit París in Barcelona—one of seven or eight *bacallà* dishes always offered by the restaurant—and, as far as I know, it was invented there. Whatever its origins, it is an extremely simple dish to make and a delicious one— though it is undeniably rather rich and is probably better suited to a chilly evening than to a sunny afternoon.

TO SERVE 4 (AS MAIN COURSE)

1–1½ pounds thick-cut salt cod, desalted (see page 79), skinned, boned, and cut into small steaks about 4 × 2 inches
Flour
Olive oil
1 cup heavy cream
2 ounces Roquefort, crumbled
White pepper

Dust the salt cod with flour, and sauté it in hot oil until golden-brown and cooked through.

In another pan, slowly heat the cream; then add the Roquefort, and simmer, stirring occasionally, until the cheese has melted. Add pepper to taste.

Pour the sauce over the fish, and serve immediately.

Bunyols de Bacallà

(SALT COD FRITTERS)

In one form or another, these little *bacallà*-and-potato puffs are a classic *tapa* in Catalonia, and are often brought as a complimentary appetizer in some of the region's better restaurants. The highly acclaimed Hispania, just northeast of Barcelona, outside the seaside town of Arenys de Mar, doesn't give them away—but their free-form parsley-flecked version is one of the best I've ever had. This recipe is theirs.

TO SERVE 4 (AS APPETIZER)

*1 pound salt cod, desalted (see page
    79) and cut into several pieces*
1 bay leaf
*2 medium potatoes, peeled and sliced
    very thin*
Olive oil
⅓ cup flour
3 eggs
2 cloves garlic, minced
2 sprigs parsley, minced
Salt and pepper

Place the salt cod and bay leaf in cold water to cover; then bring to just below the boiling point on medium heat. Cover, and let the pot stand off the heat for about 10 minutes.

Remove the salt cod from the water, and cool, setting the water aside.

When the fish has cooled, remove the skin or bones, if any, and flake the flesh with a fork.

Cook the potatoes until soft in the reserved salt-cod water; then drain, discarding the water.

In another pan, bring 1¼ cups water and 2 tablespoons oil to a boil, then remove from the heat, and slowly beat in the flour to form a batter. Beat in the eggs 1 at a time.

Mash the salt cod, potato slices, garlic, and parsley together well in a large bowl, add salt and pepper to taste; then mix the batter into the salt cod mixture.

Cook on a low flame until the mixture thickens slightly and will hold its shape when formed into balls.

Fill a cassola or other deep pan with at least 1 inch of oil (or use a deep-fryer), and heat the oil to 375°.

Form salt-cod balls in the bowl of a deep soup spoon, then fry in batches until deep golden-brown.

Drain on paper towels before serving, but serve very hot.

Brandada de Bacallà

(SALT COD PURÉE)

"Salt cod . . . has been shinning up the social ladder in the Reagan years with almost the same agility as monkfish," wrote Alexander Cockburn in *House & Garden* in mid-1986. I fear he was overstating the case somewhat, but salt cod *has* started making tentative appearances here and there at the occasional French-style neo-bistro or New American restaurant—and when it does, it's often in the form of *brandade* (*brandada* in Catalan). *Brandade* is a specialty of Provence and the Languedoc—a coarse *rillette*-like purée of salt cod with olive oil and garlic and sometimes milk and/or potatoes. It is said to have been invented in Nîmes, southwest of Avignon, and probably isn't really Catalan at all—but it is extremely popular in Catalonia today, and is certainly Catalan in spirit. This recipe is an amalgam of several French and Catalan formulas.

TO SERVE 6–8 (AS APPETIZER)

*1 pound salt cod, desalted (see page
    79) and poached, skinned (see
    note), boned, and flaked as in the
    previous recipe*
*2 pounds potatoes, baked or boiled
    until done, peeled, and riced*
4 cloves garlic, minced
1 cup mild extra-virgin olive oil
Salt and pepper
*Toast points or flat, round croutons of
    French or Italian bread*

Mix salt cod and the potatoes together well with a fork or whisk, then mix in the garlic.

Add the oil bit by bit, working it into the mixture slowly until the *brandada* has absorbed it all and reached a coarse puréelike consistency.

Salt and pepper to taste.

Spread thickly on toast points or croutons.

Note: In Provence, whatever skin may be found on the salt cod is sometimes left on and worked into the *brandada*. This makes the mixture a bit richer and smoother, and I usually do it myself.

Brandada amb Carxofes

(SALT COD PURÉE WITH ARTICHOKES)

I might as well confess at once: This is not a Catalan dish, period—and I doubt sincerely whether anything like it has ever been made in the *països catalans*. It's the creation of a chef named Michael Roberts, whose bailiwick is the contemporary Californian restaurant called Trumps in West Hollywood. It's so good, though, and makes such a nice counterpoint (or partner) to conventional *brandada*, that I can't resist including it. Anyway, there *are* some Catalan dishes that combine salt cod and artichokes—specifically in the Balearic Islands. Coloma Abrinas Vidal gives a recipe for salt cod sautéed with artichokes and peas in her *Cocina selecta mallorquina*, for instance, and Pedro

Ballester describes "meatballs" ("pilotas") of artichoke and salted fish in his book of Minorcan recipes, *De re cibaria*. If *brandada* with artichokes has not in fact been made in the *països catalans*, in other words, at least it might have been.

TO SERVE 6–8 (AS APPETIZER)

6 large artichokes (about 3½–4 inches in diameter) or 8 medium ones (about 3 inches in diameter)
1 cup mild extra-virgin olive oil
4 cloves garlic, minced
1 pound salt cod, desalted (see page 79) and poached, skinned (see note), boned, and flaked as for Bunyols de Bacallà (see page 85)
3–4 sprigs parsley, minced
Salt and pepper
Toast points or flat, round croutons of French or Italian bread

Trim the stems off the artichokes, and pull off the outer leaves. Cut each artichoke through crosswise about 1 inch above the base, and discard the top portions. Cut away the remaining fibrous exterior, leaving only the artichoke bottoms.

Bring water to a boil in a large pan, reduce the heat, then simmer the artichoke bottoms on low heat, covered, about 25–30 minutes or until very tender. Drain, and cool.

When the artichokes are cool, scoop out the chokes, gently squeeze the bottoms to remove excess moisture, and dry.

Warm the oil on low heat, and let the garlic cook in it about 5 minutes.

Mash the artichokes with a pestle or potato masher, then stir in the salt cod with a fork or whisk, and mix well.

Add the oil and garlic bit by bit, working it into the mixture slowly until the *brandada* has absorbed it all.

Stir in the parsley, and salt and pepper to taste.

Chill the *brandada* overnight, then return it to room temperature before serving. Spread thickly on toast points or croutons.

Note: As with conventional *brandada*, the salt cod skin may be worked into the mixture for added richness.

See Also:

BOLETS
(MUSHROOMS)

In the late fall of a good year, the markets of Catalonia smell like the forest—damp, earthy, as spicy as pine. It is the smell of wild mushrooms, sometimes a dozen kinds of them or more, heaped up into knobby pyramids, scattered thickly over tabletops and counters, spilling out of wooden crates and baskets, exuding their deep scents, almost glowing (in their array of browns, grays, whites, yellows, and reds) with the promise of their rich and subtle flavors.

The Spanish as a whole don't seem to trust mushrooms very much, and don't use them very often in their cooking. The Basques and the Catalans, however, with their abundant forests, their Pyrenean backyards, and their love of all good things to eat, devour mushrooms by the bushel every season—and count as sorry any season when they don't appear in plentitude. (When lack of rain severely curtailed the mushroom crop in 1985, I met Basques and Catalans who had practically gone into mourning.) Catalonia, above all, is mushroom-mad—and, though I wouldn't want to get into an argument on the subject, Catalans routinely claim to know and appreciate and consume many more kinds of mushrooms than the French or the Italians. Indeed, it has been said that some 1,458 varieties of mushrooms and related fungi have been catalogued in Catalonia—though, admittedly, by no means all of these are edible, and a good many are fiercely poisonous. Rather more modestly, Vincens Serrano, in his *Manual del boletaire català*

("Catalan Mushroom-Hunter's Handbook") identifies fifteen of the region's species as being of excellent culinary quality, thirty-eight as being good to eat, and another forty-three as being perfectly acceptable to the palate. Three of the varieties most prized in Catalan cuisine are readily available in the United States, sometimes fresh but more frequently dried or packed in oil: *ciurenys* or *surenys,* which are cepes or *porcini (Boletus edulis); rossinyols,* which are *girolles* or chanterelles *(Cantharellus cibarius);* and *rabassoles* or *múrgules,* which are morels *(Morchella vulgaris).* I've also seen, in the occasional specialty store, dried *moixernons* or St. George's mushrooms *(Calocybe gambosa),* known sometimes under their French name, *mousserons;* and *camasecs,* here called Scotch bonnet or fairy-ring mushrooms *(Marasmius oreades).* Some other kinds of mushrooms favored by the Catalans grow in the United States and might be located now and then by the dedicated mycologist— but are rarely if ever sold commercially. Among these are the mild, blue-gray *fredolic (Tricholoma terreum),* known in this country as mousy or earth-colored *Tricholoma* and related to the naked mushroom or wood-blewits *(Tricholoma nudum);* the exquisite yellow-gilled *ou de reig (Amanita caesarea)* or Caesar's *Amanita,* known in Italy as the *ovulo* or *fungho reale* ("royal mushroom") and in France, where it is unaccountably rare, as the *oronge (sic)* or *oronge de César;* and the fragrant *rovelló (Lactarius sanguifluus),* the color of oxidized bronze, which is a good deal more appetizing than its English name, "bleeding milk cap," would suggest—and which is related (and superior) to the better-known *Lactarius deliciosus.*

Truffles grow in the *països catalans*, too, incidentally. The wine town of Maury in the Roussillon is particularly famous for them. Locals reportedly seek them out by following a certain species of fly, which is said to make its home down tiny holes in the soil, beneath which the precious fungi invariably grow. In my experience, Catalan truffles, French or Spanish, don't have much to do with the black jewels of the Périgord and vicinity—though friends of mine insist that those of Olot, in Catalonia itself, can rival their more famous counterparts. The Catalan truffles *I've* had remind me of the brown truffles of Umbria in Italy—possessed of a distinctive, not unattractive nutlike flavor, but hardly any great gastronomic miracle.

Sopa de Bolets

(CATALAN MUSHROOM SOUP)

This is a simple, hearty soup of a kind eaten all over Catalonia. It is best made with fresh wild mushrooms, but a combination of fresh and (reconstituted) dried wild and/or cultivated mushrooms will work too.

TO SERVE 4 (AS APPETIZER)

2 onions, chopped
2 tomatoes, seeded and grated (see
page 7) or peeled, seeded, and
chopped
2 cloves garlic, minced
Olive oil
2 pounds assorted wild mushrooms
(see page 88), well cleaned
1 quart strong veal or beef stock
Salt and pepper
4 slices French or Italian bread,
toasted or fried in oil (see page
40)

In a cassola, Dutch oven, or soup pot make a *sofregit* (see page 38) of the onions, tomatoes, and garlic in oil.

Wash the mushrooms thoroughly, and cut the larger ones in halves or quarters, depending on their size.

Add the mushrooms to the *sofregit*, and sauté on low heat for 10–20 minutes, depending on the type of mushrooms used, or until the mushrooms have begun to shrink and weep.

Add the stock, bring to a boil; then simmer uncovered for 15–20 minutes on low heat. Salt and pepper to taste.

Place a piece of toast or fried bread on the bottom of each of four soup bowls; then ladle the soup over it.

Sopa de Fredolics

(*FREDOLIC* SOUP)

This is another very simple mushroom soup, as made by my friend Lluïsa Jausàs, in whose lovely Barcelona home I have shared many excellent meals.

TO SERVE 4 (AS APPETIZER)

*2–3 ounces European-style ham
    (prosciutto or Black Forest type),
    minced
2 cloves garlic, minced
Olive oil
2 pounds* fredolics (Tricholoma
    terreum), *wood-blewitses*
    (Tricholoma nudum), *or other
    medium-sized, fleshy,
    mild-flavored wild mushrooms,
    well cleaned and cut in half
1 quart strong veal, beef, or chicken
    stock
Salt and pepper
2 thin green onions or scallions,
    trimmed at both ends and minced*

In a cassola, Dutch oven, or soup pot, sauté the ham and garlic in a small amount of oil for about 5 minutes.

Add the mushrooms, stir well, and cook uncovered over low heat until the mushrooms give up their water, 5–10 minutes.

Add the stock, bring to a boil, then simmer uncovered for about 5 minutes. Salt and pepper to taste.

Just before serving, stir in the minced green onions.

Bunyols de Ciurenys

(CEPE FRITTERS)

The Catalans love *ciurenys* or cepes, and they love little fried things—croquettes, fritters, and the like. This recipe combines the two affections. These fritters are usually served as an hors d'oeuvre or appetizer, but they also make an unusual and delicious side dish, particularly appropriate with poultry or game dishes. Other varieties of wild mushroom may of course be substituted for cepes, though cepes seem to work particularly well in this context.

TO SERVE 4 (AS APPETIZER OR SIDE DISH)

*Salt
1½ cups flour
1 cup room-temperature milk
2 eggs, lightly beaten
Olive oil
1 package dry yeast dissolved in 2 ⅔
    tablespoons (8 teaspoons) warm
    water
2 cloves garlic, minced
1 sprig parsley, minced
1 sprig fresh marjoram, minced, or ¼
    teaspoon dried*

*1 pound cepes or other wild
   mushrooms, well cleaned and cut
   in half if large*
Pepper

Add ¼ teaspoon salt to flour; then stir in milk, eggs, 1 tablespoon oil, yeast, garlic, parsley, marjoram, and about ¼ teaspoon pepper. Mix together well to form thin batter.

Fill a cassola or other deep pan with at least 1 inch of oil (or use a deep-fryer), and heat the oil to 375°.

Dip the mushrooms in the batter, then fry them in batches until deep golden-brown.

Drain on paper towels, and salt to taste.

Bolets a la Graella

(GRILLED WILD MUSHROOMS)

I grew up not much liking mushrooms, largely because the only mushrooms in our house were those rubbery little "button" ones that came in cans and had both the flavor and the consistency of a soggy eraser. I learned to love mushrooms, along with so many other foodstuffs I had hitherto avoided, in Rome—where, at one point in my life, I used to spend a great deal of time in the company of an American expatriate who knew Roman food better than any native of the city. My mycological breakthrough came, I remember vividly, one afternoon at a little trattoria in Trastevere, where my friend had ordered something I could hardly even picture—*porcini* mushroom caps, bathed in olive oil and then grilled like meat over an open fire. One bite of the things

and I was a mushroom-lover for life. They were *better* than meat; they were better than *anything*. And ever since that day, I've had a passion for grilled mushrooms.

Now, grilled mushrooms aren't something you're likely to find in the average restaurant in Catalonia, but in backyards and impromptu picnic grounds, especially in the mountains, they are happily consumed almost anytime good mushrooms are in season and somebody has a match. For this recipe—and it's so simple it can hardly even be called a recipe—dried mushrooms simply, obviously, will not do. Neither will small mushrooms or fragile ones. And a real grill, whether fired by wood or charcoal, or even gas, is a virtual necessity.

TO SERVE 4 (AS APPETIZER OR LIGHT MAIN
        COURSE)

2–2½ pounds fresh cepes, matsutake,
   or shiitake *mushrooms, and/or
   other varieties with large, firm caps*
Olive oil
Salt and pepper

Remove the stems from the mushrooms, and reserve them for other purposes.

Wash, and dry the mushroom caps thoroughly.

Coat the mushroom caps generously on all surfaces with olive oil.

Grill the mushroom caps on a hot fire for 3–5 minutes (depending on thickness), then turn carefully, using tongs or a large spatula, and cook 3–5 minutes longer. (Be careful of possible flare-ups from excess olive oil.)

Salt and pepper to taste.

Patates amb Rabassoles

(POTATOES WITH MORELS)

To me there's something positively opulent about the combination of potatoes and wild mushrooms. I've had the two together in several forms in Catalonia—*ous de reig* sautéed with thinly sliced potatoes, diced cepes fried with little potato cubes, etc.—but this remains perhaps my favorite version of the dish.

TO SERVE 4 (AS APPETIZER OR SIDE DISH)

*1 pound fresh morels or ½ pound
    dried
2 onions, chopped
2 cloves garlic, minced
1 tablespoon lard
Olive oil
2 pounds small potatoes, peeled and
    sliced about ¼-inch thick
1 sprig fresh marjoram or ¼ teaspoon
    dried
Salt and pepper
2 sprigs parsley, minced*

Rinse the morels well, then soak them in water, changing it several times until it is clean. If you are using dried morels, reconstitute them in warm water for about 2 hours, then continue soaking them in water, again changing it several times until it is clean.

Meanwhile, in a cassola or large skillet, make a *sofregit* (see page 38) of the onions and half the garlic in the lard and a small amount of oil.

Add the potatoes and morels (cut in half lengthwise if large), and stir to coat well with lard and oil.

Add the marjoram, and salt and pepper to taste, and simmer for about 5 minutes, then barely cover with warm water.

Simmer uncovered until the potatoes are done but not falling apart and only a small amount of liquid is left (about 10–15 minutes). Pour off excess liquid, or add more if necessary.

Mix the remaining garlic with the parsley, and just before serving, sprinkle this mixture on top of the potatoes and morels.

See Also:

Ous Remenat amb Bolets, Tofones, i Manxego (Scrambled Eggs with Wild Mushrooms, Truffles, and Manchego Cheese), page 124
Peus de Porc Farcits amb Bolets (Stuffed Pigs' Feet with Wild Mushrooms), page 153
Fricandó (Braised Veal with Wild Mushrooms), page 243

CAÇA
(WILD GAME)

In the spring of 1986, taking my life in my hands, I spent a week guiding five top young American chefs and a brace of journalists around the restaurants and bars of Barcelona. As part of the package, the chefs had agreed to cook a dinner—contemporary-American in style but using Catalan ingredients—for an assortment of local restaurateurs, journalists, winemakers, and just plain food-loving citizens. One day the chefs swarmed through La Boqueria, the main Barcelona market (see pages 295–296) buying provisions for their meal, letting—as is their wont in their own country—the availability and condition of ingredients dictate their menu. Among the things they saw that most impressed them were some sweet-looking little farm-raised quails—and these (at a mere 50 cents apiece) became the main course. They also became, as it turned out, the least popular course.

After superb hors d'oeuvres of bonita tartare and fried calf's brains with deep-fried capers and sherry vinaigrette, and a beautiful California-style salad of bright raw and cooked vegetables and assorted seafood, came the quail—grilled over charcoal, still pink inside, and not bad at all. But roughly half the diners returned their quail unfinished. Everyone was very polite about it, and praised that course with all the others—but these particular birds, American-style, clearly hadn't taken off.

The next day, discussing the meal with author/chef Llorenç Torrado, who had been one of the guests, I asked him what the other diners hadn't liked—had, for instance, the quail simply been too underdone for Catalan tastes? That might have been part of it, he replied, but there was a bigger problem: "The quail weren't wild. Quail is a game bird, and we just don't think the farm-raised kind have much flavor."

Catalans love wild game, in other words, and don't take kindly to tame imitations of it. Hoofed game is appreciated, particularly *cervol* (venison) and, in the Pyrénées, *isard* (chamois or mountain antelope). Boar—*senglar*—is highly regarded, too, but it is said that the main

autoroute through Catalonia has displaced and ultimately decimated much of the region's boar population. The real favorites, though, are *llebre* (hare) and such winged wonderments as *perdiu* (partridge), *colomí* (wild pigeon), *ànec salvatge* (wild duck), *becada* (woodcock, perhaps the most delicious game bird of all—protected as an endangered species in most of Europe but still shot and consumed in Spain), the aforementioned quail or *guatlle,* and, espe-

cially in the Empordà and the Balearics, *tord* (thrush). (Balearic game connoisseurs have had bad luck lately. In 1985, a particularly dry spring and summer lessened the size of the olive crop in the islands and by extension discouraged *tords* from stopping there, as they habitually do late each summer to eat the just-formed olive fruit; in 1986, shooting of migratory game birds was forbidden on the islands due to radioactive contamination from the Chernobyl nuclear disaster.)

Unless you're a hunter yourself, you won't be able to find much wild game in the United States. Most "game" sold here is in fact farm-raised—and, though it can sometimes be quite good, it will almost inevitably lack the dark richness of the true wild variety. Still, the three recipes that follow involve sauces that are themselves rich in flavor, in different ways, and domestic fowl (even "game hens," which are among the least gamy of all such beasts) will work more than adequately in their preparation.

Perdiu a la Col, Estil Josep Pla

(JOSEP PLA'S PARTRIDGE-STUFFED CABBAGE)

The great Catalan writer Josep Pla (1895–1981) was a child of the Empordà, born in Palafrugell, and he spent much of his life in the region and devoted most of his work to it. Among his favorite concerns were the landscape of this part of Catalonia, the people who inhabit it, the sea (by which he usually meant

the tidal waters of the Costa Brava), and food—and his books on these subjects (*Aigua de Mar, Narracions, El Pagès i el seu mon, Cadaqués, De l'Empordanet a Barcelona, L'Herencia,* etc.) are both down-to-earth and lyrical. When it came to gastronomy, he was sensible and serious—noting, for example, that "Cuisine is an art of equilibrium, moderation, organization, and health . . . [and] a very difficult art, requiring a vocation, a sense of constant vigilance, a great deal of experience, and a lot of patience." And his eloquent, wide-ranging statement of his own gastronomic philosophy, *El que hem menjat* ("That Which We Have Eaten"), belongs on the shelf alongside Waverley Root, M. F. K. Fisher, and Joseph Wechsberg—or would if it had been translated into English. At the same time, he was proud of being a man of the countryside ("I'd rather converse with a peasant of the Empordà than with a Barcelona intellectual," he used to say); he scoffed at friends' attempts to introduce him to new cuisines and openly admitted many food prejudices. ("I don't like raw things, sweets, or too many salads," he once wrote. And, "Luxury, in food as in everything, depresses me.") He did become a great friend, though, of that cosmopolitan and gastronomically adventurous reviser of Catalan culinary tradition, Josep Mercader, and spent many a mealtime at Mercader's Hotel Ampurdán.

One of his favorite dishes there, apparently, was the Catalan classic known as *perdiu amb farcellets de col,* roasted partridge with cabbage dumplings. As Pla got older, however, he lost his teeth—and suddenly found those bony birds too great a challenge. Taking pity on his plight, Mercader invented a new dish for him—one in which the partridge and the dumplings became one, in a sense, with the bird losing its bones in the process. This is Mercader's recipe for that invention. It's admittedly time-consuming, but the results are unusual and very good.

TO SERVE 4 (AS MAIN COURSE)

1 large green cabbage or Savoy cabbage
Butter
Olive oil
3 partridges or 2 game hens
4 ounces thick-cut bacon, cut into
    1/4-inch slices
1 onion, chopped
1 carrot, chopped
1 leek, white part only, chopped
1 tomato, seeded and grated (see page
    7) or peeled, seeded, and chopped
1 bay leaf
2 botifarra sausages (see page 147)
2½ cups rich chicken or game stock
Flour
1 cup dry white wine
Salt and pepper
1 egg, beaten
1 clove garlic, minced
1 sprig parsley, minced
6 almonds, blanched and roasted (see
    page 39)
6 hazelnuts, roasted (see page 39)
2 teaspoons pine nuts, lightly toasted

Core the cabbage, remove and discard the tough outer leaves, and blanch the cabbage in boiling water for 8–10 minutes. Drain and cool, then remove 12 of the largest and most regularly shaped leaves, which should be tender enough to fold or roll. Dry these leaves, and set them aside.

In a cassola or Dutch oven, melt enough butter to cover the bottom of the pan, add a few drops of olive oil to prevent burning; then sauté the partridges and bacon together, browning the birds on all sides and cooking the bacon until crisp. Remove the partridges and bacon, and set aside.

In the same cassola, make a *sofregit* (see page 38) of the onion, carrot, leek, and tomato, adding more oil if necessary. When the *sofregit* is almost finished, add the bay leaf.

Return the partridges to the cassola and continue cooking over low heat.

Meanwhile, prick the sausages in several places with a fork, and sauté them in another pan, adding a bit of oil if necessary, until well-browned.

Add the sausages to the cassola, pour off the excess fat from the sausage pan, and deglaze with ½ cup of the stock. Reduce slightly, then add these juices to the cassola.

Stir about 2 tablespoons of flour into the cassola, then add the remaining stock and the white wine. Simmer uncovered until the liquid is reduced and the partridges are cooked through, about 20 minutes.

Remove the partridges and sausages from the cassola, set the partridges aside to cool, and finely chop the sausages and reserved bacon together, then return them to the cassola and mix in well.

Purée the contents of the cassola in a food processor, blender, or food mill; then return to the cassola, and simmer on low heat. Salt and pepper to taste.

When the partridges have cooled, cut each one into quarters, and completely bone them, retaining shape of each quarter as well as possible.

Wrap each boneless quarter in a cabbage leaf, folding the edges over to cover the partridge completely; then dip each stuffed leaf in beaten egg, and dust with flour.

In another pan, sauté each stuffed leaf in butter with a few drops of oil added, until lightly browned and slightly crisp. Drain the stuffed leaves on paper towels, and set aside.

Make a *picada* (see page 40) of the garlic, parsley, almonds, hazelnuts, and pine nuts, moistened with a bit of liquid from the cassola.

Add the *picada* to the cassola, and stir in well, cooking for about 5 minutes; then return the stuffed cabbage leaves to the cassola, and continue cooking until heated through (about 6–8 minutes).

Serve the stuffed cabbage leaves topped with sauce from the cassola.

Perdiu a la Vinagre

(PARTRIDGE WITH VINEGAR SAUCE)

In an address given in 1981 at the first (and thus far only) Catalan Culinary Congress (Congres Català de la Cuina), wild game expert Josep Maria Luna quoted the great French actor Sacha Guitry thus: "How beautiful life is and how agreeable the conversation when four people have just finished eating a partridge apiece!" This recipe provides just that—though in a form that Guitry might not have recognized.

The use of vinegar in Catalan cuisine dates at least from the period of the Arab conquest, and indeed one of the most popular vinegar-

based dishes in the region today—*escabetx*, which is fish or fowl first cooked and then marinated in vinegar with garlic and herbs (see page 176)—has direct Arab antecedents. Vinegar is less often employed in dishes to be eaten hot, but this preparation of partridge in a *sofregit* moistened with red wine vinegar is an old Catalan specialty that still shows up now and again on restaurant menus and home tables. I first encountered it myself at Casa Juan, a very good restaurant in Vilafranca del Penedès, the capital of Catalonia's best wine country. This recipe is based on my own attempts to re-create the dish as it is served there.

TO SERVE 4 (AS MAIN COURSE)

4 partridges or 2 game hens (see note)
Olive oil

8 onions, very thinly sliced
4 tomatoes, seeded and grated (see
    page 7) or peeled, seeded, and
    chopped
1 carrot, coarsely grated
1 sprig parsley, minced
1 cup good quality red wine vinegar
Salt and pepper

Brown the partridges in plenty of oil in a cassola or large skillet; then remove from the cassola and set aside.

Pour off the excess oil from the cassola, leaving about ½ inch on the bottom, then make a *sofregit* (see page 38) in it of the onions, tomatoes, carrot, and parsley.

Return the partridges to the cassola, add the vinegar; then simmer covered until the birds are done (about 30 minutes for partridges, 1 hour for game hens).

Salt and pepper to taste.

Note: Game hens or particularly large partridges may be split lengthwise before browning for shorter cooking time. Pheasant may also be cooked in this manner.

Guatlles amb Salsa de Magrana

(QUAIL IN POMEGRANATE SAUCE)

Salsa de magrana or *granada*—pomegranate sauce—is an unusual specialty of Majorca. Recipes calling for pomegranates (or pomegranate juice) appear in the *Libre de Sent Soví* and the *Libre del coch* (though the latter also contains a recipe for a so-called *salsa granada* that is in fact made from chicken livers, egg yolks, and spices, and doesn't involve pomegranates at all). Indeed, though the sauce described in this particular recipe is of far more recent origin, it always seems somehow medieval to me, too—something to do with its contrast of sweet and slightly sour flavors. A different version of *salsa de magrana* is sometimes served with pork or turkey (see page 152).

TO SERVE 4 (AS MAIN COURSE)

8 quail
1 tablespoon lard
Olive oil
1 onion, chopped
1 tomato, seeded and grated (see page
    7) or peeled, seeded, and chopped
1 sprig parsley, minced
1 cup chicken or game stock
Seeds of 4–5 pomegranates
Salt and pepper

In a cassola or large skillet, sauté quails in lard and a small amount of oil until golden-brown on all sides. Remove, and set aside.

In the same lard and oil, make a *sofregit* (see page 38) of the onion, tomato, and parsley.

Add the stock to the cassola, and stir well, then add the quails and pomegranate seeds (reserving a handful for garnish if desired). Simmer partially covered for about 20 minutes, or until the quails are cooked through.

Salt and pepper to taste; then remove the quails, and place them on a heated serving dish.

Pass the sauce through a sieve, then return

it to the heat, and reduce to desired thickness.

Pour the sauce over the quails, and garnish with pomegranate seeds if desired.

See Also:

Escabetx de Gallina, Colomí, o Perdiu (Pickled Chicken, Pigeon, or Partridge), page 177

cassola mallorquina, page 283

es niu, page 284

CARGOLS
(SNAILS)

"Al juliol ni dona ni cargol," warns an oft-quoted Catalan proverb—"In July, neither woman nor snail." I'll save my comments on the first part of that caveat for another time; but I must report that, one July afternoon not long ago—proverbs be damned—I set off from Barcelona with friends to the farming town of Tornabous, about sixty miles to the northwest, near Lleida, to attend a *cargolada*—an "ada" of snails. Now, the suffix *-ada* (*-ade* in the Roussillon) gets tacked onto a number of food names in the *països catalans*. There is the *calçotada*, for instance, based on green onions or *calçots* (see page 167), and the *romescada*, based on a sauce called *romesco* (see pages 222–225). The exact definition of the suffix is apparently a matter of some disagreement in the region, but for all practical purposes, an *-ada* in Catalan seems to be about the same thing as a "-rama" in English (as in "Ribs-o-Rama" or "Fish-o-Rama"): an exhaustive presentation of a single kind of food, a communal celebration of it, a pig-out. That was certainly the case, at least, in Tornabous, with those snails.

Our hosts were the owners of some local farm and orchard land (Tornabous and vicinity are noted for their apples, pears, and peaches) and their best friends, the town doctor and his wife. Traditionally, a *cargolada* is something you throw when you see old friends you haven't seen for a long time. These particular friends see each other regularly—but aren't about to let a little matter of tradition stand in the way of their passion for everybody's favorite landbound gastropod mollusk. The mollusks, in fact, outnumbered the celebrants on this particular afternoon by about 100 to one. In the kitchen, when we arrived, were four big mesh sacks of snails, alive if not exactly kicking—about four kilos of them in all, which works out to roughly 1,000 snails for the ten of us guests. This, I was told, is about average for a serious *cargolada*.

The fete commenced with delicious little black olives, wrinkled and slightly sweet, and good, cold Spanish beer. Meanwhile, several of the women of the house were working on the snails, worrying them one by one with a rough cloth to clean them, rubbing off the plasticlike veil that protects the opening to each shell. When this was done, the snails were packed in a single layer—with openings facing upward, and still very much alive—into large, flat, black rectangular iron pans lined with damp newspaper. Downstairs, in the backyard, a hot fire of vine cuttings had been started in a big brick barbecue. The trays of snails were carried down, salt was scattered over them, and, one at a time, the iron rectangles were fitted down into the barbecue, resting a few inches from the flames. As the snails cooked, more salt and some finely ground black pepper were added. After about ten minutes, the first trayful was done. Olive oil was drizzled over the snails, now charred, and the tray was taken up to the dining room.

One thing you must understand about a *cargolada* is that, though it may be dedicated to the consumption of snails, snails are by no means the only thing its celebrants consume. By the time that first tray had been set down on a trivet in the middle of the table, we had already started on a huge platter of the salt cod salad called *Esqueixada* (see page 172), on heaps of thickly sliced tomatoes and raw onions, on a salad of romaine lettuce dressed with olive oil and vinegar, and on the first two of what were to be a seemingly endless number of unlabeled bottles of good Rioja. ("You must never drink water with snails," the doctor in the house advised, "for it will surely make you sick.")

At last, though, using a battery of glorified toothpicks made from light metal, we attacked the *cargols* themselves—prizing them from their blackened shells, dipping them alternately in the *allioli* or the coarse tomato and garlic sauce that had been provided, and eventually, at one point, falling almost silent, almost hypnotized by the elemental mechanics of the operation, almost lost in the sheer primal savor of these earthy-tasting, smoky-tasting, wondrous little creatures. I managed about sixty of them myself. One of my Barcelona friends stopped with a dozen, saying that he wasn't particularly fond of snails (now he tells us!). One of our hosts reached something like 125.

And then, because this is Catalonia, where eating is taking seriously, the rest of the meal appeared—a platter of peeled strips of roasted eggplant and red pepper (called *Escalivada*, see page 169) and another of *carns a la brasa*, grilled meats, which in Catalonia usually means an assortment of thin-cut loin and shoulder lamb chops, crisp and well-done, with lengths of mild *botifarra* sausage, drained of much of its fat by the grill. We finished with a chocolate cream cake and with the inevitable postprandial *cava* or sparkling wine.

Then, leaving my fellow snail eaters in a haze of brandy and cigars, I got into my car and drove up into the Pyrénées, where I slept soundly all night long, dreaming of *cargols* and probably of a *dona* or two as well.

Cargolada

As simple as it is, the traditional means of cooking snails for a *cargolada*—which is called "*a la llauna*" or "on the tin"—is difficult to reproduce unless you have a large barbecue grill, access to vine cuttings or other hot-burning wood, and a large, heavy metal tray or two. A cast-iron skillet will do for a cooking vessel, but won't hold very many snails at one time— and will eventually suffer from too much direct high flame. I've tried cooking snails this way on a gas burner on an ordinary range, and even under a hot broiler, and—though edible and not unpleasant snails resulted in both cases—they lacked the outdoorsy, smoky flavor I find so appealing at a real *cargolada*. For those who have the requisite equipment, or who want to try their own improvisations on the theme, here is the way those snails were cooked in Tornabous.

TO SERVE 4 (AS APPETIZER OR MAIN COURSE)

*4 tomatoes, peeled, seeded, and
    coarsely chopped (not shaved)*
4 cloves garlic, minced
Salt and pepper
Olive oil
¼ cup allioli *(see page 30) per 15–20
    snails*
*12–50 snails per person (or more or
    less), depending on appetite
    (see note)*

In a mixing bowl, combine the tomatoes and garlic, add salt to taste and plenty of freshly ground black pepper, and cover the mixture with olive oil to about 1 inch above its surface. Mix again, and divide into 4 bowls.

Divide the *allioli* into 4 other bowls.

If you are using live or fresh snails (see below), clean them thoroughly with a damp, rough cloth, making sure to rub off the "veil" at the opening of each shell. (Do not rinse.)

Line the bottom of a large cast-iron skillet or other heavy metal pan or tray with four or five layers of damp newspaper, then pack the snails into the pan, openings upward, filling the pan completely so that the snails hold each other in place.

Place the pan over a very hot fire until the shells begin to blacken, about 5–10 minutes,

adding salt and freshly ground black pepper about halfway through the cooking.

Remove from the fire, drizzle with olive oil, and serve from the pan, with toothpicks or small cocktail forks and with *allioli* and to-mato-garlic sauce on the side.

Note: If you live in the country, or in an urban area relatively free from pollution, you might want to try harvesting your own snails for a *cargolada,* even those from your own garden. These must be purged of possible toxins before use, though. Methods for doing this are described in a number of cookbooks, including *The Joy of Cooking* by Irma S. Rombauer and Marion Rombauer Becker (Bobbs-Merrill, 1984) and *The Cuisine of the Sun* by Mareille Johnston (Random House, 1976).

If you don't want to, or can't, harvest your own snails, I recommend using live or at least fresh snails if possible. These are available in some ethnic markets and specialty fish markets. Canned snails, which are precooked, may of course be used—but for a *cargolada,* obviously, you'll need snails still in their shells. In whatever form you use them, I recommend that you try to find smaller snails rather than larger ones—the type called *petit gris,* for instance. It is said that at least seven different kinds of snail, each with its own distinctive flavor, are eaten in Catalonia—but the large Burgundian-style snail usually served as *escargots* in French restaurants is rarely among them.

Cargols Estil Porreres

(SNAILS PORRERES-STYLE)

Jaime Mesquida makes good wine in the town of Porreres, east of Palma on the island of Majorca. He is also a great *amateur* of Majorcan cooking, which—though it is rarely found in restaurants in its authentic state—can be some of the best and most varied in the *països catalans.* And, like many Majorcans, he is mad for snails. "In November, when the first rain falls," he told me one evening, over a glass of his light but very pleasant cabernet sauvignon

and some of his family's own superb *sobrassada* sausage, "everyone is out at night, with lanterns and flashlights, looking for *cargols*. The best are those found in the vineyards, and after them, the ones found in the forest. I picked up seven kilos of them in just two hours one night!"

Later, he took me into a kind of larder alongside his house and showed me the plywood-and-wire-mesh boxes in which some of his catch was confined, awaiting his eventual pleasure. Then he told me how his grandmother used to cook snails—the best way of all, he said. The recipe below is an approximate reconstruction of her method as Mesquida described it to me. He added that in his household snails cooked in this manner were habitually preceded by rice soup or another simple first course, and were themselves consumed with plenty of bread and wine. After eating, each member of the family was obliged to reveal how many snails he or she had accounted for—with around 100 per person being the average. Then everybody drank a glass of milk, in the belief that it would help digest the snails.

TO SERVE 4 (AS MAIN COURSE)

25–50 snails per person (or more or fewer), depending on appetite (see page 98)
2 potatoes, peeled and quartered
1 sprig each of thyme, rosemary, parsley, and spearmint (yerba buena or hierbabuena), tied together in a bouquet garni, or ¼ teaspoon each of dried thyme, rosemary, and parsley and ½ teaspoon dried mint, mixed
together well and wrapped securely in cheesecloth
Peel of 1 orange
2 onions, chopped
5 tomatoes, 4 seeded and grated (see page 7) or peeled, seeded, and chopped, and 1 whole
4 cloves garlic, minced
Olive oil
¼ pound boneless pork or European-style ham (Black Forest or prosciutto type), cut into 4 pieces
1 squab or quail, quartered
Salt and pepper
2 cups Allioli amb Ous *(see page 31)*

Preheat the oven to 350°.

If you are using live or fresh snails, clean them thoroughly with a damp, rough cloth, making sure to rub off the "veil" at the opening of each shell; then rinse well and drain.

Place the potatoes, herbs, and orange peel in a large pot, adding the snails if they are live or fresh. Cover with water, bring to a boil; then simmer for about 1 hour.

Meanwhile, in a large cassola or Dutch oven, make a *sofregit* (see page 38) of the onions, chopped tomatoes, and garlic in oil.

While the *sofregit* cooks, bake the whole tomato in a lightly oiled baking dish for 10 minutes; then remove, and cool.

Add the pork or ham and the squab or quail to the cassola, and sauté lightly, turning the bird quarters well to brown slightly on all sides. Add water to cover the birds halfway; then simmer, covered, until the birds are cooked through (about 15–20 minutes). Salt and pepper to taste.

When the potatoes are cooked, remove 1 of them (4 quarters), and rice or mash it.

Carefully peel and seed the baked tomato, and coarsely chop it. Then, in a large bowl, mix it thoroughly with the *allioli*. Add the riced or mashed potato, and mix together well with a fork or whisk. The finished mixture should have the consistency of a thick paste; thin with more *allioli* if necessary.

Drain the snails (if added to the pot in step 3) and the remaining potato quarters, reserving the liquid.

Add the snails and potato quarters to the cassola with the *sofregit,* and stir well. If you are using precooked canned snails, add them at this point. The snails should be barely covered with liquid. If the liquid in the cassola has evaporated, add reserved potato water as necessary.

Serve the snails in large bowls with toothpicks or small cocktail forks. Serve the *allioli* on the side, to be stirred in to taste.

Cargols de la Padrina Mercè

(GRANDMOTHER MERCEDES'S ROASTED SNAILS)

I first went to Balaguer, the capital of the *comarca* of La Noguera, northeast of Lleida, because of a photograph on a tourism brochure. The photo showed the town square, the Plaça del Mercadal, on a Saturday market day—appropriately enough, since *mercadal* is an old Catalan word for marketplace. The square itself was enclosed by buildings of varying ages, styles, and colors, but mostly of about the same height (four or five stories) and mostly with connecting porticoes—which imposed a kind of handsome ragged uniformity upon it. The center of the square was filled with market stands and tents, some of the latter brightly striped, at which were being sold not only meat and fish and produce but also clothing (reds and blues were big) and household utensils—and with hundreds of local citizens, hawking and haggling, standing and talking, busying this way and that. The trees that in warmer weather obviously shaded the market had been pollarded for the winter. Looming above the square on a dusty, scrub-covered hill, framed by the faint metallic gray-blue sky, was the stern Gothic church of Santa Maria.

The picture hypnotized me. It was mysterious, inviting, relentlessly evocative, fascinating. I knew that I had to see the Plaça del Mercadal on market day for myself—and one chilly January afternoon in 1986, I did just that. The square as I first saw it in person was a living double of the photograph—even the sky was the same color—and I felt as drawn to the reality as I had been to the photographic image. I spent two hours there, just wandering around, looking, sniffing the air, listening—and somehow felt part of another world, another time, much more than I had ever felt in ancient Barcelona or Tarragona or on the fantastical shores of the Costa Brava. I felt both disconnected and somehow joined to the place. And I felt as if I were, at last, really in Catalonia.

Then I went and had lunch. Balaguer has one distinguished restaurant, Cal Morell, run by one distinguished chef, Josep Maria Morell, and it was to that establishment that I repaired. My meal turned out to be simple, hearty, salty, and good, but two items stood out particularly.

One was part of a complimentary hors d'oeuvre assortment—curious little slices of some sort of root or tuber, raw but pickled, that I found quite delicious. They came from a root called *patofa*, I was told—"wild potatoes." I realized that I had seen them in the market, gnarled beige tubers that looked like a cross between ginger and indeed potatoes. To this day, I'm not sure what this substance was—the word *patofa* doesn't appear in the standard Catalan dictionaries, and my gastronomic advisers elsewhere in the *països catalans* had never heard the word nor encountered the thing I described, but food scholar Charles Perry has since suggested that the root might have been a tuber related to taro, called *Colocasia antiquorum*—a plant known to the Roman and Greek Mediterranean, though we tend to associate taro more with Polynesia today.

The other memorable feature of my meal at Cal Morell was easily identifiable—a heaping bowl of delicious snails, a specialty of this region, roasted with pork and garlic. This is the recipe which Morrell has named after his grandmother. She used to prepare it, he recalls, when he visited her as a child.

TO SERVE 4 (AS APPETIZER)

15–20 snails per person (see page 98)
1 bay leaf (if you are using live or
    fresh snails)
6 ounces boneless pork loin, cut into
    thin strips about 1½ inches long
1 head garlic, separated into cloves
    but unpeeled
Olive oil
2 tablespoons flour
1 tomato, seeded and grated (see page
    7) or peeled, seeded, and chopped
Salt and pepper
1–2 cups allioli *(see page 30)*

If you are using live or fresh snails, clean them thoroughly with a damp, rough cloth, making sure to rub off the "veil" at the opening of each shell, then rinse well, and drain.

Again, if you are using live snails, place them in a large pot with salted water to cover and the bay leaf, bring to a boil, reduce the heat, and simmer uncovered for about 30 minutes. Drain well, dry thoroughly, and set aside.

Meanwhile, preheat the oven to 500°.

In a cassola or large ovenproof skillet, sauté the pork strips and garlic cloves in about ½ inch of oil until lightly browned.

Add the cooked snails (or precooked canned snails), the flour, tomato, and salt and pepper to taste. Mix well, and cook together slowly for 10 minutes.

Roast in the oven for an additional 10 min-

utes, or until the snail shells have begun to blacken.

Serve the snails with toothpicks or small cocktail forks, and *allioli* on the side.

See Also:

Paella Valenciana, page 210
Mar i Muntanya II (Ragout of Rabbit, Snails, Monkfish, Cuttlefish, and Prawns), page 227

FAVES, CIGRONS, LLENTIES, MONGETES, I MONGETS

(FAVAS, CHICK-PEAS, LENTILS, WHITE BEANS, AND BLACK-EYED PEAS)

Legumes or pulses—favas, chick-peas, and the like—were brought to Catalonia, and to Spain in general, by the Romans. They became very popular on the peninsula, especially among the poorer classes, not least because they require comparatively little water to grow—chick-peas especially—an obvious advantage in this notoriously arid land. Though chick-peas are certainly the most important of these vegetables in most of the rest of Spain, Catalans seem fonder of favas and white beans, *faves* and *mongetes,* and both figure in some of the most basic of all Catalan dishes.

"Favas have produced in Catalonia an astonishing cuisine," author/chef Domènec

Moli has gone so far as to say, "so baroque as to be almost Valencian." (Valencian cuisine is always called "baroque" by Catalan writers, though in fact it is no more so than that of the Empordà or the Balearics.) *"Déu dóna faves a qui no té queixals,"* says a Catalan proverb, being a bit more down to earth: "God gives favas to him who has no teeth." White beans were ennobled, in nineteenth-century Catalan restaurant slang, with names like *ballarines, menuts de gallina, llagrimes de sabater,* and *perles de pagès*—"ballerinas," "chicken offal," "shoemaker's tears," and "farmer's pearls"—and, with potatoes and cabbage, were called *la sagrada familia,* "the Holy Family."

Lentils are somewhat less common, but black-eyed peas—to the occasional amazement of visiting Americans, who think of them as being the preserve of the American South—are widely eaten and appreciated, especially in the Empordà region. The same area, it might be noted, also makes a white bean dish called *cassolada empordanesa*—which some locals insist is the original of southwestern France's famous cassoulet.

Faves a la Catalana

(FAVAS WITH BLOOD SAUSAGE AND BACON)

Author Manuel Vázquez Montalbán calls this classic Catalan specialty, also known as *faves ofegades* ("smothered favas"), "one of the gastronomic pillars of the nation," alongside *Escudella i Carn d'Olla* (see page 231) and *botifarra* sausage with white beans (see page 147). "The hegemony of this supreme triad," he continues, "is indisputable." *Faves a la Catalana* is more or less the pork and beans of Catalonia—a vegetable dish above all, in which the pork products, indispensable though they may be, are more accent than substance. Catalans overcook their favas—almost all their vegetables—mightily by contemporary French or American standards, and they insist on adding sugar to most fava dishes; nonetheless, overcooked and sugary though *Faves a la Catalana* usually turns out to be, its mesh of sweet, salt, and earthy fava flavor can be most appealing.

TO SERVE 4 (AS APPETIZER OR LIGHT MAIN COURSE)

1¼ pounds shelled fresh favas (about 2 pounds unshelled) or 1 pound dried favas or two 10 ounce packages frozen favas (see note)
½ pound thick-cut bacon, with 1 thick slice cut from it and the remainder diced
2–3 green onions or scallions, minced
Olive oil
2 botifarra negra sausages (see page 147), 1 cut into ½-inch slices and 1 left whole
1 teaspoon Pernod
1 bay leaf
1 sprig fresh mint, minced, or ¼ teaspoon dried mint
A pinch of sugar
Salt

If you are using dried favas, cover with 1 quart water in a pot, bring to a boil, then simmer until almost tender (about 40–50 minutes). Drain and set aside.

Meanwhile, in a cassola or Dutch oven, sauté the diced bacon and green onions in 1 cup of oil until lightly browned.

Add the sliced *botifarra negra* and favas to the cassola, mix well, then sauté 2–3 minutes.

Add the Pernod, bay leaf, mint, sugar, bacon slice, and the whole *botifarra negra* to the cassola, and salt to taste. Stir well.

Add about 1 cup of water, or enough barely to cover the favas; cover the cassola, bring to a boil, lower the heat, and continue to cook until the favas are tender and grayish-green in color and the water has evaporated (about 15–20 minutes).

Remove the bacon slice and whole *botifarra negra*. Cut each into 4 pieces, then divide the favas evenly among 4 plates, and garnish each with a piece of bacon and a piece of *botifarra negra*.

Note: If you are using large fresh favas, blanch them after shelling in boiling water for 2–3 minutes, cool, and remove the tough outer skins. Many Spanish cookbooks suggest lima beans as a substitute for favas. Though they're about the same size, shape, and color, they are very different in flavor and texture, and I don't recommend such a substitution unless it is absolutely necessary.

Amanida de Faves amb Menta

(FAVA SALAD WITH FRESH MINT)

This is one of Josep Mercader's recipes, an inspired combination of favas (preferably small ones), thin wisps of good ham, and chopped fresh mint—a summer salad par excellence.

TO SERVE 4 (AS APPETIZER)

1¼ pounds shelled fresh favas (about 2 pounds unshelled) or two 10-ounce packages frozen favas (see notes this page and 107)

4 sprigs fresh mint, 1 whole and three finely chopped (see note page 107)

4 large leaves very crisp lettuce, very finely julienned

*4 ounces European-style ham
(prosciutto or Black Forest type),
very finely julienned*
2 ounces mild extra-virgin olive oil
*1 ounce sherry vinegar or good-quality
red wine vinegar*
1 teaspoon good-quality mustard
Salt and pepper

Cover the favas with 1 quart of water in a pot, add the whole sprig of mint, bring to a boil, then simmer until just done (10–15 minutes for fresh favas, 8–10 minutes for frozen). Drain, discard the mint, and allow the favas to cool.

Toss the lettuce, ham, and cooled favas together well.

In a bowl or blender, make a dressing of the oil, vinegar, mustard, and salt and pepper to taste; then stir in the minced mint (do not blend the mint).

Pour the dressing over the salad and toss again, adjusting the seasoning if necessary.

Note: I don't recommend the use of dried favas for this salad. Fresh mint is a must in this case; if you can't obtain it, omit the mint entirely (or, better yet, wait until you *can* obtain it).

Crema de Faves

(CREAM OF FAVA SOUP)

I've had two fava soups in the *països catalans*. One was an unpleasant-looking but delicious Minorcan purée of favas with tomatoes, green peppers, carrots, celery, turnips, and lots of garlic, served (as are most soups in the Balearic Islands) over rounds of lightly toasted bread. The other is this one, an elegant creation of the Eldorado Petit restaurants in Barcelona and Sant Feliu de Guixols—sort of a fava vichyssoise if you will.

TO SERVE 6–8 (AS APPETIZER)

*1 pound shelled fresh favas (about
1⅔ pounds unshelled) or 12
ounces dried favas or one and a
half 10-ounce packages frozen
favas (see note page 106)*
2 onions, chopped
2 tablespoons butter
Olive oil
*1 pound potatoes, peeled and thinly
sliced*
*1½ quarts chicken or strong vegetable
stock*
1 cup heavy cream
Salt and white pepper

Cover the favas with 1 quart of water in a pot, bring to a boil; then simmer until tender (about 1 hour for dried favas, 15–20 minutes for fresh favas, 10 minutes for frozen favas).

In a cassola or Dutch oven, sauté the onions, until wilted, in the butter and a small amount of oil. Add the potatoes and cooked favas to the cassola, stir in well, then cook on low heat for about 5 minutes.

Meanwhile, bring the stock to a boil in another pot; then reduce the heat, and slowly pour the stock into the cassola, stirring gently as you do so. Cook 30–40 minutes, or until the potatoes are about to disintegrate.

Purée the vegetables and stock together in

a blender or food processor or with a food mill; then return to the cassola and bring to a simmer.

Stir in the cream, and mix well; then salt and pepper to taste.

Note: This soup may be served hot or cold; I prefer it in the latter state.

Cigrons amb Mussolina d'All

(CHICK-PEAS WITH GARLIC MOUSSELINE)

Over lunch and the usual ration of food talk one afternoon, Manuel Pagès, director of the Raïmat winery, recalled fondly a dish of his childhood—chick-peas with a bit of *allioli* gratinéed on top. He didn't describe the dish in any more detail than that, but the idea sounded good, and I subsequently came up with this interpretation of it.

TO SERVE 4 (AS APPETIZER OR LIGHT MAIN COURSE)

*2 ounces thick-cut bacon, cut into
 ½-inch cubes
1 ounce European-style ham
 (prosciutto or Black Forest type),
 diced or cut into julienne strips
 about 1 inch long
Olive oil
2 onions, chopped
1 tomato, seeded and grated (see page
 7) or peeled, seeded, and chopped*

*2 cloves garlic, minced
4 cups chick-peas, cooked (about 1⅓
 cups dry)
Salt and pepper
1 cup Mussolina d'All (see page 33)*

Fry the bacon and ham together in a small amount of oil in a cassola or large skillet until lightly browned; then remove from the cassola, and drain on paper towels.

Pour off excess fat from the cassola, leaving enough to cover the bottom; then add the onions, tomato, and garlic, and make a *sofregit* (see page 38).

Add the bacon, ham, and chick-peas to the *sofregit,* mix together well, and cook briefly on low heat until heated through.

Add salt and pepper to taste; then flatten the chick-pea mixture gently with a wooden spoon or spatula and spread a layer of *Mussolina d'All* over top.

Brown the *Mussolina d'All* briefly under a broiler or with a salamander until it begins to puff up.

Amanida de Llenties

(LENTIL SALAD)

This is a delightful little salad prepared at Petit París in Barcelona.

TO SERVE 4 (AS APPETIZER)

*2 cloves garlic, peeled
2 cups red lentils, cooked (about 1
 cup dry)*

1 small leaf iceberg, red-leaf, or butter
    lettuce, cut into chiffonnade
1 small leaf escarole or radicchio, cut
    into chiffonnade
Olive oil
Tarragon vinegar
Salt and pepper
¼ pound small shrimp or crayfish
    tails, cooked and shelled

⅛–¼ pound salt cod, desalted (see
    page 79) and poached, skinned,
    and boned as for Bunyols de
    Bacallà (see page 85), then very
    thinly sliced or finely shredded
1 tomato, slightly green, very thinly
    sliced (see note)

Rub the interior of a salad bowl well with
garlic; then toss the lentils, lettuce, and escarole or radicchio together well in it.

Dress the salad lightly with olive oil and
vinegar (about 3 or 4 parts to 1), then salt and
pepper to taste, tossing gently.

Divide the lentils evenly among 4 plates,
and garnish each one with shrimp, salt cod, and
tomato.

Note: Catalans cook with ripe tomatoes and make salads
with greenish ones. The crispness and acidity of the latter
are indeed quite pleasant.

Botifarra amb Mongetes

(PORK SAUSAGE WITH WHITE BEANS)

"La mongeta es la lleguminosa reina de la cuina catalana," writes Barcelona restaurant critic Luís Bettónica—"The white bean is the leguminous queen of Catalan cuisine"—and never is it more typically Catalan than when sautéed in a *sofregit* and set next to good grilled pork sausage. The best Catalan white beans are said to come from the village of Santa Pau in the *comarca* of the Garrotxa; I've also had very good ones near Lleida and in the Empordà—long, rather thin, and cylindrical, rather than stubby and kidney-shaped like, say, navy or great northern beans. Good Spanish white beans *(alubias)* may occasionally be found in specialty markets in the United States. Otherwise, the closest equivalent is probably Italian-type *cannelli* beans. I don't particularly recommend the canned version of these beans, incidentally, because they're packed in a heavy syrup, and tend to turn to mush with even brief cooking.

TO SERVE 4 (AS MAIN COURSE)

1 tomato, seeded and grated (see page 7) or peeled, seeded, and chopped
2 cloves garlic, minced
1 sprig parsley, minced
Olive oil
4 large or 8 small botifarra *sausages (see page 147)*
4 cups white beans, cooked (about 2 cups dry)
Salt and pepper

In a cassola or large skillet, make a *sofregit* (see page 38) of the tomato, garlic, and parsley in the oil.

Meanwhile, prick the sausages in several places; then grill them on a barbecue, broil on a metal rack in a preheated broiler, or panbroil with ¼–½ cup water until done. Keep the sausages warm.

Stir the beans into the *sofregit*, salt and pepper to taste, and cook briefly on low heat until heated through.

Mound the beans in the middle of a serving platter, and arrange the sausages around them, cutting large sausages into 2 or 3 pieces and leaving small ones whole.

Note: The no-meat-day mirror image of this dish is *bacallà amb mongetes,* in which the beans, cooked exactly the same way, are presented not with sausage but with pieces of salt cod that have been dredged in flour and fried in oil.

Amanida de Mongets i Bacallà Empordà

(EMPORDÀ-STYLE BLACK-EYED PEA AND SALT COD SALAD)

Mongets, also known as *fesolets* (and not to be confused with *mongetes*), are exactly the same vegetable as the black-eyed peas so common to the American South—and, as in the United States, they come in both green-and-black and beige-and-black versions. Black-eyed peas always taste a bit "dirty" to me—in a good sense, as if they'd just been dug from the soil (though of course they grow on vines)—and the combination of that flavor with the smooth sea echoes of salt cod is most appealing, I think.

This is another recipe from the Hotel Ampurdán—this time created not by Josep Mercader but by his son-in-law and successor, Jaume Subirós.

TO SERVE 4 (AS APPETIZER)

½ pound thick-cut salt cod, desalted (see page 79), skinned, and boned
2–3 sprigs fresh mint
5 cups black-eyed peas, cooked (about 2 cups dry)
2 tomatoes, seeded and grated (see page 7) or peeled, seeded, and chopped
2 green onions or scallions, finely chopped
1 small stalk celery, very thinly sliced
12 small radishes, trimmed
¼ pound fresh mushrooms, thinly sliced
Olive oil
Red wine vinegar
Salt and pepper

Poach the salt cod as for *Bunyols de Bacallà* (see page 85), adding the mint sprigs to the water. Then drain and cool, remove any skin and bones, and thinly slice.

Divide the peas evenly among 4 serving plates, then arrange the tomatoes, scallions, celery, radishes, mushrooms, and salt cod on top.

Dress with oil and vinegar (about 3 or 4 parts to 1), and salt and pepper to taste.

See Also:

Amanida de Bacallà (Salt Cod Salad), page 174

Freginat (White Beans with Fried Pork Liver), page 152

MENUTS
(ORGAN MEATS)

"The trouble with Americans," said Carles Llavià one day, across a table at his modest but superb Cypsele restaurant in Palafrugell, "is that they think a cow has only entrecote on it." We were discussing, of course, organ meats—all those delicious but sometimes off-putting parts of the cow (or lamb or pig or whatever) that poor countries tend to eat so much more than we do. ("In America, you feed the tripe and kidneys to your dog," a Chinese chef from Hong Kong once said to me joshingly. "In Hong Kong we eat them ourselves—and then we eat the dog, too.")

Americans do eat the lesser parts of animals, of course—liver, kidneys, sweetbreads, etc. (and lungs and heart and such, ground up into unforbidding particles in sausages and such)—but a lot of us remain shy of them, too. Now, as far as I'm concerned, there's no reason in the world why anybody should eat anything he doesn't want to eat or doesn't like or doesn't *want* to like—and the last thing I'm going to do here is to embark on a little pro-offal crusade. But organ meats are essential to Catalan cuisine, and the Catalan kitchen does many good things with them. Descriptions of four of these things follow.

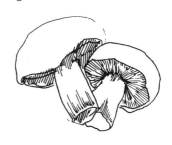

Fetge amb Ceba

(CALF'S LIVER WITH ONIONS)

This Catalan staple is basically *fegato alla veneziana*—Venetian-style calf's liver—though it seems to have developed independently in Catalonia. There was certainly extensive contact between Catalonia and Venice, of course, during the centuries when both shared power in the Mediterranean—and thus it is entirely possible, I suppose, that one people gave the dish to the other. (There are even some similarities between Catalan and the Venetian dialect of Italian.) But this is mere speculation—and, personally, I never feel much like speculating when I smell onions sautéing on the stove. A particularly delicious variation on this dish, incidentally, is sometimes made with baby goat's liver.

TO SERVE 4 (AS MAIN COURSE)

2 pounds onions, sliced paper-thin
2 tablespoons lard
Olive oil
1 cup vi ranci *(see note page 57) or*
*   dry sherry*
1½ pounds calf's liver, cut into
*   ¼-inch strips*
Flour
2 sprigs parsley, minced
Salt and pepper

In a cassola or large skillet, sauté the onions slowly in 1 tablespoon of the lard and a small amount of oil until golden-brown.

Pour the sherry over the onions, bring to a boil, partially cover the cassola, then simmer until the sherry is reduced by about half.

Meanwhile, dust the liver strips lightly with flour; then in another pan, sauté the liver on high heat in the remaining lard and a small amount of oil until browned and slightly crisp around the edges.

Add the liver to the onions, add the parsley, salt and pepper to taste; then cook briefly over high heat, stirring well, until the liquid is evaporated.

Note: This dish is traditionally served with *allioli* (see page 30).

Tripa a la Catalana

(CATALAN-STYLE TRIPE)

Tripe is popular all over Spain, and is perhaps best-known in the form of *callos a la madrileña* or Madrid-style tripe—a rich stew, slightly spicy, with ham and sausage and a pig's foot traditionally included. This Catalan version is much simpler, but equally savory. Tripe—even the ready-to-use variety now widely available—takes a very long time to cook, incidentally, and in any case this dish is better when made a day in advance and reheated.

TO SERVE 4 (AS A MAIN COURSE)

1 pound ready-to-use honeycomb tripe,
*   rinsed, blanched, and cut into*
*   thin strips about 2–3 inches long*
1 bay leaf
Flour
2 tablespoons lard

112

Olive oil
2 onions, chopped
4 tomatoes, seeded and grated (see
  page 7) or peeled, seeded, and
  chopped
2 sprigs parsley, minced
1 cup dry white wine
6 almonds, blanched and roasted (see
  page 39)
1 tablespoon pine nuts, lightly toasted
2 cloves garlic, minced
½ slice fried bread (see page 40)
Salt and pepper

Place the tripe and bay leaf in a large pot with about 2 quarts of water, bring to a boil, then simmer 5–7 hours or until the tripe is tender. (Cooking time will vary.)

Drain the tripe, and pat it dry with paper towels; then roll the strips in flour, and sauté in a cassola or large skillet in the lard and a small amount of oil until golden-brown. Drain on paper towels.

In another cassola or Dutch oven, make a *sofregit* (see page 38) of the onions, tomatoes, and half the parsley in oil.

Add the tripe to the *sofregit* and mix well; then add the wine, bring to a boil, and simmer covered on top of the stove or in a slow oven for 1 hour.

Meanwhile, make a *picada* (see page 40) of the nuts, garlic, fried bread, and the remaining parsley, moistened with a bit of tripe liquid to form a thick paste. Fifteen minutes before the tripe is done, stir the *picada* into the liquid, and salt and pepper to taste.

Note· Roasted or fried potatoes are practically de rigueur with this dish.

Cap i Pota amb Samfaina

(STEWED CALF'S HEAD AND FOOT WITH *SAMFAINA*)

This is another basic specialty of Catalan cuisine—definitive and fundamental. Though widely appreciated throughout Catalonia, by gastronomes of every stripe, it gained particular popularity among the working class of Barcelona in the first three or four decades of this century, and was often eaten in the wee hours of the morning in the precincts of the city's old municipal slaughterhouse—sort of a Catalan version of the famous onion soup around Les Halles in Paris.

TO SERVE 4 (AS MAIN COURSE)

*1 pound calf's head, cut into pieces
    about 1–1½ inches square
½ a calf's foot, split down the middle,
    or 2 pounds veal shank* (osso
    buco), *bone in
2 tablespoons lard
Olive oil
1 cup* vi ranci *(see note page 57) or
    dry sherry
½ recipe* samfaina *(see page 42) with
    1 small dried red chili pepper,
    minced, or ½ teaspoon spicy red
    pepper flakes added with the
    ingredients in step 1.
Salt and pepper*

Place the calf's head and calf's foot or
veal shanks in a large pot with water to
cover, bring to a boil; then simmer for about
1½ hours or until the meat is very tender.
Remove the meat from water, cool, bone, and
chop coarsely.

In a cassola or Dutch oven, sauté the meat
in the lard with a small amount of oil until
light golden-brown on all sides.

Remove the meat from the cassola, pour
off the excess fat, then deglaze the cassola with
sherry, cooking over medium heat until the
liquid is reduced by about half.

Return the meat to the cassola, and coat
well with sherry, then add the *samfaina* and
mix together well.

Simmer uncovered for 15–20 minutes,
adding a bit of water if necessary and stirring
occasionally.

Salt and pepper to taste.

Testicles de Toro amb All i Julivert

(BULL TESTICLES WITH GARLIC AND PARSLEY)

Florian is one of the best and most imaginative restaurants in Barcelona, noted for its
elaborate "composed" salads (including one
made with warm pasta—as much a novelty in
Spain today as it is a cliché in the United
States), its *Escabetxos* (see page 176) and sophisticated fresh fish dishes, its many preparations of wild mushrooms in season—and, again
in season, its *cuina taurina* or "cuisine of the
bull."

Florian buys prime cuts of bulls killed in
the Barcelona bullring, then offers four or five
bull-meat specials daily. The restaurant even—
somewhat   disconcertingly—identifies   the
"bull of the day" on its menu, complete with
name, weight, description, pedigree, time of
execution, and name of matador. Because
bulls, being valuable animals, are somewhat
pampered during their lifetimes, given the best
pasturage and such, Florian proprietors Javier
Garcia-Ruano and (chef) Rosa Grau call its
flesh "the most trustworthy of red meats."

Be that as it may, it is certainly *good* meat,
rich and full-flavored—and Grau certainly
knows how to cook it. She makes a delicious
kind of "oxtail stew" of bull's tail, for instance,
with old Rioja wine; she grills bull entrecote or
filet with sweet red peppers, and she turns (to
come right out and say it) the bull's testicles
into a delicate and delicious dish reminiscent
of sweetbreads or even tender veal.

It will perhaps not surprise you to learn

that the testicles of bulls killed in bullrings (or anywhere else for that matter) are not readily available in the United States. Calf testicles, though—also known as Rocky Mountain oysters and sometimes beef fries—can easily be substituted, and *are* available in some Hispanic meat markets (where they are usually called *criadillas*) and by special order from some other butchers. (Provimi and other major premium veal producers pack and sell calf testicles, and butchers who carry such brands will probably be able to obtain them for you.)

Quick sautéing in olive oil with minced garlic and parsley is a favorite Catalan cooking method (see *Calamars Saltejats amb All i Julivert*, page 138), and can be adapted to sweetbreads, veal scallops, calf's liver, and some kinds of seafood, among other things. This is Rosa Grau's recipe for bull testicles cooked in this manner.

TO SERVE 4 (AS APPETIZER OR LIGHT MAIN COURSE)

2 bull testicles or 4 calf testicles
Salt
2–3 cloves garlic, minced
2 sprigs parsley, minced
Flour
Olive oil

Remove the exterior membrane from the testicles (if it is difficult to remove, place the testicles in the freezer for about 30 minutes or until frosty, then peel), slice ⅛–¼-inch thick, and salt lightly on both sides.

Mix the garlic and parsley into flour; then dip the testicle slices in flour mixture one by one, coating them well.

Heat the oil until very hot; then quickly sauté the testicle slices, browning them lightly on both sides.

Drain on paper towels, and sprinkle with more minced parsley if desired.

See Also:

Flam de Peuada (Pigs' Foot Mousse), page 155

Peus de Porc Farcits amb Bolets (Stuffed Pigs' Feet with Wild Mushrooms), page 153

"Mousse" de Fetge de Pollastre amb Panses i Salsa de Crancs de Riu (Chicken Liver Mousse with Raisins in Crayfish Sauce), page 230

OLIVES I OLI D'OLIVA
(OLIVES AND OLIVE OIL)

One of my favorite spots in all of Barcelona is a stand marked "Conservas A. Rossel," number 15G, just to the right of the main entrance as you walk into the city's great Mercat de Sant Josep or Mercado de San José—the massive downtown food market known to absolutely everyone as La Boqueria (see page 295). What I like so much about Conservas A. Rossel is simply that *el senyor* Rossel himself generously lets potential customers (of which I am always one) taste the full range of his wares: things like Majorcan capers, plump and mild; *taperots* from Murcia, the delicious pickled fruit of the caper plant; and most of all olives, wondrous olives—tart, black little Jonquillos from Alicante; Aloreñas from Málaga, cracked,

green, and marvelously bitter; big greenish-brown Obregóns from Andalusia, spicy with cumin, bitter orange peel, oregano, and summer savory; Extremeñas, mixed green and black and purple, from Spain's western border, hot with raw garlic. . . . And the pride of Catalonia, understated by comparison, tasting only (and intensely) of themselves—the tiny, gray-ish brown, extraordinary Olives d'Arbeca or Arbequines.

There are something like 350,000 acres of olive trees in Catalonia, and about a dozen principal varieties of olives are grown—two kinds of Arbequines (the classic "de les Garrigues" and the slightly larger, rounder "del Camp de Tarragona"), Verdiells, Fargues, Morrudes, etc. The best olives are said to come from the *comarques* of the Priorat, El Baix Ebre, and Les Garrigues. The Empordà region—the Costa Brava and vicinity—used to be noted for its olives, too, but a severely cold winter in 1956 destroyed most of the region's trees, and they have never been replanted in commercial quantity.

Olives, wrote Lawrence Durrell in *Prospero's Cell*, have "A taste older than meat, older than wine. A taste as old as cold water." That taste, that flavor, is difficult to describe—especially when it's unaccompanied by spice or garlic. At its best, though, as any lover of true olives knows full well (and I don't count as true those cottony, emasculated dark black and drab green olives that are most common in America), it is a flavor of earth and herb and vegetable, a taste of salt and sour and sweet. (The traditional Catalan method for obtaining the perfect salinity for olive-curing brine was to place a very fresh egg, laid that very morning, in the bottom of a pot of water and then to add salt until the egg bobbed to the surface.) Arbequines, I think, *are* olives at their best. Barcelona author/columnist Josep M. Espinàs once wrote, in fact, that he looked forward to a day when they would be "served at table as if they were caviar." There have been times, I swear, when I'd rather *have* them than caviar.

Unfortunately—and by now you probably know this is coming—Arbequines are not, to the best of my knowledge, sold in America. (The closest substitute I've found for them are the blackish Nanni Ardoino olives from Italy, sold here under the Vall'Aurea label—not the same thing at all, but good olives nonetheless.) Olive oil *made* from Arbequines is available here, though—the most common labels being

Verge de Borges (sold nationally by Williams-Sonoma, among other merchants), Siurana, Lérida, and Montserrat—and will give you at least a ghost of the flavor of the thing. The English restaurant critic Lieutenant-Colonel Newnham-Davis, back in 1903, called Spanish olive oil "a coarse liquid, the ill taste of which remains all day in one's mouth." Today's Arbequina-based oil, which is probably the best in Spain, is quite the contrary—smooth, attractively but not overpoweringly fruity, and at least sometimes delicate almost to the point of being ethereal. (Spain, incidentally, is the world's largest producer of olive oil.)

Recent studies have shown that olive oil may in fact be better for the human system than polyunsaturated oils (corn or safflower, for instance). It apparently helps flush potentially harmful low-density lipoprotein cholesterol out of the system while increasing the beneficial high-density kind. That's one good reason for using a lot of it, Catalan and otherwise. Another good reason, though, as noted earlier, is that it's a very good cooking medium—perhaps the best and most versatile cooking fat there is.

There is some disagreement among experts on the question of how much olive oil may be heated without smoking or releasing toxins. Jaume Ciurana, in his authoritative book *Els Olis de Catalunya* ("The Oils of Catalonia") writes that good oil will retain all its flavor and nutritional value up to around 210°, and remain perfectly usable at least up to 350°. He does note, though, that extra-virgin oil keeps its characteristics better at high temperatures than lower grades—which is one reason I recommend it for cooking. (Extra-virgin oil, by international agreement, must have less than 1 percent acidity; in practice, though, most Catalan extra-virgins—almost all of which, incidentally, are based at least partially on Arbequines—do not exceed .4 or .5 percent.) Some authors report that olive oil starts smoking at around 300°, but I generally deep-fry at around 375° with the Catalan oils I've been using, and have rarely had a problem. Ciurana does note, however, that it's a good idea to stir very hot oil with a wooden spoon to avoid "hot spots" on the bottom of the pan, where toxins might form. I follow his advice.

The majority of recipes in this book call for olive oil. Here are three that call for olives themselves.

"Garum"
(ANCHOVY-OLIVE *PÂTÉ*)

The original *garum* was of course the famous fermented fish sauce of the Romans (a sauce the sound of which, incidentally, calls to mind the remark of British author Basil Collier that, "There is independent evidence . . . that the taste of Romans in matters of gastronomy was not infallible"). When Josep Mercader developed *this* version of the thing at the Hotel Ampurdán—a complex, wonderfully Mediterranean pâté or paste based on olives and anchovies (if not fermented then at least preserved)—he called it *garum* as a joke. But in fact there is apparently a legitimate Catalan connection with the Roman condiment of old. Fish caught off the coast of Catalonia—at least according to several modern Catalan culinary historians—was particularly prized by the Ro-

mans for the making of their fish sauce. "Catalan-brand" *garum*, that is, was honored even in ancient times. This updated one deserves the same attention today, I think.

TO MAKE 1–1½ PINTS (AS APPETIZER)

18 ounces Italian-style black olives, pitted
16 anchovy filets, soaked in water for 1 hour and patted dry
1 hard-boiled egg yolk
3 ounces capers
1 clove garlic, minced
1 teaspoon grainy mustard
1 tablespoon fresh parsley, minced (see note)
1 tablespoon fresh marjoram, minced (see note)
1 tablespoon fresh dill, minced (see note)
1 tablespoon fresh rosemary, minced (see note)
1 tablespoon fresh thyme, minced (see note)
1 teaspoon white pepper
¼ cup olive oil

Mix all ingredients together in a blender or food processor until light and fluffy.

Purée the mixture in a food mill or push it through a sieve with a wooden spoon.

Return to the blender or food processor, and process briefly to obtain a smooth paste.

Note: It is important to use fresh herbs in this recipe, as dried ones will not purée properly. If some varieties of herb called for are unavailable fresh, omit them. If one or more herbs is omitted, the amount of parsley used may be increased to 2 tablespoons. *"Garum"* is served at the Hotel

Ampurdán with small rounds of very crisp, slightly dried toast—Catalan melba toast, as it were—but is equally good on crackers, toast points, etc. It will keep, covered, in the refrigerator for at least ten days.

Boles de Picolat

(FRENCH CATALAN MEATBALLS WITH GREEN OLIVES)

Boles de Picolat—literally "balls of ground meat"—is one of the great Catalan specialties of the Roussillon. It's an unusual dish, made a bit mysterious by the presence of cinnamon but kept down-to-earth by the flavor of good olives.

TO SERVE 4–6 (AS MAIN COURSE)

½ pound lean ground beef
1 pound botifarra *sausage (see page 147), casings removed, crumbled*
6 cloves garlic, minced
2 eggs, lightly beaten
1 sprig parsley, minced
Salt and pepper
Flour
Olive oil
1 onion, chopped
1 tomato, seeded and grated (see page 7) or peeled, seeded, and chopped
1 small dried sweet pepper (ancho-type), soaked in water for 1 hour, stemmed, seeded, and chopped
1½ tablespoons cinnamon
½ teaspoon sweet paprika
1½ cups green olives (see note), rinsed and pitted

Combine the ground beef, sausage, garlic, eggs, and parsley in a mixing bowl. Salt and pepper to taste. Blend the mixture thoroughly with your hands; then form into small meatballs, about 1–1½ inches in diameter.

Dust the meatballs with flour; then brown them in a small amount of oil in a cassola or Dutch oven.

Remove the meatballs from the cassola and set aside, then cook the onion in the same oil over low heat until soft, adding more oil if necessary.

Sprinkle about 3 tablespoons of flour over the onions, stir in well, then add the tomatoes, chopped pepper, cinnamon, paprika, and about 1½ cups of water. Bring to a boil, then add the meatballs and olives, and lower the heat.

Simmer, covered, for about 30 minutes or until the sauce thickens. Salt and pepper to taste.

Note: Use the best green olives you can find for this recipe, since their flavor will permeate the sauce. I recommend *Picholine du Gard* olives from Provence, imported under several French labels, or Santa Barbara brand country-style olives from California, or a good grade of Spanish olive (though the best ones, alas, are not presently imported). Do not use prepitted olives, as they seem to have lost both flavor and texture in the process. *Boles de Picolat* is often served with plain white beans on the side.

Anjoni ama Urivas

(LAMB CHOPS WITH OLIVES)

This simple but effective and rather unusual recipe comes from the Catalan-speaking enclave of Alghero (l'Alguer in Catalan) on the Italian island of Sardinia—a fact, incidentally, that might surprise all those illustrious

food experts in Catalonia itself who have assured me that Alghero has no Catalan dishes of
its own. I owe this and the other Algherese
recipes in this book, which derive from traditional sources, to Loretta Cervi—a (non-Sar-
dinian) Italian living in Barcelona, where she
promotes Italian-Catalan cultural exchange.
"Anjoni" is the Algherese Catalan word for
lamb, related to the Sardinian terms *anzone*,
agnoni, and *angioni*; *urivas* is local dialect, of
course, for olives.

TO SERVE 4 (AS MAIN COURSE)

2 pounds thin lamb chops (about
½–¾-inch thick), bones in, cut
into 12 pieces of approximately
equal size
Breadcrumbs
Olive oil
6 ounces black olives (see note),
rinsed, pitted, and, if you are
using large olives, halved
2–3 tablespoons lemon juice
1 sprig fresh marjoram, minced, or ¼
teaspoon dried
Salt and pepper

Dredge the chops in breadcrumbs.

In a cassola or large skillet, sauté the chops
in a small amount of oil until slightly cripsy on
both sides. Grind an ample amount of pepper
over them as they are cooking.

Remove the chops from the cassola, and
set aside. Pour off the excess fat, then add the
olives, and sauté lightly over low heat until
soft (about 10–15 minutes).

Season the olives with lemon juice, marjoram, and salt to taste.

Return the chops to the cassola, mix well
with the olives, and cook until heated through.

Note: Though they are tedious to pit, I like the pungency
of tiny Niçoise olives in this dish. Any good-quality black
olives will do, though, especially Italian or Provençal varieties. Again, however, I advise against prepitted olives.

See Also:

Coca d'Ànec i Olives (Duck and Olive *Coca*),
page 195
Platillo de Vedella amb Olives (Veal *Platillo*
with Olives), page 241

OUS
(EGGS)

Eggs are an important part of the Catalan
diet, sometimes stirred raw into soups or stews
as thickening (especially in old-fashioned
recipes), and frequently eaten scrambled, hard-
boiled (in salads or crumbled over anchovies,
the latter especially in the Roussillon), and,
above all, in omelet form.

An omelet is a trout in Catalan; that is, the same word, *truita*, serves for both (though, where there might be some confusion, the fish *truita* is often called *truita de riu* or "trout of the river"). Why these two rather different foodstuffs should bear the same moniker, I don't know—and neither, it seems, does anybody else. One theory is that an omelet is shaped a bit like a trout, flat and elongated with a curved side—the only trouble being that a *French* omelet is shaped like that but a Catalan (or other Spanish) omelet isn't.

In Catalonia, as elsewhere in Spain, an omelet—unless it's specifically identified as a

French-style one—is a round, cakelike affair, dryish and with a relatively low percentage of egg to other ingredients (much like an Italian *frittata;* and not much like a trout). Maybe an omelet is a trout in Catalonia for the same reason that melted cheese is a "Welsh rabbit" or toast with anchovy paste and eggs is "Scotch woodcock" in the British Isles: If you don't *catch* a trout, you've got to have something more humble for dinner—something to pretend *is* a trout. In any case, omelets in Catalonia are made with all manner of things—including potatoes (the classic Catalan, and Spanish, omelet), white beans, green beans, *samfaina*, artichokes, asparagus, garlic shoots, wild mushrooms, tuna, *botifarra* sausage, apples or pears, even fried zucchini flowers (a specialty of the Garrotxa region). To the best of my knowledge, though, no one has yet come up with a *truita de truita*—and you will perhaps be relieved to hear that I have resisted the very real temptation to invent one herewith.

Truita de Patata

(POTATO OMELET)

The potato omelet (usually called the *tortilla española* or "Spanish omelet" in Castilian) is ubiquitous in Spain—eaten warm or at room temperature, a wedge of it on a plate, a piece of it cut to fit into a sandwich (!), little cubes of it impaled on toothpicks as *tapas* or hors d'oeuvres. It's hardly a uniquely Catalan dish, but it *is* a typical one, as common in Catalonia as it is anywhere else in the country.

The best *truita de patata* I've ever had was at the handsome, rustic *borda* (barn) restaurant Casa Perú, in the slate-roofed hamlet of Bagergue in the Vall d'Aran. It was thick, hot, hearty, perfect in texture, positively succulent. Of course, the mountain air and the Pyrenean scenery might have helped somewhat; the dense, delicious-tasting potatoes and light, fine olive oil and hours-old eggs from the restaurant's own chickens certainly did. The restaurant's proprietor, Angela Aunos Paba, was kind enough to give me her recipe for the dish—but, not surprisingly, it just doesn't taste quite the same in my kitchen as it did in her dining room. This slight variation on her formula, though, does produce a very good *truita*, authentically Spanish (and Catalan) in style.

TO SERVE 4–6 (AS APPETIZER, SIDE DISH, OR LIGHT MAIN COURSE)

1 pound potatoes, peeled and thinly sliced
1½–2 cups olive oil
6 eggs, lightly beaten
Salt and pepper

Sauté the potatoes on low heat in a 10- or 12-inch skillet (preferably nonstick) in enough oil to barely cover, reserving about ¼ cup. Do not allow the potatoes to brown or stick together.

Drain the potatoes on paper towels, discarding the oil; then add the potatoes to the eggs, and salt and pepper to taste.

Heat ¼ cup of oil in the same skillet until very hot; then add the potato-and-egg mixture, distributing the potatoes evenly.

Lower the heat, and allow the eggs to brown lightly, shaking the pan occasionally to prevent sticking.

Place a plate or lid over the skillet, carefully turn the omelet out onto it, then slide the omelet back into the skillet with the uncooked side down, and cook until lightly browned, adding more oil if necessary. (The omelet may be flipped several times if desired; some recipes recommend this for more even cooking.)

Serve it hot or, preferably, at room temperature, cut into wedges.

Note: Most Spanish potato omelets, Catalan and otherwise, include a bit of minced onion, sautéed with the potatoes. Angela Paba leaves out the onion, and I have respected her preference here—but feel free to add some if you wish

Truita de Samfaina

(*SAMFAINA* OMELET)

One of the most popular *truites* in Catalonia after the potato variety, this omelet makes a perfect summer luncheon when accompanied by a green salad and a light, slightly cooled red wine.

TO SERVE 4–6 (AS APPETIZER, SIDE DISH, OR
LIGHT MAIN COURSE)

2 cups samfaina *(see page 42)*
6 eggs, lightly beaten
Salt and pepper
Olive oil

Drain the *samfaina* in a strainer or colander for about 10 minutes to remove the excess oil. Reserve the oil.

Stir the *samfaina* into the eggs, and salt and pepper to taste.

Follow the procedure described in the previous recipe, cooking omelet in the reserved oil from the *samfaina,* plus additional oil if needed.

Again, serve hot or, preferably, at room temperature, cut into wedges.

Truita de Pagès

(FARMER'S OMELET)

Barcelona author/columnist Josep M. Espinàs, in a little essay called "To Dream of Omelets," proposes that "The great secret of an omelet is the balance of its ingredients." This assortment of ingredients is bright in both color and flavor, and held in perfect equilibrium, I think, by the eggs that bind the whole together.

TO SERVE 6–8 (AS APPETIZER, SIDE DISH, OR
LIGHT MAIN COURSE)

1 cup olive oil
4 ounces butter
½ a potato, peeled and diced
½ an onion, minced
½ a carrot, diced
½ a turnip, diced
½ a red pepper, roasted and peeled as
*   for* Escalivada *(see page 170) and*
*   diced*
½ cup shelled peas, fresh if possible
2–3 ounces European-style ham
*   (prosciutto or Black Forest type),*
*   diced*
8 eggs, lightly beaten
Salt and pepper

123

Heat the oil and butter on low heat in a 10- or 12-inch skillet (preferably nonstick) on low heat. Add the vegetables at approximately 1-minute intervals in the order given, add the ham, and cook them until soft but not browned.

Drain the vegetables and ham on paper towels, and pour off about two thirds of the fat from the skillet, discarding or reserving it for other cooking, and leaving the remaining oil on low heat.

Stir the vegetables and ham into the eggs, and salt and pepper to taste. (See note.)

Follow the procedure described in the recipe for *Truita de Patata* (page 122).

Serve hot or, preferably, at room temperature, cut into wedges.

Note: This same vegetable filling is very good in a folded-over French-style omelet, too.

Ous Remenat amb Bolets, Tofones, i Manxego

(SCRAMBLED EGGS WITH WILD MUSHROOMS, TRUFFLES, AND MANCHEGO CHEESE)

This is not so much a Catalan dish as a French one—but it's a specialty of the Eldorado Petit restaurants in Barcelona and Sant Feliu de Guixols, which are among the very best restaurants in Catalonia—and that makes it Catalan enough for me.

TO SERVE 6–8 (AS APPETIZER) OR 4 (AS LIGHT MAIN COURSE)

1 pound wild mushrooms (see note), washed thoroughly, dried, and coarsely chopped
Butter
8 eggs
½ a black truffle (see note)
2 tablespoons heavy cream
2 ounces Manchego or Parmesan cheese (see note), grated
White pepper

Sauté the mushrooms slowly in butter over low heat until soft.

Beat the eggs, then grate the truffle into them, and add the cream and then pepper to taste.

Melt about 2 tablespoons of butter in the top of a double boiler, add the mushrooms, and stir well; then add the egg mixture. Cook slowly, stirring constantly, for about 15–20 minutes, or until the eggs are well-scrambled, with a creamy consistency.

When eggs are almost cooked, stir in the cheese.

Note Eldorado Petit usually makes this dish using *ou de reig (Amanita caesarea)* mushrooms, but any flavorful wild mushroom will do. Bear in mind, however, that gray or brown mushrooms will give the finished eggs a gray or brown color, whereas predominately white or yellow ones will yield a lighter hue. Less expensive Italian or (if available) Spanish brown truffles work perfectly well in this dish, though a small black French truffle, even a canned one, will add more character. Manchego is Spain's most famous cheese, made in the La Mancha region near Madrid. Good Parmesan—preferably the authentic Italian variety—is a delicious substitute.

See Also:

PEIX I MARISCOS
(FISH AND SHELLFISH)

The bounty of the Mediterranean crawls by in bright blue plastic boxes on a conveyor belt; some of it still twitching and all of it still glistening from the sea—fat *gambes* (shrimp), tiny reddish-brown *popets* (baby octopi), *calamars* (squid) in half a dozen sizes, fierce-looking *raps* (monkfish), speckled *gats* ("cats"—which we call dogfish), elaborately finned *capellans* ("chaplains" or poor cod), buglike *galeres* (squill), sardines of several lengths and girths, transluscent solelike *limandes*, long ribbonlike *cintes* (bandfish—*cinta* is Catalan for "band," "tape," or "ribbon"), and on and on.

The procession passes in front of an attentive gallery of wholesale seafood dealers, seated at school desks, in tiers, as if in a lecture hall, though with fingers poised not over examination papers or notebooks but over pushbuttons with which to signal their bids for each tray of merchandise. Beyond the conveyor belt hangs a huge electronic tote board, bearing the name of each variety of creature offered and of the boat it came in on (an hour or so earlier), the weight of each lot, and the price—the last of which changes constantly, almost too fast to follow, always in a downward direction, until a buyer likes the price and grabs it.

At the far end of the belt, clerks pack each blue box with ice and attach to it a printout spewed forth by a machine connected to the tote board, confirming the identity of the seafood and of its buyer and the final price. It is now 5 P.M. or so at the wholesale fish market in Roses, on the underside of the Cape Creus on the Costa Brava. By 6 or 7 A.M. the next morning, the local fleet will be out dragging their nets for more of the same—and by lunchtime (and maybe even dinnertime tonight in some cases) the fish and shellfish they've brought in today will be on tables in the resort towns of the coast, Figueres, Girona, and Barcelona.

Roses is one of the two most important fishing ports on the Costa Brava, the other (and somewhat larger) being Palamós, roughly twenty-five miles to the south. There are at least thirty-five fishing ports along the Catalonian coastline, however, from Llança (Lansa), just down from the French border, to Deltebre, south of the Cape of Tortosa—and, of course, many more such ports in other parts of the *països catalans*, from the Roussillon to the *país valencià* and out to the Balearic Islands and Alghero. Spain has one of the longest coastlines of any country in Europe—a dramatic, ever-changing wraparound littoral, stretching from the heart of the western Mediterranean out into the Atlantic and then (with a long interruption in the person of Portugal) up to the Bay of Biscay—and seafood is, of course, an essential part of the local diet all over Spain. But in Catalonia, at least in the coastal *comarques,* fish is practically a religion, shellfish practically a cult.

Consider, for example, the words of Josep Pla's friend and traveling companion, Don Victor Rahola, as quoted in one of Pla's best books: *Aigua de mar* ("Sea Water")—which, if fish is a religion in this region, is part of the Holy Writ: "The fish of these waters so pure," he rhapsodizes at one point, "buffeted by such strong currents, enriched by this olive oil and by the subtle *sofregits* we make here, give the human blood a radiant fullness, a transcendental flight."

Not every piece of fish I've ever had in the *països catalans* has been perfect, I must admit. When a group of American chefs visited Catalonia with me on one occasion, we were served a luncheon at one of the region's most famous restaurants that included a *Romesco de Peix* (see page 223) made with shellfish of a quality that my friends—upstarts from Hamburgerland though they may have been—would never have allowed in their kitchens. Elsewhere, I've had my share of dried-out monkfish and tired shrimp and flavorless hake. On the other hand, I've also had big *gambes* lightly poached in seawater (see page 135) that were of almost unimaginable delicacy and sweetness; tiny *escupinya* clams from the harbor of Maó in Minorca, brash and tart and hauntingly delicious; perfect thick steaks of sea bream; superbly meaty tuna; tender, luscious spiny lob-

ster; tiny red mullet as silky-fleshed as a dream; rich *nero* or grouper (which Josep Pla considered to be the greatest of all fish) that seemed soaked in the very essence of the sea—some of the most remarkable seafood I've ever had, anywhere.

Many of the kinds of fish and shellfish most popular in the *països catalans* are simply unavailable in the United States—or can be found only at very high prices and usually a few days too old, in shops specializing in imported European seafood. *Orada* or gilthead sea bream (*daurade* in French), *nero* or grouper (*anfós* in the Balearics, *mero* in Castilian, *merou* in French), *escórpora* (in fact that essential constituent of *bouillabaisse* called *rascasse*), and *moll* or red mullet, for instance, are rare birds indeed on these shores. Some other varieties may be found here but lack the same character. Our Pacific lobster (or "lobster tail") is basically the same animal as the fabled *llagosta* of the Mediterranean, for instance—but a fresh *llagosta* of the best quality from the Roussillon or the Costa Brava or Minorca (the most famous of all) has about the same relation to the usual frozen lobster tail as beluga caviar does to whitefish eggs. On the other hand, we get plenty of good tuna, swordfish, shrimp (especially from the Gulf of Mexico), monkfish (though usually from larger beasts than in the Mediterranean), octopus, squid, and so on—and in the case of those aforementioned unobtainables, there are plenty of more-than-adequate substitutes. Buy the best, freshest fish and shellfish possible for these recipes, though, whatever the variety—in honor of the Mediterranean, let's say, if not in imitation of it.

Pastís Calent de Rap amb Mussolina d'All

(WARM MONKFISH TERRINE WITH GARLIC MOUSSELINE)

Spanish fish terrines, often called *pastels* (*pastisos* in Catalan), tend to be clogged up with breadcrumbs and dry as the dickens. This one is moist, eggy, and delicate. The recipe comes from Jaume Subirós at the Hotel Ampurdán, and makes good use of the mild garlic sauce, *mussolina d'all*, so favored by his late father-in-law, Josep Mercader.

TO SERVE 6–8 (AS APPETIZER)

2 pounds monkfish, halibut, or other
    firm-fleshed ocean whitefish, cut
    into 6 or 8 pieces of
    approximately equal size
Butter
5 eggs
1½ cups heavy cream
1 sprig fresh thyme, minced, or ¼
    teaspoon dried
Salt and white pepper
1 small or ½ medium tomato, seeded
    and grated (see page 7) or peeled,
    seeded, and chopped (about ¼
    cup)
2 cups Mussolina d'All *(see page 33)*

Preheat the oven to 350°.

Bake the fish in a lightly buttered baking dish or pan until very well done, about 45 minutes. (The fish should be dry.)

Remove the fish from the oven, and raise the oven temperature to 400°.

Allow the fish to cool; then shred it with your fingers or a fork, removing skin and bones if necessary.

Beat 1 egg, then add it to the fish, and slowly pour in the cream, mixing well. Season with thyme and with salt and pepper to taste. (The mixture should be thick and slightly lumpy.)

Generously butter a 2-quart loaf pan or terrine (preferably nonstick), and pour or spoon in half the fish mixture, patting the surface with a spatula to smooth it.

Beat the remaining eggs, pour half over the fish mixture, pour the tomatoes in a wide stripe down the center of the eggs, then carefully add the remaining fish mixture so that the tomatoes and eggs don't seep through.

Smooth the surface with a spatula; then pour the remaining eggs over the fish.

Bake in a *bain-marie* for 45 minutes, then remove from the oven, and cool in the pan until set.

Turn the terrine out of its pan, and cut into slices ½–¾-inch thick.

Arrange the slices on a lightly buttered cookie sheet, and cover half of each one with garlic mousseline, or arrange on broilerproof serving plates, and cover half of each one with *mussolina d'all*, allowing some to spill over the side of the terrine; then brown briefly in the broiler or with a salamander until the mousseline puffs up slightly.

Rap amb All Cremat

(MONKFISH WITH BURNT GARLIC)

Monkfish, also called anglerfish (and known in French as *lotte* or *baudroie* and in Castilian as *rape*) is one of the ugliest sea creatures you'll ever see—"large and grotesque" seafood expert Alan Davidson calls it. Seen from above, the monkfish looks rather like a banjo with two oversized, squared-off ears (actually fins) attached. It has a large, toothed mouth (a big talker in Catalan is sometimes said to have *una boca com un rap*—"a mouth like a monkfish"), and a permanent nasty scowl. Its meat, however, particularly the tail portion, is very good to eat—lobster-firm and demonstrative in flavor.

Monkfish used to be considered junk fish in the United States, but emissaries of France's nouvelle and post-nouvelle cuisine have brought it to the attention, and the tables, of American diners in recent years with something approaching a vengeance. As a result, it is by no means impossible to find in premium fish markets today, especially on the East and West Coasts—and should be sought out for recipes that call for it, since no other fish has quite the same taste or texture. Halibut or other firm-fleshed ocean whitefish may be substituted, however, if it is not available. The name of this particular dish, which is a specialty of the Costa Brava, is a bit misleading. The garlic isn't really burnt (which would give the sauce a nasty bitterness), just seriously darkened.

TO SERVE 4 (AS MAIN COURSE)

6–8 cloves garlic, peeled and sliced
Olive oil
1 slice French- or Italian-style bread
1½ pounds monkfish, halibut, or
    other firm-fleshed ocean
    whitefish, cut into 8–12 pieces
Flour
2 cups fish stock
1 sprig parsley, minced
Salt and pepper

Sauté the garlic in a small amount of oil over medium-low heat until dark brown but not burned; then remove from the pan with a slotted spoon, and set aside.

In the same oil, fry the bread quickly on both sides, adding more oil if necessary; then remove and set aside.

Dredge the fish pieces in flour, and again, in the same oil (adding more if necessary), sauté on medium heat until golden-brown on all sides; then remove, and set aside.

Deglaze the pan with the fish stock; then reduce the liquid by about one third.

Meanwhile, make a *picada* (see page 40) of the garlic, fried bread, and parsley, moistened with a bit of fish stock to make a thick paste.

When the stock is reduced, stir in the *picada*, cook for 3–4 minutes until the *picada* is well integrated into the stock; then return the fish to the pan, and simmer, partially covered, until the fish is cooked through, and the sauce is thick. (If the sauce evaporates too quickly, add more fish stock or water.) Salt and pepper to taste.

Note: As if concerned that they might not be getting their proper day's ration of garlic, residents of the Costa Brava usually garnish this dish with plenty of *allioli.*

Llobarro al Forn

(BAKED SEA BASS WITH POTATOES)

"Fish baked on a bed of thinly sliced potatoes," writes Manuel Vázquez Montalbán in his *L'Art de menjar a Catalunya*, "and seasoned with aromatic herbs, chopped onion and tomato, garlic, parsley, and lemon offers a trip to paradise without LSD." I don't know if the Catalans invented the idea of baking fish this way—the results are indeed marvelous, the potatoes infused with fish flavor and the bottom of the fish unmarred by the pan—but I first encountered it in Catalonia, and have subsequently found it all over the *països catalans*. (In Minorca, there are potatoes under the fish and breadcrumbs drizzled with cream on top—a lovely refinement.)

If this method of fish cookery *is* a Catalan invention, I would suggest that it might stand as one of the culture's greatest single contributions to Western civilization. It is simply one of the two or three best ways of cooking fish I know. *Llobarro*, also known as *llubina* or *llop* in Catalan (and *lubina* in Castilian), is particularly delicious when prepared in this manner—but virtually any variety of ocean fish will work (and I've even made the dish successfully with salmon steaks, though that's not really very Catalan). This recipe is my own, and differs a bit from Vázquez Montalbán's hallucinogenic formula.

TO SERVE 4 (AS MAIN COURSE)

Olive oil
½ pound potatoes, peeled and very thinly sliced, blanched for 3–4 minutes in boiling water, drained, and patted dry
1½–2 pounds sea bass, halibut, swordfish, tuna, or other ocean fish, cut into 4 steaks about 1½ inches thick
2 tomatoes, halved
4 cloves garlic, minced

2 sprigs parsley, minced
2 green onions or scallions, white parts only, minced
1 sprig fresh rosemary, minced, or ¼ teaspoon dried
1 sprig fresh thyme, minced, or ¼ teaspoon dried
Lemon juice
Salt and pepper

Preheat the oven to 400°.

Coat the bottom of a cassola or baking dish with oil; then layer it with potato slices, overlapping them to cover the bottom completely. Arrange the fish on top of the potatoes, and arrange the tomato halves, cut side up, alongside the fish.

Brush the tops of the fish and tomatoes, plus any exposed potato slices, lightly with oil.

Mix the garlic, parsley, green onions, rosemary, and thyme together well, then sprinkle over the fish. Lightly drizzle lemon juice over the garlic mixture, then salt and pepper to taste.

Bake for 25–30 minutes, or until the fish and potatoes are done.

Orada al Forn a la Pescador

(FISHERMAN-STYLE BAKED GILTHEAD SEA BREAM)

This is an elaboration on the preceding recipe, as served at the Hotel Ampurdán in Figueres. As noted earlier, *orada* is the gilthead sea bream (*daurade* in French and *orata* in Italian), a fish highly prized throughout the

Mediterranean. It is occasionally available in the United States at specialty fish markets, but in its absence this recipe may be made with red snapper (preferably the real thing and not the lesser so-called Pacific snapper), sea bass, or almost any other ocean fish. Manuel Vázquez Montalbán thinks that *orada* is the best fish of all to cook atop potatoes, though—and more than one Catalan fisherman, and more than one Catalan chef, agrees with him.

TO SERVE 4 (AS MAIN COURSE)

1 head garlic, separated into cloves and peeled
Olive oil
½ pound potatoes, peeled and very thinly sliced, blanched for 3–4 minutes in boiling water, drained, and patted dry
1½–2 pounds bream, red snapper, sea bass, or other ocean fish, cut into 4 steaks about 2 inches thick
2 tomatoes, peeled, gently seeded, and quartered
1 green pepper, roasted, peeled, and cut into strips as for Escalivada *(see page 170)*
16–20 small black olives (Niçoise or other), pitted
1 botifarra *sausage (see page 147), cut into ¾-inch lengths*
1 bay leaf
1 sprig fresh thyme, minced, or ¼ teaspoon dried
Salt and pepper

Preheat the oven to 400°.

Roast the garlic on a lightly oiled baking sheet or in a lightly oiled pan for 10–15 min-utes, then remove from the oven, and set aside.

Coat the bottom of a cassola or baking dish with oil; then layer it with potato slices, over-lapping them to cover the bottom completely. Arrange the fish on top of the potatoes.

Bake the fish for about 10 minutes; then add the remaining ingredients, including baked garlic cloves, to the pan, distributing the tomatoes, green pepper, olives, and sausage evenly around (but not on top of) the fish and sprinkling the thyme, salt, and pepper over the fish as well.

Continue baking for 15–20 minutes or until the fish and potatoes are done.

Tall de Tonyina al Pebre

("PEPPER STEAK" OF TUNA)

Naked male bodies, some apparently in various stages of decomposition, one seemingly carved in marble in classical style, thrash around in shallow water driving pikes and glinting butcher knives into huge, gaping, sil-very fish. Blood and ocean spray and tiny jump-ing fish and fat seabirds fill the air. In the back-ground, crowds of cloaked figures stand and stoop on a ring of rocks, some looking down on a well-rounded female nude, herself balanced on one leg, staring out to sea. It is one of Salva-dor Dalí's more violent and disturbing paint-ings—*Pesca del Atún (La Almadraba)*—a de-piction not of some ancient seaside holocaust but of a traditional method, only recently banned, of catching tuna on the Costa Brava. The *almadrava* (to give it its Catalan spelling)—the word comes from the Arabic *ma-draba,* a place for striking—occurred in little natural coves along the coastline, U-shaped inlets that could be sealed off with raised nets when tuna had swum into them. Four or five fishing families would move into each cove—the assignments were often hereditary—and set up housekeeping for six weeks or so, from about mid-August to the end of September, in little shacks on the beach. When several tuna had found their way into the cove and their egress had been blocked, the fishermen would wade into the water with long spears and slay them. The last *almadrava* in Spain was held in 1965, in a little cove just southeast of Roses on the Costa Brava—below the hill where the Almadraba Park Hotel, named in its honor, is now situated.

Jaume Subirós, proprietor of the Almadraba Park, (and of the Hotel Ampurdán in Figueres), is—appropriately—very fond of tuna, a disposition not all Catalans seem to share. Very little large tuna is caught off the Costa Brava, in fact; the boats just aren't equipped for it. (Subirós says that when Catalan fishermen come across a school of the big fish, they sometimes radio to their French counterparts a few miles up the coast to tell them where it is—and that successful French fishermen sometimes put into Costa Brava ports and give their Catalan friends a tuna or two in thanks.) Subirós occasionally makes one unusual dish in which he splits a small tuna or bonito down the middle, bones it, and then wraps it around a hambone, tying it closed and roasting it. He also uses bonito for this simple variation on *steak au poivre*—though any fresh tuna will work just fine.

TO SERVE 4 (AS MAIN COURSE)

½ teaspoon herbes de Provence *(a dried mixture of rosemary, thyme, oregano, basil, and sometimes parsley and/or savory)*
1 bottle light red wine (Torres Coronas, nonreserve Rioja or Chianti, Beaujolais, California Pinot Noir, etc.)
1½ pounds fresh tuna, cut into 4 steaks
4 tablespoons butter (½ stick)
Olive oil
2 tablespoons jus de viande *or meat extract (i.e., Bovril)*
1–3 tablespoons black peppercorns, to taste, cracked or very coarsely ground
Salt

Mix the herbs into the red wine in a bowl big enough to hold the tuna.

Marinate the tuna, completely covered with wine, for 1 hour.

Remove the tuna from the wine, and pat dry, reserving the wine; then sauté the tuna in the butter and a small amount of oil over medium-low heat, turning it once, until cooked through (about 10–15 minutes for slightly pink tuna).

Just before the tuna is done, spread *jus de viande* equally on top of each steak, sprinkle with the peppercorns and salt to taste, then turn the fish once more, and cook pepper side down for about 1 minute.

Turn the steaks over, and place on serving plates pepper side up; then deglaze the pan

132

with about ⅔ cup of the reserved wine, reducing it quickly to about ¼–⅓ cup.

Pour the wine reduction over the steaks and serve.

Tonyina Estil Cambrils

(CAMBRILS-STYLE TUNA)

The little resort and fishing town of Cambrils, just south of Tarragona, with a population of about 12,000, boasts four restaurants with one star each in the *Guide Michelin*— Can Bosch, Ca'n Gatell, Casa Gatell, and Eugenia— the latter three of which are all owned by members of the same extended family. I like all three (alas, I haven't yet visited Can Bosch), but I think my favorite remains the first one I ever visited—Casa Gatell. I recall my first meal there vividly: homemade potato chips and very mild anchovies, pale almost to the point of whiteness; a light, cool cream of *cigales* (*Scyllarides latus*, a variety of flat, short-clawed lobster much loved in the Mediterranean); some remarkable red *fideus* noodles with super-fresh baby clams (see page 200); and this dish, served tepid, rich with oil and sweet and sharp with onions, far moister than tuna usually is— and absolutely delicious. This is Casa Gatell's recipe for the dish.

TO SERVE 4 (AS MAIN COURSE)

*2 pounds fresh tuna, cut into thick
3–4-inch pieces
Mild extra-virgin olive oil*
*Salt and pepper
¼ teaspoon allspice
6 cloves garlic, thinly sliced
2 onions, sliced paper-thin
1 bay leaf*

Preheat the oven to 325°.

Place the tuna in a lightly oiled baking dish just large enough to hold it.

Salt and pepper the tuna to taste, then sprinkle lightly with allspice.

Scatter the garlic slices evenly over the tuna; then cover with sliced onions.

Pour in olive oil to cover the tuna and onions completely; then add the bay leaf on top.

Cover tightly, and bake for 1 hour.

Serve at room temperature, or slightly warm, first having removed the onions and tuna from the oil and drained them on paper towels.

Note: The traditional Cambrils accompaniment to this dish is simply cooked white beans seasoned with olive oil and salt.

Peix Espasa en Cassola

(SWORDFISH WITH RAISINS AND PINE NUTS)

As noted earlier, the identity of the author of the seminal Catalan cookbook *Libre del coch*—published in Barcelona in 1520, and possibly written thirty or more years earlier—isn't really known. He claims to have been chef to the (Aragonese) king of Naples and signs himself "Mestre Robert" ("Master Robert"), with the surname "de Nola" added in the first Castilian edition of the book, dated 1525. An early twentieth-century translator of the work, Dionisio Perez, suggests, however, that "Nola" might be a pun on the Castilian expression *"no lo hay"*—which might be roughly translated, with reference to a surname, as "he doesn't have one." Other writers have posited, not unreasonably, that the author might have hailed from the town of Nola, just east of Naples. Valencian gastronome Llorenç Millo, on the other hand, states that "most critics consider [de Nola] to have been a native of Valencia." Whoever he was and wherever he was from, one thing sure about the author of the *Libre del coch* is that he knew his seafood. At least twenty-nine varieties of fish and shellfish are specified for his recipes—all but two of them (trout and barbel) denizens of the Mediterranean, and all of them still eaten in the *països catalans* today. Among these were conger eel, tuna, dentex, hake, spiny lobster, squid, cuttlefish, octopus, and swordfish, which de Nola called *emperador*—"emperor," a common name for the fish in the Mediterranean.

This recipe is my version of one that appears in this nearly 500-year-old cookbook. The sweet-and-sour character of the dish is plainly medieval in inspiration, and the rather busy sauce might seem like a bit much to apply to so delicious a fish as this—but the dish turns out very well, I think, and is certainly a change of pace from the simple grilling that swordfish usually gets. Shark or light-fleshed tuna work well in this dish, too.

TO SERVE 4 (AS MAIN COURSE)

1½ pounds swordfish, shark, or light-fleshed tuna, about 1 inch thick, cut into pieces about 2 × 4 inches
Flour
Olive oil
1 cup dry white wine
½ cup orange juice, fresh-squeezed if possible
1 tablespoon lemon juice
16–20 almonds, blanched and roasted (see page 39)
1 sprig parsley, minced
1 sprig fresh mint, minced, or ¼ teaspoon dried
1 sprig marjoram, minced, or ¼ teaspoon dried
⅓ cup golden raisins or sultanas, plumped in warm water for 10 minutes
⅓ cup pine nuts, lightly toasted
Salt and pepper

Dredge the swordfish pieces in flour, then brown lightly on all sides in a cassola or large skillet in a small amount of oil.

Remove the fish from the cassola, and drain it on paper towels. Deglaze the cassola with the wine, orange juice, and lemon juice, and reduce the liquid by half.

Meanwhile, make a *picada* (see page 40) of the almonds and herbs, moistened with a bit of liquid from the cassola; then add to the pan along with the raisins and pine nuts, stirring the ingredients together well.

Return the fish to the cassola, and heat through; then salt and pepper to taste.

Truita de Riu Andorrana

(ANDORRAN-STYLE TROUT)

The lakes and rivers of the Spanish Pyré-nées teem with fish—tench, barbel, carp, even what is known in Catalan as *blac-bas.* Freshwater crayfish (called *crancs de riu* or "river crabs") are common, too. But the region's most popular fish by far is trout. Local trout has been famous since medieval times, in fact, when it was salted like herring and shipped throughout Catalonia. (The town of Llivia, now a Spanish enclave surrounded by French territory, once sent an annual tribute of 1,100 salted trout to the Count of Barcelona.) Today, of course, Catalans like their trout fresh—nowhere more so than in the Pyrenean suzerainty of Andorra. This simple, tasty way of treating trout is a specialty of El Celler d'en Toni in Andorra la Vella, where it might precede a hearty *civet* of *isard* (chamois).

TO SERVE 4 (AS APPETIZER OR MAIN COURSE)

4 trout, cleaned, rinsed, and dried
Flour
Butter
Olive oil
4 ounces European-style ham
(prosciutto or Black Forest type),
cut into julienne strips about 2
inches long
4 cloves garlic, minced
4 sprigs parsley, minced
Salt and pepper

Dust the trout with flour; then sauté in a cassola or large skillet in butter and a small amount of oil until browned on both sides and cooked through.

Remove the trout from the cassola, and keep warm; then quickly sauté the ham, garlic, and parsley, with salt and pepper to taste, in the same pan, adding more butter if necessary.

Distribute the ham mixture evenly on top of the trout.

Gambes a la Sal, Estil Deniá

(DENIÁ-STYLE SHRIMP IN SALT WATER)

Deniá is an attractive resort town roughly halfway between Valencia and Alicante, which claims to have been founded by the Phocaean Greeks and to have drawn its name from a temple to Diana built in the vicinity by the Romans. This almost daringly simple method of cooking shrimp is typical of Deniá, although I first encountered it not in the *païs valencià* at all but at the elegant Eldorado Petit in

Barcelona—whence this recipe derives. It is important to use the freshest shrimp possible in this dish, incidentally, since the shrimp remains only about half-cooked. The purpose of the serious application of ice, in fact, is to arrest the cooking completely the moment the shrimp comes from the water.

TO SERVE 4 (AS APPETIZER)

3 quarts seawater (see note), or 3
*   quarts water with 3 ounces salt*
*   added*
2 pounds large shrimp, heads on,
*   rinsed*
Additional salt
Crushed ice

Bring the water to a rolling boil in a large pot.

Cover the bottom of a large tray or serving platter with crushed ice; then cover the ice completely with a clean kitchen towel or large napkin. Spread another towel or napkin of the same size on a table or counter and fill the center of it with crushed ice, leaving 2 or 3 inches bare on each side.

Boil the shrimp for 3 minutes, then quickly remove them from the water, arrange in a single layer on the tray or platter, salt to taste, and place the second towel or napkin on top of it, smoothing out the ice so that all the shrimp is covered.

Lift the top towel or napkin off the shrimp after about 1 minute, and serve immediately.

Note: If you have access to unpolluted seawater, collect about 3½ quarts of it and let it stand for about 1 hour, until the sand and other impurities fall to the bottom. Carefully pour, siphon, or scoop out the required amount.

Gambes amb All Confit

(SHRIMP WITH BAKED GARLIC)

This is a recipe from the Le Sardinal restaurant in Banyuls, just north of the Spanish border in the Roussillon. The basic idea is purely Catalan (compare this dish with *Rap amb All Cremat,* page 128), but the recipe is a French refinement, created by Le Sardinal's chef, Jean-Marie Patrouix.

TO SERVE 4 (AS MAIN COURSE)

2 heads garlic, separated into cloves
*   but unpeeled*
16–20 very large shrimp, heads on
2 cups heavy cream
Olive oil
Salt and pepper

Preheat the oven to 400°; then bake the garlic cloves on a lightly oiled baking sheet or in a lightly oiled skilled for 20–30 minutes or until soft but not creamy.

Cool the garlic, then slip it from its skins, setting aside as many cloves as there are shrimp.

Remove the shrimp heads and mash the remaining garlic. Pour the cream into a saucepan, add the shrimp heads and mashed garlic, and simmer until the liquid is reduced by half. Strain the cream and return it to the saucepan; then salt and pepper to taste. Keep the sauce warm.

Devein the shrimp, and sauté them slowly in a small amount of oil until just cooked but not browned.

Divide half the sauce among the centers of four warm serving plates; then arrange the shrimp extending out from the centers like the spokes of a wheel, with 1 whole garlic clove between every two shrimp. Drizzle the remaining sauce over the shrimp and garlic, thinning it slightly with more cream if necessary.

Cotzas a la Marinara

(ALGHERESE MUSSELS, SAILOR-STYLE)

I'm always surprised, considering their heroic consumption of seafood in general, that the people of the *països catalans* don't seem to eat more bivalves. Clams are admittedly popular in the region of Valencia and the Balearic Islands (the latter boasting some of the finest in the world—Minorca's *escupinyes*), but in Catalonia itself, I've rarely encountered them outside of a paella or an occasional fish soup. Oysters are much prized in the region's fancier restaurants, but are a luxury item, usually imported from France. (Oyster culture was important in Roman times around Tarragona, but has long since all but disappeared.) Mussels, again, show up in paella and fish soup, but are served by themselves, simply steamed, relatively rarely.

An exception in this last case, though, must be made for Alghero, the Catalan-speaking outpost on the island of Sardinia. Here, simply cooked mussels are a great favorite in fishermen's cafés and serious restaurants alike. This recipe, which calls mussels by the local name *cotzes* (related to the Italian *cozze*)

rather than the Catalan *musclos,* is one of the best of all Algherese preparations of them.

TO SERVE 4 (AS APPETIZER)

2 cloves garlic, minced
2 sprigs parsley, minced
½ cup fresh basil, minced, or 1
*   teaspoon dried*
Olive oil
2 anchovy filets, soaked in water for 1
*   hour and patted dry, then mashed*
*   with a fork or with a mortar and*
*   pestle*
¼ cup dry white wine
¼ cup white wine vinegar
4 dozen mussels, cleaned (see note
*   page 36)*
Pepper

Sauté the garlic, parsley, and basil quickly in enough oil to cover the bottom of a pot large enough to hold the mussels.

Stir the anchovies, wine, and vinegar together in a bowl, then add to the pot.

Add the mussels, and steam, covered, until they have opened (about 3–4 minutes).

Toss the mussels briefly with the sauce, then divide among four bowls or serving plates.

Season the remaining sauce with pepper to taste, then serve on the side, for dipping.

Calamars Saltejats amb All i Julivert

(SQUID SAUTÉED WITH GARLIC AND PARSLEY)

One of the simplest and best preparations of squid imaginable is this traditional Catalan specialty. Ideally, it is made with miniature squid (*calamarcets,* no more than an inch or an inch-and-a-half long including the tentacles) or with equally tiny octopi *(popets),* but these aren't sold in the United States to the best of my knowledge, and larger squid, cut up as for frying, work perfectly well.

TO SERVE 8 (AS APPETIZER) OR 4 (AS MAIN COURSE)

Olive oil
Coarse salt
1–1½ pounds squid, as small as
*   possible, cleaned and thoroughly*
*   dried, then cut into ½ inch rings,*
*   with tentacles left whole*
4 cloves garlic, minced
2 sprigs parsley, minced

Heat the oil until almost smoking in a cassola or large skillet.

Scatter coarse salt in the cassola; then add the squid and cook very quickly, for about 1 minute, stirring constantly with a wooden spoon.

Add the garlic and parsley, toss for a few seconds, and serve.

Calamars Farcits amb Salsa de Xocolata

(STUFFED SQUID WITH CHOCOLATE SAUCE)

At first glance, this unusual combination of squid, ground pork, and chocolate will probably sound about as unlikely and unappetizing as the aforementioned salt cod with honey (see page 83)—but, like that dish, it is quite wonderful and quite traditionally Catalan.

TO SERVE 4 (AS MAIN COURSE)

1 pound squid, cleaned and
*   thoroughly dried*
½ pound ground pork
1 onion, finely diced
1 small carrot, finely diced
2 cloves garlic, minced
2 sprigs parsley, minced
Olive oil
¼ cup breadcrumbs
½ cup pine nuts, lightly toasted
Salt and pepper
1 cup fish, shellfish, or chicken stock
½ cup dry white wine
10–12 almonds, blanched and roasted
*   (see page 39)*
1 ounce chocolate (see page 40),
*   coarsely grated*
2 slices fried bread (see page 40)

Remove the heads and tentacles from the squid, and set the bodies aside. Mince the heads and tentacles, then mix them well with the ground pork. (The mixture may be processed in a food processor if desired.)

In a cassola or large skillet, make a *sofregit* (see page 38) of the onion, carrot, garlic, and parsley in oil; then add the pork mixture, breadcrumbs, and half the pine nuts, mixing together well and cooking until the meat is well done. Salt and pepper to taste; then remove the mixture from the cassola, and drain on paper towels or in a colander.

Preheat the oven to 350°.

When the pork mixture is cool, lightly stuff the reserved squid bodies with it. (Do not overstuff, or the squid will shrink and tear while cooking.)

Bake the squid in a single layer, uncovered, in a lightly oiled baking dish, for about 20 minutes.

Meanwhile, deglaze the cassola with the stock and wine, simmering until it is reduced by about half.

While the liquid reduces, make a *picada* (see page 40) of the almonds, remaining pine nuts, chocolate, and fried bread, moistened with a bit of the liquid to make a thick paste.

Add the *picada* to the reduced liquid, stir in well, return to the boil, and salt and pepper to taste.

Pour over the stuffed squid, or spoon onto serving plates, and set the squid on top of the sauce.

Croquetes de Llagosta
(SPINY LOBSTER CROQUETTES)

Llagosta or spiny lobster is *Palinurus vulgaris*, known to the French as *langouste*—a creature once described by early-twentieth-century British wit William Caine as "a lobster that has learned to concentrate itself in one place." It is also more or less the same thing we call Pacific lobster, rock lobster, or lobster tail. Don't try to tell a Minorcan or a Majorcan that, though. They're convinced that their version of the thing is sui generis, unparalleled anywhere in the world. It even commands a higher price sometimes, by as much as 25 or 30 percent, than imported *llamàntol*, true lobster. This recipe, my own version of a delicious appetizer I've eaten several times in Majorca, is usually made from leftover scraps—but unless you eat a lot of spiny lobster to begin with, you probably won't have enough such scraps yourself; a whole tail or two will do just fine.

TO SERVE 4 (AS APPETIZER)

2 onions, minced
1 tomato, seeded and grated (see page 7) or peeled, seeded, and chopped
2 cloves garlic, minced
1 sprig parsley, minced
Olive oil
Butter
½ cup flour
1½ cups milk
1 egg, beaten, and 2 egg yolks
½ pound spiny lobster (lobster tail) or Maine lobster meat, cooked and shredded
1 cup breadcrumbs
Salt and pepper

Make a *sofregit* (see page 38) of the onions, tomato, garlic, and parsley in oil; then drain on paper towels or in a colander.

Melt 2 tablespoons of butter in a saucepan, stir in the flour, and cook for about 2 minutes; then slowly pour in the milk, stirring constantly until the mixture thickens.

Beat the 2 egg yolks into the mixture, and cook another minute or so, or until very smooth. Whip in 1 tablespoon of butter; then stir in the *sofregit* and shredded lobster.

Pour the lobster mixture into a lightly buttered dish, then flatten with a spatula, and dot and spread the top with a small amount of soft butter (to keep a skin from forming). Refrigerate 2–3 hours until the mixture can be molded.

Shape the lobster mixture into small balls or cylinders, no more than 2–2½ inches in diameter; dip into beaten egg, then roll in breadcrumbs seasoned with salt and pepper.

Let the croquettes rest on a wire rack.

Meanwhile, fill a cassola or other deep pan with at least 1 inch of oil (or use a deep-fryer), and heat the oil to about 375°.

Fry the croquettes in oil until golden-brown on all sides; then drain on paper towels before serving.

Civet de Llagosta

(SPINY LOBSTER STEW)

Llagosta is a favorite shellfish all over the *països catalans*, even in the inland reaches of the Roussillon. In fact, the wine region of Maury, just northwest of Perpignan, considers *llagosta* to be one of its most important local specialties—and the day after major holidays, such as the annual Maury town fete, the garbage is said to be literally strewn with lobster shells. "People even used to make a point of keeping the carapaces whole," according to winery proprietor Bernard Dauré, "and arranging them on the top of their garbage sacks so that the garbage collector would notice them and spread the word that so-and-so had *eight* or *ten* or *twelve* for his holiday dinner. It became such a status symbol that there were even people who would collect carapaces and sell them to others who wished to exaggerate their consumption."

This recipe, a classic of French Catalonia, is more typical of the seaside than of Maury, but it is a rich, serious, quite extraordinary preparation of this honored crustacean. It comes from French Catalan food writer Eliane Thibaut-Comelade's comprehensive two-volume work, *La Cuisine catalane* (L. T. Jacques Lanore, 131 rue P. V Couturier, 92242 Malakoff, France).

TO SERVE 4–6 (AS MAIN COURSE)

4 spiny lobsters, each cut into 4–6
serving pieces, with the coral and
the creamy interior of the head
removed and set aside
Olive oil
6 ounces cognac
1 tablespoon lard
2 onions, chopped
3 shallots, minced
2 carrots, diced
1 tomato, seeded and grated (see page
7) or peeled, seeded, and chopped
½ pound European-style ham
(prosciutto or Black Forest type),
diced
½ bottle medium-dry Banyuls (see
page 253), medium-dry sherry, or
tawny port

1½ cups fish or shellfish stock
1½ cups veal or beef stock
Bouquet garni of 1 sprig each of fresh
    thyme, rosemary, and parsley, or
    ¼ teaspoon each of dried thyme,
    rosemary, and parsley, mixed
    together well and wrapped
    securely in cheesecloth
6 cloves garlic, minced
1 sprig parsley, minced
Cayenne
Salt and pepper

In a cassola, Dutch oven, or large pot, sauté the lobster quickly in a small amount of oil until it turns red; then flame it with cognac, and when the flames burn out, remove the lobster, and set it aside.

Add the lard to the cassola, with more oil if necessary, and make a *sofregit* (see page 38) of the onions, shallots, carrots, and tomato. When the *sofregit* is cooked, add the ham, mix well, and cook an additional 3 minutes.

Add the Banyuls, both stocks, the bouquet garni, garlic, parsley, a pinch of cayenne, and salt and pepper to taste and bring to a boil.

Simmer the contents of the cassola, partially covered, for about 20 minutes, or until the mixture has thickened slightly. Add the reserved lobster, and cook for about 10 minutes more, or until the lobster is heated through.

Remove the lobster pieces from the cassola, and arrange them on a warm serving platter.

Add the coral and creamy interior of the lobster head, stir well, and reduce over medium heat for about 1 minute.

Pour the sauce over the lobster, and serve.

All-i-Pebre de Llagostins

(PRAWNS WITH GARLIC AND PAPRIKA)

All-i-pebre, literally "garlic-and-pepper," is the great specialty of the Albufera, the huge marshy lagoon south of Valencia. Every village in the region—El Saler, El Palmar, Perellonet and Perello, Silla, Catarroja, Sollana, Sueca, and the rest—has its own *allipebreteros* or *all-i-pebre* specialists (always "uncles"), and each one has its own slightly different recipe. *All-i-pebre*, writes Llorenç Millo, who is the reigning contemporary expert on Valencian cuisine, "is not a dish appropriate to fine tablecloths and clear crystal; its time is in the morning . . . halfway between the freshness of the dawn and the midday heat; its place the tavern. . . . The guests . . . will sit around the stewing pot, will dip their bread into it, will pass the wine flask along and will celebrate happily a successful deal."

Midmorning might not seem like an appropriate time to eat a rich, slightly spicy dish like this—but on the other hand, say Valencians, it's *too* rich to eat at night. Unless otherwise specified in the *país valencià*, an *all-i-pebre* is always made from eel—preferably the good eel caught in the Albufera itself. But *all-i-pebres* can be made, quite authentically, from other kinds of seafood and even from meat. This particular one, served at one of the better traditional restaurants in Valencia, El Plat, is made with *llagostins*, a variety of prawn known scientifically as *Penaeus caramote*—a particularly large and meaty species. Any kind of prawn will do, though, and shrimp can be used as well—as fresh as possible in either case, please.

TO SERVE 4 (AS MAIN COURSE)

1 head garlic, separated into cloves, 4
*   cloves peeled and minced, the rest*
*   scored once lengthwise but*
*   unpeeled*
½ cup olive oil
2 cups fish or shellfish stock
1 bay leaf
½ teaspoon cayenne
Salt and pepper
1 sprig parsley, minced
1 cup pine nuts, lightly toasted
1 slice fried bread (see page 40)
24 large prawns or shrimp, heads and
*   shells on*

Sauté the unpeeled garlic in the oil for about 10 minutes to flavor the oil, then remove and discard the garlic or set it aside for another use.

Add the fish stock, bay leaf, and cayenne to the oil, and salt and pepper to taste. Simmer for about 10 minutes.

Meanwhile, make a *picada* (see page 40) of the minced garlic, the parsley, pine nuts, and fried bread. Moisten the picada with a few drops of the cooking liquid, and then stir it into the pot.

Add the prawns to the liquid, and simmer about 5 minutes, or until done.

Pop Estofat amb Patates

(STEWED OCTOPUS WITH POTATOES)

This is one of the best preparations of octopus I know—a simple stew in which the beast itself becomes very tender and unforbidding, topped by the unexpected but delightful textural contrast of little cubes of fried potato. The recipe is based on a famous specialty from Sol Ric, widely considered to be the best restaurant in Tarragona.

TO SERVE 4 (AS APPETIZER OR LIGHT MAIN COURSE)

1 onion, chopped
2 cloves garlic, minced
1 sprig parsley, minced
Olive oil
3 pounds octopus, cooked (see note
*   page 143), with tentacles cut into*
*   1–2-inch lengths and body cut*
*   into 1-inch squares*
1 teaspoon sweet paprika
Salt and pepper
1–1½ pounds potatoes, peeled and cut
*   into ½-inch squares*

In a cassola or Dutch oven, make a *sofregit* (see page 38) of the onion, garlic, and parsley in oil.

Add the octopus, paprika, and salt and pepper to taste, and stir well.

Simmer covered for about 20 minutes, or until the octopus is very tender, stirring occasionally.

Meanwhile, fry the potatoes in olive oil, and drain on paper towels.

Just before the octopus is finished cooking, put the potatoes on top of it (do *not* mix in), then cook for about 5 minutes longer.

Note: In the United States virtually all octopus is sold already cooked.

See Also:

EL PORC
(THE PIG)

One bright, crisp January morning not long ago, I found myself outside a little 1912-vintage farmhouse in the countryside near Lleida with about a dozen other people, waiting for the matador. Now, the matador we were awaiting wasn't the kind who dances around a dusty ring in sequined finery and slays brave bulls with a flashing sword. This one would arrive in blood-stained dark blue overalls, carrying an array of big knives, a hatchet, and a butane torch. *Matador* simply means "one who kills" in Catalan (as in Castilian), and this one's prey would be not bovine but porcine: He was coming to slaughter a pig.

Pig killing—called the *matança del porc* in Catalan—is an annual event in Catalonia and vicinity, and a formalized one (as indeed it is in much of the world). Catalan writers sometimes speak of it as a kind of ritual sacrifice, in fact, fraught with almost religious significance—a significance which, indeed, it once had, as an act that set Spanish Christians dramatically apart from their nonpork-eating Moorish conquerers. It is also, as author-chef Domènec Moli has noted, "an excuse for a party, for a reunion of family and friends around the table." (As with most Catalan rituals, there is a big meal attached.)

The pig isn't killed for fun, of course. It has been fattened for months for precisely this purpose, and, before the day of the *matança* is over, its body will have yielded up—by dint of much hard work on the part of the pig's owners and their friends—food worth literally thousands of grams of protein and hundreds of thousands of calories, in a form (i.e., a variety of sausages and hams) that can be stored for at least a year without refrigeration and drawn upon as needed. If this is a ritual, then, it is one with extremely practical results.

A *matador* must work quickly at a *matança*. He slaughters as many as four or five animals a day in season (from about mid-December to early February, and later in the high Pyrénées)—few farmers do it with their own hands anymore—and the last of them must have met its fate by midmorning at the latest, to leave time for the butchering and sausage-making that follows (and that must be completed by day's end so that the fresh meat doesn't spoil). Thus, when our own *matador* finally arrives—about an hour late, to an amiably sarcastic *"Bona tarda"* ("Good afternoon") from the assembled multitude—he and his assistant set promptly to their task. I won't describe the slaughter itself here; it's a fascinating process, but not exactly an appetizing one. I will say, though, that the pig this particular morning was a female, about seven months old, grown to a weight of about 275 pounds on a diet of barley, corn, fruit, and table scraps; that she did not go nobly to her death but that her agony was over in a minute or two; and that, if the slaughter is indeed a ritual, the *matador* and his assistant conduct it in a remarkably dispassionate, unceremonious manner.

By the time the *matador* leaves, what was so recently an animal is now large hunks of meat, and our own work begins. Tiny scraps of flesh are cut from two different sections of the pig, and one of our number takes them off to the local veterinarian, who will test them immediately for trichinosis and other diseases.

One of the women takes a blue plastic tub filled with the pig's blood into the farmhouse kitchen, where she will knead fresh crustless white bread into it, as stuffing for the *botifarra negra* or blood sausage that will be made. The rest of us start to work at a big concrete table covered in white cloth, wielding an odd collection of knives, boning the meat and chopping it into small pieces. (As I work, I am reminded of the story that Castilian troops, several hundred years ago, fearing a Catalan uprising, outlawed knives in local households—except for one, which had to be chained to the kitchen table.) The prime cuts—the loin, the smaller

ribs, the tongue, etc.—are set aside to be taken back to town and eaten in the next few days. The feet, highly prized in Catalonia, are cleaned and similarly marked for early consumption. Most of the organs, along with some uncured bacon and the *galtes* or jowls (which make great eating), go into a huge copper cauldron bubbling away on a wood fire in one corner of the yard—all but the liver, which disappears into the kitchen with a few other pieces of meat, to be turned (I later learn) into lunch.

Meanwhile, two of the women disappear, taking the pig's intestines back to their house in town to rinse them thoroughly—there is no running water on the farm—and clean them with salt and vinegar. Around the table, we have by now divided all the meat into three piles—some with meat alone, some with meat and fat, some with meat and fat and organs—each intended for a different kind of sausage. A small, home-sized meat grinder has been set up—almost the entire pig is about to be fed into its 4-inch maw!—and, bit by bit, the three piles are ground. Onions are chopped and fed through the grinder, too. Black pepper is pulverized in a tiny old wooden mill, emerging wonderfully fragrant. One man seasons the meat—20 grams of salt and 9 of pepper for each kilo of pork is his formula—working the seasoning into each pile with his hands. Some meat is mixed with blood-soaked bread for the *botifarra negra*. The women have returned with the cleaned intestines, already cut into short lengths, and these are now cut further, and one end of each is tied off. Cats forage in a basket for the few useless bits of meat that remain. It is time for lunch.

We eat the region's traditional *matança* meal—a big pot of wonderful white beans, cooked in lard with onions and fried bits of pork meat and liver (see page 152), and then fried pork chops. With it, we have roasted sweet red peppers drenched in olive oil, long pickled green ones, plump green olives, sliced green tomatoes with more olive oil, good local bread, canned peaches from the farm itself. We drink unlabeled young Rioja, mineral water, local young red wine in a *porró* (see page 289), coffee spiked with brandy. The man who had gone to the veterinarian returns—now that we've already eaten some of the pork—to say that everything is fine. ("Oh, I would have come back earlier if there'd been a problem," he assures us blithely.) And then it's back to work. . . .

Now the sausage-making itself begins. A sausage tube is attached to the grinder, and the long, arduous filling process starts. One person feeds meat into the grinder and cranks it; a second holds the sausage casing (i.e., the length of intestine) and shapes the sausage as it fills, pressing out air bubbles and finally twisting it off the tube and tying off its open end. Most of the finished sausages are pricked with a small nail (so the skins won't break) and cooked in batches in the still-bubbling cauldron—a quarter hour for the small ones, a half hour for the big ones, a full hour for one immense blood sausage called the *bisbe* or "bishop." One variety, an all-meat sausage called *fuet* or "whip" (for its long thin shape), is not cooked, but will be hung on racks to dry, salamilike. By sundown, barely, the work is done. Two-hundred-and-seventy-five pounds of pig has been turned into about 110 pounds of sausage in five varieties—the beast inverted, her outsides packed into her insides—with plenty of meat leftover in whole form. The ritual is finished; the party is over.

There are seventeen officially recognized varieties of sausage in Catalonia alone, and a number of subvarieties—and probably as many again in the país valencià, in the Balearics, and in the Roussillon, plus maybe eight or ten kinds in Andorra. (Alas, I have no experience of the sausages of Alghero, though doubtless there are some.) Needless to say, the American cook's chances of finding sausages here that resemble those homemade, artisanal ones whose manufacture I've just described are pretty thin—and commercially made Catalan sausages (Catalonia alone has over 500 producers of same) are unavailable here, due to federal government restrictions on the importation of pork products. There are acceptable substitutes for the varieties of sausage called for in this book, however.

Botifarra. This is perhaps the most common Catalan sausage of all—the one you get grilled with white beans or wild mushrooms, crumbled up in stuffings, etc. It's simply a white pork sausage, medium-coarse in texture and usually seasoned only with salt and pepper. Under its Castilian name, butifarra blanca, and in a domestically made version, it is sometimes available at Spanish or Hispanic markets and it may be ordered by mail (as butifarrita) from the La Española company in California (see page 305). The easiest stand-in to find, though, is mild Italian sausage—but the kind made without fennel. If you want to try making your own botifarra, there's a recipe for it in The Foods & Wines of Spain by Penelope Casas (see bibliography). Casas uses garlic, white wine, and several spices, which most Catalan botifarra-makers— the artisanal ones, at least—don't use, so I

would suggest omitting them from her recipe and doubling the amount of pepper.

Botifarra Negra. This "black botifarra" is blood sausage—made, as we have seen, with bread soaked in pig's blood. It differs from boudin noir, the French blood sausage, in that it is somewhat coarser, with a slightly higher fat content, and more mildly seasoned. The French variety, available at some charcuteries or specialty butchers in the United States, is a reasonable substitute, though—as is morcilla, the traditional Spanish blood sausage, which may be found at Spanish and Hispanic markets (and through La Española). Use the variety without rice, though, if possible.

Sobrassada. This is a Majorcan specialty, a soft, almost pâtélike pork sausage flavored with garlic and paprika and often eaten simply spread on bread. (Penelope Casas gives a recipe for a version of sobrassada in The Foods & Wines of Spain.) A domestic version (sobrasada in Castilian) is sometimes available at Spanish and Hispanic markets (and, again, is sold by La Española). Otherwise, the closest match is Mexican pork chorizo, though it's spicier than sobrassada. Despite the similarity of name, Italian soppressata is not at all the same thing and is not a good substitute.

One more Catalan sausage that should be mentioned, even though it isn't called for in this book, is botifarra dolça—sweet botifarra. This is a specialty of the Empordà region, where it is widely believed to be a leftover from the Moorish conquest (though, since the Moors didn't eat pork, this seems unlikely). In any case, it is in effect lean pork sausage cured with sugar instead of salt (though a small amount of salt is usually added), and sometimes flavored with cinnamon and lemon juice—and, Moorish or not, it apparently *is* a remnant of medieval times. It's usually eaten after a meal, as dessert (!), often with sweet fried bread. As unlikely as this might sound, it is in fact quite delicious, and I highly recommend that you try it if you visit the Empordà and find it on a restaurant menu. (And, again, Penelope Casas offers a recipe for it in *The Foods & Wines of Spain.*)

Pork is eaten in many forms other than sausage in the *països catalans,* of course. It is, in fact, the most important meat in Catalan cuisine by far; it is impossible to imagine the cuisine without it—impossible, almost, to imagine even a single meal (of the traditional sort, anyway) that isn't touched by some pork product or other. Simple grilled or fried pork chops, almost always thin-cut and always well-done (*"L'anyell sagnant i el porc cremat,"* says a proverb; "Lamb bloody and pork burnt"), and usually served with white beans, are a typical Catalan repast. I won't bother giving a recipe for that, because there's nothing to it. What follow are some slightly more unusual pork recipes—two for pâté (rare in the *països catalans* outside the Pyrénées) and five others of various sorts—including one for that *matança*-day dish of white beans and pork liver.

"Pâté" del Camp

(COUNTRY-STYLE PÂTÉ)

The French Catalan Pyrénées are lovely, full of wooded draws and amber cliffs and fruit trees, dotted with little towns with little names

like Llo, Hix, Err, and Ur (the last of whose name, English author Basil Collier once noted, "may be Hebrew, Basque, or Ligurian: If it is Hebrew it means fire; if it is Basque it means water; if it is Ligurian it may mean anything at all. . . .").

The cooking of the region, as in most mountain quarters, is hearty and sometimes a bit gruff; the great specialties include roasted snails (see pages 103–104), wild game, such rich stewlike soups as *braou-bouffat* ("good eating" in local dialect) and *ouillade,* and, maybe most of all, *embotits—charcuterie* in French—a mouthwatering catalog of hams, sausages, and pâtés. I had one of the best country-style pâtés (the kind the French call *pâté de campagne*) of my life in this region one afternoon, as a part of an assorted sausage plate at the resolutely Catalan Hostalet de Vivès in the town of Vivès, not far from the border crossing at Le Perthus. This is the Hostalet's recipe.

Our raw materials are different from those of the French Pyrénées, of course, so an American-made version of this pâté won't taste quite like the one in Vivès does—but it's a splendid pâté nonetheless.

TO SERVE 10–12 (AS APPETIZER)

12 ounces lean ground pork shoulder or loin
6 ounces pancetta (unsmoked bacon) or blanched salt pork, cut into thin strips (see note)
4 ounces pork fatback (see note)
3 ounces pork or calf's liver (see note)
2 ounces chicken liver
½ onion, minced
3 tablespoons cognac

2 eggs, lightly beaten
2 teaspoons cornstarch
½ pound pork caul fat (see note),
   rinsed thoroughly and patted dry
1 head garlic, separated into cloves
   and peeled
Salt and pepper

Preheat the oven to 350°.

Combine all ingredients except the garlic and pork caul fat in a large bowl, and work together well with your hands, then add about 1 teaspoon each of salt and pepper.

Put the mixture through the fine blade of a meat grinder, or process in a food processor until smooth.

Sauté about 1 teaspoon of the mixture, and taste for seasoning. Correct if necessary.

Line a 1½-quart terrine or loaf pan with the pork caul fat. (The caul fat should hang over the sides of the pan.)

Pack the pork mixture down into the terrine, arrange the garlic cloves on top, then fold the caul fat over the top of the mixture.

Seal the top of the terrine with aluminum foil or a tightly fitting cover; then bake in a *bain-marie* filled halfway with boiling water for 1½–2 hours or until done. (To test for doneness, remove the foil or cover, and examine the caul fat; if there are no pink juices seeping up from the meat, the pâté is done. If you are using a meat thermometer, the temperature for doneness should be about 175°.)

When done remove the pâté from the *bain-marie,* allow to cool, remove foil or cover, and seal with plastic wrap, then weight down by inverting the terrine cover and placing some heavy object (a 2-pound can or 2-pound bag of rice or dried beans, for instance) on top, or

place a 2-pound bag of rice or dried beans directly on the plastic wrap, pushing it down gently so that weight is evenly distributed.

Refrigerate the terrine, weighted, overnight. Remove the weights, and serve, or allow to rest another 2–3 days, unweighted, in the refrigerator before use.

Note: Pancetta, which is more or less unsmoked bacon, can be found at many Italian, Spanish, and Hispanic markets. Salt pork, fatback, pork liver, and caul fat are available at specialty butchers and ethnic meat markets (especially those serving Hispanic communities), or can be special-ordered from many conventional meat markets.

"Pâté" Casolana
(HOME-STYLE PÂTÉ)

The Vall d'Aran, west of Andorra in the very heart of the Spanish Pyrénées, is dramatically beautiful—carpeted in lush pastureland, wooded with pines and beeches, surrounded by high craggy peaks, dotted with little villages full of fieldstone houses with slate roofs, most of them built around starkly pretty Lombardic Romanesque churches with beaklike steeples. Spain has laid claim to the valley since the thirteenth century, but almost until our own time it has remained as isolated as Andorra (it is said that anti-Franco partisans lived here openly for years after the end of the Spanish Civil War). And, like Andorra, it has been poor but self-sufficient until very recently. It has even retained its own language, Aranese, a dialect of Gascon.

But life in the Vall d'Aran started to change in the late 1960s, when Spanish ski champion Luís Arias promoted a major ski center on the slopes of the region's Mount Baqueira. Today, though the valley's great natural beauty remains almost untouched, and though life goes on much as it has always done for most of its inhabitants, there are concentrations of ski chalets, apartments, and discos here and there, and the resort community of Baqueira-Beret and the nearby towns of Viella and Artiés can get pretty hectic during skiing season. One nice thing its newfound popularity has brought to the Vall d'Aran, though, is a profusion of good restaurants—not only upscale places like the superb French-Aranese Casa Irene (one of the best restaurants in all of Catalonia) and the first-rate Basque establishment called Patxiku Kintana, but also a number of homey little *bordes* or "barns"—many of which really *were* barns or stables—serving simple, hearty, honest dishes at reasonable prices. One of the best of these is Et Restillé ("The Manger" in Aranese) in the village of Garós, noted for its grilled trout with mountain herbs, its grilled homemade *botifarra* sausage, its *olla aranesa* (a rich meat and vegetable soup)—and for its pâté, served in earthenware crocks with slabs of great country bread. This is Et Restillé's recipe.

TO SERVE 10–12 (AS APPETIZER)

1 pound pancetta (unsmoked bacon)
    or blanched salt pork, cut into
    thin strips (see note page 149)
6 ounces lean ground pork shoulder or
    loin
3 ounces lean bacon
6 ounces pork or beef liver (see note
    page 149)
½ a pork caul fat (see note page 149),
    rinsed thoroughly and patted dry
2–4 bay leaves
Salt and pepper

Preheat the oven to 350°.

Combine all ingredients except the bay leaves and pork caul fat in a large bowl, and work together well with your hands, then salt and pepper to taste.

Put the mixture through the fine blade of a meat grinder, or process in a food processor until smooth.

Sauté about 1 teaspoon of the mixture, and taste for seasoning. Correct if necessary.

Cut the caul fat into four approximately equal pieces, then use them to line four 1-cup crocks, pushing fat firmly against the sides of the crocks and allowing any leftover fat to hang over the sides. (You may also use two 2-cup crocks, with the caul fat cut into two pieces instead of four.)

Pack the pork mixture down into the crocks, dividing it evenly between the four (or two), then press 1 bay leaf lightly into the top of each pâté and fold the overhanging caul fat over the top.

Seal the top of the crocks with aluminum foil or tightly fitting covers; then bake in a *bain-marie* filled halfway with boiling water for 1½ hours or until done. (To test for doneness, remove the foil or cover, and examine the caul fat; if there are no pink juices seeping up from the meat, the pâté is done. If you are using a meat thermometer, the temperature for doneness is about 175°.)

When done, remove the pâtés from the *bain-marie*, allow to cool, remove foil or cover, and seal with plastic wrap. Weight down the pâtés with some heavy object (a can of tomatoes or bag of rice or dried beans of the appropriate size, for instance), pushing it down gently so that weight is evenly distributed.

Refrigerate the pâtés, weighted, overnight. Remove the weights, and serve, or allow to rest another 2–3 days, unweighted, in the refrigerator before use.

Farcellets de Col

(PORK AND CABBAGE DUMPLINGS)

A *farcel* in Catalan is a bundle or a bolt of cloth. These "little bundles" aren't stuffed cabbage rolls exactly, but rather dumplinglike mixtures of shredded cabbage and ground pork, bundled up in a thin flour crust. I know of at least one other variety of *farcellets* in Catalonia, *farcellets de Calella* (named for a coastal town north of Barcelona)—which are in fact packets of very thinly sliced veal or beef wrapped around a forcemeat of crumbled sausage and hard-boiled egg (a bit like the *oiseaux sans têtes* or "headless birds" of Niçoise cookery)—and *farcellets de col* themselves are sometimes made, as an accompaniment to partridge or other game, simply out of cabbage bound with egg.

This version, though, is very popular in the region, and also appears with game—as well as in other contexts. The recipe comes from an attractive Barcelona restaurant, adept at mixing old and new, called Senyor Parellada, where it is served as an appetizer.

TO SERVE 6 (AS APPETIZER OR SIDE DISH) OR 4 (AS LIGHT MAIN COURSE)

1 small green cabbage or ½ a larger
*   cabbage (about 1 pound in all)*
1 onion, chopped
2 tomatoes, seeded and grated (see
*   page 7) or peeled, seeded, and*
*   chopped*
Olive oil
¼ cup dry white wine
1¾ cups chicken, veal, or beef stock
1 pound lean ground pork
¾ cup breadcrumbs
Flour
Salt and pepper

Boil the cabbage in salted water until bright green and slightly tender; then drain, and set aside to cool. When cool, shred the cabbage.

Meanwhile, make a *sofregit* (see page 38) of the onion and tomatoes in oil.

When the *sofregit* is finished, add the wine and 1¼ cups of stock, bring to a boil, then reduce the heat to medium, and cook until the liquid is almost gone.

Remove from the heat and allow to cool; then stir the pork, breadcrumbs, and cabbage into the *sofregit*, mix well, and add salt and pepper to taste.

Shape the mixture into balls 2–2½ inches in diameter and then into sausage-shaped dumplings 2–2½ inches long and about 1–1½ inches thick.

Preheat the oven to 350°.

Roll *farcellets* lightly in flour, then sauté in hot oil until golden-brown and cooked through.

Drain on paper towels, then place in a lightly oiled baking dish, pour the remaining stock over the *farcellets,* and bake for about 5 minutes.

Llom de Porc amb Salsa de Magrana

(PORK LOIN WITH POMEGRANATE SAUCE)

This recipe, inspired by one appearing in Coloma Abrinas Vidal's *Cocina selecta mallorquina,* offers a variation on Majorca's famous *salsa de magrana* or *granada*—pomegranate sauce—this one with the added color and sweet bite of the pomegranate seeds themselves. The same recipe, incidentally, adapts nicely to chicken or turkey breast.

TO SERVE 4 (AS MAIN COURSE)

*1½ pounds boneless pork loin, cut
    into 8 steaks
1 tablespoon lard
Olive oil
1 onion, chopped
Seeds of 1–2 pomegranates
½ cup pomegranate juice (see note)
½ cup dry white wine
½ cup half-and-half, at room
    temperature
Salt and pepper*

Sauté the pork in a cassola or large skillet in the lard and a small amount of oil until golden-brown on both sides. Remove from the cassola and set aside.

In the same oil and lard mixture, make a *sofregit* (see page 38) of the onion; then add the pomegranate seeds, pomegranate juice, wine, and half-and-half, and reduce over medium-low heat until thick.

Return the pork to the cassola, turning so that it is well-coated with sauce, and heat through (adding a small amount of water if the sauce has thickened too much). Salt and pepper to taste.

Note: Canned or bottled pomegranate juice, available at Middle Eastern markets, may be used for this recipe, but I recommend the fresh juice when pomegranates are in season. To obtain about ½ cup of juice, roll 2 medium-sized pomegranates (older ones, which have just started to shrivel, are the sweetest) gently but firmly on all sides over a kitchen counter or other hard surface. Puncture 1 side of each one carefully with a sharp knife, and squeeze the juice into a bowl.

Freginat

(WHITE BEANS WITH FRIED PORK LIVER)

This is the traditional lunch dish on the day of the *matança del porc* in the region of Lleida, as described on page 144. It is a very simple dish, more beans than meat, and one that depends on the strong flavor of the pork liver to make it work. There is no real substitute for the liver—though a less interesting *Freginat* can of course be made with pork meat alone. The meat is cut into tiny slivers on *matança* day, by the way, because fresh-killed meat tends to be rather tough. The term *freginat* simply means "fried," though it usually implies a dish of fried organ meats of some kind—and is applied to a variety of dishes in different precincts of the *països catalans.*

TO SERVE 4 (AS MAIN DISH)

2 onions, chopped
Lard
4 ounces thick-cut bacon, diced
4 ounces boneless pork meat
(shoulder, loin, leg, etc.), cut into
thin slivers
4 ounces pork liver (see note page
149), cut into thin slivers
6 cups white beans, cooked (about 3
cups dry)
Salt and black pepper

In a cassola or Dutch oven, soften the onions in a small amount of lard.

In another pan, sauté the bacon, pork meat, and liver together in a small amount of

lard until cooked through and slightly crisp. Drain off excess fat.

Add the white beans to the cassola and sauté, stirring well to coat them lightly with lard and mix them with onions, then add the cooked meats to the beans with a slotted spoon, and mix well.

Salt to taste, and add plenty of freshly ground black pepper; then simmer for about 5 minutes longer.

Peus de Porc Farcits amb Bolets

(STUFFED PIGS' FEET WITH WILD MUSHROOMS)

Pigs' feet are a bother. They're also delicious, with sweet, succulent meat and a very pleasant flavor. They're eaten in a number of ways in the *països catalans:* Chef Ignasi Domènech, in his classic book *La Teca,* for instance, describes *"un bon plat català"* composed of boiled pigs' feet boned and cut into little pieces, rolled in flour, and then fried and served with mild *allioli* and fried potatoes. They're also sometimes simply stewed with a classic Catalan *sofregit* of onions, tomatoes, garlic, and parsley, or served in a sort of ragout with snails (a dish to which only serious trenchermen need apply). And at the elegant Via Veneto restaurant in Barcelona, they're boned whole and stuffed with a complex forcemeat, then sealed in pork caul and served in wild mushroom sauce—a sophisticated preparation that yields remarkable results—and incidentally just the kind of "new Catalan cuisine" I like the best, for the way it fancies up and refines a dish without for an instant betraying its Catalan identity. If you've never had pigs' feet, incidentally, this would be an excellent (if not exactly typical) introduction to them.

TO SERVE 4 (AS MAIN COURSE)

4 pig's feet, split in half
2 onions, 1 whole, 1 chopped
1 carrot
1 bay leaf
12 peppercorns
4 tomatoes, seeded and grated (see
    page 7), or peeled, seeded, and
    chopped
Olive oil
1 pound lean ground pork
¼ pound European-style ham
    (prosciutto or Black Forest type),
    minced
1 black truffle, minced (optional)
2 eggs, lightly beaten
2 slices French or Italian bread, crusts
    removed, soaked in milk
½ cup dry sherry
Salt and pepper
½–1 pound pork caul fat
Flour
Lard
1 cup dry white wine
12 almonds, blanched and roasted (see
    page 39)
¼ cup pine nuts, lightly toasted
2 cloves garlic, minced
1 sprig parsley, minced
1 slice fried bread (see page 40)

¾ pounds fresh wild mushrooms or 2
ounces dried wild mushrooms
(rehydrated), cleaned and cut into
julienne strips

Carefully tie the pigs' feet in several places, then wrap in cheesecloth to help them keep their shape. Poach in a large pot of water with the whole onion, the carrot, bay leaf, and peppercorns for 2½–3 hours, or until tender.

Remove the pigs' feet from the pot, strain, and reserve 2 cups of liquid, and set aside the pigs' feet to cool.

Meanwhile, in a cassola or Dutch oven, make a *sofregit* (see page 38) of the chopped onion and the tomatoes in oil.

As the *sofregit* cooks, carefully bone the pigs' feet, wrap them in plastic wrap to conserve shape, and cool in the refrigerator.

Mix the ground pork, ham, truffle (if desired), eggs, milk-soaked bread, and sherry together, and salt and pepper to taste.

Divide the stuffing equally among the pigs' feet, pressing it into the cavities formed by removal of the bones.

Wrap each stuffed pig's foot in caul fat to hold the stuffing in place, then dredge lightly in flour, and sauté in a small amount of oil and lard until dark golden-brown.

Pour off excess fat from pan, then add the *sofregit*. Stir in 1 cup of reserved broth and the wine, and simmer for about 20 minutes, adding more broth if the liquid evaporates.

Make a *picada* (see page 40) of the almonds, pine nuts, garlic, parsley, and fried bread, moistened with a few drops of broth.

Remove the pigs' feet from the pan, and

keep warm. Add the *picada* and wild mushrooms to the pan, stir well, and sauté 5–10 minutes or until the sauce is thick.

Return the pigs' feet to the pan, heat through for about 5 minutes longer, and serve with sauce spooned on top.

Flam de Peuada

(PIGS' FOOT MOUSSE)

Literally, a *peuada* is a trampling, or a stamping on someone's foot. It's also, traditionally, a kind of pigs' foot stew with rice. The idea of a flan made *from* a pigs' foot stew—*Flam de Peuada*—is an old one, probably dating from medieval times. It is a specialty, not surprisingly, of the Empordà region, where it is often sweetened and eaten as dessert. (The Empordà, don't forget, is the home of *botifarra dolça*, sweet pork sausage, also considered a confection.) Jaume Subirós of the Hotel Ampurdán has published a recipe for this kind of flan, which includes not just the feet of the pig but its ears, muzzle, tail, and jowls, some chicken livers, assorted vegetables and spices, sugar, a bottle of champagne, a dozen eggs, and a pint of cream—a recipe I hope you will forgive me for not reproducing in more detail here. The modest but superb Esteve restaurant in Molins de Rei, just outside Barcelona, however, has another version of *Flam de Peuada*—turning it into a delicate, subtly delicious mousse served as a first course—and *this* recipe I will gladly provide.

TO SERVE 4 (AS APPETIZER)

6 pig's feet, washed, split, tied at 2-inch intervals, and securely wrapped in cheesecloth
4 ounces thick-cut bacon, diced
10 ounces ricotta or farmer's cheese
4 eggs, lightly beaten
⅔ cup heavy cream
¼ cup flour
Butter
Salt and pepper
Breadcrumbs
1 pound wild mushrooms (see page 88), washed and halved or quartered (depending on size)

Place pig's feet in a large pot and cover with 4–5 quarts of water. Bring to a boil, then reduce the heat and simmer, covered, for 3–4 hours or until the meat is very soft.

Drain the pigs' feet, and allow to cool; then remove the lean meat and a small quantity of soft fat, and set aside.

Fry the bacon until crisp, drain on paper towels, then mince very fine.

Preheat the oven to 350°.

Finely chop the pigs' feet meat and fat, and mix with the bacon. Then, in a large bowl, work the meat mixture into cheese, eggs, cream, flour, 3 tablespoons butter, and salt and pepper to taste.

Whip the mixture well with a whisk or process in a food processor or blender until smooth.

Butter four 1-cup soufflé molds, divide the mixture evenly among them, top each one with a scattering of breadcrumbs, and dot each one with butter.

Bake the molds in a *bain-marie* for 30–40 minutes or until puffed up and done.

Meanwhile, sauté the mushrooms in butter until soft.

When the mousse is done, unmold each one onto a warm serving plate, and top with sautéed mushrooms.

See Also:

Arròs amb Crosta (Rice with an Egg Crust), page 64

Faves a la Catalana (Favas with Blood Sausage and Bacon), page 105

Botifarra amb Mongetes (Sausage with White Beans), page 110

Pomes Farcides (Pork-Stuffed Apples), page 185

Fideus a l'Estil de Lleida (Lleida-Style Pasta), page 202

PART FOUR: THEMES AND VARIATIONS

One thing that helps make Catalan cuisine a real cuisine and not just a collection of dishes, I think, is the way it constantly refers back to itself, recycles its own ideas, adapts one technique or ingredient to more than one use. As open as it is to outside influences, it remains at the same time a kind of closed system. There's something tight-knit about it, something *interwoven*. I've already quoted author Nèstor Luján's observation that Catalan dishes vary not just from place to place but even from family to family; thus there are usually numerous recipes (all equally traditional, equally genuine) for any given dish.

Beyond that, though, one dish has a way of suggesting another in Catalan cuisine, or of taking off from it: *Escalivada* implies *samfaina*, that is; a partridge *en escabetx* foreshadows a partridge *a la vinagre; Mar i Muntanya* is, in spirit anyway, a simplification of the baroque, surrealistic *Es Niu.* This is a cuisine of themes and variations, in other words—and thus one that can perhaps best be represented not as a string of individual recipes but as a series of recipe clusters, of little groupings with their own sense of order (a sense that puts a chicken dish in the chapter on *Esqueixada,* which is salt cod salad; a sense that places a noodle dish in the paella chapter and a rice dish in the *fideus* noodle chapter).

Each of the following chapters, then, is a grouping of just that sort—each based on an important Catalan dish or class of dishes, each offering at least one basic recipe and (in all but one case) at least one variation on the theme. The chapters are divided into five broad categories: *Amanides i Entrants* (Salads and Appetizers), *Pans i Pastes* (Breads and Pastas), *Plats Principals* (Main Courses), *Llaminadures, Formatges, i Begudes* (Pastries and Desserts, Cheeses, and Drinks), and *Miscel·lània* (A Miscellany)—this last section followed by a brief chapter on culinary *Llegendes i Curiositats,* which are just what they sound like.

AMANIDES I ENTRANTS
«SALADS AND APPETIZERS»

AMANIDA CATALANA
(CATALAN SALAD)

Catalan cuisine, frankly, isn't known for the variety and originality of its salads. Except perhaps at specialty stalls in big-city markets, there are rarely more than one or two kinds of lettuce available in any one season in the *països catalans* (the Spanish ones, anyway). Less common greens like *mâche* (corn salad or lamb's lettuce in English; *herba de canonge,* "canon's grass," in Catalan); and arugula or rocket (*ruca* in Catalan) are known only to country folk and the occasional specialist. Other than lettuce, the standard salad ingredients are tomatoes (eaten slightly green and firm in this context), raw onions, olives, and roasted peppers, in various combinations.

Traditionally, salads are not mixed or tossed; each ingredient keeps its own counsel. The Catalan word for salad is *amanida,* from the verb *amanir,* "to season" (as indeed our own word "salad" comes from the Latin *sal,* "salt")—but the only seasonings commonly employed for such dishes hereabouts are olive oil, salt, and *sometimes* vinegar. Even black

pepper, so well-liked and oft-used in Catalan cooking, is almost never ground onto a salad as it might be in the United States. Exceptions to these rules include a few regional specialties (e.g. *Xató,* see page 163) and, of course, the creations of certain contemporary-style restaurants—the Caesar saladlike *amanida de la patrona* at Petit París in Barcelona, for instance, or the warm pasta salad at the same city's Florian. Otherwise, the standard *Amanida Catalana* can be pretty boring stuff. But it can also, if you use top-quality ingredients, be quite delicious and refreshing in its very simplicity.

Amanida Catalana
(CATALAN SALAD)

There is no fixed formula for a Catalan salad. It's made up of whatever fresh and/or preserved (i.e., pickled or oil-packed) vegetables happen to be available at the time, usually with the addition of anchovies and some variety of ham or sausage, or perhaps a bit of tuna or herring. There *are* rules for its construction, though. As noted, the salad's ingredients are never mixed together; again as noted, slightly green and firm tomatoes are favored over ripe ones; vegetables should be dressed with oil and salt only, except for the onion, on which a bit of vinegar may be used (but *never*, say Cata-lans, use vinegar on tomatoes); and whatever sausage or fish might be utilized (not counting anchovies) should stay far away from any dressing, even plain oil—lest their flavor be (as one writer on the subject has put it) "dis-

figured." With those strictures (which you are free to disregard, of course) in mind, here is a recipe not for "Catalan salad" but for *a* Catalan salad.

TO SERVE 4 (AS APPETIZER)

*2 red (if possible) or green bell
    peppers, roasted, peeled, and cut
    into strips as for* Escalivada *(see
    page 170)*
½ onion, sliced paper-thin
*16 small, light green leaves romaine
    lettuce (from heart of lettuce)*
*2 stalks celery, cut into sticks about
    ½ × 3 inches*
2 tomatoes, slightly green, thinly sliced
*24–32 good-quality black or green
    olives (see notes pages 119, 120)*
*16–20 thin slices small salami or
    peperoni*
*8 anchovy filets, soaked in water for 1
    hour and patted dry*
Mild extra-virgin olive oil
Red wine vinegar
Salt

Divide the bell pepper strips and onion slices evenly among 4 large salad plates or dinner plates, arranging them in the middle of each plate.

Divide the remaining space on each plate into four sections with four lettuce leaves per plate, evenly spaced.

Divide the celery, tomatoes, olives, and salami evenly, placing 1 item in each divided section of each plate.

Crisscross 2 anchovy filets across the bell pepper strips on each plate.

Drizzle oil on the bell pepper strips, onion slices, celery, tomato slices, and lettuce leaves.

Drizzle a few drops of vinegar over the onions.

Salt to taste.

Note: Among other ingredients that might be incorporated into an *Amanida Catalana* are carrots, green onions or scallions, radishes (in Catalonia, usually the long, thin kind), slices of hard-boiled egg (or crumbled hard-boiled egg), canned tuna, ham, and plain herring (i.e., not in cream, mustard sauce, etc.).

Amanida Valenciana

(VALENCIAN SALAD)

This is a variation on the preceding recipe, but one in which the ingredients (tomatoes included) are mixed together and dressed with oil and vinegar. Salads of approximately this composition, sometimes mixed and sometimes separated, are nearly ubiquitous in Valencia and vicinity.

TO SERVE 4 (AS APPETIZER)

*1 small head of lettuce, preferably
    romaine, separated into leaves and
    then torn into large pieces*
*2 tomatoes, slightly green, thinly
    sliced, and then halved*
*36–40 good-quality green olives (see
    note page 119)*
1 carrot, grated
Mild extra-virgin olive oil
Red wine vinegar
Salt

4 small scallions, trimmed
2 hard-boiled eggs, sliced

Mix the lettuce, tomatoes, olives, and carrot together in a large salad bowl, and toss well.

Dress the salad with oil and vinegar (about 3 or 4 parts to 1), and salt to taste.

Divide the salad evenly among 4 plates, then garnish each one with scallions and egg slices.

Trempó

(MAJORCAN SALAD)

This is a typical Majorcan summer vegetable salad, sometimes augmented with late-summer fruit. It is important to let the vegetables and oil "marry" a bit—and it is considered a very sensible thing in Majorca to wipe up whatever oil and juices might remain in the bottom of the cassola with pieces of good country-style bread.

TO SERVE 4 (AS APPETIZER)

2 onions, sliced paper-thin
4 tomatoes, slightly green, thinly
sliced
2 green bell peppers, seeded, cored,
and sliced into thin rings
2 apples or pears, cored and thinly
sliced (optional)
Mild extra-virgin olive oil
Salt

In a cassola or other large, flat-bottomed bowl, arrange onion slices; then layer them

with tomato slices followed by green pepper rings followed by apple or pear slices if desired.

Drizzle plenty of oil over top of salad, and salt to taste.

Let salad rest in cool place 1–2 hours before serving.

Xató

(SALT COD AND TUNA SALAD WITH *ROMESCO* DRESSING)

Every January in the coastal town of Vilanova i la Geltrú, about halfway between Barcelona and Tarragona, six or seven thousand local citizens and their guests crowd into the town square to take part in a *xatonada popular*—a food-filled festival built around the rather simple, rather delicious salad called *Xató*.

Xató—the name is pronounced almost exactly like the French word *château*—is an invention of Vilanova i la Geltrú. Unless of course it's an invention of the neighboring town of Sitges, about five miles to the north. The two municipalities dispute the question, each one offering putative historical and cultural evidence to back up its case, each ragging the other mercilessly over the matter. (I once heard the president of the Vilanova Rotary Club suggest publicly, and of course with a smile, that perhaps Cádiz [on the coast of Andalusia, at least 500 miles away] might like to lay claim to the dish as well—the point being that it was no less likely a candidate than Sitges.)

Wherever it's from, it is a popular salad in Catalonia today—to the point that Barcelona restaurant critic Carmen Casas has called it "the most important salad of our [i.e., Catalan] cuisine." It was apparently a fisherman's dish originally, and purists say it should be made with slightly wilted escarole—because escarole that had been out on a fishing boat all day would surely have wilted. In some towns, *Xató* is invariably served with a wedge of room-temperature *truita* or omelet (see pages 120–122) on the side—usually a serious one, filled with sausage or ham or at least white beans—and indeed this combination makes a delightful light lunch or supper. *Xató* is traditionally a dish consumed on *Dijous Gras* or "fat Thursday," as well—a pre-Lenten holiday resembling our (and France's) *Mardi Gras*, but with a five-day head start.

TO SERVE 4 (AS APPETIZER)

½ cup Tarragona-style Romesco *sauce (see page 224)*
Mild extra-virgin olive oil
1 head escarole or salad bowl lettuce, rinsed and dried
½ pound salt cod, desalted (see page 79), skinned, boned, and finely shredded
4 ounces good-quality canned tuna (see note), crumbled
Salt
8 anchovy filets, soaked in water for 1 hour and patted dry

Put the *romesco* sauce in the bottom of a large salad bowl, then thin with 2–3 tablespoons olive oil, mixing together well with a fork or small whisk.

Tear the escarole leaves into large pieces,

then toss them briefly in *romesco* sauce with the salt cod and tuna.

Salt to taste if necessary.

Divide the salad among four plates, and crisscross two anchovy filets on top of each.

Note: Xató *was originally made with dried, salted tuna—for which good-quality canned Italian or Spanish tuna, packed in olive oil, is probably the best easily available substitute. Simply cooked fresh tuna will work, too, of course—but in this case I really think the canned variety is better. In the town of Vendrell, incidentally, olives are added to the* Xató. *In the town of Sant Pere de Ribes, thinly sliced raw onions and sliced tomatoes (slightly green as usual) might get tossed in. Feel free to mix and match as you wish.*

See Also:

LA CALÇOTADA

Nothing I had thus far seen or eaten in the *països catalans* quite prepared me for my first *calçotada*. As noted earlier, an *-ada* is the communal celebration (and largescale consumption) of a single kind of food—in this case *calçots*, leek-sized green onions, blackened over open fires and served with a spicy nut sauce related to Tarragona's famous *Romesco* sauce (see pages 222–225). The capital of the *calçotada*, the city in which it is said to have been born (apparently in the late 1800s), is Valls, just north of Tarragona. ("A good *calçotada*," someone once wrote, "must have: as a backdrop, the Serralada de Miramar [the region's most prominent mountain range]; as scenery, a Vallenc farmhouse; as orchestra pit, the town of Valls with its tall church steeple.") Valls restaurants like Masia Bou and Casa Félix are almost *calçotada* factories, sometimes serving literally thousands of people between them in a single day at the height of the season (roughly January through April). On this particular January afternoon, though, I had been invited by the Tarragona Rotary Club to attend *their* annual version of the feast (*calçotades* are best staged on a large scale, and thus are often sponsored by clubs or fraternal organizations), and they prefered a smaller restaurant in another town—El Celler in Salomo, a bit southeast of Valls.

El Celler occupies an old chalky-white, tile-roofed farmhouse with a large pebbled courtyard and, giving onto it, a semienclosed veranda hung with bundles of dried herbs, long red-orange dried chilis curved like Christmas stockings, and strings of last summer's tomatoes, somehow not yet either dried or rotted—something to do with the circulation of the cool winter air, apparently. The *calçots* are cooked in the middle of the courtyard, bunched together on cot-sized black mesh grills (old iron bed frames themselves were used traditionally) fueled with hot-burning vine cuttings, and the eating usually takes place either in the courtyard or on the veranda. On this occasion, though, the sky was heavy

gray and the air was damp, so we retired to the cavernous wine cellar, half a level underground, for which the restaurant is named. By the time the *calçotada* officially began, around 2:30 (this being Spain, after all, where only the tourists eat lunch before 2 or dinner before 10), some eighty or ninety people had filled the room, crowding around the long paper-covered tables and upended wine casks with which it had been furnished—a mix of Rotary Club members not just from Tarragona but from Reus, Vilanova i la Geltrú, Vilafranca del Penedès, and Barcelona (an expected contingent from Andorra having been snowed in), plus their guests, their mates, and their children. Everyone was nicely dressed—sometimes almost chic, sometimes almost stodgy—but the atmosphere was casual and festive, with something like a picnicky feel about it. Buoyed by the first thick swell of animated chatter, we dug into our appetizers—bowls of tiny charred-black hazelnuts, still hot, and of olives, illuminated by needle-nosed *porrons* of fresh young local white and red wine (the white made here, in this very cellar). Then came the *calçots*. . . .

Calçots are indeed green onions, but they're hardly the everyday supermarket variety. They take as long as a year-and-a-half to grow, starting with seed onions planted in September or October (always when the moon is waning, say traditionalists), then transplanted about two months later when the shoots have pushed up through the ground. In late June or early July, they're harvested and stored in a dry place while they germinate again; then, in August or September, they're trimmed and replanted—this time in trenches. As they begin to sprout once more, earth is packed around the new growth to blanch it (as is done with celery and Belgian endive)—and this is how *calçots* get their name, from the verb *calçar*, to put on shoes or boots. (The Catalan word for shoe, in fact, is the almost identical, *calçat*. Compare the Italian word *calzone*, "big stocking," meaning a stocking-shaped turned-over pizza.) By the time the *calçots*—as many as twelve or thirteen of them from each large onion, seven or eight from each smaller one—are finally harvested in January and the ensuing few months, they have become not only much larger than the usual green onion or scallion but much milder and sweeter. And, because of their "shoes" of soil, at least half their length is white.

Calçots are grilled an hour or two before they are to be served, then wrapped tightly in newspaper and plastic and allowed to "steam"—which makes them butter-tender and loosens their burnt outer skin. They're brought to the table piled in the hollows of long terra-cotta roofing tiles (this keeps them warm), and eaten in the following manner: A *calçot* is grasped in the left hand by its blackened base and in the right hand by the inner green leaves at its top, then the black part is slipped off and discarded. The glistening white end of the *calçot* is next dipped into the aforementioned spicy nut sauce—formerly called *salvitjada* and now known mostly just as *salsa per calçots*—then lowered into the mouth with one's head thrown back jauntily, and bitten off about where the green part starts. As might be imagined, this is messy work, and everyone wears bibs at a proper *calçotada* and retires frequently to a nearby sink or pump to rinse off the soot.

This, then, was what I saw around me on that January afternoon at El Celler: eighty or ninety Rotarians (and friends and relatives of Rotarians), the commercial and social cream of Tarragona and vicinity, standing around with big checkered napkins tied around their necks in front of tables now heaped with the tangled black and green remains of *calçots*, their hands blackened, their faces smeared with pinkish sauce and peppered with flecks of charred green-onion skin, their heads tipped back, if not to eat a *calçot* then to swallow a jet of wine from a *porró*—the lot of them chattering gaily between gulps and bites, gossiping and laughing raucously, absolutely unconcerned about how they might look or what somebody else (a boss, a spouse, an American visitor) might think of how much they were eating, thoroughly at ease with themselves and their companions, and thoroughly—proudly—voracious. The whole scene seemed a perfect definition to me, vivid and sensuous, of the Catalan attitude toward eating—of the fact, among other things, that it was *all right* to love food in this society.

You will probably realize by now, of course, this being Catalonia, that there is more to a *calçotada* than just hazelnuts and olives and green onions with spicy nut sauce. I read once that in the French Catalan onion capital of Toulouges, at *their* version of a *calçotada*, individuals sometimes wolf down as many as a dozen *calçots* each. Hah! At the annual Gran Festa de Calçotada in Valls a few days before the Tarragona Rotary event, a young man from the city of Reus had won the *calçot*-eating contest by consuming 190 of the things in half an hour!—and even our own group at El Celler managed at least 20 or 25 per person, with some of us (yes, I said *us*) handling more like

35 or 40. And then we filed into an adjoining room for lunch—grilled *botifarra* sausages with white beans and *allioli*, grilled lamb chops, curly endive salad, ice-cream cake, and of course more wine, plus sparkling *cava*, coffee, and assorted alcohols. Irving Davis, in his privately published *A Catalan Cookery Book*, says that roast chickens are usually included in a *calçotada* luncheon, too. I'm sure at least some of our number missed them.

La Calçotada

The problem with reproducing a *calçotada* in America is simply finding the *calçots*. I see no reason why they can't be grown here, of course, according to the vague directions given on page 165; I'm trying it myself, in fact, in coastal Southern California, though I haven't yet reaped my first crop as I write this. In the meantime—a year-and-a-half admittedly being a long time in advance to worry about what you're going to have for lunch on a particular late winter afternoon—ordinary green onions or scallions will do. They won't have the long, sweet white portion *calçots* have, but if you choose the fattest ones possible, at least an inch in diameter, you'll be able to get the general idea. Leeks won't work, incidentally; they're wrong in both flavor and texture.

Theoretically, a *calçotada* should involve a lot of people—a dozen, a score, a hundred. Cooking enough green onions for a large crowd, however, will tax most backyard barbecues—and there's no reason why you can't prepare a miniversion of the feast for four or six (or even two). The following recipe, then,

gives quantities for one person only, so that you can expand it as needed. The *salsa* formula is approximately that used by El Celler, as given to me by the restaurant's proprietors, Maria-Teresa Cornet and Ramon Lluís. As usual in such matters, there are, of course, numerous variations possible (one of which appears on page 168).

TO SERVE 1 (AS APPETIZER)

1 tomato, whole and unpeeled
12–20 large green onions or scallions
    (or more according to size of
    green onions and appetite)
30 almonds, blanched and roasted (see
    page 39)
3 cloves garlic, roasted as for
    Mussolina d'All (see page 33) and
    squeezed from their skins
¼ teaspoon dried spicy red chili (see
    note page 168), very finely
    minced
Pinch of cayenne
½ teaspoon red wine vinegar
Olive oil
½ teaspoon salt

Roast the tomato for about 10 minutes, or until blackened on all sides, on a medium-hot barbecue or gas grill; then carefully remove and set aside to cool.

Increase the heat on the barbecue (adding vine cuttings or other hot-burning wood if you are not using a gas grill); then grill the green onions in batches until well-blackened on all sides.

As the green onions are removed from the grill, wrap them in several layers of newspaper. When all are cooked, wrap the newspapers tightly in a plastic garbage bag, and set them aside to steam for 1–2 hours.

Meanwhile, slip the skin off the tomato, cut in half, and carefully squeeze out seeds. Chop the tomato finely.

Pulverize the almonds with a mortar and pestle or in a spice mill; then add garlic, dried chili, cayenne, and salt, and mix together thoroughly until a thick paste forms.

Transfer the mixture to a small bowl, and barely cover with oil.

Let mixture rest for 1–2 minutes; then add tomatoes and vinegar, and mix in well. Add more oil, salt, and/or dried chili or cayenne if desired. Sauce should be thick but still slightly liquid in consistency.

Note: Calçotada purists say that the chili used must be the kind called *bitxo*—though in fact *bitxo* is a generic name for spicy red chilis, and applies to different varieties in different parts of the *països catalans.* The chilis most often used for *calçot* sauce in Valls, Salomo, and vicinity, are about 5–7 inches long, bright red with orange and/or yellowish highlights, and curved at the end. I know no exact equivalent available in the United States but have had good results with the smaller, straighter *arbol* chilis often sold in Mexican or Caribbean markets here. Any spicy dried chili will probably suffice—though genuine *calçot* sauce is usually only very slightly spicy.

Salsa per Calçots

(*CALÇOT* SAUCE)

There are probably as many variations on the sauce for *calçots* as there are people grilling the things in the first place. One recipe in my possession calls for sixteen different ingredients—almonds, hazelnuts, pine nuts, walnuts, tomatoes, garlic, a hard-boiled egg, a beaten egg, bell pepper, two kinds of dried chilis, parsley, mint, salt, oil, and vinegar. Most of them, like this one, which is adapted from a valuable little book called *El Romesco* by the late Antoni Adserà, are quite a bit simpler. This sauce, which uses hazelnuts as well as almonds, is less spicy than the preceding one (since it omits the dried chili), but a bit more pungent—using more garlic and a raw tomato.

TO MAKE 1–1 ¼ CUP

10 hazelnuts, roasted (see page 39)
10 almonds, blanched and roasted (see page 39)
1 tomato, seeded and grated (see page 7) or peeled, seeded, and chopped
1 head garlic, separated into cloves, roasted as for Mussolina d'All *(see page 33), and squeezed from its skins*
1 sprig parsley, minced
Pinch of cayenne
½ teaspoon salt
1 teaspoon red wine vinegar
3 tablespoons olive oil

Pulverize the hazelnuts and almonds with a mortar and pestle or in a spice mill, then transfer to a large bowl, blender, or work bowl of the food processor.

Add tomato, garlic, and parsley, and mash, blend, or process together well until smooth.

If you are using a blender or food processor, transfer the mixture to a large bowl, and stir in cayenne, salt, vinegar, and oil. Mix well by hand, and allow to stand for at least 2 hours before serving.

Calçots Fregits

(DEEP-FRIED *CALÇOTS*)

This recipe, from the Esteve restaurant in Molins de Rei near Barcelona, uses green onions or scallions of normal size, does not require a roaring open-air fire, and doesn't get your hands dirty.

TO SERVE 4 (AS APPETIZER)

2 eggs, lightly beaten
⅔ cup flour
2 teaspoon yeast (see page 7)
¼–⅓ cup water
Salt and pepper
Olive oil
48 green onions or scallions, trimmed
*   at both ends*

Make a batter of the eggs, flour, yeast, water, and salt and pepper to taste.

Fill a cassola or other deep pan with at least 1 inch of oil (or use deep fryer), and heat the oil to about 375°.

Pour the batter into a loaf pan long enough to accommodate the green onions; then dip the scallions into it one by one, and transfer them immediately to the hot oil.

Fry the green onions in batches for about 2 minutes or until golden-brown. Drain them on paper towels, and serve immediately, either alone or accompanied by *Salsa per Calçots* (page 168).

See Also:
ROMESCO, pages 223–225

ESCALIVADA

The verb *escalivar* in Catalan means to cook in hot ashes *(caliu)* or embers, and *Escalivada*—sometimes spelled *escalibada*—is simply an arrangement of vegetables that have been thus cooked. Eggplant and bell peppers are its most common constituents in the *països catalans* today—but you can cook almost *any* vegetable this way, and tomatoes, onions, and even potatoes are sometimes prepared *en escalivada.*

Escalivada is usually served as an appetizer, often along with *Esqueixada* (see page 172) or some other saladlike first course, or as a side dish to accompany grilled meats, roast chicken, and the like. (I have never seen it served as an accompaniment to fresh fish, but I see no reason why that wouldn't be quite good as well.) Carles Camós at the Big Rock restaurant in Platja d'Aro makes an extremely simple and delicious appetizer called *tosta d'escalivada*, which is simply good, thick toast topped with *Escalivada* and a few local anchovies (this would be wonderful, if not particularly Catalan, made with *pain brioche*, I think); and Luís Albajar at Ara-Cata in Barcelona serves an *Escalivada* including tomatoes and baby onions alongside foie gras— a truly inspired combination.

Escalivada

Escalivada actually cooked in hot ashes, or at least on a wood-burning barbecue or grill, is incomparably better than any other version—simply because the vegetables take on a slightly smoky taste that is quite extraordinary. As noted, though, the dish can be made in an oven—which is how it's done at most Catalan restaurants and in many Catalan households today.

TO SERVE 4 (AS APPETIZER OR SIDE DISH)

*8 Japanese eggplants (or 4 small
    regular eggplants)*
*4 red (if possible) or green bell
    peppers*

*4 small onions (3–4 ounces each)
    (optional)*
Mild extra-virgin olive oil
2 cloves garlic, minced
Salt

To roast the eggplants, peppers, and onions, set them directly onto the coals, or wood embers that are lightly covered with gray ash and glowing, turning vegetables frequently with tongs until they have blackened on all sides. Or grill the vegetables over a very hot fire on a barbecue or gas grill, again turning them frequently with tongs until they have blackened on all sides. Or coat the vegetables lightly with oil and roast in a preheated 375° oven for 30–40 minutes or until soft but not mushy. Or broil the vegetables as close to the flame as possible in a hot broiler, turning them frequently with tongs until they have blackened on all sides.

When the vegetables are cooked, place each kind in a separate paper bag, and close it tightly, then let vegetables "steam" and cool for about 10–15 minutes.

Remove vegetables from bags, and peel them.

Cut eggplants into long strips; seed peppers, and cut them into long strips; slice onions into rings, or leave them whole.

Divide vegetables evenly among four serving plates, drizzle them with oil, scatter minced garlic over them, and salt to taste.

"Mousse" Freda d'Escalivada

(COLD *ESCALIVADA* MOUSSE)

This dish, created by Josep Mercader at the Hotel Ampurdán in Figueres, typifies to me the new Catalan cuisine. It's based on a traditional, ancient Catalan specialty but is a refinement of it; it keeps the original flavors but lightens them; it is coolly contemporary but with a flavor of the past.

TO SERVE 6 (AS APPETIZER)

1 pound potatoes
Olive oil
1–2 onions, roasted, peeled, and sliced
*   as for* Escalivada *(see page 170)*
3–4 red bell peppers (see note),
*   roasted, peeled, seeded, and cut*
*   into strips as for* Escalivada
2–3 Japanese eggplants (or 1 small
*   regular eggplant), roasted, peeled,*
*   and cut into strips as for*
*   Escalivada*
1–2 tomatoes, roasted, peeled, and
*   seeded as for* Escalivada
6 cloves garlic, roasted as for
*   Escalivada and squeezed from their*
*   skin*
1 tablespoon red wine vinegar
Salt and pepper

Preheat oven to 400°.

Rub the potatoes with oil, then roast for 1 hour. Remove from the oven, cool, peel, and coarsely chop.

Purée all the vegetables including the gar-

lic together in a food processor or blender until smooth and very well mixed. Add the vinegar and 1–2 tablespoons of oil to taste. Salt and pepper to taste.

Refrigerate for at least 3 hours, or overnight, then serve with toast points or crackers as a spread or dip.

Note: It is very important to use red peppers, not green ones, in this recipe, for the sake of the color.

Pastís Fred d'Escalivada amb Vinagreta d'Anxoves

(COLD *ESCALIVADA* TERRINE WITH ANCHOVY VINAIGRETTE)

As I've already observed about the late Josep Mercader of the Hotel Ampurdán, he was a deliberate inspiration to other chefs as well as a culinary pioneer, and many of his dishes have been copied or used as starting points for the dishes of others. One such dish is this *Escalivada* terrine from Sa Punta, an excellent restaurant on a pine-covered hillside just off the Platja de Pals on the Costa Brava. Like the previous recipe, it is a contemporary reinterpretation of *Escalivada*—but it is completely different in flavor and texture and overall character.

TO SERVE 6–8 (AS APPETIZER)

4 *red bell peppers, roasted, peeled,*
    seeded, and cut into strips as for
    Escalivada *(see page 170)*
2 *onions, roasted, peeled, and sliced as*
    for Escalivada
4 *Japanese eggplants (or 2 small*
    regular eggplants), roasted, peeled,
    and cut into strips as for
    Escalivada
18 *anchovy filets, soaked in water for*
    1 hour and patted dry
White pepper
1 *cup heavy cream*
6 *eggs*
Butter (for pan)
Mild extra-virgin olive oil
2 *tablespoons red wine vinegar*

Preheat oven to 350°.

Purée vegetables with 12 of the anchovy filets in a food processor or blender, or pass through a food mill, then season with white pepper to taste.

Beat the cream and eggs together; then add to vegetable mixture.

Pour vegetable mixture into a buttered 1½-quart loaf pan or terrine; then bake in a *bain-marie* for 1 hour or until a knife inserted in middle of terrine comes out clean.

Remove the terrine from the oven, and cool to room temperature; then refrigerate.

Make a vinaigrette with 1 cup olive oil, vinegar, remaining anchovy filets, a few drops of water, and white pepper to taste; mashing the anchovy filets well with a fork, and whipping the dressing with a whisk until slightly fluffy (or mixing it in a blender).

Serve the terrine in slices, very cold, topped with vinaigrette.

_____

Note: Sa Punta serves this terrine garnished with a few shreds of lettuce and red cabbage, a few small sorrel leaves, and a few thin slices of tomato, neatly arranged on each plate. As with the previous recipe, incidentally, it is important to use red peppers rather than green ones, to avoid obtaining a mud-colored terrine.

ESQUEIXADA
(SHREDDED SALT COD SALAD)

Esqueixada is another definitive Catalan dish, a light, cool, simple, refreshing salad, especially popular in warm weather and equally appropriate to casual home-cooked meals and elegant restaurant menus. In a way, it's the Catalan seviche, since it's made with raw (though in this case, of course, salt-cured and dried) fish, "cooked" only by its marinade. It's a more delicate dish than its New World counterpart, though, both in the comparative mildness of its seasonings and in the soft, almost buttery consistency the fish itself attains.

The name *Esqueixada* comes from the Catalan verb *esqueixar*, meaning to tear or shred—and if there's one thing virtually everyone who makes the dish agrees upon, it's that the salt cod in it should never be sliced or chopped, but always shredded with the fingers. Beyond that, there is the usual disagreement as to particulars: I've seen recipes calling for as many as thirteen ingredients and others with as few as three. (This latter recipe, which is author-chef Llorenç Torrado's, appears on page 173.) Whatever goes into it (within reason), however, it's a delicious dish—and, as Paula Wolfert once pointed out, "[Its] transformation of salt cod from dry slabs to savory succulence is truly miraculous."

Esqueixada

(SHREDDED SALT COD SALAD)

The traditional *Esqueixada* is made with salt cod, tomatoes, onions, oil and vinegar, salt, and sometimes a scattering of olives as garnish. This version, from the innovative Barcelona restaurant Florián, is *almost* traditional—but is dressed up colorfully with little bits of green and red pepper. Omit them if you wish.

TO SERVE 4 (AS APPETIZER)

1 pound salt cod, desalted (see page 79), skinned, boned, and finely shredded with the fingers.
1 small onion, sliced paper-thin and separated into rings
½ green bell pepper, seeded and finely diced
½ red bell pepper, seeded and finely diced
2 tomatoes, seeded and grated (see page 7) or peeled, seeded, and chopped
Mild extra-virgin olive oil
Good-quality red-wine vinegar
Salt and pepper
2 ounces black olives (see note page 120)

Combine the salt cod, onion, peppers, and tomato in a cassola or salad bowl, and mix together well.

Dress with the oil and vinegar (about 3 or 4 parts to 1) to taste, then marinate at room temperature for 2–3 hours.

Salt and pepper to taste, garnish with olives, and serve.

Esqueixada Estil Llorenç Torrado

(LLORENÇ TORRADO'S SHREDDED SALT COD SALAD)

Llorenç Torrado is a well-known Barcelona-based chef and author. He seems to have worked at most of the traditional Catalan restaurants in town at one time or another, but now mostly cooks privately and as a demonstration chef for Catalan food products. As an author, he has written or co-written masterful works on Catalan olive oil and *embotits* (sausages and the like), among other things, and recently compiled an encyclopediac guidebook to La Boqueria, the main Barcelona market (see page 295), in honor of its 150th anniversary. His own version of *Esqueixada* is bare-bones simple, and is probably not fit study for freshmen in the school of salt cod.

TO SERVE 4 (AS APPETIZER)

1 pound salt cod, cut into large pieces and skinned and boned, but not desalted
Mild extra-virgin olive oil
Good quality red-wine vinegar

Finely shred the salt cod with the fingers; then place it in a large bowl with plenty of water to cover. Soak 15–20 minutes, working fish frequently with the hands.

Dry, and drain the salt cod, place it in a cassola or salad bowl, and dress with oil and vinegar (about 3 or 4 parts to 1), then marinate 15–20 minutes and serve.

Amanida de Bacallà

(SALT COD SALAD)

This is an elegant, upscale interpretation of *Esqueixada* from the elegant, upscale Eldorado Petit restaurants in Barcelona and Sant Feliu de Guixols. It should be served on black plates if possible, to emphasize the ivory-white translucence of the salt cod.

TO SERVE 4 (AS APPETIZER)

*1 pound thick-cut salt cod, in 1 piece,
    desalted (see page 79), skinned,
    and boned*
Mild extra-virgin olive oil
*2 sprigs fresh thyme (omit if fresh
    thyme is not available)*
*3–4 sprigs fresh cilantro (preferably)
    or Italian parsley*
Black peppercorns
*2 cups white beans, cooked (about 1
    cup dry) and cooled*
1 head butter lettuce, julienned
*16 tender, pale-colored celery leaves
    (from heart of celery)*
1–2 heads mâche (optional)
½ lemon

Freeze the salt cod 1–2 hours or until it is firm but not frozen through; then, with a very sharp knife, slice it paper thin. (Slices should be translucent.)

Place the salt cod slices in a *cassola* or large, flat bowl, cover lightly with oil, add the thyme, cilantro, and a generous scattering of peppercorns, and marinate in the refrigerator for 24 hours.

When you are ready to serve, remove the salt cod slices from the marinade, scraping off the peppercorns and herbs. Strain the oil, and set it aside.

Divide the white beans equally among the centers of four serving plates; then arrange the salt cod slices so that they cover part of the beans but extend out onto the bare plate.

Fill the remainder of each plate with four small piles of the julienned lettuce, separating each pile with 1 celery leaf and a leaf or two of *mâche* (if available).

Add the juice of ½ lemon to the reserved oil, and mix well, then drizzle the dressing lightly over everything on each plate.

Esqueixada de Lluç amb Caviar

(MARINATED HAKE SALAD WITH CAVIAR)

Strictly speaking, this sophisticated appetizer isn't an *Esqueixada* at all, since the fish it uses not only isn't salt cod, but is chopped and not shredded. (Note that the previous recipe, which called for the salt cod to be sliced, doesn't call itself an *Esqueixada*—though it is clearly an elaboration of one.) In any case, though, it is unusual and very good, and contains at least an echo of the *Esqueixada* idea. The recipe comes from Sa Punta, off the Platja de Pals on the Costa Brava.

TO SERVE 4 (AS APPETIZER)

*1½ pounds hake, true cod, halibut, or
    other firm-fleshed ocean whitefish*
Mild extra-virgin olive oil
Sherry vinegar
2 sprigs parsley, minced
*1 ounce green peppercorns, rinsed and
    drained*
*1–2 ounces beluga or sevruga caviar
    (or more, according to taste
    and/or budget)*
3–4 lettuce leaves, julienned
*4–8 tender, pale-colored celery leaves
    (from the heart of the celery
    stalk)*
Paper-thin lemon slices

Wash and thoroughly bone the hake; then chop fine, and dry on paper towels.

Place the hake in a cassola or bowl, and cover it with oil and vinegar (about 3 or 4 parts to 1). Add parsley and green peppercorns to the bowl, and mix together well, then marinate, refrigerated, for 48 hours.

When ready to serve, drain the hake in a colander, and remove most of the green peppercorns by hand; then divide the fish equally among four serving plates.

Top each serving of hake with caviar, and garnish the plates with julienned lettuce, celery leaves, and lemon slices.

Note: This dish may be served either cold or at room temperature.

Esqueixada de Pollastre

(SHREDDED CHICKEN SALAD)

This is my own version of a dish I found, under the same name, in Joseph Cunill de Bosch's 1907-vintage book *La Cuyna catalana*. I wouldn't go out and kill the chicken for it, but it's a nice way to deal with leftovers—for instance, the chicken that comes out of the stockpot.

TO SERVE 4 (AS APPETIZER)

*1–1½ pounds boneless chicken
    (preferably white meat), cooked
    and shredded with the fingers*
*½ onion, sliced paper-thin and
    separated into rings*
*2 tomatoes, seeded and grated (see
    page 7) or peeled, seeded, and
    chopped*
*4–5 tablespoons mild extra-virgin olive
    oil*
*Dash of good quality red-wine vinegar
    or sherry vinegar*
Salt and pepper
3–4 lettuce leaves, julienned

Mix chicken, onion, and tomatoes together well; then dress with oil and vinegar, and salt and pepper to taste.

Marinate 3–4 hours at room temperature; then serve garnished with julienned lettuce.

ESCABETXOS
(PICKLED FISH AND FOWL)

Dishes preserved *en escabetx—en escabeche* in Castilian—are nearly universal. With the inevitable differences in spelling and fine points of technique, *escabetxos* exist all over Spain, in Mexico, in Central and South America, in the Caribbean (most notably in Jamaica), in France, Italy, and Belgium, and in parts of Eastern Europe—among other places. The basic idea is simple. Some variety of fish or fowl (or, occasionally, vegetable) is first cooked and then marinated or pickled in oil and vinegar, almost always with garlic and herbs and/or spices included. It is a simple means of preservation—much quicker and easier than, say, salting and drying a piece of cod—and has been said to have saved millions of lives throughout history by keeping food safe from spoilage under the most adverse conditions.

The dish was apparently invented, in a different form, in Persia or the Arab world, and its name derives ultimately from the Perso-Arabic word *sikbāj*, "vinegar stew." The Arabs made *sikbāj* mostly with meat (lamb, principally), and only rarely with fish. Three recipes for *"escabeyg"* appear in the fourteenth-century *Libre de Sent Soví*, so the concept had obviously gained some popularity in the Catalan world by that time. Catalan etymologist Juan Corominas, argues, in fact, that the Catalans probably introduced the whole idea to Europe in the first place; if the word had entered the Romance languages directly through Castilian, Corominas points out, the Castilian tongue would have rendered *"sikbāj"* as *"es-cabej"* or *"escabege"* or the like—instead of as *"escabeche,"* in obvious imitation not of the Perso-Arabic but of the Catalan form. Despite its near-universality, then, *escabetx* might truly be said to be a Catalan dish—at least in its European and post-European version. It's certainly good, and easy, enough to be one. . . .

Escabetx de Sardines
(PICKLED SARDINES)

One of the great champions of *escabetxos* in Catalonia is the Florian restaurant in Barcelona, which often offers two or three different varieties of the dish. This is one of their recipes.

TO SERVE 4–8 (AS APPETIZER)

2 pounds fresh sardines (see note page 177)
Salt
1 cup flour
1 quart or liter mild extra-virgin olive oil
1 cup good-quality white wine vinegar
1 head garlic, separated into cloves and peeled
2–3 bay leaves
1 sprig fresh thyme and/or 1 sprig fresh rosemary (omit if fresh herbs are not available)
½ teaspoon sweet paprika

Clean and wash the sardines, removing the heads if desired, then dry thoroughly inside and out.

Add salt to taste to the flour; then dredge the sardines lightly in it.

Sauté the sardines in a cassola or large skillet over medium-low heat in ¼–½ cup of oil, turning once, until light golden-brown and cooked through (about 5–6 minutes).

Drain the sardines on paper towels; then layer them in a cassola or glass or earthenware bowl.

In a saucepan, mix the remaining oil with the vinegar, garlic, bay leaves, herbs, and paprika, and bring to a full boil.

Remove from the heat, and immediately pour the hot liquid gently over the sardines, making sure they are completely covered. (Add more oil if necessary.)

Cover with foil or a lid, and marinate, in the refrigerator or at room temperature, for at least 3 days. (Sardines preserved in this manner should last at least a month.)

Serve at room temperature, lightly drained.

Note: I think sardines are the best fish for *escabetx*, but any small whole fish may be used—as, for that matter, may trout—with the cooking time adjusted up or down accordingly.

Escabetx de Gallina, Colomí, o Perdiu

(PICKLED CHICKEN, PIGEON, OR PARTRIDGE)

This is another *escabetx* from Florian—a truly elegant and unexpected appetizer or light summer lunch dish.

TO SERVE 4–5 (AS APPETIZER OR LIGHT MAIN COURSE)

2 small chickens or 6 pigeons (squabs) or partridges
Salt
4 cups mild extra-virgin olive oil
2 cups good-quality red wine vinegar
2 tablespoons whole black peppercorns
5 bay leaves
2 heads garlic, separated into cloves and peeled
4–6 green onions or scallions, trimmed at both ends
1 bunch thyme

If you are using chickens, cut them into quarters. Leave the pigeons or partridges whole. Salt the birds lightly.

Add all the other ingredients to a Dutch oven or large pot, and bring to a boil; then immediately add the birds to the pot.

Lower the heat, and simmer 45 minutes (for pigeons or partridges) or 2 hours (for chickens).

Remove pot from the fire and cool to room temperature. Refrigerate for 24 hours or more.

To serve, cut the pigeons or partridges into quarters and arrange 4–6 pieces on each plate. If you are using chickens, cut off the drumsticks, thighs, and wings, and distribute them whole among serving plates; then cut breast meat into ¼-inch slices, and distribute it equally among plates. Moisten birds with a bit of cooking liquid, and garnish with a few whole peppercorns.

Note: Florian, known (among other things) for its very beautifully designed plates, serves this *escabetx* on black or other dark-colored china with a garniture of watercress, pickled baby onions, and sometimes strips of pickled sweet red pepper or pimiento.

Pesc ama Vi i Salvia

(FISH WITH WINE AND SAGE)

This dish—which comes from Alghero, the Catalan enclave on the Italian island of Sardinia—is not exactly an *escabetx*, though it's certainly in the same family. The use of olive oil as a last-minute condiment is a typically Italian touch, I think, and is not much done in Catalonia.

TO SERVE 4 (AS APPETIZER OR LIGHT MAIN COURSE)

3 cups dry white wine
1 cup good-quality white wine vinegar
Salt
1½ pounds sea bass, halibut, or other firm-fleshed ocean whitefish, cut into pieces about 1 × 3 inches
6–8 fresh sage leaves, or ½ teaspoon dried sage, wrapped securely in cheesecloth
Mild extra-virgin olive oil

In a large pot, bring the wine and vinegar to a boil, and continue to boil slowly for 5 minutes. Lower the heat, and salt to taste.

Add the fish carefully to the simmering liquid, adding more wine to cover if necessary. Add the sage, cover, and poach fish for about 10 minutes. (Do not let the liquid return to a boil.)

Remove the pot from the heat, uncover, and allow the fish to cool to room temperature in liquid.

When it is cool, carefully remove the fish pieces from the liquid and drain; then divide equally among four serving plates, and drizzle with oil.

FARCITS I FARCIDES

(STUFFED VEGETABLES AND FRUIT)

In his book *L'Art del menjar a Catalunya*, author Manuel Vázquez Montalbán compares the Basque and Catalan versions of the stuffed pepper: "The Basque ones are more sophisticated," he writes, "more *haute cuisine.* The Catalan ones are more natural—we just wash the pepper, stuff it with ground pork or veal mixed with garlic, parsley, pepper, and a bit of flour or maybe an egg to bind it, and then stick it in the oven."

Stuffed vegetables of this kind—*farcits* (masculine) and *farcides* (feminine) in Catalan—he continues, "are still found in private kitchens run by old mothers and ancient grandmothers." In fact, *farcits*, both traditional and otherwise, are found in kitchens run by just about everybody in the *països catalans.* Stuffed peppers are common, from the Empordà to the *país valencià*—in the Valencian regions of Alcoi and Boicarent, large peppers are called *bajoques* or "pods," as in bean or pea pods (sometimes causing Catalans from other regions, when they hear of *bajoques farcides*, to think very curious things indeed about local dining habits)—but onions, zucchini, eggplant, tomatoes, artichokes ("a Kierkegaardian vegetable . . . metaphysical and mysterious," Vázquez Montalbán has called it), lettuce and cabbage leaves, and even apples, pears, and peaches are also stuffed—and there isn't a corner of the whole region, from Andorra to Alghero and Perpignan to Alicante, that doesn't number at least one or two stuffed vegetable (and occasionally fruit) dishes among its specialties. Stuffed vegetables, of course, are "poor" food—food in which a small quantity of precious meat (or fish) is made to go a long way. Like so many dishes born of necessity, though, they're too good to save for times of penury—and, as several of the following recipes demonstrate, they can be fancied up quite nicely as well.

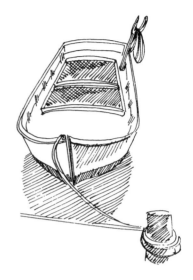

Pebrots de "Piquillo" Farcits amb Brandada de Bacallà

(SWEET RED PEPPERS STUFFED WITH SALT COD PURÉE)

Peppers stuffed with salt cod or other fish, puréed and otherwise, are found all over northern Spain. The combination of flavors and textures just simply works extraordinarily well. The best peppers for this dish, most specialists in the matter agree, are the kind known (even in Catalonia) by the Castilian name *piquillo* or "little beak." These are small (2–3 inches in diameter and 3–4 inches long), bright red, and very sweet, with a pointed (beaklike) bottom—more or less what we call pimientos (though that word describes sweet peppers of all kinds in Castilian). The best *piquillos* come from the Navarra region, and they are usually employed—even in the best places—not fresh but preroasted and packed in glass jars. If anything, this seems to make them even sweeter (and certainly more tender) than they would be straight from the garden.

TO SERVE 6 (AS APPETIZER OR LIGHT MAIN COURSE)

8 medium-large red peppers or 16 piquillo *peppers or pimientos (see note), roasted and peeled as for Escalivada (see page 170), with ribs and tops removed*
3–4 cups Brandada de Bacallà *(see page 85)*
Olive oil
2 cups heavy cream
Salt and pepper

Preheat oven to 350°.

Fill 6 medium-large peppers or 12 *piquillos* with *brandada*, setting the remaining peppers aside.

Place the filled peppers, cut side up (if you are using medium-large peppers) or on their sides (if you are using *piquillos*), in a lightly oiled baking dish just large enough to hold them.

Bake the peppers for about 20 minutes, or until the filling is heated through.

Meanwhile, purée the remaining peppers in a food processor, blender, or food mill.

Bring the cream to a boil, then reduce the heat to a simmer, and stir in enough pepper purée to obtain a rich, red color. Salt and pepper to taste.

Divide the sauce evenly among 6 plates, covering the bottom of each, and arrange pepper or peppers atop the sauce (see below).

Note: Spanish pimiento-type peppers or *piquillos* are sometimes available in jars in the United States, and are recommended. There is also a brief fresh pimiento season here. Any red or green bell pepper or other sweet pepper may be used, though (but remember that red peppers are sweeter than green ones, and hence work better). The peppers may be served without the sauce if desired.

Pebrots Farcits amb Porc i Calamars

(SWEET RED PEPPERS STUFFED WITH PORK AND SQUID)

Squid and pork end up together in a number of Catalan dishes (see, for example, *Calamars Farcits amb Salsa de Xocolata*, page 138), and, unlikely though it might seem, they go very well together. This recipe is typical of the Empordà.

TO SERVE 6 (AS APPETIZER OR LIGHT MAIN COURSE)

¾ pound squid, cleaned and coarsely chopped
½ pound ground pork
2 onions, chopped

½ carrot, chopped
2 sprigs parsley, minced
2 cloves garlic, minced
Olive oil
2 pounds very ripe tomatoes, seeded and grated (see page 7) or peeled, seeded, and chopped, or 2½ cups canned tomatoes (preferably Italian plum-type), chopped
½ teaspoon sugar
¼ cup breadcrumbs
¼ cup pine nuts, lightly toasted
6 medium-large red peppers or 12 piquillo peppers or pimientos (see note this page), roasted and peeled as for Escalivada (see page 170), with ribs and tops removed
Salt and pepper

Mix squid and pork together well; then put through the finest blade of a meat grinder, or process in a food processor until very smooth.

In a cassola or large skillet, make a *sofregit* (see page 38) of 1 onion, the carrot, parsley, and garlic in oil.

Meanwhile, in another pan, make a *sofregit* of the remaining onion; then add tomatoes and sugar and salt to taste, stir well, and simmer gently, uncovered, for about 45 minutes, stirring occasionally.

When the first *sofregit* is cooked, add squid-and-pork mixture to the cassola; then stir in the breadcrumbs and pine nuts. Sauté until the squid and pork are well cooked, and salt and pepper to taste.

When the tomato sauce has simmered for 45 minutes, pass it through a sieve or food mill; then return it to the pan, and continue simmering, uncovered, for 15 minutes longer.

Preheat oven to 350°.

Remove squid-and-pork mixture from the cassola, and place it in a strainer to drain off the excess fat.

Fill the peppers with squid-and-pork mixture, dividing it equally between them; then place them, cut side up (if you are using medium-large peppers) or on their sides (if you are using *piquillos*), in a lightly oiled baking dish just large enough to hold them.

Pour the tomato sauce evenly over the peppers; then bake for about 20 minutes, or until the filling is heated through.

Pebrots Farcits amb Ànec

(SWEET RED PEPPERS STUFFED WITH DUCK)

Chef Antonio Ferrer, proprietor of Barcelona's noted La Odisea restaurant, offers yet another variation on the classic Catalan stuffed pepper, this one filled with a delicate, elegant forcemeat of ground duck—given extra richness by the unexpected addition of calf's brains to the filling (these are very important and should not be omitted unless it is absolutely necessary)—and cloaked in béchamel sauce (*beixamel* in Catalan). Though French in origin, not Italian as some writers have claimed (it was named for the eighteenth-century French courtier Louis de Béchamel), this sauce is very popular not just in the *països catalans* but all over Spain—and is very easy to make.

TO SERVE 6 (AS APPETIZER OR LIGHT MAIN COURSE)

1 onion, chopped
2 leeks, white part only, chopped
1 carrot, chopped
2 cloves garlic, minced
1 sprig fresh thyme, minced, or 1/3 teaspoon dried
1 bay leaf
Olive oil
1 1/2 pounds boneless duck meat, minced (see note page 182)
1 duck or chicken liver, quartered
1/3 pound calf's brains, chopped
1 cup ruby port
1 cup dry white wine
Salt and pepper
1 slice stale or lightly toasted French or Italian bread, soaked in milk
2 cups milk
Butter
4 tablespoons flour
6 medium-large red peppers or 12 piquillo peppers or pimientos (see note page 180), roasted and peeled as for Escalivada (see page 170), with ribs and tops removed
2–3 sprigs parsley, minced

In a cassola or Dutch oven, make a *sofregit* (see page 38) of onion, leeks, carrot, garlic, thyme, and bay leaf in oil.

Preheat oven to 325°.

Add the duck meat, liver, and calf's brains to the finished *sofregit*, and cook until golden; then add the port and white wine, and salt and pepper to taste. Simmer, uncovered, about 10 minutes, until the liquid has evaporated.

Add the bread to the cassola, and stir in well; then bake the mixture in the preheated oven for about 30 minutes.

Meanwhile, make a béchamel sauce. Heat the milk in a saucepan (being careful not to let it boil) and at the same time, in another pan, melt 3 ounces butter over a low heat and slowly stir in the flour. Cook 3–5 minutes, stirring constantly, until a thick roux forms (do not let the roux burn); then slowly stir in the hot milk, and salt and pepper to taste. Continue cooking, stirring constantly, until the sauce becomes smooth and thick; then remove from the heat, and set aside.

When the meat mixture is baked, allow it to cool enough to handle. Then put it through the finest blade of a meat grinder or process in food processor until very smooth.

Raise the oven temperature to 350°.

Divide the mixture equally between the peppers; then place them, cut side up (if you are using medium-large peppers) or on their sides (if you are using *piquillos*), in a lightly buttered baking dish just large enough to hold them.

Pour béchamel sauce evenly over the peppers; then bake for about 20 minutes, or until the filling is heated through and the sauce has begun to brown. Sprinkle with minced parsley.

Note: Turkey or chicken (preferably dark meat) may be substituted for duck, though duck has a more pronounced flavor.

Rotllos de Brandada de Bacallà

(CABBAGE ROLLS WITH SALT COD PURÉE)

This is an unusual version of stuffed cabbage, filled with a silky-smooth, potatoless *brandada.* The recipe comes from the pleasant Barcelona restaurant La Dida ("The Wet-Nurse").

TO SERVE 4 (AS APPETIZER OR LIGHT MAIN COURSE)

1 pound salt cod, desalted (see page 79), skinned, and boned
8 cloves garlic, peeled and thinly sliced
1 cup olive oil
1½ cups heavy cream
1 large green cabbage
Butter
3 onions, thinly sliced
1 tomato, seeded and grated (see page 7) or peeled, seeded, and chopped
1 red bell pepper, roasted, peeled, and cut into strips as for Escalivada *(see page 170)*
Salt
6 dried pasilla, ancho, or other mild or mildly spicy chilis, soaked in warm water 1–2 hours or until plumped, then seeded and coarsely chopped
½ cup silvered or grated almonds (optional)

Poach the salt cod as for *Bunyols de Bacallà* (see page 85); then drain, reserving the cooking water and setting the salt cod aside.

Cook the garlic slices in oil until they begin to brown, then remove immediately, discard garlic, and set the oil aside.

Bring one cup of cream almost to a boil, then keep warm over very low heat.

Meanwhile, mash the salt cod with a fork or potato masher; then slowly add about ½ cup of the reserved garlic oil, working in well. Add the warm cream and enough of the reserved cooking water to make a medium-thick paste (about the consistency of Cream of Wheat). Set aside.

Core the cabbage, and remove the tough outer leaves, then blanch 5–6 minutes in salted water. After blanching, plunge the cabbage immediately into cold water; then remove 8–12 of the biggest and most perfectly formed leaves, trimming the tough ribs if necessary.

Fill the leaves with the salt cod mixture, and roll them carefully into the shape of *canalons (cannelloni)*, tucking in the ends. Set them in a buttered baking dish.

In the remaining oil, make a *sofregit* (see page 38) of onions, tomato, and red bell pepper; then add about ½ cup of the reserved cooking water. Add the dried chilis, and simmer about 20 minutes.

Purée the *sofregit* mixture in a blender or food processor, or pass through food mill, then strain through fine sieve. Return the mixture to the heat, add the remaining cream, salt to taste, and reduce the sauce over low heat until thick.

Meanwhile, preheat the oven to 350°.

Bake the cabbage rolls for about 15 minutes, or until heated through.

Serve the cabbage rolls topped with sauce, and sprinkle with grated almonds (if desired).

Cebas Farcides

(MEAT-STUFFED ONIONS)

I sat down in a little restaurant called Ca N'Aguedet in the town of Es Mercadal on the island of Minorca one summer evening a few years back—a delightful place, I must add, bare-bones simple but friendly and neat as a pin—and asked to see a menu. The waiter shook his head. "I have a better idea," he said. Then he motioned me into the kitchen with him. He showed me everything—stuffed vegetables, cauldrons of aromatic soup, fresh fish awaiting further instructions, even a peppery roast suckling pig—which he stole me a bite of, risking a playful slap from the chef (who might well have been his grandmother). The roast pig was delicious, and I settled on that at once as a main course. To begin with? He nodded toward a tray of meat-stuffed onions, gratinéed with breadcrumbs, and gave me a look that said, The smart money's on those things. I took his advice and was glad I did; the onions were wonderful—sweet and meaty and just crunchy enough. This recipe is my attempt at re-creating them.

TO SERVE 4 (AS APPETIZER OR LIGHT MAIN COURSE)

8 medium-large Spanish onions, peeled
Olive oil
6 ounces ground veal
3 ounces ground pork
2 ounces bacon, ground or very finely minced
1 sprig parsley, minced
1 sprig fresh thyme, minced, or ¼ teaspoon dried
1 sprig fresh marjoram, minced, or ¼ teaspoon dried
2 tablespoons breadcrumbs
2 tablespoons Manchego, Gruyère, white cheddar, Gouda, or other firm white or yellow cheese
1 egg, lightly beaten
Salt and pepper
2 cups tomato sauce (as for Pebrots Farcits amb Porc i Calamars page 180) (optional)

Slice off a small piece at the root end of each onion, so it will sit flat; then slice off the top of each onion about ½–¾ inches down. With a grapefruit knife or sharp paring knife, hollow out the onion, leaving walls about ½ inch thick (and being careful not to cut through the bottom). Set aside the onion cores.

Cook the hollowed onions 4–5 minutes in ample boiling, salted water; then drain, and set aside to cool.

Mince the reserved onion cores, and sauté in a small amount of oil until soft; then add the veal, pork, bacon, and herbs, and continue cooking until the meat is browned.

Mix the breadcrumbs, cheese, and egg into the meat mixture, and salt and pepper to taste.

Preheat oven to 350°.

Stuff the onions with the meat mixture; then bake in a lightly oiled baking dish until the onions are slightly soft and cooked through (about 40–50 minutes).

Serve plain or, if desired, with tomato sauce.

Patates a la Catalana

(CATALAN-STYLE STUFFED POTATOES)

Stop the presses! Stuffed baked potato skins are Catalan! Well, maybe. I found this recipe in the great French gastronome Austin de Croze's *What to Eat and Drink in France* (published back in 1931), wherein he describes it as a specialty of the Roussillon. I must admit that I've never run across the dish there myself, but it's a good version of this now-popular specialty, and I feel no qualms about including it here.

TO SERVE 4 (AS APPETIZER OR SIDE DISH)

2 large baking potatoes
2–3 tablespoons shallots, minced
Butter
4 anchovy filets, soaked in water for 1
  hour and patted dry
2 hard-boiled eggs
1 red (if possible) or green bell pepper,
  roasted, peeled, and cut into strips
  as for Escalivada *(see page 170)*
1 tablespoon chives, minced
¼ cup crème fraîche *or sour cream*
Salt and pepper
2 sprigs parsley, minced

Bake the potatoes at 425° for 1 hour, or until done.

Cut the potatoes in half, and carefully scoop out the insides with a spoon. Set the scooped-out portion aside, and return the potato skins to the oven for about 5 minutes or until slightly crisp.

Sauté the shallots in a small amount of butter until soft.

Rice or mash the potatoes, then stir in shallots.

Coarsely chop the anchovies, eggs, and bell pepper strips together. Stir in minced chives, and add to the potato mixture. Stir in *crème fraîche*, mix well, and salt and pepper to taste.

Refill the potato skins with the potato mixture, drizzle melted butter over each one; then return to 425° oven for about 20 minutes or until golden-brown.

Garnish with minced parsley.

Pomes Farcides

(PORK-STUFFED APPLES)

Pears or apples stuffed with meat are common to the Empordà region of Catalonia and to the Balearic Islands—two regions which, as noted earlier, share many culinary ideas. Such dishes are *also* known in far-off Persia, and I wondered if the concept could somehow have traveled all the way from there to Mediterranean Spain. Probably not, says food-and-language scholar Charles Perry (whose special province is Middle Eastern food history), since such dishes are *not* known to the Arabic-speaking Mediterranean, which would presumably have been the way station in such a journey; it's probably just a case of parallel development. Curiously, this dish is sometimes known in Catalonia as *relleno*—which is the *Castilian* word for "stuffed."

TO SERVE 4 (AS APPETIZER)

1 ounce plain marzipan
1 tablespoons breadcrumbs or 2–3
  butter cookies, crumbled
½ teaspoon anisette
¼ pound ground pork
1 egg, lightly beaten
½ cup sugar
¼ teaspoon cinnamon
Salt and pepper
¼ cup pine nuts, lightly toasted
¼ cup golden raisins or sultanas,
  plumped in warm water for 10
  minutes
4 large baking apples (about 1 pound
  each), preferably pippins or the
  Red Roma variety
½ cup dry white wine
2 cups warm water
Salt and pepper
½ cup slivered or grated almonds
  (optional)

In a food processor or by hand, work together the marzipan, breadcrumbs, and anisette; then mix well with the pork, egg, half the sugar, the cinnamon, and a pinch each of salt and pepper.

If you are using a food processor, transfer the mixture to the bowl. Mix in the pine nuts and raisins by hand; then set the mixture aside.

Core the apples, being careful not to cut through the bottom. Then slice off the top of each one about ½ inch down, and discard. With a grapefruit knife or sharp paring knife, remove enough apple pulp from each apple to make room for about ¼ cup of filling.

Chop the removed apple pulp, and add to the meat mixture; then stuff the apples with the mixture, letting it protrude slightly from the top and rounding it off.

Preheat oven to 325°.

Mix remaining sugar with wine and water; then pour half the liquid into a baking dish just large enough to hold the apples. Add the apples, and bake for 1¼ hours, basting occasionally and adding more of the remaining liquid to the dish if necessary. (Apples should be soft but still firm enough to hold together.)

Just before serving, sprinkle with the slivered almonds if desired.

See Also:

Albergínies Farcides amb Anxoves (Stuffed Eggplants with Anchovies), page 48
Albergínies d'Anfós (Eggplant "Sandwiches" with Grouper Mousse), page 50
Perdiu a la Col, Estil Josep Pla (Josep Pla's Partridge-Stuffed Cabbage), page 94
Pomes Farcides amb Crema Catalana (Apples Stuffed with Catalan "Burnt Cream"), page 248

PANS I PASTES
«BREADS AND PASTAS»

PA AMB TOMÀQUET
(CATALAN TOMATO BREAD)

Having lunch at Els Perols de l'Empordà in Barcelona one day with a local-born friend, I ordered some mild Palamós anchovies as an appetizer. They arrived accompanied by a basket of toast, a cruet of olive oil, and a single whole ripe tomato. Now, though I'd only been in Catalonia for a week or so at this point, I'd already noticed that Catalans somehow ate tomatoes with their bread—but the specifics had thus far escaped me.

Making a stab at it, I put a piece of toast on my plate, cut the tomato in half, then started thinly, primly slicing it and layering it on the toast. My Catalan companion laughed good-naturedly, put a piece of toast on her own plate, cupped the remaining tomato half in her hand, and simply rubbed it on the toast—squeezing it lightly as she did so, as one might squeeze a lemon half to anoint a piece of fish. Then she turned the toast over and repeated the action on the other side. Next, she drizzled oil from the cruet over the toast and shook a bit of salt on it—first on one side, then on the

other. Finally, she reached her fork cut for a couple of anchovies and laid them across her concoction, then gestured to her plate as if to say, *"Voilà!"* She had just shown me how to make the most basic, and probably the best-loved, Catalan dish of all—*Pa amb Tomàquet,* literally "bread with tomato."

Josep M. Espinàs once pointed out, in one of his wise and witty food columns for the magazine *Serra d'Or,* that the Catalan word for bread, *pa,* is, along with the universal *ma,* "the first and most basic infantile syllable." Thus, he argues—tongue at least slightly in cheek—bread is more basic to Catalan culture than to any other. There is even a word in Catalan, he points out, for someone who eats a lot of bread—*panarra.* And the sausage, herring, or cheese that a Catalan might mate with bread to make a sandwich, he suggests, is really just a pretext to eat more of the thing itself.

Be that as it may, it is certainly the case that bread is greatly loved, and greatly eaten, in the *països catalans.* (A Minorcan proverb says, *"Ahon no hi ha pa, es juliol hi ha fred"*—"Where there is no bread, July is cold.") And, since butter has not traditionally been consumed in great quantity in the region—outside of Minorca and the Pyrénées, at any rate—it makes sense that the Catalans would long since have figured out some nondairy means of moistening and flavoring this most favored food.

The first moistening and flavoring agent, of course, was simply olive oil—a substance generously applied to bread not just in Catalonia and vicinity, but virtually everywhere such oil is produced—and a few other places besides. (In Catalonia, a wishy-washy politician is sometimes said to be *pa sucat amb oli,* "bread soaked with oil.") Elizabeth David, who has done so much to introduce Mediterranean cooking to the English-speaking world, described a French Catalan peasant dish which she called *el pa y all*—fresh bread rubbed with garlic and sprinkled with salt and a few drops of olive oil—in her *French Country Cooking,* first published in 1951. When the book came out, David recently told an interviewer, "one reviewer remarked rather tartly that she hoped we British would never be reduced to breakfasting off so primitive a dish." Today, of course, the children of David's first readers—in London as in New York or San Francisco—would probably consider good bread drizzled with good oil, at lunchtime if not necessarily for breakfast, to be a great gastronomic treat (though alas neither good bread nor good oil is anymore within the scope of the average peasant's budget).

The Catalans went a bit further than mere oil, though. Lots of folks bring bread and tomatoes together, of course. Italians sometimes spoon chopped tomato pulp onto *bruschetta* or *fettunta*—their versions of bread with oil and garlic; in Provence, thin slices of tomato might be applied; in America, for that matter, we celebrate the BLT. But only in the *països catalans,* to the best of my knowledge,

does anyone rub tomato straight on bread (and only *then,* incidentally, worry about the oil). Indeed, the whole idea is perfectly Catalan in its practicality. You've got some bread that's a day or two old and starting to dry out, and you've got too many tomatoes (everybody who grows tomatoes has too many tomatoes at least occasionally). . . . Say, why not combine the two, using up the tomato surplus and revivifying the old bread simultaneously—and come up with a whole new, delicious kind of food in the process?

Author Nèstor Luján has found a written reference to *Pa amb Tomàquet* in Catalonia as early as 1884. The dish might well have been invented earlier still, of course, but not too much earlier, since the tomato didn't reach the region until the sixteenth century and didn't become everyday fare until the eighteenth. Barcelona photographer and restaurateur Leopold Pomés has written an entire book on Catalan tomato bread—a lighthearted, affectionate, wittily illustrated little tome called *Teoria i práctica del pa amb tomàquet*—"The Theory and Practice of Bread with Tomato." In it, he offers his own imaginative version of how the dish might first have been conceived: "An artist from the Empordà, one summer day, returning to his house intoxicated by the blue sea, his skin still impregnated with salt, saw a red sun on the horizon—and, combining his great hunger with his inborn love for the products of his own countryside, wished to pay homage to the sun and give peace to his demanding stomach at the same time. He took some red tomatoes and the flat surface and slightly uneven texture of a big slice of bread—a wonderful canvas for the work he was creating—then covered the bread completely in red, without the usual dilution of watercolor, and, being both an accomplished artist and a noted gourmand, polished it voluptuously with the golden brilliance of that most exquisite varnish, olive oil."

Pomés also writes, somewhat less fantastically, of his own fond childhood memories of *Pa amb Tomàquet*—of how it was his usual after-school treat, and how, when his mother kindly tried to offer him something more elaborate when she could, he would balk and insist on the same old tomato bread. This is something of a common theme among Catalans: *Pa amb Tomàquet* arouses great nostalgic passion, great Proustian stirrings of sensuous recollection. It is Catalan comfort food, almost the very bread and butter (as it were) of Catalan cultural identity.

Pa amb Tomàquet

(CATALAN TOMATO BREAD)

Plain *Pa amb Tomàquet,* made with good bread, good oil, and a nice ripe tomato, is its own reward—a self-sufficient treat. It is also, however, a versatile accompaniment to all manner of other foodstuffs. The most common accoutrements to Catalan tomato bread are anchovies or slices of mountain ham. Sardines, herring, or little rounds of *botifarra* sausage are traditional, too. Casa Perú in the hamlet of Bagergue, near Salardú in the Vall d'Aran, serves an exquisite do-it-yourself *Pa amb Tomàquet* with cloves of garlic (a refinement that, surprisingly enough in this garlic-loving land, is not usually added to tomato bread) and with both local ham and slices of superb yellow-white Pyrenean cheese. A Barcelona businessman of

my acquaintance has been eating *Pa amb Tomàquet* with fresh peeled figs crushed on top since childhood—a confection I expressed enough skepticism about one evening that he interrupted a serious dinner in his elegant private dining room to fetch me an example. (It was delicious!) Leopold Pomés, in his *Teoria i práctica del pa amb tomàquet* reports that superstar Catalan singer-songwriter Lluís Llach likes to alternate bites of a piece of tomato bread held in one hand with a bar of dark chocolate held in the other. Myself, I've found that little rounds or squares of *Pa amb Tomàquet,* treated on one side only (and with little or no salt) make a perfect foil for smoked salmon and even caviar.

Beyond such exotic variations (and beyond the traditional accompaniments mentioned above), I see no reason why virtually any kind of leftover meat, fish, or fowl, thinly sliced or crumbled (as appropriate), wouldn't taste just fine in this Catalan context—and a one-sided application of tomato, oil, and salt, incidentally, makes great dressing for sandwiches. (If you serve conventional *Pa amb Tomàquet* moistened on one side only, however, it is said in Catalonia to be a sign that you come from a large family—the implication being that large families can't afford to waste oil or tomatoes on both surfaces.)

TO SERVE 1 (AS APPETIZER)

1–2 thick slices country-style French or Italian bread or sourdough bread (see note)
1 small-medium fresh tomato, very ripe (see note)
Mild extra-virgin olive oil
Salt
2–4 anchovy filets, soaked in water for 1 hour and patted dry, or 1–2 very thin slices European-style ham (prosciutto or Black Forest type)

Grill the bread lightly on a wood-burning fire or barbecue (if possible), or toast it lightly in the toaster or under a broiler (turning once in the latter case).

Cut the tomato in half crosswise; then rub both sides of the toast (including the crust) with the cut side, squeezing gently as you do, to leave a thin red film, including some seeds and bits of tomato flesh, on both surfaces.

Drizzle oil on both sides of the toast to taste, then salt to taste.

Place anchovies or ham on top of the toast, and serve with knife and fork. (See above for serving variations.)

Note: The better the bread, obviously, the better the *Pa amb Tomàquet.*

Fresh, truly ripe tomatoes, preferably homegrown (and preferably *not* those sad, cottony, artificial-pink ones all too often sold in our supermarkets), are called for, too. If these aren't available, coarse homemade tomato sauce may be substituted, as may, in a pinch, good-quality canned tomatoes (ideally the Italian pear-shaped ones), well-drained of their packing juices.

Pamboli amb Tomàtiga

(MAJORCAN TOMATO BREAD)

Pamboli is a contraction of the words *pa amb oli,* bread with oil; *tomàtiga* is the Majorcan word for tomato. This version of tomato bread, suggested by a recipe in Luís Ripoll's *Cocina de las Baleares,* is quite different from the Catalan interpretation. It uses sliced tomatoes rather than squeezed-out tomato juice and pulp, it addresses one side of the bread only, it admits the possibility of vinegar (never added to Catalan *Pa amb Tomàquet*), and it uses an assortment of final toppings I've never seen put on bread in Catalonia proper. It is nonetheless a delicious, if somewhat more pungent, dish.

TO SERVE 1 (AS APPETIZER)

1–2 thick slices country-style French or Italian bread or sourdough bread (see note this page)
1 small-medium fresh tomato (see same note)
Mild extra-virgin olive oil
Salt
Good-quality red-wine vinegar (optional)
6–8 medium-sized black olives or 10–12 Niçoise olives, pitted and coarsely chopped
1–2 teaspoons capers (to taste), rinsed and dried
1 tablespoon samphire, fresh or pickled, finely chopped (optional; see note page 191)

Toast bread as in previous recipe.

With a very sharp knife, cut 4–5 paper-thin (translucent) slices from the tomato. Arrange them across the surface of the toast, one side only, and press slightly into toast with spatula or dinner knife.

Drizzle oil over tomatoes to taste; then salt to taste.

Carefully shake a few drops of vinegar over tomatoes (not too much) if desired.

Mix olives, capers, and, if desired, samphire together; then spread over surface of tomatoes and serve with knife and fork.

Note: Samphire is a European coastal plant *(Crithmum maritimum),* related to the carrot and to parsley and also called pousse-pierre, pousse-pied, cristmarine, sea fennel, and sea bean. It is bright green or yellow-green in color and resembles a thicket of tiny, many-twigged branches. It has a vivid, salty, strangely pleasant flavor, and adds unusual character to *Pamboli amb Tomàtiga* in Majorca. (It is also very good in salads, especially with seafood.) Samphire, both fresh and in glass jars (pickled), is occasionally available at specialty food shops in the United States. *Pamboli amb Tomàtiga* is sometimes eaten as a light lunch or supper in Majorca, accompanied by an ample wedge of some Spanish-style omelet or other (see pages 120–124).

COQUES

The *coca* (plural: *coques*) is more or less the Catalan pizza—a flat pastry base for a wide variety of toppings (both sweet and savory), usually made of simple bread dough and usually in the shape of an elongated oval (except in the Balearics, where it is often round). The word itself apparently derives from the Latin *coquere,* to cook, and is used not only in Cata-lan but in the old Occitan tongue of neighboring Toulouse and vicinity (though in that region it generally refers to a kind of sweet cake).

Coques differ from pizzas not only in their usual shape but in the fact that cheese and herbs are rarely added, and that they are traditionally served at room temperature. Often, too, they bear a single topping rather than a combination of them—just onions, say, or just anchovies.

I learned how to make *coques* from Rossend Colomé and Pau Carbó, the bakers of the wine village of Pla del Penedès, west of Barcelona, whom I met not in Catalonia at all, but in Brentwood, California. In 1985, Penedès winegrower and Southern California restaurateur Jean Leon, who had just opened La Scala Presto in Brentwood as a casual offshoot of his La Scala restaurant in Beverly Hills, imported Colomé and Carbó to the new establishment for a week to try to make Penedès-style bread and *coques* in the restaurant's pizza ovens. The bread was less than a success (the ovens were too hot, and anyway, Carbó later told me, American flour has too much gluten in it for his bread-making style, and simply didn't rise correctly). The *coques,* on the other hand—simple ones, elaborated only with sugar, pine nuts, and a drizzle of anisette—were a minor triumph, almost identical in texture and flavor to the very good ones the bakers make daily back in Pla.

At this writing, La Scala Presto is still turning out *coques* according to their recipe, to rave notices from customers who most likely have no idea where Catalonia is. Colomé and Carbó, meanwhile, returned to their hometown as celebrities: *"Els Estats Unis admiren els pans i les coques del Pla del Penedès,"* read a front-page headline in the local newspaper when they got back—"The United States admires the breads and *coques* of Pla del Penedès."

Coques have, admittedly, yet to take America by storm—perhaps they await their Wolfgang Puck—but they're easy to make and offer a delightful and at least slightly exotic alternative to pizza itself.

Coca de Pinyons

(PINE NUT *COCA*)

This is the basic *coca* recipe (as adapted for American ingredients) given to me by Rossend Colomé and Pau Carbó, the bakers of Pla del Penedès. Though sugar and pine nuts are called for as topping, a wide range of other

items may be substituted (see note). This particular version, which may be served warm or at room temperature and which should be slightly chewy in texture, is usually eaten for breakfast or as a sort of midmorning snack— sometimes with a modest glass of *cava* (Catalan "champagne") or sweet wine of one variety or another.

TO MAKE 1 LARGE OR 2 SMALL *COQUES*

1 package dry yeast dissolved in 2⅔ tablespoons (8 teaspoons) warm water
3½–3¾ cups flour
2 teaspoons salt
1¼ cups water
Olive oil
Sugar
¼ cup pine nuts (not toasted)
Anisette

Knead the yeast, flour, salt, water, and 2–3 tablespoons oil together by hand or in an electric mixer with a dough hook. (If you are using the mixer, knead for about 5 minutes at low speed.) Finished dough should be smooth and elastic.

Place the dough in a large bowl in a warm place, brush the top lightly with oil, and allow to rise for 1 hour.

Preheat the oven to 450°.

Punch the dough down and, if you are making 2 *coques*, divide into 2 equal parts.

Pat the dough out into a long, flat oval shape, about 6 inches wide, 18–24 inches long, and ½ inch thick. (For 2 *coques*, retain ½ inch thickness and reduce other dimensions proportionately.)

Place the *coca* on an oiled cookie sheet, and brush the top lightly with oil; then lightly score the dough diagonally in a crisscross pattern at 1–1½ inch intervals. Form a low rim around the edges of the dough.

Sprinkle the top of the dough amply with sugar, and scatter pine nuts evenly over the surface. Drizzle lightly with anisette.

Bake 10–15 minutes, or until golden-brown.

Note. Other *coca* toppings common in Catalonia, which may be substituted for sugar and pine nuts, include the following: thinly sliced onions or red or green peppers (lightly sautéed in oil and well drained before adding to dough); thinly sliced tomatoes or zucchini (added raw); anchovy filets or thinly sliced pieces of *botifarra* sausage (see page 147); pitted and coarsely chopped black and/or green olives; small cubes of thick-cut bacon (partially cooked before adding); Swiss chard or a mixture of chard and spinach (cooked, well-drained, and chopped), and small or thinly sliced wild mushrooms (raw). Some combination of these and/or other similar ingredients may of course be used—but to remain authentically Catalan, don't mix too many of them together on any one *coca*. An exception to this rule comes in the next recipe.

Coca amb Recapte

(*COCA* "WITH EVERYTHING")

This is the one *coca* with which the Catalans go wild, express their individuality (or that of their region), use up leftovers, break the rules. In Catalan, *recapte* means provisions, food stores, victuals, and a *Coca amb Recapte* is thus a *coca* that raids the larder, throws in a little bit of everything. (In some areas, the same dish is called a *coca enramada*, a garnished or "garlanded" *coca*.) Author Josep M. Espinàs notes that a *Coca amb Recapte* is "by definition local, and, what's more, *localist*." Each *comarca* of Catalonia has its own version, he continues, "And everybody says of their *Coca amb Recapte*, 'This is an authentic specialty of this *comarca* alone.'"

The only strictures limiting such a *coca* are that it be colorful (which usually implies some combination of tomatoes and/or red peppers with one or more green vegetables) and that at least one kind of meat or fish be included—ham, sausage, pork loin, anchovies, herring, sardines, etc. Some suggested toppings are given below—but use your imagination, mix and match, have fun. Try to use only the highest-quality ingredients, though. Remember: The honor of your *comarca* is at stake.

TO MAKE 1 LARGE OR 2 SMALL *COQUES*

1 recipe coca *dough as given on page 192, brushed with olive oil (omit sugar, pine nuts, and anisette)*
2–3 small zucchini, unpeeled, sliced paper-thin
2–3 red (if possible) or green bell peppers, seeded and thinly sliced
1–2 onions, sliced paper-thin
Olive oil
½ pound botifarra sausage (see note page 147), thinly sliced

Preheat oven to 450°.

Sauté the vegetables together for 4–5 minutes in oil, drain, then spread them evenly over the top of the *coca* (dividing equally if you are making 2 *coques*).

Arrange the *botifarra* slices on top of the vegetables.

Bake 10–15 minutes or until golden-brown.

Note: Coca amb Recapte is best served at room temperature, or slightly warm, rather than hot.

Coca de Sant Joan

(SAINT JOHN'S DAY *COCA*)

This is a sweet, egg-enriched *coca*—lighter and thicker than most varieties—traditionally served on the eve of Saint John's Day, June 23. A similar confection is traditional a month later, on July 24, for the eve of the feast of Sant Jaume or Saint James the Greater. It is good breakfast material any day of the year.

TO MAKE 1 LARGE OR 2 SMALL *COQUES*

2 cups sugar
5–6 cups flour
1 teaspoon salt
2 packages dry yeast dissolved in ⅓ cup warm water
1 cup room-temperature milk
4 eggs, lightly beaten
¼ pound butter, melted
1 tablespoon grated lemon rind
8–10 slices candied pineapple (red, green, and yellow), cut into thirds or quarters
½ cup red and green candied cherries, halved
¾ cup candied orange peel, cubed
1 cup pine nuts (not toasted)

194

If you are working by hand, combine 1 cup sugar with 4 cups flour and the salt; then stir in yeast, milk, 3 eggs, the butter, and lemon rind. When this is well mixed, work the remaining flour into the dough ¼ cup at a time until the dough takes shape (1–2 cups more total). When the dough is ready, turn it out onto a floured board, and knead until it is smooth and elastic.

If you are using an electric mixer, combine 1 cup sugar, the salt, yeast, milk, 3 eggs, butter, and lemon rind with the mixer paddle; then replace the paddle with the dough hook, and add the flour 1 cup at a time until the dough takes shape (5–6 cups total), and becomes smooth and elastic. Turn out onto a floured board, and turn several times.

Allow the dough to rise in a warm place, in a bowl covered with a towel or in a sealed plastic bag, for about 1 hour, or until doubled in size.

Punch the dough down, and divide it in half if you are making 2 *coques*. Shape with the hands until each *coca* is about twice as long as it is wide and about ½–1-inch thick.

Place the *coca* on a lightly oiled cookie sheet, and allow it to rest for 15 minutes; then brush with the remaining beaten egg.

Meanwhile, preheat the oven to 450°.

Distribute candied fruit and pine nuts evenly over the top of the *coca*; then sprinkle the remaining sugar over the top.

Bake the *coca* 20–25 minutes or until golden-brown.

Cool to room temperature before serving.

Coca d'Ànec i Olives
(DUCK AND OLIVE *COCA*)

This is a turnover *coca*—a *calzone*, if you will—popular in the Roussillon.

TO MAKE 1 *COCA*

1 onion, chopped
2 tomatoes, seeded and grated (see page 7) or peeled, seeded, and chopped
Olive oil
1½ cups raw boneless duck meat (about 2½ pounds bone-in duck), skin removed, cut into strips
3–4 ounces European-style ham (prosciutto or Black Forest type), diced
1 cup good-quality green olives (see note page 119), pitted, blanched, and halved
½ cup anisette
Duck or chicken stock
Salt and pepper
4 eggs, beaten
1 basic coca *recipe (see page 193, steps 1, 2, and 4), doubled in size*

In a cassola, Dutch oven, or large skillet, make a *sofregit* (see page 38) of onion and tomatoes in oil. Add duck and ham, and cook until lightly browned, adding more oil if necessary. Add the olives, and stir well.

Deglaze the pan with anisette; then add stock to cover, and simmer, uncovered, about ½ hour, adding a bit more stock if necessary, until the duck is very tender, and the liquid has evaporated.

Add salt and plenty of fresh-ground black pepper to taste.

Let the mixture cool slightly; then add ¾ of the beaten eggs, and mix well.

Preheat the oven to 350°.

Roll out the *coca* dough into a large circle about ½ inch thick; then place the filling on one half of the dough, leaving about 1 inch of dough uncovered around the edge.

Fold the uncovered half of the circle over on the top of the filling, to form a large half-circle; then crimp the edges of the *coca*. Brush the *coca* on both sides with the remaining egg mixed with a few drops of water.

Bake for 45 minutes or until dough is golden-brown and crisp. Serve at room temperature, cut into 2-inch slices crosswise.

Note: This *coca*, a good appetizer or light lunch main course (with a salad on the side), is also an unusual and very satisfying picnic dish.

FIDEUS
(CATALAN PASTA)

After a trip to Spain in the mid-nineteenth century, Alexandre Dumas *père* wrote, "In Italy, where one eats badly, the few good inns tell you, 'Sir, we have a French chef.' In Spain, where one eats abominably, the good places tell you, 'Sir, we have an Italian chef.'" Italian food, indeed, became something of a rage in urban Spain in the 1800s—especially in Bar-

celona, with its long history of mercantile contact with Italy. Italian chefs and restaurateurs had become commonplace in the Catalan capital by the turn of the century, in fact, and indisputably helped to establish the fine dining tradition that persists there to this day. Perhaps the greatest culinary gift Italians brought to the region, however, was pasta—which has become, in a wide variety of forms, an integral part of the Catalan diet.

But Italians weren't the first to introduce pasta to Catalonia. The Moors were. Food and language scholar Charles Perry has argued convincingly that the first pasta-makers of Southern Europe were probably the Greeks (the Greek word *itria* is the oldest recorded word for noodles in the Mediterranean), and that this Greek specialty was first adopted by the Arabs (as *iṭriyah*) and then brought by them into Spain in the eighth or ninth century A.D.—where it became known as *alatria*, the name under which it appears in two recipes in the *Libre de Sent Soví* (c. 1324), the first known Catalan cookbook. That name has pretty much died out in the *països catalans* today (though a pasta called *aletria* is still made in Murcia), but another pasta name (and form) imported by the Moors still thrives: *fideus*.

Fideus is very short, very thin pasta—little noodles an inch or two long, about the thickness of Italy's narrow-gauge *vermicelli* or *spaghettini*. I call it simply Catalan pasta, because it is, in a sense, Catalonia's own. The only pasta form that rivals it in popularity in the region, *canalons* (see pages 203–206), remains close to its Italian model—sometimes almost indistinguishably so. *Fideus* doesn't *have* an Italian model. The word itself has a complicated and somewhat disputed etymology, but it apparently derives originally from the Arabic word *fāḍa,* meaning to be abundant or to overflow (as in, presumably, an overloaded cooking pot), and seems to have entered the Romance languages—as *fideos* in Castilian, *fedelini* in Italian, *fidei* in Swiss French, etc.— by way of Mozarabic (the dialect of Spain's Arabicized Christians) and then Catalan. What is certain is that it first showed up in the latter language in 1429, a good 170 years before the earliest appearance of the word *fedelini* in Italian, and that a recipe for it is given in the influential *Libre del Coch* (1520).

In any case, *fideus* isn't prepared like Italian pasta at all. To begin with, it is never cooked *al dente,* and if it is sometimes firm to the tooth, it's only because it has been *overcooked* and hardened a bit in the oven. And it isn't boiled separately in water and then moisted with sauce as most Italian pasta is, but rather thrown into the pot with the other ingredients and cooked along with them.

Fideus a Banda

(CATALAN PASTA AND RASCASSE, IN TWO COURSES)

Fideus a banda is one of the greatest, and one of the simplest, of all Catalan dishes. It is a two-part affair by definition. Its name literally means *"fideus* apart," and it thus consists of noodles cooked in fish stock first, which are later ("apart" from the noodles) followed by the fish from which the stock was made—traditionally rascasse or scorpionfish (*escórpora* in Catalan), that ugly but intensely flavored deni-

zen of the Mediterranean (said poetically in France and the *països catalans* alike to somehow assimilate the savor of the laurel trees, pines, and wild thyme that grow at the sea's edge) that is considered by the French to be the single indispensable constituent of authentic bouillabaisse.

A close relative of *fideus a banda* is *fideus rossejats* or simply *rossejat,* which is the same dish but without the fish course to follow. The name comes from the verb *rossejar,* which my Enciclopedia Catalana dictionary defines as "to be slightly blond" (an almost universal concept, incidentally, which perhaps only the Catalans have found a word for)—a reference to the fact that the raw *fideus,* as in *Fideus a Banda,* is always sautéed in olive oil before cooking, so that it takes on a blondish golden hue. (The sizzling action of sautéing might also be responsible for the old Barcelona restaurant name for *fideus—xerraires,* "chatterboxes.")

It is important to remember that *fideus rossejats* and the noodle portion of *Fideus a Banda* aren't noodles covered with a sauce, like Italian pasta; instead, they are noodles which have *drunk* a sauce, absorbed it, become one with it. Please don't be tempted to "improve" the dish by adding fish or shellfish directly to it, or by stirring in the *sofregit* instead of straining it out as directed. (If you want to do those things, see the recipe for *Fideuà* on page 216.) The beauty of the thing in the first place is its very purity and simplicity. If made properly and well, it doesn't need improving—because it is already perfect.

This particular recipe comes from chef Carles Camós, owner of the highly rated Big Rock restaurant in Platja d'Aro on the Costa Brava. He stresses that this is his own interpretation of the dish. "You might like it more or less than some other versions," he says frankly, "but it is mine." I like it more.

TO SERVE 6 (AS APPETIZER AND MAIN COURSE IF MADE WITH FISH; AS APPETIZER IF MADE WITH NOODLES ALONE)

2 onions, chopped
4 tomatoes, seeded and grated (see page 7) or peeled, seeded, and chopped
4 cloves garlic, minced
2 sprigs parsley, minced
Olive oil
1½ pounds rascasse (scorpionfish) or other full-flavored rockfish, cut into 6 serving pieces (see note; omit for fideus rossejats)
2 quarts strong fish stock
12 ounces fideus noodles (see note)
Salt and pepper
1–2 cups Allioli Negat (see page 32), to taste
1–2 cups Allioli Autèntic (see page 30) or Allioli amb Ous (see page 31) to taste (omit for fideus rossejats)

In a cassola, Dutch oven, or large skillet, make a sofregit (see page 38) of onions, tomatoes, garlic, and parsley in oil.

Add the fish to the cassola, and coat well with the sofregit. (Omit this step if you are making fideus rossejats.)

Add the stock to the cassola, and simmer, covered, for 30 minutes, removing the fish (if added) after 10 minutes and setting it aside.

Meanwhile, in another cassola or large skillet, sauté fideus in a small amount of oil over medium-low heat, stirring constantly until the noodles are light golden-brown. (Do not allow the noodles to burn.) Alternatively, toss fideus in oil until well-coated; then roast on a cookie sheet in a preheated 350° oven, shaking occasionally, until light golden-brown.

When the stock has finished simmering, strain out and discard sofregit. In a saucepan, reduce the stock to about 6 cups over medium heat.

Reheat the fideus in the cassola, and add 1 cup stock. Stir well until the liquid is absorbed; then repeat this step until all but 1 cup of stock is used up, and fideus is cooked. (Fideus should be soft and thickly liquid.) Salt and pepper to taste.

Serve Allioli Negat with fideus at the table, to be stirred in to taste.

If you are serving the fish, heat it briefly in the remaining cup of stock (do not overcook), then serve with Allioli Autèntic or Allioli amb Ous, to be added to taste at the table.

Note: Rascasse or scorpionfish is sometimes available at specialty fish markets in the United States, and I highly recommend its use for Fideus a Banda. If it is not available, monkfish, redfish, or ocean perch may be substituted—or, if necessary, any other flavorful ocean fish.

Fideus noodles (fideos in Castilian) are available at most Spanish and Hispanic markets. The Italian version, fedelini (also called fidelini or fideo), is sold at many Italian markets, often coiled into "nest" form rather than cut into short lengths but it can easily be broken into pieces of approximately the right size. If necessary, vermicelli, spaghettini, capellini, or other thin straight noodles may be used, broken into 1–2-inch lengths. Do not use egg pasta, though, as it will turn to mush when cooked fideus-style.

For his own delicious version of the dish, which is somewhat drier than Camós's, Lluís Cruanyas of the Eldorado Petit restaurants in Barcelona and on the Costa Brava stirs some Allioli Negat into the fideus when it is done, then browns the noodles for 5 minutes or so under a hot broiler or salamander, which both fluffs the fideus up a bit and gives it a tasty top crust.

Arròs a Banda

(RICE AND RASCASSE, IN TWO COURSES)

In Valencia and vicinity, near the vast rice fields of La Albufera, a delicious *a banda* dish is made with rice instead of *fideus*. It is prepared virtually identically to its pasta counterpart, except that saffron is usually added—but Valencian connoisseurs sometimes claim that their version is superior because rice absorbs the stock, and thus the flavor of the fish, more fully than *fideus* does. Valencian gastronome Llorenç Millo, in fact, recounts the story of one local food lover who, encountering *Arròs a Banda* for the first time, promptly broke into tears. When asked why he was crying, he replied, "Because I am forty years old and I am thinking of all the years I have lost before tasting this rice." As with the previous recipe, incidentally, this one may also be made as a single course without the fish.

TO SERVE 6 (AS APPETIZER AND MAIN COURSE IF MADE WITH FISH; AS APPETIZER IF MADE WITH NOODLES ALONE)

2 onions, chopped
4 tomatoes, seeded and grated (see page 7) or peeled, seeded, and chopped
4 cloves garlic, minced
2 sprigs parsley, minced
Olive oil
6–8 threads saffron, lightly toasted
1½ pounds rascasse (scorpionfish) or other full-flavored rockfish, cut into 6 serving pieces (see note page 198; omit if you are making rice alone)
2 quarts fish stock
6 cups short-grain rice (see page 63)
Salt and pepper
1–2 cups Allioli Autèntic *(see page 30)* or Allioli amb Ous *(see page 31) to taste (omit if making rice alone)*

Follow instructions for *Fideus a Banda* (page 197), crumbling saffron threads into *sofregit* when cooked and substituting rice for *fideus*.

If you are making rice *and* fish, serve *Allioli Autèntic* or *Allioli amb Ous* with the fish at the table, to be added to taste.

Note: Allioli Negat (page 32) is rarely eaten in the region of Valencia, and the rice portion of *Arròs a Banda* is usually eaten without additions of any kind. However, no stern Valencian gastronomic inquisitor is likely to materialize at your elbow if you want to add a dab of *Allioli* of any kind to your rice—*Negat, Autèntic,* or *amb Ous.*

Fideus Vermells amb Cloïsses

(RED CATALAN PASTA WITH CLAMS)

One of the most memorable seafood dishes I've ever encountered in Catalonia (which, I can assure you, is really saying something) is this one—sort of a Catalan version of spaghetti with red clam sauce, as prepared at the superb Casa Gatell in Cambrils. The clams used there are small, sweet ones, with zigzag markings reminiscent of an American Indian basket pattern. I believe these are called in English "golden carpet shells" *(Venerupis aurea).* Any high-quality, very fresh clams will do, though—small ones if possible.

TO SERVE 6 (AS APPETIZER)

2 onions, chopped

6 tomatoes, seeded and grated (see page 7) or peeled, seeded, and chopped
4 cloves garlic, minced
Olive oil
1 pound each rascasse (scorpionfish) and monkfish, or 2 pounds total assorted full-flavored rockfish, cut into large pieces
12 ounce fideus noodles (see note page 198)
Salt
6–12 dozen fresh clams (depending on size) (see note page 201)
1–2 cups Allioli Autèntic (see page 30) or Allioli amb Ous (see page 31), to taste

In a cassola, Dutch oven, or large skillet, make a *sofregit* (see page 38) of onions, tomatoes, and garlic in oil.

Add the fish to the cassola, coat well with *sofregit,* and sauté until the fish is lightly browned.

Add 2 quarts water, bring to a boil, then reduce the heat, and simmer, covered, for 30 minutes.

Meanwhile, in another cassola, cook *fideus* in a small amount of oil over a medium-low heat, stirring constantly until the noodles are golden-brown. (Do not allow noodles to burn. See page 198 for alternate cooking method.)

Strain the fish and *sofregit* from the liquid, and discard them; then reduce the stock to about 6 cups over medium heat.

Reheat the *fideus* in cassola, and add stock, stirring well. Cook over medium heat until the *fideus* is tender and soupy; then salt to taste, and stir in clams.

Continue cooking 2–3 minutes, or until clams have opened. (Discard any clams that do not open.)

Serve with *Allioli Autèntic* or *Allioli amb Ous* at the table, to be added to taste.

Note: Clams added directly to *fideus* might release some sand. To avoid this, soak them overnight in salted water to cover.

Cassola de Fideus Negres

(CATALAN BLACK PASTA)

This variation on *Arròs Negre,* or Black Rice, comes from the excellent Sa Punta restaurant, off the Platja de Pals on the Costa Brava.

TO SERVE 6–8 (AS APPETIZER) OR 4–6 (AS MAIN COURSE)

2 onions, chopped
1 green pepper, cut into thin strips
Olive oil
1 pound small cuttlefish or squid, cleaned and cut into small pieces, with ink sacs set aside (see note page 67)
½ pound botifarra *sausage (see page 147), cut into ½ inch pieces*
½ pound monkfish, cut into small pieces with skin and bones removed
2 tomatoes, seeded and grated (see page 7) or peeled, seeded, and chopped

2 quarts fish stock
Salt and pepper
1 pound fideus *noodles (see note page 198)*
2 cloves garlic, minced
1 sprig parsley, minced
6–8 threads saffron, lightly toasted

In a cassola, Dutch oven, or large skillet, make a *sofregit* (see page 38) of onions and green pepper in oil.

Add the cuttlefish or squid and sausage pieces, stir well, and cook until lightly browned. (Add more oil if necessary.)

Stir in the monkfish, then add tomatoes, stir well, and simmer for about 5 minutes.

Meanwhile, bring the stock to a boil, then keep warm over a low flame.

Add the *fideus* to cassola, stirring well so that each piece is well coated with sauce.

Place ink sacs in a sieve, hold it over the cassola, and crush the sacs with the back of a spoon. Pour a few tablespoons of water through the sieve to extract more ink. Stir well.

Add 1 cup hot fish stock to the cassola, stir well until the liquid is absorbed; then repeat this step until all the stock is used up and the *fideus* is cooked. (*Fideus* should be soft and thickly liquid.) Salt and pepper to taste.

Mix garlic, parsley, and saffron together, and stir into *fideus;* then remove from heat and serve.

Fideus a l'Estil de Lleida

(LLEIDA-STYLE PASTA)

Fideus isn't always cooked with fish or shellfish, of course. The important Catalan capital of Lleida (Lérida in Castilian), west and slightly north of Barcelona by about 95 miles, was a forbidding hilltop citadel in medieval times, and, as such, was occupied by the Moors for almost 400 years—until the twelfth century. Typical of Lleida today, this particular *fideus* dish, in which the noodles are cooked in a cassola with assorted meats, is said to date from precisely that century and to be an invention of the Moorish kitchen—though of course the Moors didn't make the dish with pork, which was forbidden to them. I find it one of the most savory of all Catalan pasta dishes.

TO SERVE 6 (AS APPETIZER OR LIGHT MAIN COURSE)

6 ounces botifarra *sausage (see page 147), coarsely chopped*
1 tablespoon lard
Olive oil
2 onions, chopped
1 red (if possible) or green bell pepper, seeded and cut into thin strips
1 bay leaf
3 tomatoes, seeded and grated (see page 7) or peeled, seeded, and chopped
2 cloves garlic, minced
12 hazelnuts, roasted (see page 39)
1 sprig parsley, minced
½ slice fried bread (see page 40)
½ teaspoon paprika

5–6 threads saffron, lightly toasted
12 ounces fideus *noodles (see note page 198)*
Salt and pepper
4–5 cups chicken or vegetable stock
½ cup grated Parmesan or Gruyère-type cheese
8 thin-cut pork chops (about 1½ pounds total)

In a cassola or Dutch oven, sauté the *botifarra* sausage in lard and a small amount of oil for about 5 minutes; then add the onions, red bell pepper, and bay leaf, and cook for 5 minutes more. Add the tomatoes to the cassola, and simmer, uncovered, for 10–15 minutes.

Meanwhile, make a *picada* (see page 40) of garlic, hazelnuts, parsley, fried bread, paprika, and saffron, moistened with a few drops of oil.

Stir *fideus* noodles into the cassola, coating well with vegetables, then stir in the *picada*, and allow to simmer for about 5 minutes.

Meanwhile, bring the stock to a boil; then stir about 1 cup of it into the *fideus*. Reduce the stock to a simmer, and continue adding it to the *fideus*, about 1 cup at a time, stirring frequently, until the liquid is absorbed and the *fideus* is tender. Salt and pepper to taste.

Remove the *fideus* from the heat, sprinkle with cheese, and allow to rest for 5–10 minutes.

Meanwhile, quickly sauté the pork chops in a small amount of oil until cooked through and slightly crisp. Just before serving the *fideus*, arrange the pork chops on top.

See Also:

Fideuà (Valencian Pasta "Paella"), page 216

CANALONS

If Barcelona has a heraldic dish, a single culinary presentation so well-loved and widely eaten in the city as to be virtually emblematic of it, it is *canalons*—the Catalan version of Italy's famous *cannelloni*—apparently introduced into the region during the great wave of Italian immigration in the nineteenth century. Just why Barcelona, and indeed Catalonia as a whole, should have taken this Italian specialty to heart (and to table) with such enthusiasm is hard to say. Perhaps *canalons* were seen as a kind of wintertime substitute for the stuffed vegetables so popular in the region in the spring and summer. (Though *canalons* are eaten twelve months a year in Catalonia, they are particularly popular late in the year, and are the traditional dish of Saint Stephen's Day, December 26.) Or perhaps it's just that *canalons* are so easy to make and so good.

I take it as a measure of their universality and adaptability, incidentally, that the two best restaurant versions of the dish I've ever

had in Catalonia were at one of the region's most modest eating places, the home-style Hostal La Pequeña in Riudellots de la Selva (near Girona), and one of its most elegant, Reno in Barcelona.

Canalons a la Barcelonesa

(BARCELONA-STYLE *CANALONS*)

The traditional Barcelona interpretation of *canalons* seems to have been borrowed from Italy's *cannelloni Rossini,* both being stuffed with ground pork and chicken livers and seasoned with nutmeg and white pepper. The filling offered here is a bit more elaborate, but it is still typically Barcelonese. Catalan *canalons* are also sometimes stuffed with spinach, veal, beef, fish (see page 206), calf's or lamb's brains, calf's liver, and various kinds of game, or some combination of such ingredients.

TO SERVE 6 (AS APPETIZER OR LIGHT MAIN COURSE)

1 onion, chopped
2 cloves garlic, minced
1 tomato, seeded and grated (see page 7) or peeled, seeded, and chopped
1 tablespoon lard
Olive oil
6 ounces boneless chicken or turkey meat, finely ground
3 chicken livers, minced
6 ounces veal, finely ground
6 ounces pork, finely ground
4 tablespoons breadcrumbs

1 egg, lightly beaten
1 sprig fresh thyme, minced, or ⅓ teaspoon dried
½ teaspoon nutmeg (freshly ground if possible)
Salt and pepper
18 canaló wrappers or 3 sheets fresh pasta (12 × 16 inches) cut into 18 rectangles, each 5⅓ × 6 inches (see note page 205)
Butter
1 recipe béchamel sauce (as for Pebrots Farcits amb Ànec, page 181)
½ cup grated Parmesan cheese

In a cassola or large skillet, make a *sofregit* (see page 38) of onion, garlic, and tomato in lard and a small amount of oil.

Add the chicken, chicken livers, veal, and pork to the cassola; then cook over medium heat for about 10 minutes, stirring frequently.

Mix the breadcrumbs with the egg; then stir in thyme and nutmeg and salt and pepper to taste. Stir the mixture into the cassola, then remove from heat, and set aside.

Cook the *canaló* wrappers in plenty of boiling salted water, a few at a time, for about 3 minutes; then remove them carefully from the water with a slotted spoon, and drain them on clean absorbent towels. (Do not use paper towels.)

Preheat the oven to 400°.

Spoon a small amount of meat mixture down one side of each *canaló* wrapper, covering no more than one third of its surface; then carefully roll each wrapper into a tube, starting from the meat side. As the *canalons* are filled, place them seam side down and side by side in a lightly buttered baking dish just big enough to hold them. Pour béchamel evenly over *canalons*, then sprinkle with Parmesan cheese.

Bake the *canalons* until the filling is heated through and the cheese has turned golden-brown (about 15–20 minutes).

Note: Canaló (*canelone* in Castilian) wrappers are sold in Spanish and Hispanic markets. Pasta sheets, either homemade or the kind found in Italian markets, may be substituted and cut into the appropriate size as indicated above. I recommend against using prerolled *manicotti* or *cannelloni* shells, as they tend to sweat when baking. But very good *canalons* (more correctly called *crespons* in Catalan) may be made with crepes (either homemade or store-bought) instead of pasta, without adjusting the above recipe (though crepes, of course, needn't be boiled before stuffing).

Canalons d'Ànec

(*CANALONS* WITH GROUND DUCK)

Using the same duck forcemeat he stuffs sweet peppers with, Barcelona poet/chef Antonio Ferrer of the city's La Odisea restaurant serves this unusual and delicious variation on conventional Barcelona-style *canalons*.

TO SERVE 6 (AS APPETIZER OR LIGHT MAIN COURSE)

1 recipe duck filling (as for Pebrots Farcits amb Ànec, *page 181)*
18 canaló *wrappers or 3 sheets fresh pasta (12 × 16 inches) cut into 18 rectangles, each 5⅓ × 6 inches (see note this page)*
Olive oil
1 recipe tomato sauce (as for Pebrots Farcits amb Porc i Calamars, *page 180)*
½ cup grated Parmesan cheese

Preheat oven to 400°.

Cook and fill the *canaló* wrappers as for recipe on page 204, then place them seam side down and side by side in a lightly oiled baking dish just big enough to hold them. Spoon the tomato sauce evenly over *canalons;* then sprinkle with Parmesan cheese.

Bake the *canalons* until the filling is heated through and the cheese has turned golden-brown (about 15–20 minutes).

Canalons de Peix al Cabrales

(*CANALONS* WITH FISH MOUSSE IN BLUE CHEESE SAUCE)

As popular as *canalons* are in Catalonia, there were times, until recently, when the traditional meat-filled Barcelona-style version of the dish was simply never eaten—on Fridays and other Catholic fast or abstinence days, to be precise. What was the *canalons*-loving Catalan to do on such meatless occasions? Why, eat *canalons* stuffed with spinach (another literal Italian borrowing) or—less commonly but more interestingly—with fish, of course. This version of that latter idea comes from the Barcelona restaurant Le Camembert.

TO SERVE 6 (AS APPETIZER OR LIGHT MAIN COURSE)

10 ounces hake, sea bass, halibut, or other firm-fleshed ocean whitefish
10 ounces monkfish
Bouquet garni made of 1 sprig each of fresh tarragon, marjoram, and basil, or ¼ teaspoon each of dried tarragon and marjoram and ½ teaspoon dried basil, mixed together well and wrapped securely in cheesecloth
2–3 large mint leaves, or ¼ teaspoon dried mint added to herb mixture above
1 shallot, minced
2 cloves garlic, minced
Butter
2½ cups heavy cream
Salt and pepper

3–4 ounces Cabrales (Spanish blue cheese), Roquefort, or other good-quality blue cheese
18 canaló wrappers or 3 sheets fresh pasta (12 × 16 inches) cut into 18 rectangles, each 5⅓ × 6 inches (see note page 205)
1 tablespoon almonds, blanched and roasted (see page 39) and finely ground

Place the hake, monkfish, and herbs in a pot, and cover with water, then simmer for 15 minutes. (Do not boil.) Remove the hake, and set it aside to cool; then let the monkfish continue simmering with herbs for 20 minutes longer. Remove the monkfish, and set it aside to cool, discarding the herbs but reserving the water.

Sauté shallot and garlic in 2 tablespoons butter; then flake or mince the cooled fish, and sauté it briefly in the same pan.

Add ½ cup cream to the fish mixture, and salt and pepper to taste. Stir well, then remove from the heat, and set aside. (The mixture should be very thick.)

Crumble the blue cheese, and mix it with the remaining cream in a small saucepan; then simmer, stirring continually, until the cheese is melted and well integrated into the cream.

Preheat oven to 400°.

Cook and fill the *canaló* wrappers as for *Canalons a la Barcelonesa* (page 204), using the fish water for cooking; then place them seam side down and side by side in a lightly buttered baking dish just big enough to hold them. Spoon the cheese sauce evenly over the *canalons*, then sprinkle with ground almonds.

Bake *canalons* until the filling is heated through and the cheese sauce has begun to brown slightly (about 15–20 minutes).

PLATS PRINCIPALS
«MAIN COURSES»

PAELLA

One cool, bright, early afternoon in January, I left my temporary quarters in El Saler, near the marshes of La Albufera just south of Valencia, and drove northwest to the little inland village of Benisano. If you know any Latin, the town's name might suggest "good health" to you, but what I was looking for wasn't a doctor or a mineral spa. I was after the salutary effects of a genuine *Paella Valenciana,* as prepared by one Rafael Vidal, who had been dubbed by local gastronomes on one occasion as *Mejor Paellero* or Best Paella Maker of the entire Valencia region (a region where, as a Spanish restaurant guide has pointed out, there seems to be a *paellero* under every rock).

Vidal's establishment, the Restaurante Levante, turned out to be a plain-looking, underlighted place on Benisano's main drag—at first glance, nothing more than a rather dingy workingman's bar. But on a table in a little hallway at the back of the room was a huge paella pan (itself called a paella in most of the *països catalans,* and a *paellera* in the rest of Spain, but known here on paella's home ground, perversely enough, as a *caldero*), probably four feet across, partially covered with a cotton towel. And beyond the hallway, through a

bead curtain, was an actual dining room—a bit brighter than the bar, pleasantly if simply furnished, and almost completely full of customers, most of them men and many of them in business suits.

Shown to one of the few remaining tables, I was promptly addressed by a waiter. "What will you have?" he asked.

"What have you got?" I answered.

"Well, paella, of course, for the main dish," he said, "but first you can have cuttlefish fried with garlic and parsley, deep-fried squid, or *bacallà* with red peppers." I chose the last of the three—a dish known locally as *esgarrat,* meaning "shredded" (as does *esqueixada,* see page 172)—in fact a bowl of roasted red pepper strips mixed with bits (shreds) of salt cod, dressed in good olive oil enlivened with minced raw garlic—a dish that got my palate's attention right away. Then came the paella. . . .

Had this been my first encounter with authentic *Paella Valenciana,* I would have been shocked. To begin with, it came not at all the way most of us imagine paella—in a steaming-hot paella pan decorated with bright green peas and pieces of red pepper and garnished with whole shrimp and mussels; it was simply heaped onto a ten-inch plate, at room tempera-

ture. (That big *caldero* in the hallway contained the day's full ration of the dish, cooked
in the morning and scooped up as needed; most
aficionados of paella prefer it tepid, not hot.)
More astonishing, though, would have been
the paella's contents—which were nothing
more than little hunks of rabbit and chicken,
some broad green beans and pale yellow butter
beans, a hint of tomato and onion, more than
a hint of saffron, and rice, rice, rice. There were

no peas or red peppers, no ham or sausage or
meat of any kind, no fish or shellfish, period.
Yet this paella was as historically and traditionally correct as it was delicious. This was a real
Paella Valenciana.

Rice was brought to Valencia by the Moors
in the eighth or ninth century A.D., but the
region earned its reputation as Spain's great
rice capital only after 1238, when Jaume I of
Aragon, in an attempt to contain an incipient

malaria epidemic, restricted rice plantings in Catalan-held territories to the marshlands of La Albufera, practically in Valencia's backyard. Because La Albufera is separated from the Mediterranean by a narrow strip of solid land, and because rice growers are after all farmers and not fishermen, it was natural that early rice dishes of the region looked inland for raw materials—to the *huertas* (*hortes* in Catalan), the lush network of orchards and market gardens that cover the nearby countryside. (One exception was the eel, plentiful in the marshes, which was combined with rice early in Valencian gastronomic history—and which still shows up with some regularity in various paellas.)

Today, of course, seafood has become de rigueur for most kinds of paella, in Valencia as in neighboring Catalonia, which has adopted the dish and fashioned its own versions of it—and beyond the borders of Spain (for paella is the most international of all Spanish dishes), it is universally considered to be a seafood dish by definition. What is understood in Valencia, and usually understood in Catalonia, however, is that whether it contains seafood or not, paella is above all a *rice* dish—and it is ultimately good rice, not good seafood (or whatever) that makes a paella great.

As that erudite and charming specialist in Valencian cuisine Llorenç Millo has noted, "A paella can be as savory in the shade of a tree, out in the country, with the rice accompanied only by some snails and runner and butter beans as one served in the most luxurious dining room, adorned with crayfish and lobsters."

Millo also offers five traditional rules (with a bit of a wink in his eye) for the proper enjoyment of this famed Valencian specialty:

(1.) It must be eaten outdoors, preferably in the shade of an old vine or a wide-topped fig tree, and ideally when the mild noontime breeze that local peasants used to call *El Paellero* is blowing. (2.) It must be eaten only at midday—it being considered self-evident by Valencians that a properly made paella will be too rich and heavy for the evening meal. (3.) It must be served directly from the *caldero*. (4.) It must be dished up with a spoon made out of boxwood. (5.) The only proper topics of conversation during the consumption of a paella (it being assumed that those sitting around in the open air at noontime eating it are male) are women, bullfighting, and crops—and above all, political controversies and philosophical declarations are to be avoided. In this last context, Millo recounts this story about Valencia's most famous author, Vicente Blasco-Ibáñez (author of *Blood and Sand* and *The Four Horsemen of the Apocalypse*): One afternoon, after attending a political meeting at a small inland village near Valencia, the noted novelist was invited to help polish off a monumental paella. As he dug in, one of the locals, seeking to show off his intellectual knowledge to the distinguished guest, asked, "Don Vicente, what do you think of Schopenhauer?" The author looked up from his plate, fixed the man with a stare, and responded, *"Schopenhauer?* Shut up and eat, man! Shut up and eat!"

Millo's strictures aside, there *are* some rules—or at least some guidelines—that should be followed if you want to make a good paella. First, use short-grain (or round-grain) rice, not the long-grain variety so often called for in American paella recipes. Valencian rice is preferable, of course, and can sometimes be found in this country. In its absence, the next best thing is Italy's *aborio* rice—the kind used for risotto—and Blue Rose or Japanese short-grain rice will also do. (The shorter, fatter grains absorb the flavor of the cooking liquid more readily and stay moist inside even when their exteriors get crusty.)

Second, if you can't use a real paella pan or *caldero,* at least use a vessel that is as wide and as shallow as possible. (Sometimes the wideness gets out of hand: Paella master Antonio Galbis, for instance, cooks an annual "paella for 1,000" at his Hostal Galbis in Alcudia de Carlet, using 220 pounds of rice and 250 pounds of chicken, among other ingredients, in a *caldero* roughly 12 feet in diameter—oiled from the inside with a janitor's pushbroom.) The point is that the liquid added to the dish must be cooked off evenly and relatively quickly, so the broadest possible surface—the greatest possible area of contact between rice and pan bottom—is desirable.

Third, paella should always be cooked on top of a flame, not in the oven (though, for practicality's sake, it can be finished in the oven; see below). In Valencia, in fact, a true paella is cooked not on a stove at all but over an open wood fire. Serious paella connoisseurs are very firm on this point—some even specifying a preferred variety of wood. At first, I thought this was just some anachronistic folkway or a pose struck for the tourists—but then one *paellero* demonstrated to me how live flames lapping around the edges of the *caldero* actually create a kind of mini-atmospheric inversion on the surface of the vessel, keeping the top of the rice moist with steam and flavoring the dish a bit with wood smoke, even as the rice on the bottom of the pan and around the edges takes on the *socarrat* or sweetish dark

brown crust so prized by paella lovers. Since wood-fire cookery isn't practical for everybody, I recommend using a round barbecue, very hot, or, more practically still, a very large gas burner, a smaller burner with a heat diffuser, or, as a last resort, two burners—turning the cooking vessel frequently so that it heats evenly. Do not try to make a paella on an electric burner; it will create a hot spot in the middle of the pan and burn the rice.

Three final paella rules: First, never stir a paella once the rice has been added (though it is permissible to pat the rice down into flatness if necessary); this is not risotto. Second, never add more liquid than called for. If the paella seems to be drying out too quickly, reduce the heat; conversely, if it is still soupy when the cooking is almost finished, increase the heat slightly. Third, always let a paella rest for 5 or 10 minutes when it comes off the flame, to allow its flavors to marry. Anyway, the plain truth is that, for whatever reasons, paella simply doesn't taste as good hot as it does merely warm.

Oh, and one more thing: Don't overdo it. Don't load your paella up with everything you can think of, and don't add too much or many of the ingredients you choose. Remember that paella is above all a celebration of *rice;* everything else—seafood or otherwise—is just gravy.

Paella Valenciana

"You know, dear Colman," the Majorcan journalist and food expert Pablo Llull said to me quite earnestly one afternoon, "you simply *cannot* write that paella is a Catalan dish." His point, of course, was that paella is an invention of Valencia, not of Catalonia. (The cooking of his island isn't Catalan either, he was quick to add, and anyone seeking Majorcan cooperation in studying the subject had better not go around saying that it is; I took the hint.) I've already argued for a broad definition of Catalan cuisine, though—that it is the cooking of the *països catalans* and not just of Catalonia itself; anyway, Catalonia has taken up paella enthusiastically and made it its own.

Nonetheless, it must certainly be admitted that the original paella, the definitive one, is Valencia's classic version—the kind known at least since the nineteenth century as *Paella Valenciana*. "The abuses committed in the name of *Paella Valenciana*," wrote Catalan author Josep Pla in one of his essays, "are excessive—an authentic scandal." Indeed, as the dish is served in much of the world—and it *is* served, from Toronto to Tokyo, Stockholm to Santiago—it would be all but unrecognizable to the average Valencian. (I have a recipe, clipped from a Los Angeles newspaper a few years back, for a "paella" made with leftover turkey, canned chopped clams, sliced pepperoni, and Spanish rice mix—in a microwave!)

At the same time, there is no official recipe for paella in its homeland, no single agreed-upon interpretation of the dish. Even so confident an authority as Llorenç Millo demurs. "Paella has as many recipes as there are villages," he says, "and nearly as many as there are cooks, so I will be very careful not to become pedantic and give a master formula." As it happens, though, without being a pedant about it, he *does* provide a master formula for the dish in his book on Valencian gastronomy,

La Taula i la cuina ("The Table and the Kitchen"). This recipe is based on that formula, and on several other traditional paella recipes.

TO SERVE 6–8 (AS APPETIZER) OR 4–6 (AS MAIN COURSE)

24 snails (optional; see note, page 100)
½ pound rabbit, cut into small serving pieces
Olive oil
1½ pounds chicken, cut into small serving pieces
1 onion, chopped
3 tomatoes, seeded and grated (see page 7) or peeled, seeded, and chopped
4½ cups hot chicken stock
1 pound assorted white beans, butter beans, and Italian-style broad beans or string beans (see note page 212), cooked and drained
1 sprig fresh rosemary (see same note)
1 pound short-grain rice (see page 63)
Salt

If you are using live or fresh snails, clean them thoroughly with a damp, rough cloth, making sure to rub off the "veil" at the opening of each shell; then rinse well, and cover with salted water in a pot, bring to a boil, and simmer until done (about 30 minutes). Drain and set aside. If you are using canned snails, drain and set aside.

In a paella, cassola, or other wide, flat-bottomed pan, sauté the rabbit pieces in a small amount of oil until golden-brown; then remove them, drain, and set aside.

In the same oil, sauté the chicken pieces until golden-brown; then remove them, drain, and set aside.

Pour off the excess fat; then make a *sofregit* (see page 38) of onion and tomatoes in the remaining fat.

Return the rabbit and chicken pieces to the pan, and stir well to coat with *sofregit;* then add the stock, and simmer for 10 minutes.

Add the snails, the rosemary, and the beans; stir well, salt to taste, then stir in rice.

Cook over medium-high flame (see page 210) without stirring for 20–25 minutes or until the rice is done and the liquid has evaporated. (Do not allow the rice to burn; a dark brown crust on the bottom and sides of the pan, however, is desirable.)

When the paella is finished, let it stand 5–10 minutes off heat before serving.

Note: Three kinds of beans are traditionally used in an authentic *Paella Valenciana: ferraúres,* which are Italian-style broad green beans; *tavelles,* which are white beans (*mongetes* in Catalan; see page 104); and *garrofóns,* which are butter beans or large pale yellow (or beige) limas. Conventional string beans may be substituted for the *ferraures,* and green limas or favas may be used in place of *garrofóns* if necessary.

Ideally, of course, fresh beans would be used in all cases. Since fresh white beans are virtually unobtainable in the United States, however, and fresh limas are rare, dried beans make a perfectly acceptable substitute—and indeed are usually used in Valencia itself. Italian-style broad green beans are difficult to find fresh, but are commonly available frozen—and are one of the few vegetables that seem to freeze quite well. Use canned beans only as a last resort, as they are the least flavorful and the most likely to turn mushy.

The vegetables in a paella should be very soft and almost integrated into the rice. If you insist on crisper vegetables, you can merely blanch them (or, in the case of dried beans, cook them partially) before adding them to the paella. Valencian chefs never put both snails and rosemary into the same paella. This fact always mystified me, until I happened upon a reference, in quite another context, to the fact that snails in the Mediterranean world often *feed* on rosemary and would thus bring the herb with them into the paella! This isn't likely to be a consideration with American snails.

Paella Valenciana amb Mariscos

(VALENCIAN PAELLA WITH SHELLFISH)

This is a paella in more familiar form—with mussels and shrimp and/or crayfish added. Again, the recipe is based on the formula offered by Llorenç Millo in *La Taula i la cuina.*

TO SERVE 8–10 (AS APPETIZER) OR 6–8 (AS MAIN COURSE)

*2 pounds chicken, cut into small
    serving pieces*
Olive oil
5½ cups chicken stock
*12 mussels, cleaned (see note page
    36)*
*½ pound shrimp and/or small prawns
    (scampi), heads and shells on*
*½–¾ pound assorted white beans,
    butter beans, and Italian-style
    broad beans or string beans (see
    note page 212), cooked and
    drained*
*1 tomato, seeded and grated (see page
    7) or peeled, seeded, and chopped*
1 tablespoon sweet paprika
6–8 threads saffron, lightly toasted
*1⅓ pounds short-grain rice (see page
    63)*
Salt

In a paella, cassola, or other wide, flat-bottomed pan, sauté the chicken pieces in a small amount of oil until golden-brown; then remove them, drain, and set aside.

Meanwhile, bring stock to a boil; then reduce the heat and simmer.

Pour off excess fat from the paella; then add the mussels and shrimp and/or the crayfish, beans, tomato, and paprika, and stir well.

Add the stock, return chicken to pan, and simmer for 10 minutes; then crumble saffron into pan, and salt to taste.

Stir in the rice; then cook over a medium-high flame (see page 210) without stirring for 20–25 minutes or until the rice is done and the liquid has evaporated. (Do not allow the rice to burn; a dark brown crust on the bottom and sides of the pan, however, is desirable.)

When paella is finished, carefully arrange the mussels and shrimp and/or crayfish on top of the rice, using tongs and being careful not to leave the rice uneven (top should be flat); then let stand 5–10 minutes off heat before serving.

Paella Parellada

("RICH MAN'S" PAELLA)

Standing in the lobby of the Hotel Colón in Barcelona one evening, I heard a guest—an American in his fifties—ask concierge Joan Domingo where he and his wife could get a good paella that evening. "What kind of paella do you have in mind?" Domingo asked—for he is the kind of concierge who knows the difference. "One with *everything,*" the American replied. "You know—shrimp, mussels, clams, lobster, fish, sausage, chicken, veal, peas . . . *everything.*" Domingo recommended what I'm sure was a very good restaurant nearby, where the couple doubtless got exactly what they wanted. What they got, though, was probably something very different from any paella they could have found in Valencia.

Catalan writers like to describe Valencian food, and especially paella, with words like "baroque," "polychrome," or (as Nèstor Luján once put it) "gloriously heterodox." Ironically, though, the most polychromatic paellas of all are those of Catalonia—and especially of wealthy, sophisticated Barcelona. These are paellas whose main purpose seems to be to show off the riches of the nearby sea and the surrounding fields and mountains, with the rice—so important in Valencian paella—sometimes becoming not much more than an anonymous backdrop. Such paellas, I hasten to add, can be very good—and certainly at least one of them deserves a place in this chapter. And perhaps the most famous non-Valencian paella of all is this one, *Paella Parellada*—a dish not only polychromatic, not only full of the local bounty, but somehow almost decadent in its basic conception.

Paella Parellada is named for a young Barcelona dandy of the early years of the century, Juli Parellada. He lived on the Carrer de Canuda, in the elegant family palace that later became the Barcelona Atheneum, and spent most of his inherited income on clothes, flowers, perfumes and colognes, and restaurants. One of his regular stops was the Café Suís (or El Suizo), known at one time as the city's single most expensive eating place. One day, Parellada, bored with the usual Café Suís menu, is said to have asked a waiter named Jaume Carabellido to concoct some special rice dish for him. Carabellido disappeared into the kitchen, conspired with the chef, and eventually returned with an immense paella, noteworthy not only for the sheer quantity and variety of its ingredients, but for the fact that every piece of fish, shellfish, fowl, and meat had been shelled, skinned, and/or boned. It was a lazy man's delight—a paella that could be eaten without the slightest effort on the diner's part. Parellada loved it, and from then on demanded it often.

Set Portes (Siete Puertas) and other of the city's restaurants quickly took it up, and soon it had become a Barcelona classic—usually bearing Parellada's name, incidentally, but sometimes called paella (or simply *arròs*) *sense entrebancs* (*sin tropiezos* in Castilian)—"without impediments"—or *tot pelat*—"completely peeled." Under whatever name, it is truly, as restaurant critic Luís Bettónica has noted, "a paella for sybarites."

TO SERVE 6–8 (AS MAIN COURSE)

1 chicken, cut into 6–8 serving pieces, then boned and halved (and skinned if desired)
Olive oil
½ pound boneless pork loin, cut into 6–8 thin scallops
6–8 small pork sausages (breakfast sausages, etc.)
½ pound monkfish, cut into 6–8 small pieces, skinned and boned
½ pound sea bass, halibut, or other firm-fleshed ocean whitefish, cut into 6–8 small pieces, skinned and boned
6–8 large shrimp, peeled
3 onions, chopped
4 medium artichoke hearts, halved and sprinkled with lemon juice
½ pound squid, cleaned and cut into rings

2 tomatoes, seeded and grated (see page 7) or peeled, seeded, and chopped
5½ cups chicken stock
1 pound short-grain rice (see page 63)
½ cup fresh or frozen peas
4 red (if possible) or green bell peppers, roasted, peeled, and cut into strips as for Escalivada *(see page 170)*
4 cloves garlic, minced
2 sprigs parsley, minced
6–8 threads saffron, lightly toasted
Salt
24 mussels, cleaned (see note page 36), cooked in salted water until open, and shelled

In a paella, cassola, or other wide, flat-bottomed pan, sauté the chicken pieces in a small amount of oil until golden-brown; then remove them, drain, and set aside.

Sauté the pork scallops and sausages in the same oil until crisp; then remove them, drain, and set aside.

Sauté the fish and shrimp in the same oil, adding more if necessary, until lightly browned; then remove them, drain, and set aside.

Sauté the onions, artichokes, and squid in the same oil until onions soften slightly; then add tomatoes, stir in well, and add 1 cup stock. Bring to a boil, then reduce heat and simmer for 10 minutes.

Return the chicken and pork scallops to the pan; then add rice and pepper strips (reserving 10–12 strips for decoration).

Add remainder of stock, and increase the flame to medium-high.

Make a *picada* (see page 40) of garlic, parsley, and saffron, moistened with a few drops of stock, and stir into the pan.

Stir in fish, and shrimp, and salt to taste.

When the stock is partially evaporated, arrange the mussels, sausages, and reserved red pepper strips on top of the rice, and continue cooking until the rice is done and liquid has evaporated (about 20–25 minutes total cooking time after the remainder of the stock is added).

When the paella is finished, let it stand 5–10 minutes off the heat before serving.

Paella amb Verdures

(PAELLA WITH VEGETABLES)

This is my version of an excellent all-vegetable paella served every Wednesday at El Plat in Valencia, one of the city's most able specialists in Valencian cuisine.

TO SERVE 4–6 (AS MAIN COURSE), 6–8 (AS APPETIZER), OR 8–10 (AS SIDE DISH)

2 onions, chopped
3 leeks, white parts only, chopped
4 tomatoes, seeded and grated (see
*   page 7) or peeled, seeded, and*
*   chopped*
Olive oil
6 medium artichoke hearts, halved and
*   sprinkled with lemon juice*
3 red (if possible) or green bell
*   peppers, roasted, peeled, and cut*
*   into strips as for* Escalivada *(see*
*   page 170)*
½ head cauliflower, broken into
*   florets*
½ cup fresh or frozen peas
5½ cups chicken or vegetable stock
4 cloves garlic, minced
2 sprigs parsley, minced
Salt
1 pound short-grain rice (see page 63)

In a paella, cassola, or other wide, flat-bottomed pan, make a *sofregit* (see page 38) of onions, leeks, and tomatoes in oil.

Stir in the artichoke hearts and pepper strips (reserving 10–12 strips for decoration).

Stir in the cauliflower florets and peas, and add 1 cup stock.

Bring to a boil; then simmer for 10 minutes.

Stir in the garlic and parsley, then add the remaining stock. Salt to taste.

Stir in the rice; then cook over medium-high flame (see page 210) without stirring for 20–25 minutes or until rice is done and liquid has evaporated.

Arrange the reserved red pepper strips on top of the rice about 5 minutes before cooking is completed.

When paella is finished, let stand 5–10 minutes off heat before serving.

Fideuà

(VALENCIAN PASTA "PAELLA")

Fideuà is sometimes just the Valencian name for what is known as *fideus rossejats* or *rossejat* (see page 197) in more northerly climes, but *fideuà* can also be, in effect, a paella made with noodles instead of rice. Unlike paella, though, it is always based exclusively on seafood, having been invented, it is said, by Valencian fishermen—who traditionally cooked it in an old porcelain washbasin on shipboard, using any fish or shellfish they didn't expect to be able to sell. The dish can also be made in a paella or cassola, of course, with good-quality seafood of a more exalted nature.

TO SERVE 6–8 (AS APPETIZER) OR 4–6 (AS MAIN COURSE)

1½ pounds shrimp and/or small prawns
*   (scampi), heads and shells on*

1 pound monkfish, cut into 4–8 pieces
Olive oil
2 tomatoes, seeded and grated (see
    page 7) or peeled, seeded, and
    chopped
2 quarts fish stock
6–8 threads saffron, lightly toasted
Salt
1 teaspoon sweet paprika
2 cloves garlic, minced
1 pound fideus noodles (see note page
    198)

In a paella, cassola, or other wide, flat-bottomed pan, sauté the shrimp and then the monkfish in a small amount of oil until golden-brown; then stir in the tomatoes, and simmer on low heat for about 5 minutes.

Meanwhile, bring the stock to a boil in another pan, and let simmer, covered.

Crumble the saffron into the pan; then stir in the paprika and garlic, and salt to taste.

Add the *fideus* to the shrimp and monkfish in the paella, stirring well so that each piece is well coated with sauce; then add the stock to the pan, stir thoroughly once only, and cook over medium-high flame (see page 210) without further stirring for 20–25 minutes or until the *fideus* is tender and the liquid has evaporated.

When the *fideus* is cooked, carefully remove the shrimp and/or the small prawns from the noodles, using tongs and being careful not to leave the *fideus* uneven (the top should be flat), and arrange them on top of the *fideus*. Brown top of shrimp and *fideus* briefly in a hot broiler or with a salamander if desired. Let stand 5–10 minutes off heat before serving.

See Also:

ARRÒS (RICE), pages 62–67
Arròs a Banda (Rice and Rascasse, in Two Courses), page 199

CALDERETA, SUQUET, I SARSUELA
(FISH AND SHELLFISH SOUPS AND STEWS)

Few dishes evoke the Mediterranean—the sea itself, the sun, the salt, the sensuality of food, the ease of life (real or imagined)—as vividly as a savory seafood soup or stew. There's an old saying in the region that a fish swims three times—first in water, then in oil (as it's being cooked), and finally in wine (as it's washed down the gullet with a glass or two of something cool). Fish soups sneak in a fourth swim, this time in water *and* oil (and sometimes, for that matter, wine as well), that seems to tie the rest together. (In a fish soup, oil and water *do* mix, or at least pretend to.)

So warm and fresh and aromatic, these dishes seem particularly complete, and thus unusually satisfying. They're seaside soul food. There's nothing mystical about fish soups, though. In the *països catalans* as elsewhere in the Mediterranean, they're mostly fishermen's dishes to begin with, often thrown together on the boats themselves as an improvised working lunch—and thus they ought to be quick and simple, as befits offhand galley cooking.

Fish-stew specialists, be they fishermen, home cooks, or even restaurant chefs, all seem to stress this fact: Don't put too much into the pot, they counsel; use the freshest seafood possible (preferably just pulled out of the water, of course), and then let it speak for itself.

Caldereta de Llagosta

(MINORCAN SPINY LOBSTER SOUP)

It is said in Minorca that when God had finished creating the larger and more beautiful island of Majorca next door, Saint Peter approached the Supreme Being and asked if he, Peter, might not try his hand at making something, too. "All right, Peter," God replied. "You can make Minorca." Saint Peter did so—but, frankly, he didn't do a very good job. Seeing this, God had a problem: He didn't want to hurt Saint Peter's feelings, but on the other hand He felt sorry for the people who would inhabit the island Peter had created. Then He had an idea. "I'll tell you what, Peter," He said. "I'll switch with you now. You take care of the Majorcans, and I'll take care of the Minorcans."

Thus, say Minorcans, are they so blessed today; and one of their greatest blessings, probably every one of them would agree, is the quality of their seafood—most of all the tiny *escupinya* clams from Maó harbor, as sweet and flavorful and briny-fresh as oysters, and the famous *llagostes* or spiny lobsters of the island's northern coast, served grilled with *allioli* or *maionesa* or in the pure and simple soup called *caldereta*.

A *caldereta* can be made with fish, with *escupinyes*, with *dàtils* (sea dates), even with *patjalides* (limpets)—but the *llagosta* version is almost legendary, especially as prepared in the pretty little fishing village of Fornells.

Penelope Casas, incidentally, in *The Foods & Wines of Spain*, notes that *caldereta de llagosta* is "oddly similar" to the classic French lobster preparation known alternately as *à l'américaine* or *à l'amoricaine*, and adds a new twist to the debate over which of the two names is correct by wondering if the dish might not originally, in fact, have been called *à la menorquina*. Seafood expert Alan Davidson lends some credibility to this suggestion in his authoritative *Mediterranean Seafood* by pointing out that the famous French specialty is clearly of Mediterranean origin, and that both forms of its name (the first suggesting that it is an American invention and the second that it comes from Amorica—an old name for Brittany) "are inappropriate and lack historical basis or even plausibility." (And the French, remember, did hold Minorca for a time in the eighteenth century.)

In any case, whatever other dishes it might have inspired, the authentic *Caldereta de Llagosta* remains a quintessentially Minorcan dish—so much so that the standard recipes for it generally begin, "First, take a live Minorcan *llagosta*. . . ." This is considered essential. I once asked one Fornells chef for his own recipe for the dish, and he replied, "But what good will it do you? You can't make a *caldereta* in America, because you don't have our *llagosta* there." We don't, of course—but with top-quality fresh or (better yet) live spiny lobster (also known as Pacific lobster, rock lobster, etc.), or, for that matter, with true lobster, it is certainly possible to make a very good *cal-*

dereta far from this blessed island. I cannot stress highly enough, however, the importance of using the best and freshest crustaceans possible for this dish.

TO SERVE 4 (AS MAIN COURSE)

1 onion, minced
1 green pepper, seeded and minced
2 tomatoes, seeded and grated (see
*   page 7) or peeled, seeded, and*
*   chopped*
2 cloves garlic, minced
2 sprigs parsley, minced
Olive oil
Four 1–1 1/4-pound spiny lobsters or
*   true lobsters (live if possible)*
Salt
4 thin slices French or Italian bread,
*   lightly toasted and allowed to dry*
*   out*

In a cassola, Dutch oven, or soup pot, make a *sofregit* (see page 38) of onions, green pepper, tomatoes, garlic, and parsley in oil.

Meanwhile, cut the lobsters horizontally into 4–6 pieces each across the tail, detaching and setting aside the heads and appendages. If you are using true lobsters, crack the claws gently with a mallet or hammer, and add to the tail pieces. (If you are using live crustaceans, first sever the spinal cord with a sharp knife where the head joins the body, then remove and discard the stomach.)

Scoop the coral and creamy interior out of the heads, scramble with a fork in a small bowl, and set aside.

Place the heads and appendages in a small pot, and cover them with water. Bring to a boil; then simmer until the *sofregit* is finished.

When the *sofregit* is finished, stir the coral mixture into it; then add the lobster pieces, turning with tongs so that they are well-coated with the vegetables.

Strain and reserve the lobster water, discarding the heads and appendages. Add 4 cups of lobster water to the cassola, and bring it to a boil; then reduce the heat to medium, and cook for about 10 minutes, turning the lobster several times. Salt to taste.

Place a slice of toast on the bottom of each of 4 large soup plates, divide the lobster pieces evenly between them, then ladle in soup.

Note: Soup may be served first, over the toast, with lobster as a second course—though I prefer it all together, messy though it can be to eat. Some chefs advise that you make the soup a day ahead and refrigerate it overnight; then reheat it just before serving. I prefer it freshly made.

Suquet

(CATALAN FISH AND POTATO SOUP)

The *països catalans* know countless varieties of fish and shellfish soups and stews: not just the aforementioned *caldereta* (itself in many forms), but the closely related *panadera*, also from Minorca; the even simpler *borrida* of Majorca and *olla de peix* of the southern Costa Brava; the *bullinada* of the Roussillon, which, it has been said, "yields nothing to the bouillabaisse of Marseille"; even *"bullavesa"* itself—among many others. Perhaps the most famous of all, though, is the Empordà region's straightforward, succulent *suquet*. Jaume Subirós of the Hotel Ampurdán in Figueres, in fact, considers *suquet* to be his region's most famous dish of any kind—meat, fish, or fowl.

The name comes from the verb *suquejar*, to seep or exude, the idea being that the fish bleeds its flavor into the sauce. As with *caldereta*, in fact, the quality of the main ingredient is of utmost importance. Again, this is a very simple dish—one first made by fishermen on their boats, with little more than oil, water, onions and/or green peppers, garlic, tomatoes (or sometimes just tomato juice), potatoes, and whatever portion of their catch was too rough and plain for sale. The version offered here, though gussied up a bit with brandy, is little more than that—though it comes from the sophisticated kitchen of Carles Camós at the Big Rock restaurant in Platja d'Aro, who was kind enough to let me look over his shoulder as he made the dish one day.

TO SERVE 6 (AS MAIN COURSE)

2 pounds very fresh rascasse (scorpionfish), monkfish, rockfish, ocean perch, redfish, sea bass, halibut, or a combination of any two of the above, cut into serving pieces (see note)
Flour
Salt and white pepper
Olive oil
2 sprigs parsley, minced
4 cloves garlic, minced
¾ cup cognac or good-quality Spanish brandy
1 onion, chopped
2 tomatoes, seeded and grated (see page 7) or peeled, seeded, and chopped

1½–2 pounds potatoes, peeled and sliced about ⅛-inch thick
Fish stock
1 slice fried bread (see page 40)
12 almonds, blanched and roasted (see page 39)

Dredge the fish lightly in flour seasoned with salt and white pepper; then sauté it in a cassola, Dutch oven, or soup pot in a small amount of oil (adding more if necessary) until golden-brown.

Sprinkle the parsley and half the garlic over the fish, add brandy, and carefully ignite. When the flames die out, remove the fish from cassola and set aside.

In the same cassola, adding more oil if necessary, make a *sofregit* (see page 38) of onion and tomatoes; then add potatoes and enough stock to cover. Cook covered for about 15 minutes, or until the potatoes are almost done.

Meanwhile, make a *picada* (see page 40) of remaining garlic, fried bread, and almonds, moistened with a few drops of oil.

Stir the picada into the cassola when the stock has almost finished cooking; then add the fish and continue cooking until the fish is heated through. Salt and pepper to taste.

Note. If you are using monkfish, do not remove it from the cassola in step 2. Make the *sofregit* in a separate pan, and add it to the cassola with the potatoes and the stock, then cook all ingredients together for 20 minutes. (Monkfish takes longer to cook than other varieties.)

Sarsuela

(SEAFOOD "OPERETTA")

If *suquet* is Catalonia's most famous fish soup, *sarsuela* is its most notorious. A Barcelona restaurant dish of the nineteenth century, *sarsuela* throws everything into the pot, embarrassing itself with riches. British author Anthony Burgess once referred to it rather drily as "a very inclusive seafood anthology." Catalan Josep Pla, on the other hand, spoke of "these horrible *sarsueles* served in restaurants, without any culinary sense and with certain peril to the stomach."

Sarsuela has a bad reputation among many serious Catalan chefs (and among virtually all Catalan fishermen) both because it seems too much of a good thing and because, in unscrupulous hands, it can provide an easy way to use up bad fish. Nonetheless, if well made with good ingredients, it can be a delight.

Its name, spelled *zarzuela* in Castilian, in fact means a kind of operetta or musical comedy—the implication being that this is a sort of variety-show of a dish, presumably not to be taken too seriously.

There is no one standard recipe for *sarsuela*, but this one is based on several versions of the dish I've had in Barcelona. Needless to say, the selection of fish and shellfish used is almost infinitely variable. The late, highly respected Catalan chef Ignasi Domènech, incidentally, says that a *sarsuela* made with lobster should be called an *opera*—an obvious upgrading. I've included lobster (or spiny lobster) here, but it may certainly be omitted.

TO SERVE 4 (AS MAIN COURSE)

One 1–1¼-pound spiny lobster or true lobster (optional), cut into serving pieces (see page 218)
4 prawns (scampi) or large shrimp, heads and shells on
1 pound rascasse (scorpionfish), rockfish, ocean perch, redfish, or any combination of the above, cut into serving pieces
4 small filets of Pacific, rex, or true sole
Flour
Olive oil
2 onions, chopped
3 tomatoes, seeded and grated (see page 7) or peeled, seeded, and chopped
3 cloves garlic, minced
½ cup rum
1 bay leaf
¼ teaspoon cinnamon
¼ teaspoon allspice
½ cup vi ranci (see note page 57) or dry sherry
Fish stock
4 squid, cleaned and cut into rings
16–20 clams (see note page 201)
Salt and pepper

In a cassola, Dutch oven, or soup pot, sauté all the fish and shellfish except the squid and clams, in batches, in a small amount of oil until lightly browned. Drain and set aside.

In the same oil, adding more if necessary, make a *sofregit* (see page 38) of onions, tomatoes, and garlic.

When the *sofregit* is finished, return the sautéed fish and shellfish to cassola, add the rum, warm slightly, and carefully ignite.

When the flames die out, add the bay leaf, cinnamon, allspice, *vi ranci,* and enough stock to cover the fish and shellfish halfway. Bring to a boil, and simmer for 10 minutes, turning the fish and shellfish several times.

Add the squid and clams, salt and pepper to taste, and cook for 5 minutes longer.

See Also:

Civet de Llagosta (Spiny Lobster Stew), page 139

Romesco de Peix (Tarragona Seafood Stew), page 223

ROMESCO

"I don't think there are many cities in the world," Josep Pla once wrote, "that have, in addition to an incomparable past, a splendorous present and a uniquely beautiful location, a sauce of their own." The city he's talking about is Tarragona, the fabled old Roman capital (and now modern business center) sixty miles or so down the coast from Barcelona, and the sauce is *Romesco*—a Catalan classic based on pulverized almonds and hazelnuts, dried sweet peppers, and tomatoes. The word *romesco,* in fact, has three meanings in the region: It is a variety of dried pepper, small, ruddy-red, and medium-mild, also called the *nyora* (*ñora* in Castilian); it is a sauce; and it is a great seafood dish—perhaps the most interesting of all Catalan fish soups or stews. Local

tradition in Tarragona sometimes maintains that it is of Roman origin (hence its name), and journalist Angel Muro, in his book *El Practicón,* published in 1894, extended its pedigree even further back, suggesting that it had been eaten by the Celts in Tarragona and was in fact originally a Phoenician invention. A bit more modestly, another Tarragona journalist, Antonio Alasá, used to claim that a representative of the city had offered it to Jaume I of Aragon, The Conquerer, when he visited the region after his victory in Majorca in 1232, and that by the end of the thirteenth century, it was common among local fishermen.

The only trouble with all this supposed history, of course, is that the single most important ingredient of the sauce—the one without which, by common agreement, it would not be *Romesco*—is the *nyora* pepper, and peppers, an import from the New World, weren't planted in Catalonia until the sixteenth century. In reality, whatever its antecedents, the dish seems to have first appeared in the nineteenth century.

Scholar Charles Perry, who has made a special study of peppers both sweet and hot, tells me that he *thinks* the *nyora* pepper is the variety scientifically called *Capsicum annuum grossum/provar. pomiforme/sub-var. Conc. humilirotundum Haz.* So there. Whatever it is, it is not available in the United States—but I've had good luck substituting ancho peppers (called pasilla in California, though elsewhere that name refers to a spicier dried pepper) or small New Mexican peppers.

TO SERVE 6 (AS MAIN COURSE)

*3 pounds assorted ocean fish (see note
page 224), cut into small steaks
about 1-inch thick*
Flour
Olive oil
*1 dried ancho pepper (see page 222),
soaked in warm water for 1 hour,
seeded, and minced*
1 small spicy dried red pepper, minced
*1 head garlic, separated into cloves
and peeled*
1 slice fried bread (see page 40)
1 sprig parsley, minced
*12 almonds, blanched and roasted (see
page 39)*
12 hazelnuts, roasted (see page 39)
½ cup dry white wine
2–3 cups fish stock
*½ pound medium-sized prawns,
shrimp, clams (see note page
201), or mussels (see note page
36), in their shells*
Salt and pepper

Romesco de Peix

(TARRAGONA SEAFOOD STEW)

When Francesc Vizcarro Llambrich, win-
ner of the 1981 Concurs de Mestres Romes-
caires de Tarragona (Tarragona Master
Romesco-Makers Competition), was asked
what the secret of his winning recipe was, he
replied, "Black pepper." The late Antoni Adserà, whose little volume *El Romesco* is the
definitive study on the subject, quotes this anecdote as an illustration of the fact that there
really *are* no secrets for making *Romesco* (also
sometimes known as *romescada,* a name im-
plying large quantity and communal consumption)—other than the chef's native ability and
the quality of the fish. About the former, neither you nor I can do a thing; we've either got
the knack or we haven't. But, about the latter,
again, I cannot stress strongly enough the importance of using the finest, freshest fish and
shellfish possible, in this as in all Catalan
dishes. It really will make a difference. This is
my version of Adserà's *Romesco* recipe.

Dredge the fish lightly in flour, then sauté
in a cassola or Dutch oven in a small amount
of olive oil until golden-brown. Drain, and set
aside.

In the same oil, sauté the ancho or pasilla
pepper, the spicy red pepper, and half the garlic
cloves, until the garlic is light golden brown.
Remove the peppers and garlic from the cassola
with a slotted spoon, and set aside, reserving
oil.

Make a *picada* (see page 40) of sautéed
peppers and garlic, remaining raw garlic, fried
bread, parsley, and nuts, diluted with a few
drops of white wine.

Add the *picada* to the oil in the cassola, adding more oil if necessary, and stir in 1 tablespoon flour. Sauté for 1 minute; then add 2 cups of the fish stock and the remaining wine, bring to a boil, lower heat, and simmer for 5 minutes or until the liquid thickens.

Add the sautéed fish and raw shellfish to the liquid, adding more fish stock if necessary to barely cover.

Simmer on medium heat for 10 minutes, uncovered, and salt and pepper to taste.

Note. Virtually any kind of ocean fish may be used in a *Romesco de Peix,* but there should be at least three different varieties. Recommended fish include monkfish, swordfish, halibut, sea bass, turbot, rascasse (scorpionfish), cod, rockfish, ocean perch, and redfish.

Romesco I

(TARRAGONA-STYLE *ROMESCO* SAUCE)

In a little brochure on Catalan food specialties published by the Hostal Vora la Mar in Tamariú on the Costa Brava—far from Tarragona—*Romesco* is described as "the queen of Catalan sauces." This is a bit surprising, because the usual Catalan opinion outside the province of Tarragona is that *Romesco* is just some sort of amusing regional curiosity, not at all a serious sauce on the order of those four great Catalan classics, *allioli, sofregit, picada,* and *samfaina.*

This attitude, I think, is quite unfair. *Romesco,* I would argue, ought to be considered as the fifth classic sauce of Catalan cuisine—not only because it is attractive, full of personality, and uniquely Catalan, but also be-cause, like the other four, it has applications throughout the Catalan culinary idiom. We've just seen how it intensely flavors a fish stew; earlier, we've seen variations on it used as a sauce for *calçots* or green onions (see page 168) and as a salad dressing (see page 163). In the form presented here—a faithful adaptation of the city of Tarragona's official *Romesco* recipe—it can be used to accompany virtually any kind of simply cooked fish or shellfish —poached, grilled, fried, etc. The next recipe extends the possibilities still further.

TO MAKE 1–1 ¼ CUPS

*3 dried ancho peppers (see page 222),
    soaked in warm water for 1 hour,
    seeded, and minced*
*1 small piece fresh serrano or jalapeño
    pepper (½–1-inch long, to taste),
    minced*
Mild extra-virgin olive oil
2 tomatoes
6 cloves garlic, minced
*24 almonds, blanched and roasted (see
    page 39)*
24 hazelnuts, roasted (see page 39)
2 sprigs parsley, minced
2 slices fried bread (see page 40)
*2 teaspoons good-quality red wine
    vinegar*
Salt

Preheat the oven to 350°.

Sauté the fresh and dried peppers briefly in a small amount of oil.

Bake the tomatoes in a lightly oiled baking dish for 10 minutes; then remove and cool.

With a mortar and pestle (preferably) or in a food processor or spice mill, make a thick paste of the garlic and sautéed peppers.

Work the nuts, parsley, and fried bread into a mixture, mixing well.

Carefully peel and seed the tomatoes, and coarsely chop.

Work the tomatoes into the mixture, then add vinegar and 2–3 tablespoons of oil and salt to taste. Mixture should be thickly liquid.

Romesco II

(JOSEP MARIA MORELL'S *ROMESCO* SAUCE)

This unorthodox *Romesco* sauce, which contains no nuts and which is cooked instead of mostly raw, is a creation of Josep Maria Morell, owner/chef of Cal Morell in Balaguer—in the province of Lleida, a good many miles from Tarragona. It probably shouldn't even be called *Romesco,* in fact, but Morell calls it that, and it's very good, so who am I to argue? This sauce is delicious with fish, pork or ground beef, and even scrambled eggs.

TO MAKE 1–1¼ CUPS

1 dried ancho pepper (see page 222), soaked in warm water for 1 hour, seeded, and minced
2 cloves garlic, minced
1 sprig parsley, minced
Mild extra-virgin olive oil
½ onion, chopped
1 bay leaf
¼ cup good-quality red wine vinegar
3 tomatoes, seeded and grated (see page 7) or peeled, seeded, and chopped

½ a small spicy dried red pepper, minced
½ teaspoon cayenne
1 slice fried bread (see page 40)
1 cup chicken or vegetable stock
Salt and pepper

Make a *picada* (see page 40) of ancho or pasilla pepper, garlic, and parsley, moistened with about 1 tablespoon oil.

Sauté onion in a small amount of oil until golden and soft, then stir in the *picada.*

Add the bay leaf and vinegar, cook covered for 3 minutes, then add the tomatoes, spicy pepper, cayenne, fried bread, and stock. Bring to a boil; then lower heat and simmer, covered, for 30 minutes.

Remove the bay leaf, then strain out the solids, and purée them with ¼ cup liquid in a food processor or blender. Strain them through a food mill or fine sieve; then stir ¾ cup of the remaining liquid back in. Salt and pepper to taste. Discard the remaining liquid.

See Also:

La Calçotada, page 167
Salsa per Calçots (*Calçot* Sauce), page 168

MAR I MUNTANYA
("SEA AND MOUNTAIN")

If the Empordà region—the *comarques* of the Alt and Baix Empordà in Catalonia's (and thus Spain's) far northeastern corner—was indeed, as legend has it, born out of the union of a shepherd and a Siren, then *Mar i Muntanya* ("sea and mountain") must have been the main course at the wedding banquet. *Mar i Muntanya*, to be a bit less poetical about it, is sort of like Catalan "surf'n'turf"—a mix of seafood (most often spiny lobster, prawns, or shrimp, but sometimes other things as well) and one or more landbound creatures (usually chicken but sometimes rabbit and/or snails).

Unlike surf'n'turf, though, it doesn't merely pose its main elements next to each other awkwardly on a plate ("Say . . . what's this *shrimp* doing here?"): It cooks them together intimately, insisting that they drink in each other's flavors; it marries them—becoming thus symbolic of the Empordà's own happy confluence of land and sea.

It has been said that *Mar i Muntanya* was an invention of the seaside town of Calella de Palafrugell, just north of Palamós—but the idea of mating shellfish and poultry in the same pot dates at least from Roman times and has been widespread throughout the Empordà for as long as anyone can remember. In classical French cooking, chicken is sometimes served with a garnish or sauce of shrimp or freshwater crayfish (as in *poulet à la Nantua*, for instance)—the idea apparently being that the somewhat pedestrian bird will be ennobled by the savor of some distinguished crustacean or other. In the Empordà, at least to begin with, it was just the opposite: Chicken was expensive, taking time to raise and money to feed, while every cast of the net brought up prawns and shrimp and spiny lobster. Before refrigeration, of course, there was no way to ship this ample bounty inland and thus not much of a market for it. It had to be used up locally, and one way of doing this was to add it to the chicken stew—not to enhance the fowl so much as to extend it, to make it go further. Today, alas, it is the shellfish that is expensive—and even in its homeland, *Mar i Muntanya* is often now primarily a chicken dish. Even in this somewhat enervated state, however, it is a splendid dish—and a definitively Catalan one.

Mar i Muntanya I

(CHICKEN AND PRAWN RAGOUT)

I'm particularly fond of this interpretation of *Mar i Muntanya*, which is more or less a classic one, not only because I like the way it tastes but also because it was the first Catalan dish I ever made myself—or rather helped to make. I was in Sant Feliu de Guixols one balmy evening in July with my friends Luís and Charlie and their families (and the latter's Pyrénées shepherd dog or *gos d'atura*, Murphy), at a house the two take turns renting every summer. A communal dinner was in the making, with everybody drifting in and out of the kitchen lending a hand. Luís offered me a beer—a common Catalan aperitif—and asked if I wanted to help. "Of course," I said. The next thing I knew, I was frying bread, chopping onions and tomatoes, cleaning anchovies, and grating chocolate—a series of seemingly disconnected tasks which, at the time, I couldn't quite imagine adding up to anything coherent. (Surely we weren't going to put the chocolate and the anchovies into the same pot?) Eventually, though, everything became clear.

The anchovies were a first course, soaked and rinsed to rid them of their excess salt, patted dry, arranged on a large plate in an attractive crisscross pattern, and served with toasted French bread slathered with butter—delicious! Next, there were some tiny local mussels, steamed in their own juices and then generously bathed in lemon juice, and a salad of sliced tomatoes and cucumbers and whole green onions (separate, not mixed). The onions and tomatoes I had chopped were for the *sofregit* with which to start the main course, the *Mar i Muntanya* that was to be the evening's centerpiece, and the bread and chocolate were for the *picada* that would complete the dish.

The finished product was superb, if I do say so myself—as everyone agreed later in the evening over wedges of sweet melon and sweeter peaches and glass after glass of *cava*. This is the recipe I scribbled down between chores that night.

TO SERVE 4 (AS MAIN COURSE)

1 chicken, cut into 8 serving pieces
Olive oil
8–12 prawns (scampi) or large shrimp,
  heads and shells on
2 onions, chopped
4 tomatoes, seeded and grated (see
  page 7) or peeled, seeded, and
  chopped
½ cup dry white wine
Dash of Pernod
4 cloves garlic, minced
2 sprigs parsley, minced
1 slice fried bread (see page 40)
1 ounce chocolate (see page 40),
  grated

8 almonds, blanched and roasted (see
  page 39)
Salt and pepper

In a cassola or Dutch oven, sauté the chicken pieces in a small amount of oil until golden-brown. Remove them, drain, and set aside.

In the same oil, sauté the prawns in their shells until bright red. Remove them, drain, and set aside.

Pour off the excess fat, and then, in the same cassola, make a *sofregit* (see page 38) of onions and tomatoes.

Return the chicken pieces to the cassola, and add 2 cups water. Bring to a boil; then reduce the heat, and simmer, uncovered, for about 20 minutes.

Add the wine and Pernod, return to a boil; then reduce the heat again, and continue simmering. After 10 minutes, return the prawns to the cassola; then simmer for 20 minutes more or until the chicken is very tender, adding more water if necessary.

Meanwhile, make a *picada* (see page 40) of garlic, parsley, bread, chocolate, and almonds, moistened with a bit of cooking liquid.

About 10 minutes before the cooking is completed, salt and pepper to taste, then stir in the *picada*.

Mar i Muntanya II

(RAGOUT OF RABBIT, SNAILS, MONKFISH, CUTTLEFISH, AND PRAWNS)

This rather more elaborate—almost baroque—version of *Mar i Muntanya* comes from the attractive traditional-style Mas dels Arcs restaurant, on the outskirts of Palamós.

TO SERVE 4 (AS MAIN COURSE)

40 snails (see note page 100)
1 rabbit, cut into 8 serving pieces
Olive oil
4 prawns (scampi) or large shrimp,
  heads and shells on
1 pound monkfish, cut into 4 pieces
1 onion, chopped
1 tomato, seeded and grated (see page
  7) or peeled, seeded, and chopped
2 cloves garlic, minced
3 sprigs parsley, minced
1 cuttlefish, diced, or 2 squid, cut into
  rings
2 cups strong fish stock
1 slice fried bread (see page 40)
1 rabbit liver, lightly sautéed in oil
8 almonds, blanched and roasted (see
  page 39)
1 dried ancho pepper (see page 222),
  soaked in warm water for 1 hour,
  seeded, and minced
Salt and pepper

If you are using live or fresh snails, clean them thoroughly with a damp, rough cloth, making sure to rub off the "veil" at the opening of each shell; then rinse well and cover with salted water in a pot, bring to a boil, and simmer until done (about 30 minutes). Drain and set aside. For canned snails, drain and set aside.

In a cassola or Dutch oven, sauté the rabbit pieces in a small amount of oil until golden-brown. Remove them, drain, and set aside.

In the same oil, sauté first the prawns in their shells (until bright red) and then the monkfish (until golden-brown), adding more oil if necessary. Remove them, drain, and set aside.

In the same oil, again adding more if necessary, make a *sofregit* (see page 38) of onion, tomato, garlic, and ⅔ of the parsley.

Add the cuttlefish or squid pieces to the *sofregit*, and mix in well; then add the fish stock.

Return the rabbit to the cassola, and simmer, uncovered, for 15 minutes or until the rabbit is tender.

Meanwhile, make a *picada* (see page 40) of fried bread, rabbit liver, almonds, minced dried pepper, and the remaining parsley, moistened with a bit of cooking liquid.

When the rabbit is tender, stir the *picada* into the cassola, salt and pepper to taste; then add snails, prawns, and monkfish, and cook for 5 minutes more or until all ingredients are heated through.

Mar i Muntanya III

(RAGOUT OF RABBIT, PORK, SOLE, AND MUSSELS)

This is a more sophisticated, French-style *Mar i Muntanya*, as it might be prepared in the Roussillon—a *mer et montagne*, it might be called, and indeed *is* called in the book this recipe is adapted from, the first volume of French Catalan chef/author/nutritionist Eliane Thibaut-Comelade's *La Cuisine catalane* (L. T. Jacques Lanore, 131 rue P.V Couturier, 92242 Malakoff, France).

TO SERVE 4 (AS MAIN COURSE)

*16–20 mussels, cleaned (see note page
    36)*
3 ounces thick-cut bacon, diced
Olive oil
Flour
1 rabbit, cut into 8 serving pieces
*½ pound boneless pork loin, cut into
    4 thin scallops, or 4 thin-cut loin
    pork chops*
*4 small filets of Pacific or rex sole or
    ½–¾ pound sole cut into 4
    pieces*
1 onion, chopped
½ cup vi ranci *(see note page 57) or
    dry sherry*
½ cup tomato sauce as for Pebrots
    Farcits amb Porci Calamars *(see
    page 180)*
1 sprig parsley, minced
4 cloves garlic, minced
*½ pound fresh mushrooms, wild if
    possible (see page 88)*
4–6 threads saffron, lightly toasted
Salt and pepper

In a large pot, steam the mussels in ½ inch of water for 3–4 minutes or until they open; then cool them, remove them from their shells, and set them aside.

In a cassola or Dutch oven, sauté the bacon in a small amount of oil; then remove it, drain, and set aside.

Lightly flour the rabbit pieces, and sauté them until golden-brown in the same oil; then remove them, drain, and set aside.

Repeat this action with the pork and then the sole, adding more oil if necessary.

In the same oil, again adding more if necessary, sauté the onion until soft; then deglaze the cassola with *vi ranci* and 1 cup water.

Add the tomato sauce, parsley, garlic, mushrooms, and saffron; mix well, salt and pepper to taste, and simmer for 5 minutes.

Return the bacon, rabbit, and pork to the cassola, cover, and simmer for 15–20 minutes or until the rabbit is very tender.

Add the sole and mussels and simmer, uncovered, for 5 minutes more.

"Mousse" de Fetge de Pollastre amb Panses i Salsa de Crancs de Riu

(CHICKEN LIVER MOUSSE WITH RAISINS IN CRAYFISH SAUCE)

This dish isn't a *Mar i Muntanya* at all, and it isn't a main course, but it does mate poultry (or at least poultry liver) with crustaceans—in this case, freshwater crayfish. The recipe comes from the excellent El Castell restaurant in La Seu d'Urgell, a few miles from Andorra and about twenty-five from the French border, and is thus not surprisingly rather French in flavor. But the dish ends up being also, I think, a logical "new Catalan" extension of the basic *Mar i Muntanya* idea.

TO SERVE 6 (AS APPETIZER)

4 chicken livers, cleaned and coarsely chopped
2 ounces beef marrow, chopped
½ cup milk
1⅔ cups half-and-half or heavy cream
3 eggs
½ teaspoon nutmeg (freshly ground if possible)
Butter
Salt and white pepper
⅓ cup golden raisins or sultanas, plumped in warm water for 10 minutes
20 freshwater crayfish, cleaned
1 carrot, chopped
1 leek, white part only, chopped
1 onion, chopped
1 bay leaf
1 cup cava, champagne, or other sparkling wine
1 fresh black truffle, very thinly sliced (optional)
2 sprigs parsley, minced

Soak the chicken livers and marrow in milk for about 3 hours.

Preheat oven to 400°.

Drain livers and marrow, discarding the milk; then mix both well with ⅔ cup half-and-half, eggs, nutmeg, about ¼ teaspoon white pepper, and about ½ teaspoon salt. Purée in a blender or food processor until smooth; then pass the mixture through a fine sieve or food mill.

Butter six ½-cup molds generously, scatter raisins evenly on bottoms of the molds, then pour in the liver mixture, dividing it evenly. Bake in a *bain-marie* for 25–30 minutes or until done.

Meanwhile, crack the shells of 8 crayfish; then sauté them with the carrot, leek, onion, and bay leaf in butter for about 10 minutes. Add the *cava*, bring to a boil, and cook for 2–3 minutes; then add the remaining half-and-half. Continue boiling for another 2–3 minutes; then pass the sauce through a fine sieve, return to pan, and continue cooking until reduced to about 1¼ cups. Salt and pepper to taste.

Just before serving, steam the remaining crayfish until done (about 3–4 minutes).

To serve, allow the mousse to cool for about 5 minutes; then very carefully unmold onto warm plates. Gently pour sauce over mousses, then garnish with 2 crayfish per person, truffle slices (if desired), and parsley.

ESCUDELLA I CARN D'OLLA

(CATALAN SOUP WITH BOILED MEATS AND VEGETABLES, IN TWO COURSES)

There's a Catalan proverb that says, *"No és fa bona olla amb aigua sola"*—"A good soup isn't made with just water." Taking this advice to heart, the people of the *països catalans* tend to like big, serious soups, soups filled almost to excess with assorted meats and vegetables: heroic soups like the *ouillade* or *ollada* of the Roussillon, thick with pork, cabbage, and potatoes, traditionally cooked in two pots simultaneously and then mixed (pots which were never washed out, never allowed to cool); the *olletes* and *gaspatxos* of the *país valencià*, the former rich with white beans and sausages and sometimes huge cornmeal dumplings, the latter (unrelated to the *gazpacho* of Andalusia except in name) crowded with game birds and wild rabbit and perfumed with aromatic herbs; the legendary *"sopa sens aigua, foch, ni olla"* of the Balearics, made "without water, fire, or pot" (pork and/or chicken and six or eight moist vegetables baked in a hollowed-out pumpkin in the leftover heat of a baker's oven); the many fish soups and *sopes* of Catalonia itself, and the same region's *Escudelles;* and, above all, *Escudella i Carn d'Olla,* the very flesh and blood of Catalan bourgeois cooking—a soup and a stew and practically a way of life, all in the same pot.

Escudella i Carn d'Olla—an *escudella* is a bowl and by extension a bowl of soup; *carn d'olla* is meat from the *olla* or pot—is "the

oldest and most traditional dish of Catalan cuisine," author/chef Josep Lladonosa has written. Gironan gastronome Jaume Fàbrega calls it one of the idiom's "culinary chromosomes." Singer/songwriter and food-lover Lluís Llach maintains that it reflects "all the wisdom of the (Catalan) people." Author Manuel Vázquez Montalbán hails it as "the *Summa Theologica* of Catalan cuisine," and says that it was "for the Catalan bourgeoisie its pedigree . . . its credential as a society without pretensions, one that knew how to do things and that had adopted a European, democratic attitude."

And just what is this ancient, definitive, symbolic dish, exactly? It's the Catalan version of *cocido* or *pot au feu* or *bollito misto* or boiled dinner—root vegetables, cabbage, chickpeas, meatballs, chicken, sausages, etc., simmered together for hours to produce a rich, complex broth and then served in two parts: first the broth itself, in which some rice or pasta has been cooked at the last minute, then the vegetables and meats.

Some scholars consider it a direct descendant of the *adafina* of Spain's Sephardic Jews; others point out that the basic notion of such a hodgepodge is common to most of the world's cuisines, developing independently almost everywhere that there were pots, vegetables, and meats. Most Catalans seem content to let anybody think whatever they want about the dish; *they* know it is theirs and theirs alone. During the nineteenth century, which was the period of *Escudella i Carn d'Olla*'s greatest popularity in Catalonia, in fact, many families ate it for dinner six or seven times a week—adding minor variation only by altering the nature of the starch stirred into the soup (rice one day, *fideus* another, semolina another still, and so on, and even this according to the same fixed schedule week after week). Greater love for a dish hath no people.

Escudella i Carn d'Olla

(CATALAN SOUP WITH BOILED MEATS AND VEGETABLES, IN TWO COURSES)

It is said that after the great French Catalan military hero Maréchal Joffre had won the Battle of the Marne in 1914, stopping the German advance on Paris, his chef recited to him a magnificent menu for the victory banquet—to which Joffre responded that what he really had in mind in this moment of glory, thanks, was . . . yes, *Escudella i Carn d'Olla.*

One sees his point. Catalan hyperbole aside, it must be admitted that the dish is indeed an unusually comforting and restorative one—just the thing to soothe travails, salve wounds, revivify beleaguered spirits. It is, indeed, as Garrotxan chef Domènec Moli once wrote, ''a sumptuous, splendiferous dish, which marries the virtues of the vegetables with those of the meat, generating an unimprovable broth and a dish both strong and flavorful.'' True connoisseurs of *Escudella i Carn d'Olla,* in fact, will tell you that that unimprovable broth is the most important aspect of the dish—''an extract of a thousand essences'' and ''a résumé of the ingredients of the pot,'' Manuel Vázquez Montalbán has called it.

There's really no secret to the broth's richness—just long, slow cooking and high-quality

ingredients—and don't leave out the bones or the pig's foot (the latter of which adds not only flavor but thickness of body). And whether or not *Escudella i Carn d'Olla* sounds like your idea of a good way to celebrate a victory, it certainly can warm a chilly night or feed a hungry multitude.

TO SERVE 8 (AS APPETIZER AND MAIN COURSE)

8 ounces dried chick-peas (see note page 233)
6 ounces thick-cut bacon, diced
1 pig's foot, halved
1 small whole ham bone or 1–1½ pounds ham hocks
1 pound veal or beef bones
1 pound stewing veal, cut into pieces about 2 inches square
1 green cabbage, quartered
2 stalks celery
2 carrots
2 turnips, halved
1 chicken, cut into 8 serving pieces
10 ounces botifarra *sausage (see page 147), casing removed, or 10 ounces ground pork*
4 ounces ground veal or beef
2 eggs, lightly beaten
2 cloves garlic, minced
2 sprigs parsley, minced
2 tablespoons breadcrumbs
Pinch of cinnamon
Flour
4 medium potatoes, peeled and halved
2 botifarra negra *sausages (see page 147)*
Salt and pepper
8 ounces fideus *noodles (see note page 198) or large shell pasta*
Olive oil

Soak the chick-peas overnight in cold water, then drain.

In a large soup pot, add the bacon, pig's foot, ham bone, and veal bones to about 6 quarts of water; bring to a boil, and simmer, partially covered, for ½ hour. Skim as necessary.

Add the veal, cabbage, celery, carrots, and turnips; uncover, and continue simmering for 45 minutes.

After 45 minutes, add the chicken pieces, and cook 45 minutes longer, adding more water if necessary to cover the ingredients.

Meanwhile, crumble the *botifarra* sausage or ground pork into a large bowl; then add the ground veal, eggs, garlic, parsley, breadcrumbs, and cinnamon, and work together thoroughly until all the ingredients are well integrated and slightly sticky. Form the mixture into 2 cylindrical shapes, about 5–7 inches long and 2½–3½ inches thick. Roll the cylinders lightly in flour, and set them aside.

When the chicken has cooked for 45 minutes, add the potatoes and ground meat cylinders to the pot, again adding more water if necessary, and simmer 20 minutes longer.

After 20 minutes, add the *botifarra negra* sausages, then simmer for 10 minutes longer. Salt and pepper to taste.

Strain out three quarters of the broth, and transfer it to another pot, allowing the meats and vegetables to rest off heat, uncovered, in the original pot.

Bring the transferred broth to a boil; then add pasta, return to a boil, and cook 10–15 minutes or until the pasta is very tender (not *al dente*).

Divide soup and pasta evenly between 8 bowls and serve.

To serve second course, reheat meats and vegetables briefly in remaining broth, then strain out broth, reserving for another use (see below). Divide meats and vegetables evenly between 8 plates, cutting vegetables and *botifarra negra* into 8 pieces each and cutting meat cylinders into 1–1½ inch slices. Drizzle meats and vegetables lightly with olive oil.

Note: It is important for this recipe to use dried chick-peas, not canned ones, since they must cook in the broth to lend their flavor to it, and canned ones, already cooked, would disintegrate with long cooking. Leftover broth is delicious by itself, but I also like cooking rice in it as a side dish for pork or veal chops.

ESTOFAT DE BOU
(CATALAN BEEF STEW)

During the Franco era, when even *Playboy* was banned in Spain (and even *men*, if we are to believe James Michener in his book *Iberia*, were sometimes arrested for going topless), whole busloads of Spanish Catalans used to cross the border into France on Saturday nights and head up to Perpignan to see films like *Emmanuelle* and *Last Tango in Paris* and just in general to celebrate the weekend in permissive Gallic style. "Perpignan was wonderful when they'd come to town," a local resident told me once with obvious nostalgia (now that Barcelona and the Costa Brava have far surpassed the Roussillon in terms of open sexual divertissements). "The hotels, bars, and restaurants were full, for that night at least, and everybody had a good time." Then, on Sunday mornings, the Catalans would climb back into their buses, head west to Lourdes to cleanse their souls, and return to Spain.

But according to author Josep Pla, who spent much of his life a few miles from the French border, the flesh shown in erotic movies wasn't the only kind Spanish Catalans crossed into France to find. Perpignan was also the source of another sensual pleasure not easily obtainable in their own territory: beef. Catalans simply don't raise, or eat, much of this noble meat themselves. Pla, who loved good beef, called Catalan cuisine "a cuisine without beef," in fact—and noted that a nonbeef-eating people might well believe they had a complete diet anyway, but if they traveled abroad (even just to Perpignan) and tasted a good beef dish, upon returning home, they'd suddenly feel cheated by its absence. Thus, Catalans living near the French border sometimes acquired a taste for the thing and found themselves drawn back to France to find high-quality representations of it (most of which, Pla notes, came from Normandy or Brittany anyway, the Roussillon not being great beef country either).

There's a practical reason for the lack of beef in the *països catalans.* In a country with relatively little pasture land, bringing beef cattle to maturity would simply take too much time and space, and too much fodder. (Even those bullring bulls whose meat is so popular in some quarters are mostly fattened up in other parts of Spain and imported.) There are dairy herds, of course, especially in the Pyrénées, but cattle raised specifically for meat rarely make it past the point of being veal. This happens to be fine with the Catalans, however, since they are great fans of veal—that of the region of Girona being particularly favored—and, unlike beef, veal *is* much eaten in Cata-

lonia and vicinity. (Josep Pla accuses the Catalans of being infanticides in matters culinary, citing their love of veal as primary evidence.)

Bearing all this in mind, it is perhaps not surprising, then, that the single most famous beef dish in the *països catalans* is not some local variation on steak tartare or châteaubriand, but beef long stewed on a slow fire in a closed pot—*Estofat de Bou*—precisely the kind of dish you'd want to make if the source and quality of your beef were irregular and uncertain.

The word *estofat* derives from the Catalan verb *ofegar,* "to smother or suffocate," and the dish is thus by definition a stew "smothered" in a pot with a tight-fitting lid. Josep Pla once proposed, quite reasonably I think, that "Cuisine is the art of resuscitating cadavers, not of remurdering things already dead"—but I think he would have made an exception in this case, admitting that doing violence to beef in this manner does it good.

Estofat de Bou I

(CATALAN BEEF STEW)

This is a classic Catalan recipe. With slight variations, it has appeared in countless books on Catalan cuisine. This particular version is based on a formula I found in the November 1943 edition of the now-defunct Castilian-language Barcelona household magazine *Menaje.*

TO SERVE 4 (AS MAIN COURSE)

2 ounces thick-cut bacon, diced
1½ pounds beef chuck or other
stewing beef, cut into chunks
about 1½ inches square

1 cup vi ranci *(see note page 57) or
dry sherry*
2 onions, chopped
4 cloves garlic, minced
*1 sprig each of thyme, marjoram, and
parsley, tied together in a bouquet
garni, or ¼ teaspoon each of dried
thyme and marjoram, mixed
together well and wrapped
securely in cheesecloth, plus one
sprig parsley*
1 bay leaf
1 tablespoon flour
Salt and pepper
*¾ ounce chocolate (see page 40),
finely grated*
¼ teaspoon cinnamon
*1 pound new potatoes (if possible) or
small red potatoes, peeled and cut
into ½-inch slices*
1 botifarra *sausage (see page 147), cut
into ½ inch slices (optional)*

In a cassola or Dutch oven, sauté the
bacon on low heat in its own fat until golden-
brown; then remove with a slotted spoon and
set aside.

Sauté the beef chunks in bacon fat until
lightly browned; then return bacon to the cassola, and deglaze with *vi ranci.*

Add the onions, garlic, and herbs to the
cassola, and stir in flour; then add 1 pint water
and salt and pepper to taste.

Simmer, covered, for 2½ hours, stirring
occasionally.

After 2½ hours, stir in the chocolate and
cinnamon, and add potatoes.

Continue simmering, still covered, for ½
hour longer or until the potatoes are soft but
not disintegrated. Add more water if necessary.

If desired, fry the *botifarra* slices in their
own fat until golden-brown.

Before serving, remove the bouquet garni.
Garnish the *estofat* with fried *botifarra* pieces
if desired.

Estofat de Bou II

(CATALAN BEEF STEW WITH ORANGE PEEL AND BLACK OLIVES)

To be perfectly honest, I'm not sure this is
really a Catalan recipe at all. I first had the dish
some years ago at a little Catalan restaurant in
Paris called La Sardana, where it was *described*
as Catalan. The combination of orange peel and
black olives stewed with meat, however, is typical of Provence—and I wonder if the dish
might not have wandered over to Catalonia
from there. I certainly haven't run across it in
any of the Catalan sources I've consulted
(which have been legion); on the other hand,
the ingredients are all typically Catalan, and
the dish is a good one—so here it is, based on
my recollections of the way it was served at La
Sardana.

TO SERVE 4 (AS MAIN COURSE)

5 ounces thick-cut bacon, cut into
  ½-inch cubes
Olive oil
2 pounds lean beef round, skirt steak,
  or stewing beef, cut into pieces
  about 1½-inch square
2 onions, chopped
2 cups full-bodied red wine (Priorat,
  Côtes-du-Rhône, Petite Sirah, etc.)
1 ounce fresh orange peel (peel of
  about 1 medium-sized orange),
  pith removed, cut into very fine
  julienne strips about 1-inch long
2 bay leaves
4 cloves garlic, minced
2 sprigs parsley, minced
1 cup Niçoise olives or other
  good-quality Provençal, Italian, or
  Spanish black olives, pitted
Salt and pepper

In a cassola or Dutch oven, sauté the bacon in a small amount of oil until lightly browned. Remove and set aside.

In the same oil, sauté the beef in batches until well-browned. Remove it, and set aside with the bacon.

In the same oil, adding more if necessary, make a *sofregit* (see page 38) of onions.

Preheat oven to 325°.

When the *sofregit* is ready, return the beef and bacon to the cassola; add the red wine, orange peel, bay leaves, garlic, and parsley, bring to a boil, then remove from heat.

Cut a piece of cooking parchment to fit snugly inside the cassola; then carefully push it down so that it covers the beef mixture, rest-ing lightly on top of it. Cover the cassola, and bake for 3½–4 hours, adding olives and salt and pepper to taste after 2 hours.

Note: Estofat should be very thick, with very little liquid, and the meat should be falling apart. It is best to make this dish at least 24 hours in advance. If it has been refrigerated overnight, skim excess fat off the top before reheating.

Estofat de Quaresma

(CATALAN VEGETABLE STEW)

Any favorite Catalan meat dish which *can* be adapted to fish or vegetables *is* adapted to fish or vegetables. That's one of the imperatives of a strongly Roman Catholic society that both loves to eat and seeks (or at least used to seek) to observe the laws of dietary abstinence. *Estofat de quaresma* literally means "Lenten stew," and was thus a dish created for the pre-Easter period, during which the faithful were obliged to abstain from meat on many occasions. Today, regardless of one's religious orientation, it makes an agreeable vegetarian main course, but is also a nice side dish to accompany meat or fowl. The recipe is adapted from Ferran Agulló's classic *Llibre de la cuina catalana,* first published in 1933.

TO SERVE 4 (AS MAIN COURSE) OR
6–8 (AS SIDE DISH)

1½ cups dried fava beans, butter
  beans, or lima beans (see note
  page 237)
2 slices fried bread (see page 40),
  chopped or crumbled
Olive oil

3 onions, minced
1 head garlic, separated into cloves
and peeled
4 tomatoes, seeded and grated (see
page 7) or peeled, seeded, and
chopped
1 large sprig fresh mint, or ½
teaspoon dried
2 sprigs parsley
2 pounds red potatoes, scrubbed and
quartered but unpeeled
1 pound shelled fresh peas (see below)
Salt and pepper
2–4 ounces butter to taste, softened

Soak the beans overnight in cold water, then drain.

In a cassola or Dutch oven, briefly sauté the breadcrumbs in a small amount of oil over low heat; then stir in the onions, garlic, tomatoes, mint, parsley, and beans. Add about 1 cup of water and simmer, covered, for about 15 minutes.

Add the potatoes, and simmer for about 15 minutes more, adding a bit more water if necessary.

Add the peas, mix well, and simmer for about 15 minutes more or until the beans are done. Salt and pepper to taste.

Remove the parsley and mint sprigs if desired, then stir in butter.

Note: Dried beans are preferable in this recipe, so that they can be cooked the full 45 minutes and thus add their flavor more fully to the pot. If you are using canned beans, strain their liquid into the pot and add the beans themselves 5 minutes before the cooking is finished. For frozen beans or peas, add them 10 minutes before cooking is finished. Do not use canned peas.

See Also:

Platillo de Vedella amb Olives (Veal *Platillo* with Olives), page 241
Platillo de Xai amb Pèsols (Lamb *Platillo* with Green Peas), page 242

PLATILLOS

"The *platillo*," warns a little volume on the subject called *Platillos de l'Empordà*, "is a dish of difficult and disputed definition." I'll say. The word itself, a Castilianism in Catalan, literally means "little plate" or "saucer." *Platillos* aren't small in size, though, like *tapas;* they're small in gastronomic stature, in the nature of their ingredients—or at least they were to begin with. Maybe. They are in general sauced dishes, stews or ragouts. According to some sources, they are by definition based on such things as offal, poor cuts of meat (lamb breast, chicken necks, etc.), or leftovers, simmered with fresh seasonal vegetables, often including wild mushrooms. Others maintain that it is slow cooking and dramatic combinations rather than poverty of ingredients that defines the *platillo*, and that the genre thus encompasses such dishes as *Ànec amb Peres* (Duck with Pears, see page 69), rabbit with prunes or snails, and the elaborate *plat de les set delicies* or "dish of the seven delicacies"—those being veal, pork, lamb, chicken, rabbit, meatballs, and wild mushrooms.

Still others marry the two concepts, arguing that true *platillos* mix rich and poor—like the legendary *es niu* (see page 284) or the less well-known *plat del dimoni* or "devil's plate" of partridge, dove, *botifarra negra*, bacon, snails, chicken-blood "meatballs," and the livers, necks, wings, feet, and gizzards of ducks and/or chickens—plus favas, peas, and other vegetables. *Platillos de l'Empordà* reports that, in principle, there's no such thing as a *platillo* of fish or shellfish—that what appear to be such are in fact *suquets* or whatever; no less an authority than Josep Pla, though, says that there most certainly *are* fish *platillos*—and that *suquet* is one of them. By some definitions, even roast partridge with stuffed cabbage rolls (a Catalan favorite) and pork-stuffed apples (see page 185) are *platillos*. *Estofats*, on the other hand, are not. Why not? Well, er, because they're *estofats*, that's why. . . .

What is certain about *platillos* is that they are a specialty of the Empordà region, and what is probable about them is that they are a remnant of medieval and possibly even Roman eating habits in Catalonia. Meals in those earlier times in the region were usually served in two courses—first a roast of some kind (meat, fish, game, or fowl), then a sauced dish, cooked in a cauldron overhanging the roasting fire and based on scraps or discards from that roast, trimmed off and set to stew beforehand. (Later, the stew was sometimes eaten first.) It was these latter dishes that apparently developed into *platillos*. They thus began as glosses or asides, and like the predella paintings on the borders of Renaissance altarpieces, they were complex in themselves but still subservient to a larger work. I have no doubt, then, that originally they *were* made only from poor materials. I also have no doubt that, just as the experimentation common to predella paintings eventually found its way into the artistic mainstream, so did the culinary elaborations with

which these minor products were enhanced eventually find themselves applied to nobler substances.

Today, then, *platillos* can be made with good cuts of meat. They can also be made, I would maintain—citing Josep Pla and a number of contemporary Empordanese chefs as my authorities—with seafood. And they can certainly stand alone, as main dishes, without a roast at hand. That still doesn't define them once and for all, of course, or establish incontrovertibly what is or is not a *platillo*—but it's the best I can do, given the confusion of the Catalans themselves over the matter.

Platillo de Sèpia amb Verdures

(CUTTLEFISH *PLATILLO* WITH VEGETABLES)

This elaborate dish, truly a "grand" *platillo* if that's not a contradiction in terms, was created by the late Josep Mercader at the Hotel Ampurdán in Figueres. It is admittedly complicated and time-consuming to prepare, but the resulting dish is formidable in appearance, and complex and immensely varied in flavor—and I think it's well worth the bother.

TO SERVE 6–8 (AS MAIN COURSE)

4 pounds cuttlefish (see note page 240) or squid
4 carrots, 1 whole, 1 chopped, and 2 cut into sticks about 2 inches long and ½ inch in diameter
2 leeks, 1 whole and 1 chopped
8 ounces hake, grouper, sea bass, halibut, or other firm-fleshed

ocean whitefish, in 1 piece
6 ounces thick-cut salt cod, desalted
    (see page 79), skinned, and boned,
    in 1 piece
2 onions, chopped
2 tomatoes, seeded and grated (see
    page 7) or peeled, seeded, and
    chopped
6 cloves garlic, minced
6 sprigs parsley, minced
2 tablespoons lard
Olive oil
12 green onions or scallions, trimmed
    to 4-inch lengths
1 turnip, cut into sticks about 2
    inches long and 1/2 inch in
    diameter
4 baby artichokes, stems and tough
    outer leaves removed, quartered,
    or 6–8 artichoke hearts, halved
2 cardoons, peeled and cut into sticks
    about 2 inches long and 1/2 inch
    in diameter (optional)
6 small red potatoes, peeled and
    quartered
1 slice French or Italian bread, crust
    removed, soaked in milk
1 egg
Pinch of nutmeg (freshly ground if
    possible)
Salt and pepper
Flour
1 stalk celery, chopped
1 bay leaf
2 sprigs fresh thyme, chopped, or 1/4
    teaspoon dried
2 sprigs fresh oregano or marjoram,
    chopped, or 1/4 teaspoon dried
10 almonds, blanched and roasted (see
    page 39)

10 pine nuts, lightly toasted
2 tea biscuits (Carr's Wafers, Lorna
    Doone cookies, etc.)
1 ounce chocolate (see page 40),
    grated
Anisette
1 tablespoon cuttlefish or squid ink
    (see page 66)
1 cup muscat wine (see note page
    240)

Clean the cuttlefish, carefully removing and reserving the ink sacs (see note page 67), then cutting off and reserving the tentacles and heads. Peel or scrape the skin off the cuttlefish, and reserve. Cut the cuttlefish bodies into 2 1/2–3-inch squares. If you are using squid, cut it in half crosswise. If you are using small cuttlefish or squid, leave whole.

Add the tentacles, heads, and skin to a pot with the whole carrot and leek, the hake, the salt cod, and water to cover. Bring to a boil; then reduce the heat, and simmer, uncovered, for 30 minutes.

Meanwhile, in a cassola or Dutch oven, make a sofregit (see page 38) of onions, tomatoes, half the garlic, and half the parsley in the lard and a small amount of oil.

At the same time, in another pan, sauté the carrot sticks, green onions, turnips, artichokes, cardoons (if used), and potatoes, one vegetable at a time, in a small amount of oil until lightly browned. Drain and set aside. Set pan aside. Do not clean.

Strain the stock, reserving the hake and salt cod, and discarding the vegetables; then add 2 cups of stock to the sofregit, stir well, and continue simmering.

Meanwhile, finely chop the hake and salt cod, and mix with the bread, egg, half of the remaining garlic and parsley, and nutmeg, and salt and pepper to taste. Form the mixture into balls about 1–1½ inches in diameter; then sauté them in the vegetable pan, adding more oil if necessary, until lightly browned. Add to the cassola.

Dredge the cuttlefish pieces in flour seasoned with salt and pepper; then sauté them in the vegetable pan, adding more oil if necessary, until lightly browned. Add to the cassola.

Wrap the chopped carrot and leek, celery, bay leaf, thyme, and oregano securely in cheesecloth, and add to the cassola.

Add vegetables in this order: green onions, carrots, turnips, artichokes, cardoons (if used), and potatoes, and continue simmering for about 15 minutes.

Make a *picada* (see page 40) of almonds, pine nuts, tea biscuits, chocolate, and remaining garlic and parsley, moistening it with a few drops of anisette and then mixing it well with the cuttlefish ink.

Add the *picada* to the cassola, then stir in the wine. Stir well, bring to a boil, then reduce the heat, and simmer for 10 minutes longer.

Remove the cassola from the heat, remove the herbs and vegetables wrapped in cheesecloth, and let the *platillo* rest for 5–10 minutes before serving.

Note: Use fresh cuttlefish if possible; otherwise, try to obtain fresh squid. The dish may be made with frozen cuttlefish or squid, but to the detriment of its flavor.

For muscat wine, use Muscat de Rivesaltes or Muscat de Beaumes de Venise from France if possible, or Quady Essencia from California, or a medium-dry California Muscat of Alexandria or Muscat Canelli.

Platillo de Mandonguilles de Lluç

(*PLATILLO* OF HAKE QUENELLES)

This dish is sort of a stripped-down relative of the previous one—a simple combination of delicate fish quenelles and green peas. The recipe is based on one appearing in a book called *Art de ben menjar (Llibre català de cuina)*, "The Art of Eating Well (Catalan Book of Cuisine)" by Marta Salvia, published in Barcelona earlier this century—probably in the late twenties or early thirties (the book is undated)—and later revised by Joan Cabané, the famed maître d'hôtel of Barcelona's original Hotel Colón.

TO SERVE 4 (AS MAIN COURSE)

1½ pounds hake, grouper, sea bass, halibut, or other firm-fleshed ocean whitefish
1 egg, lightly beaten
¼ teaspoon cinnamon
2 sprigs parsley, minced
Flour
Salt and pepper
Olive oil
3 onions, chopped
3 tomatoes, seeded and grated (see page 7) or peeled, seeded, and chopped
3 cloves garlic, minced
1 pound shelled fresh peas (see note page 241)
3 cups fish stock
2 tablespoons almonds, blanched and roasted (see page 39)

Poach the hake in salted water to cover until done (about 15 minutes); then drain and set aside to cool.

When the fish is cool, remove the skin and bones, shred the fish with a fork, and mix well with the egg, cinnamon, and half the parsley. Form the mixture into balls about 1–1½ inches in diameter, dredge in flour seasoned with salt and pepper, and sauté in a small amount of very hot oil until golden-brown.

In a cassola or Dutch oven, make a *sofregit* (page 38) of onions, tomatoes, garlic, and remaining parsley in oil.

Add the peas and fish quenelles to the *sofregit*; then add the fish stock, and simmer, covered, for about 20 minutes. Uncover, and cook for 10 minutes more, or until liquid reduces and thickens.

Crush the almonds as for a *picada* (see page 40), moisten with a few drops of cooking liquid, and stir into the cassola. Salt and pepper to taste, and simmer 5 minutes more.

Note: If you are using frozen peas, add them when the cassola is uncovered.

Platillo de Vedella amb Olives

(VEAL *PLATILLO* WITH OLIVES)

This recipe, from the book *Platillos de l'Empordà*, belongs to Tomàs Carreras, proprietor of the Sa Gambina restaurant in Cadaqués, on the Costa Brava.

TO SERVE 4–6 (AS MAIN COURSE)

2 onions, chopped
1 head garlic, separated into cloves and peeled, with 2 cloves minced and set aside
1 stalk celery, chopped
2 carrots, chopped
1 red (if possible) or green bell pepper, seeded and chopped
Olive oil
3 pounds veal brisket or other stewing veal, cut into strips about 2–2½ inches long and ½–1 inch thick
Flour
Salt and pepper
2 cups dry white wine
2 bay leaves
2 sprigs parsley, minced
8 almonds, blanched and roasted (see page 39)
8 hazelnuts, blanched and roasted (see page 39)
1 slice fried bread (see page 40)
4 cups veal or beef stock
1 cup tomato sauce as for Pebrots Farcits amb Porc i Calamars *(see page 180)*
1 cup green olives, rinsed and pitted (see note page 119)

In a cassola or Dutch oven, make a *sofregit* (see page 38) of onions, garlic cloves, celery, carrots, and bell pepper in oil.

Meanwhile, dredge the veal in flour seasoned with salt and pepper, and sauté it in small batches in a small amount of oil until golden-brown, adding more oil as necessary. Drain on paper towels, and set aside.

Pour off excess oil; then deglaze the pan with half the wine.

Add the veal and pan juices to the cassola; then stir in the remaining wine, and add bay leaves. Cook on medium heat until the liquid is reduced by half.

Meanwhile, make a *picada* (see page 40) of minced garlic, parsley, nuts, and fried bread, moistened with a few drops of liquid from the cassola and a few drops of olive oil.

Add the stock, tomato sauce, olives, and picada to the cassola and stir well; then cover the cassola, and simmer over the lowest possible heat for 4 hours, stirring occasionally. (The *Platillo* may also be cooked in a preheated 275° oven for 4 hours.)

Platillo de Xai amb Pèsols

(LAMB *PLATILLO* WITH GREEN PEAS)

Peas are well-loved in the Empordà—not "the scandalously bright and dense Persian green" of frozen peas (as author Josep M. Espinàs once put it), but the duller hue—and more vivid flavor—of fresh local ones. Catalans don't like their peas *al dente*, though. As with most vegetables in this cuisine, peas are cooked until they're very soft, almost mushy. This treatment may well be antithetical to contemporary French and American trends, but the plain truth is that vegetables of good quality cooked in this manner reveal a delicious (if untrendy) flavor of their own. This recipe, again from *Platillos de l'Empordà*, was created by María Àngels Aupí, an accomplished home cook and also owner of the Tot Pell ("All Leather") boutique in Figueres.

TO SERVE 6–8 (AS MAIN COURSE)

3 onions, chopped

3 tomatoes, seeded and grated (see page 7) or peeled, seeded, and chopped

1 sprig fresh thyme, minced, or ¼ teaspoon dried

1 sprig fresh oregano or marjoram, minced, or ¼ teaspoon dried

Olive oil

4½–5 pounds small loin or shoulder lamb chops

Flour

Salt and pepper

8 baby artichokes, stems and tough outer leaves removed, halved, or 8 artichoke hearts, halved

½ teaspoon cinnamon

2 bay leaves

2 pounds shelled fresh peas (see note)

6–8 threads saffron, lightly toasted

4 cloves garlic, minced

2 sprigs parsley, minced

18 almonds, blanched and roasted (see page 39)

18 hazelnuts, roasted (see page 39)

2 slices fried bread (see page 40), soaked in ¼ cup vi ranci (see note page 57) or dry sherry

In a cassola or Dutch oven, make a *sofregit* (see page 38) of onions, tomatoes, thyme, and oregano in oil.

Meanwhile, dredge the lamb chops in flour seasoned with salt and pepper, and sauté them in batches in a small amount of oil until golden-brown, adding more oil as necessary. Drain them on paper towels, and set aside. Set the pan aside. Do not clean.

Dredge the artichoke halves in flour seasoned with salt and pepper, and sauté in the same pan, adding more oil if necessary. Drain them on paper towels, and set aside.

Add the cinnamon and bay leaves to the cassola, then salt and pepper to taste. Add lamb chops and 4 cups water; then simmer, covered, for 1 hour.

Add the artichokes and peas, and continue cooking for 20 minutes.

Meanwhile, make a *picada* (see page 40) of saffron, garlic, parsley, nuts, and fried bread, moistened with a few drops of water from the cassola if necessary.

Stir in the *picada*, and cook for 10 minutes longer.

Note: If you are using frozen peas, add them along with the *picada*.

Fricandó

(BRAISED VEAL WITH WILD MUSHROOMS)

In French culinary terminology, *fricandeau* is either topside (rump) of veal or veal loin *(noix de veau)*, usually braised. The Catalan version of the word, *fricandó*, first appeared in 1767, according to author Nèstor Luján, describing a dish made from chicken. Today, in Catalonia, *fricandó* is veal again, though the cut may vary. My mushroom-loving friends in Barcelona and the Empordà tell me that the best mushrooms to use with this dish are *rossinyols de pi*, which, as far as I have been able to figure out, are simply *rossinyols* (chanterelles, *Cantharellus cibarius*, see page 88) collected in the forest. (*Pi* is Catalan for "pine.") Author Manuel Vázquez Montalbán, on the other hand, singles out morels as the best accompaniment—and in reality any flavorful wild mushroom, fresh or dried, will do nicely.

TO SERVE 4 (AS MAIN COURSE)

1 onion, chopped
1 tomato, seeded and grated (see page 7) or peeled, seeded, and chopped
Olive oil
1½ pounds boneless veal topside, shoulder, leg, or loin, thinly sliced as for scaloppine
Flour
Salt and pepper
1½ pounds fresh wild mushrooms or dried wild mushrooms reconstituted in warm water, cut into large slices
1 cup dry white wine
1 cup veal or beef stock

In a cassola or large skillet, make a *sofregit* (see page 38) of onion and tomato in oil.

Meanwhile, dredge the veal pieces in flour seasoned with salt and pepper, and sauté them in batches in a small amount of oil until golden-brown, adding more oil as necessary. Drain them on paper towels, and set aside.

Add the veal pieces and mushrooms to the cassola, stir in 2 tablespoons flour; then add white wine. Bring to a boil; then reduce heat and simmer, uncovered, for 5 minutes.

Add the stock and salt and pepper to taste, and continue simmering for 30–45 minutes longer, or until the veal is tender and the sauce has thickened. Add more stock if necessary.

See Also:

Ànec amb Peres (Duck with Pears), page 69
Oca amb Naps (Goose with Turnips), page 70
MAR I MUNTANYA ("SEA AND MOUNTAIN"), pages 225–230
and perhaps
Pomes Farcides (Pork-Stuffed Apples), page 185
Suquet (Catalan Fish and Potato Soup), page 219
ESTOFAT DE BOU (CATALAN BEEF STEW), pages 233–237

LLAMINADURES, FORMATGES, I BEGUDES «PASTRIES AND DESSERTS, CHEESES, AND DRINKS»

LLAMINADURES
(PASTRIES AND DESSERTS)

"El català," writes Eliane Thibaut-Comelade plainly and indisputably, *"es llaminer"*—"The Catalan is fond of sweets." There are, for instance, at least fifty traditional associations of specific sweetmeats with specific holidays in the region—*Panellets* (see page 57) for All Saints' Day, marzipan fruits and vegetables for Twelfth Night's Eve, cream-stuffed pastries in the form of fish for Easter, and so on. That the Catalan sweet tooth is no recent development may be seen by the fact that, despite the overall paucity of food shops in Barcelona before the seventeenth century, that city had its first pastry shop as early as 1382—very early indeed, considering that a great gastronomic capital like Paris didn't get *its* first one (which was Ragueneau, whose proprietor figures as a character in *Cyrano de Bergerac*) until 1608.

Though French- and Italian-style desserts and baked goods eventually became commonplace in the *països catalans*, the region's first pastries (which remain among its most popular) were Moorish in inspiration, and thus included lots of pine nuts and almonds, candied

fruits, marzipan, and flaky pastry (Charles Perry argues convincingly that rough puff pastry or *demifeuilleté* was a creation of Moorish Spain)—as in the delicious *bisbalenc* of La Bisbal d'Empordà, which is a long, flat, strudel-like confection filled with a sort of sweet squash paste and topped with pine nuts and sugar. The most famous of all Spanish sweets, the *turrons* or nougats of Xixona (Jijona in Castilian) in the dramatically beautiful mountains of the *país valencià* north of Alicante, are likewise of obvious Moorish descent. The basic form of the coiled pastry *ensaïmada* of the Balearics seems Moorish, too—though a definitive ingredient of the thing is lard *(saïm)*, which was hardly part of the average Moorish diet. (*Ensaïmades*, dusted with sugar, are eaten plain or with coffee, used as the basis for a kind of custard cake called *greixonera*, and sometimes served with ice cream on top—but Majorcans also eat them, during the last week before Lent, embellished with thin slices of *sobrassada* sausage and candied squash. I tried this specialty one spring morning at one of Palma's best bakeries, the Horno Santo Cristo, and thought it was about as good a thing as I had ever eaten.) And in introducing large-scale cultivation of citrus trees into the *països catalans*, the Moors might even be said to have brought the region its simplest and in a sense its most curious dessert of all, *suc de taronja*—which, though offered and consumed as an alternative to ice creams and pastries in restaurants all over Catalonia, is in fact nothing more than a glass of freshly squeezed orange juice—a rare example of Catalan gastronomic restraint.

The pastry and dessert recipes that follow range from the Moorish-derived to the blatantly French, from the medieval to the just-made-up.

Menjar Blanc

(ALMOND-MILK PUDDING)

Menjar Blanc, literally "white food," is said to have been invented in the monasteries around Reus, near Tarragona, sometime in the eighth or ninth century. (It should be noted that the French also claim it, under the name "blancmanger," as a creation of the Languedoc—but this claim isn't taken very seriously in Catalonia.) Catalans, even (especially?) Catalan monks, have always been notoriously clever at circumventing the dietary obligations of the Catholic Church—that is, observing the letter of the law on matters of fast and abstinence, while continuing to eat as well as possible under the circumstances—and *Menjar Blanc* apparently developed in the first place out of just such circumvention. In medieval times, the Church forbade not only animal flesh during Lent and other periods of abstinence, but even the milk of animals. The "milk" of almonds, on the other hand, was permitted—and Catalans began using this substance to enrich a variety of savory dishes.

Menjar Blanc, the most famous and enduring of these preparations, began not as a dessert at all, then, but as a kind of thick gruel made of pulverized chicken or seafood with spices, steeped in almond milk. Both the *Libre de Sent Soví* and the *Libre del coch* contain recipes for this kind of *Menjar Blanc.* In Catalonia today, however, the dish has pretty much left its medieval origins behind to become a mild, subtly delicious sweet pudding with a ghost of almond flavor. For the record, though, it should be noted that in giving a recipe for the *Menjar-Blanc*-like Ibizenco Christmas pudding called *salsa* in his privately published *A Catalan Cookery Book,* Irving Davis mentions that an old woman on the island advised him that, even for a dessert, the almond milk was better made with chicken broth than with mere water! The adventurous may wish to try that refinement on the recipe herewith.

TO SERVE 4–8 (AS DESSERT)

½ pound almonds, blanched and
*   finely ground*
1 tablespoon cornstarch
⅔ cup rice flour (see note page 247)
½ cup sugar
2 teaspoon grated lemon rind
1 teaspoon vanilla

Mix the ground almonds with 1 quart water in a bowl, cover, and refrigerate for 2 hours; then process the mixture very briefly (3–4 turns) in a blender at slow speed.

Strain the mixture through several layers of cheesecloth, compacting almonds and pressing all liquid out of the cloth into a saucepan.

Stir in the remaining ingredients, and

cook over low heat, stirring constantly, until thickened. Continue cooking and stirring about 7–8 minutes longer, or until no raw flour taste remains.

Pour into eight ½-cup or four 1-cup molds, and refrigerate until set.

Note: Rice flour is available at Asian markets and in health food stores. *Menjar Blanc* may be served plain, topped with toasted slivered almonds, or accompanied by fresh fruit or a simple fruit purée or unsweetened *coulis.*

Menjà-Blanc Frit

(FRIED ALMOND-MILK PUDDING)

This is a recipe from Minorca suggested by one appearing in Pedro Ballester's book on the cooking of that island, *De re cibaria.*

TO SERVE 4 (AS DESSERT)

½ recipe Menjar Blanc *(see recipe on page 246)*
Breadcrumbs
Butter
Powdered sugar

Before *Menjar Blanc* sets, pour into a lightly buttered square pan, about 8 × 8 inches. Chill for at least 3 hours.

Unmold, and cut carefully into 2-inch squares, then roll in breadcrumbs. (*Menjar Blanc* will be very delicate, so use as light a touch as possible.)

Fry the squares in butter until golden-brown; then drain them on paper towels, and dust with powdered sugar.

Crema Catalana

(CATALAN "BURNT CREAM")

Crema catalana is a rich custard usually covered with a sheet of caramelized sugar—and thus as a rule is virtually identical to the popular French dessert called *crème brûlée.* I say "usually" because purists claim that it is the nature of the custard and not its sugar topping that defines the dish, and that the sugar may in fact be omitted. At least one important restaurant in Catalonia, the highly rated Hispania in Arenys de Mar, just north of Barcelona, offers it both with sugar and without. Whatever its original form might have been, though, the vast majority of *crema catalana* served today does have a caramelized crust—and the dish is even sometimes known as *crema cremada,* which means "burnt cream."

Despite its similarity to *crème brûlée,* it should be noted, the Catalans claim to have invented *crema catalana*—and they may well have done so, since burnt cream was not at all well-known in France until recent years. (It isn't mentioned, for instance, in either Escoffier's *Le Guide culinaire* or the *Larousse gastronomique.*) The English, on the other hand, sometimes claim it as their own, noting that it has an ancient history in the dining halls of Cambridge University—and James Beard notes that burnt cream appears in a seventeenth-century recipe collection from Dorset. Manuel Vázquez Montalbán, who sometimes seems to disdain all contemporary Catalan cooking, says that most of what's offered as *crema catalana* in modern-day Catalonia resembles the real thing about as much as *"el caviar de plàstic"* resembles *"el caviar Beluga Beluga."* I hope he would class the *crema catalana* this recipes yields in the latter category.

TO SERVE 4 (AS DESSERT)

1 pint half-and-half
Peel of ½ lemon
½ cinnamon stick
3 egg yolks
¾ cup sugar

Heat the half-and-half, lemon peel, and cinnamon stick in a saucepan over medium heat until just boiling; then remove them from heat immediately, discard the lemon peel and cinnamon stick, and allow to cool.

Beat the egg yolks with ¼ cup sugar until thick; then strain the cooled half-and-half into the eggs, stirring constantly.

Reheat the custard mixture in a heavy-bottomed saucepan over low heat, stirring constantly until it thickens slightly and coats the back of a wooden spoon. Allow it to cool slightly.

Pour the custard into four 1-cup ramekins, custard cups, or 4–5-inch *cassoles* (see below). Allow it to set, then sprinkle each with a thin layer of sugar and caramelize until dark amber in color (see note).

Note: Sometimes, the sugar atop *crema catalana* is caramelized with a red-hot poker, pressed across the top in successive motions (though the ramekin must be very full for this to work, so that the lip doesn't prevent the poker from touching the sugar), or with a kind of branding iron made especially for this purpose. The sugar can also be caramelized under a very hot broiler, with a salamander (but make sure that the ramekins you're using can withstand the heat), or even with a miniacetylene torch.

Still another method is to line a cookie sheet with foil and butter it amply, then sprinkle ½ cup of sugar evenly in 4 circles the same diameter as the ramekins and broil in a hot broiler for about 5 minutes or until the sugar reaches the desired color. Allow the sugar to cool, then carefully

peel it from the foil and set one circle on top of each ramekin of custard.

The best dishes to use for *crema catalana* are small *cassoles* designed especially for this purpose. These *cassoles* and the aforementioned branding irons are available at Williams-Sonoma (see page 305) and at some of the other shops listed on pages 304–305.

Pomes Farcides amb Crema Catalana

(APPLES STUFFED WITH CATALAN "BURNT CREAM")

Stuffed apples are traditional in Catalonia, as is *crema catalana.* Whoever first got the idea to combine the two dishes deserves a medal. These are the best baked apples I've ever tasted.

TO SERVE 4 (AS DESSERT)

4 large baking apples
Butter
½ cup sugar
½ recipe crema catalana *(see recipe on page 247), without caramelized sugar*

Preheat the oven to 350°.

Core the apples, being careful not to cut through the bottoms; then pare a 1-inch strip from around the top of each.

Arrange apples in a lightly buttered baking dish just big enough to hold them.

Bring ½ cup water to a boil; then stir in half the sugar and pour the mixture over the apples.

Bake, uncovered, basting occasionally, for 30–40 minutes or until the apples are tender, and the skin begins to crack.

Remove the apples from the oven, and allow them to cool for about 10 minutes, continuing to baste occasionally.

Fill each apple with *crema catalana* (some may be left over), then sprinkle the top of each with the remaining sugar, and place it under a hot broiler or salamander until the sugar is dark brown.

Allow it to cool slightly before serving.

Flam de Poma amb Puré de Maduixa

(APPLE FLAN WITH STRAWBERRY PURÉE)

This lovely dessert is a specialty of the Restaurant La Riera in Sant Martí Vell in the Empordà region.

TO SERVE 8–10 (AS DESSERT)

6 large apples (about 2½ pounds),
preferably Golden Delicious,
peeled, cored, and coarsely
chopped
¾ cup plus 1 tablespoon sugar
1½ cups heavy cream
5 eggs
½ pound fresh strawberries, washed,
hulled, and drained
2 teaspoons kirsch

Preheat the oven to 350°.

In a large saucepan, slowly cook the apples with ¼ cup sugar and about 2 tablespoons water until soft (about 10 minutes). Remove them from the heat, and set aside to cool.

Meanwhile, in a small saucepan, combine ½ cup sugar with about 2 tablespoons water, and cook over medium heat until the sugar begins to caramelize; then continue cooking while stirring with a wooden spoon until the sugar turns dark amber.

Immediately pour the caramelized sugar into a 2-quart mold, quickly turning the mold from side to side to coat the sides and bottom evenly. Set aside to cool.

Scald 1 cup of the cream, then set it aside to cool.

Purée the apples.

Beat the eggs, and slowly stir them into the scalded cream; then strain the egg mixture into a large bowl. Stir in the apple purée; then pour the mixture into prepared mold.

Bake the flan in a *bain-marie* for about 1½ hours, or until a knife inserted into its middle comes out clean. Remove from the oven, and allow to cool to room temperature.

Before serving, purée the strawberries; then thoroughly mix in the remaining cream, kirsch, and 1 tablespoon sugar. Unmold the flan, and slice carefully, then serve topped with strawberry purée, or pour a shallow pool of puree onto each serving plate, and place the flan on top of it.

Puding de Patata

(SWEET MINORCAN POTATO CAKE)

This unusual *puding*—really more a moist cake—is made at the Rocamar restaurant in Maó (Mahón), the capital of Minorca, by Zulema Borrás, wife of chef and co-owner Josep Borrás.

TO SERVE 6 (AS DESSERT)

1 pound potatoes
3 eggs, separated, with whites stiffly
beaten
1 cup sugar
Zest of 1 lemon, grated
Butter
½ cup sliced almonds (optional)
Powdered sugar

Boil the potatoes in their skins until done; then cool them slightly, peel, and pass through a food mill or ricer.

Meanwhile, preheat the oven to 350°.

In a large bowl, work the egg yolks, sugar, and lemon zest into the potatoes, then slowly add the beaten egg whites.

Pour the mixture into a buttered 2-quart baking dish or pie pan; then bake for 20 minutes or until a toothpick inserted into the middle of the cake comes out clean.

If desired, sprinkle sliced almonds over the top of the cake 10 minutes before the baking is finished.

Cool, and invert the cake onto a serving platter; then dust with powdered sugar.

Flaó

(IBIZENCO MINT AND CREAM CHEESE TART)

This light and refreshing dessert, which is more or less a flan in a crust, is typical of Ibiza—but a remarkably similar recipe appears in the medieval *Libre del coch* under the heading "Els Flaons."

TO SERVE 6–8 (AS DESSERT)

2 cups flour, sifted
Butter
2 tablespoons lard
5 eggs
1 cup plus 1 tablespoon sugar
1 teaspoon active dry yeast
½ cup milk
1 pound cream cheese or fresh ricotta
*   cheese*
8–10 fresh mint leaves, preferably
*   spearmint, 2 of them minced (see*
*   note)*
¼ cup Pernod

Preheat the oven to 350°.

Combine the flour, 2 tablespoons butter, lard, 1 egg, 1 tablespoon sugar, yeast, and milk in a large bowl to form a piecrustlike dough.

Roll the dough out between 2 large sheets of wax paper; then press into a lightly buttered flan tin or pie pan, about 10 inches wide and 2 inches deep.

Combine the cheese and remaining sugar in a food processor or blender, or mix together thoroughly with a wire whisk; then add the remaining eggs, minced mint leaves, and Pernod, and mix together very well.

Pour the cheese mixture into the crust, and bake for about 20 minutes.

Arrange the remaining mint leaves in a spoke pattern on top of the tart, allowing 1 for each serving, then continue baking 10 minutes longer or until the filling is set and light brown in color.

Allow to cool to room temperature before serving.

Note: Fresh mint is essential for this dish; if you can't find any, make some other dessert instead—for instance, the *Gató de Formatge* which follows.

Gató de Formatge

(MAJORCAN-STYLE CHEESECAKE)

Bartolomé ("Tomeu") Esteva has been in the kitchen since 1932, when he was eleven, first cooking and then teaching other people how to cook. He has spent most of his career on the island of Majorca, where he was born—eighteen years of it as an instructor at the highly regarded local hotel school—but is proud of having also cooked briefly, he says, in France, Belgium, Holland, Germany, Denmark, Finland, and Bournemouth (!), and even at the North Pole. Through his travels, he has accumulated an incredible collection of nineteenth- and twentieth-century menus from all over Europe (with Majorca and Catalonia, reasonably enough, predominating)—at least 4,000 of them in all.

He has also accumulated a lifetime's worth of recipes, which he is now in the process of standardizing and cataloging for the busy and ambitious local restaurant association, the Asociación Empresarial de Restauración de Mallorca—for whom, in his semiretirement, he works as a consultant. Esteva was kind enough to offer me a selection of these recipes one afternoon, over a glass of homemade liqueur, which he concocts from his own formula of fourteen medicinal herbs, but which he himself is no longer allowed to touch, he says ruefully—because of his health. This is one of them—a traditional Majorcan dessert refined with the "Tomeu" touch. *Gató,* incidentally, is an obvious borrowing from the French *gâteau,* or "cake."

TO SERVE 6–8 (AS DESSERT)

2 cups flour, sifted
1 teaspoon active dry yeast
1 cup milk
Butter
Pinch of salt
¾ cup sugar
¾ pound fresh ricotta or pot cheese
4 eggs
1 heaping teaspoon cornstarch
1½ cups heavy cream
2 teaspoons grated lemon rind

Juice of ½ lemon
⅓ cup golden raisins, plumped in dark rum (preferably Jamaican) to cover for ½ hour, then drained

Combine the flour, yeast, milk, 4 tablespoons of butter, salt, and a pinch of sugar in a large bowl to make a dough; then knead until very smooth. Set the dough aside in a bowl, and let it rise in a warm place for ½ hour.

Preheat the oven to 350°.

Roll the dough out between 2 large sheets of wax paper to a thickness of about ¼-inch; then press into a lightly buttered flan tin, pie pan, or mold.

Combine the cheese, the remaining sugar, and the eggs in a food processor or blender, or mix together thoroughly with a wire whisk until very creamy; then stir in cornstarch, cream, lemon rind, and lemon juice.

Pour the cheese mixture into the crust and allow to rest 10 minutes; then bake for about ½ hour or until the filling is set, sprinkling raisins on top of the cheesecake after the first 20 minutes.

Allow to cool briefly, but serve slightly warm.

Pastís de Xocolata amb Banyuls

(CHOCOLATE CAKE WITH BANYULS)

Chocolate reached Spain from the New World in 1585, and in the next hundred years or so became a certifiable rage throughout the country—especially in the form of a hot drink. Historian Jaume Reventòs, pointing out correctly that the chocolate of Mexico was unsweetened and noting that the Empordà region of Catalonia had long since developed, by the time of chocolate's arrival, a cuisine that combined sugar freely with other strong flavors, suggests that the Empordanese might have been the first to mix cacao and sugar—thus creating chocolate as we know it. Less speculative is the fact that the world's first mechanical chocolate factory was established in Barcelona in 1780 and that chocolate has remained extremely popular in the *països catalans*—to the extent that Josep M. Espinàs is able to claim, "In Catalonia, chocolate is eaten like *escudella*—which is to say every day."

Catalans, however, express their love of chocolate in rather different ways than we (or, for that matter, their neighbors the French) do. Chocolate candy and chocolate-flavored cookies are well-loved in the region, as is hot chocolate—and, as we have seen, chocolate is often used as a minor flavor component in savory dishes; but chocolate desserts—mousses, cakes, elaborate pastries, and so on—are rare. There are no (or precious few) chocolate *dégustation* plates as there are in some restaurants in France, no confections bearing names like "chocolate decadence" or "death by chocolate" as we have in the United States. Chocolate ice cream and an occasional chocolate-cream-filled pastry are about the extent of it. Of all the places chocolate may be found in the Catalan diet, after a meal isn't very often one of them.

But clearly this book—like any cookbook worthy of the name these days—had to have at least one excessive chocolate recipe, and if I

couldn't find one in the *països catalans*, clearly I had to invent one. (I should say that recipe tester Linda Zimmerman had to invent one for me, or rather to fashion one after my basic idea.)

The notion was to use typically Catalan nutmeats—almonds, hazelnuts, and pine nuts—and somehow to incorporate the great French Catalan fortified wine called Banyuls. Banyuls is widely considered, not just in French Catalonia but in southwestern France in general, to be the only wine that can be drunk with chocolate. (Even the noted Gascon chef André Daguin holds this to be true.) Banyuls itself is rather chocolaty, but has a spicy, woody character, too, which sets it against the taste of chocolate very nicely—and it occurred to me that applying it to chocolate cake might produce a wondrous effect indeed. I must modestly say that I think I was right. Banyuls isn't easy to find in the United States, but it *is* available here—most often from the region's largest shipper, Templers. If you can't find it, ruby port may be substituted.

TO SERVE 10–12 (AS DESSERT)

½ pound plus 6 tablespoons sweet
butter, softened
¾ cup sugar
1 pound semisweet chocolate, broken
into pieces
6 eggs
1½ cups almonds, blanched and
roasted (see page 39), then ground
in a food processor or spice mill
1½ cups hazelnuts, roasted (see page
39), then ground in a food
processor or spice mill
1¼ cup Banyuls
1 tablespoon cornstarch
3 ounces unsweetened chocolate
⅓ cup pine nuts, lightly toasted
2 cups heavy cream, well-chilled

Preheat the oven to 375°.

Butter the sides and bottom of a 9-inch cake pan with 1 tablespoon butter. Cut a piece of parchment or wax paper to fit the bottom of the pan, set it in place, butter with 1 table-spoon butter, and dust with a bit of sugar.

Melt 12 ounces of the chocolate in a double boiler.

Meanwhile, beat ½ pound butter with the sugar until pale and very creamy; then beat the eggs into the butter one by one. Add the melted chocolate, ground nuts, ¼ cup Banyuls, and cornstarch, and stir together well.

Pour the mixture into the cake pan, and bake for 35 minutes.

Remove the pan from the oven, cool for 5 minutes, then gently run a dull knife around the edges of the pan to loosen the cake. Invert it on a rack, remove the paper from the bottom,

and cover the top of the cake with another rack. Allow to cool.

Meanwhile, melt the remaining butter and semisweet chocolate and the unsweetened chocolate in a double boiler.

At the same time, reduce the remaining Banyuls to half its volume in a small saucepan. Stir half the reduced Banyuls into the melted chocolate, and beat together vigorously. Let the remaining Banyuls chill in the refrigerator for at least half an hour.

Remove the cake from the racks, setting it on a serving plate; then slowly pour the glaze over the cake, smoothing over the sides and top. Sprinkle with pine nuts.

Allow the glaze to set before serving. (Cake may be refrigerated unglazed, then glazed and served cold.)

Just before serving, whip the cream with the remaining Banyuls until fluffy, and use as garnish on wedges of cake.

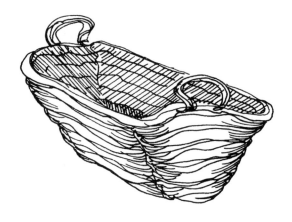

Refresc de Menta

(MINT SORBET)

This light, tart, refreshing, easy-to-make sorbet, rather Italianate in style, is a specialty of the Hotel Ampurdán in Figueres.

TO SERVE 4 (AS DESSERT)

¾ cup sugar
1 large bunch fresh mint (see note),
  thoroughly washed
¼ cup freshly squeezed lemon juice

Add the sugar to 1 quart water, and bring to a boil; then add mint, first cutting off 4 evenly formed sprigs and setting them aside. Reduce heat, and simmer for about 10 minutes.

Remove the pan from the heat, cover, allow to cool, then refrigerate for 10–12 hours.

Strain out mint, and discard; then add lemon juice to syrup, and stir in well. Process according to manufacturer's instructions in the ice cream maker of your choice (see note).

Garnish each dish of sorbet with 1 sprig of mint.

Note: Use fresh mint only; this recipe won't work with dried mint.

I highly recommend the Donvier Chillfast Ice Cream Maker for this and other ice cream or sorbet recipes in this book. It is inexpensive (about $30 for the one-pint size, $40 for the one-quart), fast (it makes ice cream or sorbet in about 20–30 minutes), and very easy to use. The Donvier is widely available at department stores, cookware stores, discount stores, etc.

Refresc de Muscat de Rivesaltes amb Figues i Menta

(SORBET OF MUSCAT DE RIVESALTES WITH FIGS AND MINT)

This recipe is not at all Catalan, but was created by the noted French pastry chef Gaston Lenôtre for a French-government-sponsored *"Les Produits du Roussillon"* promotion. It uses one of French Catalonia's best wines, the luscious muscat from the Rivesaltes region.

TO SERVE 6 (AS DESSERT)

1 bottle Muscat de Rivesaltes,
  well-chilled (see note)
12–18 ripe figs, peeled
12–18 fresh mint leaves

Simply pour a very cold bottle of Muscat de Rivesaltes into the ice cream maker of your choice (see note below) and process according to the manufacturer's instructions. The wine will freeze into sorbetlike form.

Carefully open each fig from the top with your thumbs and spread it open into 4 segments, like the petals of a flower.

Arrange 2 or 3 figs on each plate, and divide the sorbet equally among them, placing 1 scoop or rounded spoonful in each.

Garnish each scoop of sorbet with a mint leaf.

Note: Muscat de Rivesaltes is available in the United States, but not always easy to find. The more widely distributed Muscat de Beaumes-de-Venise may be substituted, as may Quady Essensia, a similar muscat from California.

Gelat de Canyella amb Culis Calent de Maduixes

(CINNAMON ICE CREAM WITH WARM STRAWBERRY *COULIS*)

This truly brilliant juxtaposition of flavors (and temperatures) was conceived by Rosa Grau, co-owner and chef of the innovative Florian restaurant in Barcelona.

TO SERVE 6–8 (AS DESSERT)

1 quart half-and-half
2 cinnamon sticks
1 tablespoon cinnamon
8 egg yolks
1¾ cups sugar
2 cups fresh strawberries, hulled (see note)
1 tablespoon freshly squeezed lemon juice

Scald the half-and-half with cinnamon sticks and cinnamon, then set aside to cool.

Beat the egg yolks with 1 cup sugar, until thick and lemon-yellow in color.

Remove the cinammon sticks from the half-and-half, and slowly whisk the egg mixture into it.

Allow the mixture to cool to room temperature, then refrigerate until well-chilled.

Process according to the manufacturer's instructions in the ice cream maker of your choice (see note page 255).

Meanwhile, purée the strawberries with the lemon juice and the remaining sugar, pass the mixture through a sieve; then heat gently until the sugar has dissolved and the *coulis* is warmed through.

To serve, divide the *coulis* equally between 6 or 8 plates, allowing it to cover the bottom of each; then top with 1 or 2 scoops of ice cream.

Note: I don't like frozen strawberries, but you may certainly use them if you wish. If decent fresh strawberries aren't available, though, I recommend substituting raspberries or other fresh berries.

Gelat de Crema Catalana

(CATALAN "BURNT CREAM" ICE CREAM)

Several Catalan chefs take credit for creating this dish, and indeed several of them might very well have come up with it independently (it is, after all, nothing more than a deftly simple alchemical transformation of one extremely popular kind of Catalan dessert into another, custard into ice cream). But as far as I can tell, the first person actually to serve a frozen *crema catalana* was the prolific Josep Mercader at the Hotel Ampurdán in Figueres. His idea, apparently, was that a warm or room-temperature version of the dessert might seem too rich after a big Catalan meal, but if you turned that richness cold, it seemed to cut through all that had come before. In any case, the results are quite wonderful—and, incidentally, almost impossible for the unsuspecting to identify.

TO SERVE 4 (AS DESSERT)

1 pint half-and-half
Peel of 1/2 lemon
1/2 cinnamon stick
3 egg yolks
3/4 cup sugar
Butter
1/2–3/4 cup blanched and roasted almonds (see page 39), roasted hazelnuts (see page 39), or roasted walnuts, or any combination of these, still warm and coarsely chopped (optional)

Make *crema catalana* according to the first three steps of instructions on page 247, but when cool, pour it into a large bowl, and refrigerate until well-chilled.

Place the remaining sugar in a saucepan with 2 tablespoons warm water, and simmer on low heat, shaking the pan gently but not stirring, until the sugar caramelizes and turns dark brown. Immediately pour it out onto a room-temperature, lightly buttered cookie sheet so

that it forms a thin sheet. Allow it to set, and when it has hardened, crack it into small pieces, and stir them into the chilled *crema catalana.*

Process according to manufacturer's instructions in the ice cream maker of your choice (see note page 255).

When serving, top with warm roasted nuts if desired.

_____

Note: When *gelat* is made according to the instructions above, the caramelized sugar will soften in the ice-cream-making process. In some versions of this dessert, cracked sugar is stirred in just before the ice cream is finished, so that it remains crunchy—also a nice effect. Alternately, caramelize about 1/4 cup additional sugar, harden and crack it as above, and then mix it with the nuts to be sprinkled on top of the ice cream.

"Cassata" de Fruites Seques amb Culis de Kiwi

(FROZEN CUSTARD WITH PINE NUTS, HAZELNUTS, AND WALNUTS, WITH KIWI *COULIS*)

Fruites seques literally means "dried fruits" in Catalan, but in common usage the phrase refers to roasted nuts. This frozen custard, in the style of an Italian *cassata*, is one of the signature desserts at the Eldorado Petit restaurants in Barcelona and on the Costa Brava. In defense of kiwi, I must say that, although it may have become a rather silly gastronomical cliché in the United States in recent years, it is really quite a delicious fruit—and both its acidity and its pale green color offset the creamy-sweet beige *cassata* very nicely. However, Eldorado Petit also sometimes serves this dessert with a *coulis* of strawberries (see page 256), if you prefer to try that—or perhaps a sort of yin-yang-patterned combination of the two.

TO SERVE 6–8 (AS DESSERT)

1½ cups sugar
½ cup pine nuts, lightly toasted
40 to 50 hazelnuts, roasted (see page 39)
40 to 50 walnuts, roasted
Butter
2 cups heavy cream
6 egg whites
3 kiwis, peeled

Caramelize half the sugar as for the recipe on pages 256–257, and while it is still liquid, stir in the pine nuts, hazelnuts, and walnuts; then immediately pour it out onto a room-temperature, lightly buttered cookie sheet and let set, also as for that recipe. When it is hardened, break into small pieces; then process into smaller pieces in a food processor or blender. Set aside.

Whip the cream and egg whites separately; then carefully fold the egg whites into cream. Slowly stir in the crushed nut mixture.

Pour the *cassata* into a rectangular 8-cup mold, and freeze for 24 hours or more.

When ready to serve, purée the kiwis with the remaining sugar and about 3 tablespoons water. Unmold the *cassata* by quickly running the bottom of the mold under hot water, then gently shake it from the mold. Cut into serving

pieces, 2 per person; then divide the *coulis* among 6–8 plates, and arrange *cassata* slices on top.

Peres amb Vi Negre

(PEARS POACHED IN RED WINE)

Both the French and Spanish Pyrénées are noted for the quality of their fruit, above all pears and apples. This simple, unusual recipe, taking advantage of fine local produce, comes from the Boix restaurant—an unexpected treasurehouse of gastronomic delights in the Cerdanya region on the Spanish side of the border.

TO SERVE 4 (AS DESSERT)

1½ bottles light- or medium-bodied red wine (for instance, Catalonia's Torres Sangre de Toro or Coronas, or Californian Pinot Noir or Gamay Beaujolais)
1 cup sugar
3 tablespoons whole black peppercorns
1 cinnamon stick
4 large, firm, ripe pears (see note page 259)

Mix the wine, sugar, peppercorns, and cinnamon stick together in a saucepan, and slowly bring to a boil.

Meanwhile, peel the pears; then cut them in half, and remove the seeds and stems.

Add the pears to the boiling liquid; then immediately reduce the heat, and poach the pears for 10–12 minutes or until tender. (Do not allow the liquid to come to a boil again.)

Remove the pears from the liquid, and cool to room temperature. Reserve the liquid, and just before serving, moisten pears with a bit of it.

Note: I like to make this recipe with comice pears, which, anyway, are about my favorite variety in the United States. Any good, sweet pear will do, though, including Anjou, bosc, Bartlett, or seckel. If the pears are particularly large or small, adjust the cooking time accordingly. Pears may also be cooled in the cooking liquid; the dessert turns out sweeter that way, because the syrup thickens and clings to the fruit—but remember that the pears will continue cooking as the liquid cools and thus might overcook.

I love black pepper in any form, incidentally, and thus like to scatter *my* pear with some of the peppercorns from the liquid, which I happily crunch away on with each bite of pear. I realize, however, that this might not be to everyone's taste.

Figues amb Aniset

(FIGS WITH ANISETTE)

Figs are very popular in Catalonia and, as often as not, are served with some application or other of anise flavoring, either in solid or liquid form—as in the dried fig cakes of the Priorat, for instance, pressed with aniseed and bay leaves. This recipe—too simple even to be called a recipe, really—is popular all over the region.

TO SERVE 4 (AS DESSERT)

2½–3 pounds fresh figs
Anisette

Carefully peel the figs, then halve them lengthwise.

Divide the figs evenly among four plates, cut side up, and drizzle with anisette.

"Mousse" de Figues

(FIG MOUSSE WITH WALNUTS)

This lovely recipe, from the Hotel Ampurdán in Figueres, is hardly more complicated than the preceding one.

TO SERVE 4–6 (AS DESSERT)

1 pint heavy cream
3 pounds fresh figs
2 ounces walnuts, roasted and
*   chopped, with 4–6 left whole*
Anisette

Whip cream, and set aside.

Halve the figs lengthwise; then, with a spoon, gently scoop out the pulp into a bowl.

Mix the pulp together a bit with a fork, then add it to the cream. Next, add the chopped walnuts and a few drops of anisette, and beat the mousse for several minutes with a wire whisk.

Refrigerate the mousse for 3–4 hours, then serve with a whole walnut, opened into 2 halves, garnishing each dish.

Bunyols

(CATALAN FRIED PASTRIES)

Bunyols (called *brunyols* in the Empordà, and related to what are known as *buñuelos* in the rest of Spain) are popular all over the *països catalans.* Said to have been invented (like so many other Catalan culinary delights) as Lenten fare—a kind of compensation for all that fasting and abstinence (rather like our own somewhat more sober hot cross buns)— *bunyols* are simply free-form little fritters of egg batter, suggesting wild mushroom caps (chanterelles, maybe) in shape and color, dusted with sugar and preferably eaten hot. *Bunyols* are traditionally associated with Saint Joseph's Day, and the ones sold on that occasion by street vendors in Valencia, which are very hot indeed, are something of a miracle in my book. One variety of *bunyols,* called *bunyols de vent* ("of the wind") for their airy texture, are almost ethereally light; the classic *bunyol,* though, as Josep Pla notes, should offer "a slight resistance to the tooth—but not too much, of course."

This recipe was developed for American kitchens with the help of Lluís Cruanyas of the Eldorado Petit restaurants in Barcelona and on the Costa Brava, and that of his chef at the former location, Joan Figueres.

TO MAKE 40–50 *BUNYOLS*

3 eggs
¾ cup plus 1 tablespoon sugar
2 teaspoons cinnamon
1 teaspoon salt
2 teaspoons anisette

½ cup milk
1 package active dry yeast dissolved in
  2⅔ tablespoons (8 teaspoons)
  warm water
3–3½ cups flour
Olive oil

Beat the eggs with ¾ cup of sugar; then stir in 1 teaspoon cinnamon, the salt, anisette, milk, and yeast. Add the flour gradually until a slightly sticky dough has formed; then cover the mixing bowl with plastic wrap, and allow the dough to rise in a warm place for 2½ hours.

When the dough has risen, heat at least 1 inch of oil in a heavy skillet or cassola to about 325° (or use a deep-fryer). Do not let the oil get too hot or the *bunyols* will cook too quickly and remain raw inside.

Scoop out about ½ teaspoon of dough in a teaspoon; then use another teaspoon to push the dough out into oil. Repeat the process, frying the *bunyols* in small batches until the dough is all used up. As they are done, remove them from the oil with a slotted spoon, and drain on paper towels.

Sprinkle them with the remaining cinnamon and sugar mixed together well, and serve slightly warm.

Neules

(CATALAN ROLLED COOKIES)

Valentí and his wife run a little general store in the front room of their house in Tortella, a village in the Garrotxa best known for its production of caned chairs. Here, they sell the local basics—chocolate, olive oil, pasta, canned tuna, rice, almonds, potatoes, dried beans, soap and detergents, wine and beer—and also operate a tiny bar, really no more than a few bottles of vermouth, strong wine, brandy, and anisette on a marble shelf within easy reach of the customers (who help themselves). Out back, though, on a little terrace beyond the kitchen (with its marble washbasin and wood-burning stove), is the machine that used to be the real focal point of Valentí's life, and the thing that drew most of his clientele.

It is a *neuler*, an old cast-iron contraption consisting of four double-sided pans, resembling small waffle irons, each about five inches in diameter, mounted on spokes extending from a central hub so that they can be rotated past three little fire pots. Each spoke is attached to the hub with a ball-and-socket hinge so that the pans can be flipped over, allowing each surface to be exposed to the flame in turn. They are designed to cook batter. Valentí is a master cookie maker—or, rather, he was until 1984. He specialized in two varieties of cookie, similar to one another, both rolled—*cubanets* (usually known by their Castilian name, *cubanitos*) or "little Cubans," so called for their cigarlike shape, and *Neules, nuela* meaning "fog" or "mist" in Catalan—a reference, I suppose, to their lightness.

Valentí's cookies are reputed to have been the best in the Garrotxa—and hungry *cubanet* or *neula* fans came even from the Costa Brava to buy his wares. But he shut down his machine and stopped making cookies, because his neighbors had begun to complain about the wood smoke drifting through their windows,

and because he had heard about lawsuits brought against artisanal bakers. What if a man already sick ate one of his *Neules,* for instance, and got worse—couldn't he be held liable? Anyway, he was getting old, and the general store took up enough time as it was.

In 1985, however, Valentí made *Neules* and *cubanitos* one last time. He is a fanatical admirer of "Barça," the Barcelona football (soccer) team—so fanatical, in fact, that his doctor forbids him to watch their games on television, because he gets so excited that he starts breaking things—and when Barça won the national championship that year, he simply couldn't help himself. He fired up his contraption, baked hundreds of cookies, and gave them out to one and all like a new father handing out, well, cigars. The cast-iron has been cool since then and will remain so.

Unfortunately, I wasn't around when Barça won. I have never tasted Valentí's *Neules*—and it would be presumptuous of me to think that I could reproduce them (in an ordinary oven, yet)—but with the help of recipe tester Linda Zimmerman, I have been able to come up with something at least approximating the *Neules* sold in good bakeries in Catalonia today. They turn out to be simple cookies, but very tricky to make. I sometimes think I could probably just go out and buy some cookies very much like these (they resemble the *tuiles* of France a bit, though they're completely rolled instead of just curved, tilelike), and nobody would know the difference, but I always feel a sense of accomplishment at having made them myself. . . . And I always feel a little sad that Valentí doesn't make them still.

TO MAKE ABOUT 30 *NEULES*

Butter
¼ cup flour plus flour for cookie
  sheets
3 egg whites
½ cup sugar
Pinch of salt
2 ounces melted butter

Preheat the oven to 400°.

Lightly butter and flour 2 or 3 cookie sheets.

Beat the egg whites, sugar, and salt together until frothy; then beat in ¼ cup flour and the melted butter.

Pour batter, about 1 tablespoon at a time, onto the prepared cookie sheets, letting each tablespoon spread into a very thin, almost transparent oval about 4 inches in diameter.

As each sheet is filled, bake on the middle rack of the oven 6–8 minutes or until evenly browned. (If the cookies brown unevenly, turn the sheet frequently.)

Remove the sheet from the oven, and immediately lift one cookie with a metal spatula, transfer it to a work surface, and as quickly as possible, roll into a tight cylinder. (See note.) Cookies may be rolled around the handle of a wooden spoon or some other thin round form, or they may be rolled free-form.

Repeat the process—cleaning, buttering, and flouring the cookie sheets as they're used—until the dough is used up.

Allow the cookies to cool completely; then store in an airtight container.

Note: It is important to work as quickly as possible when rolling *Neules*. Try baking only 2 or 3 at a time until you get the hang of it. Cookies must be rolled while still warm. If they cool off too much, place in a hot oven for several seconds until they soften a bit.

See Also:

Albergínies Dolçes (Fried Eggplant with Sugar or Honey), page 53
Panellets (Catalan Marzipan Cookies), page 57
Coca de Pinyons (Pine-Nut *Coca*), page 192
Coca de Sant Joan (Saint John's Day *Coca*), page 194
FORMATGES (CHEESES), pages 262–266

FORMATGES
(CHEESES)

The matter of cheese has been a great disappointment to me in the *països catalans*. I must hasten to add that I don't mean the cheese itself, for there are a number of superb ones produced in the region: the smoky, winy Formatge de la Vall d'Aran; the nicely sourish La Selva, a bit like a good Caerphilly or Wensleydale when young; the chalky, intense, delicious Montsec, La Garrotxa, and Santa María d'Olot; the forthright, Cantal-like Serrat; the firm, waxy Urgellet from La Seu d'Urgell, resembling a farmhouse Gouda (and from the same region, a fresh, tart goat cheese whose name I never was able to discover, that's both covered and shot through with finely ground black pepper); the excellent leaf-wrapped *chèvre* of La Vall de Ruitlles; the many fine Tomme-style cheeses of the French Catalan Pyrénées; the famous Mahón cheese of Minorca (the only cheese in the *països catalans*, and one of only four in all of Spain, to have been granted a *denominación de origen* by the Spanish government). . . .

No, the trouble isn't the cheese. The trouble is *finding* the cheese. To begin with, Catalans just aren't used to eating cheese after a meal. Thus the region's restaurants, even those of cosmopolitan pretension and/or high gastronomic quality, rarely offer much of a cheese selection—and what there *is* is usually French (with Roquefort and Camembert seeming to predominate), save for the (non-Catalan) La Mancha region's ubiquitous Manchego. The one exception to the rule is Catalonia's own *mató* (with its close relative, *recuit*), a fresh, ricottalike cheese traditionally eaten with honey or preserves (see page 264)—but that's really more of a dessert than a cheese course. Another problem is that, beyond *mató* (and *recuit*) and the aforementioned Mahón, most of the region's cheeses are still made with artisanal methods and thus in artisanal quantities, and—the encouragement of both the Spanish and the Catalan governments notwithstanding—are very poorly distributed. The same restaurateurs and shop owners who celebrate with happy chauvinism the quality of local fish, vegetables, baked goods, and so on, turn their backs on local cheeses—partly, it's true, because they haven't found much of a custom for them, but also partly because they're just so darned hard to come by.

I hope that this situation will change one day and that the recent great revival of interest in Catalan cuisine and Catalan raw materials will eventually extend to cheese as well. In the meantime, though, if you find yourself in Barcelona with a hunger for local *formatge,* you might want to visit the Cannes Bar (Doctor Joaquim Pou, 4), which offers tasting samples of some thirty or thirty-five Spanish cheeses, at least a dozen of them from Catalonia and vicinity (including a stunningly good La Garrotxa)

or to investigate such shops as Lafuente (Fernando, 29), Semon (Ganduxer, 31), Tivoli (Caspe, 12), or Casa Guinart, at the entrance to the La Boqueria market. (La Vall de Ruitlles *chèvre* and other rustic cheeses are sometimes available at the artisan's market held on the first Friday of every month on the Plaça del Pi.) Shops or markets carrying at least a few local cheeses in other corners of the *països catalans* include these: Casa Bonet in Sant Feliu de Guixols (Rambla Vidal, 24, just down the street from the noted Eldorado Petit restaurant); Colmado Roig in Lleida (Plaça S. Joan, 4); La Favorita in Palma de Mallorca (Mercat des Tenis); the Mercat Pagès ("Farmer's Market") in Ibiza; Marquet (Avinguda Carlemany) and Aleix (Avinguda Miquel Mateu) in Les Escaldes (Andorra); Viuda de Vela (Don Juan de Austria, 26) and Mantequerías Lauria (Lauria, 12) in Valencia; and Bremen in Alicante (Mayor, 22). I include no shops or markets in the Roussillon in this brief list because the above remarks about the paucity of cheese in the *països catalans* don't apply to its French precincts—which, being French, eat plenty of cheese, after meals and otherwise. A few Spanish cheeses are imported into the United States (most commonly Manchego, the lightly smoked San Simón from Galicia, and the blue-veined Cabrales from Asturias), but I have yet to see any Catalan varieties sold here. I hope this situation, too, may one day be remedied.

Mel i Mató

(FRESH CHEESE WITH HONEY)

The difference between *mató* and its cousin, *recuit*, is mostly one of form and texture. *Mató*, which is often sold in the shape of an inverted shallow bowl impressed with a sort of waffle pattern, greatly resembles true fresh ricotta, being slightly granular and rather, well, cheeselike in consistency. *Recuit*, usually packed into little terra-cotta pots or *cassoles*, is much smoother, with the look and substance of very thick clotted cream, and much less like ricotta, despite its similarity in name. Just to confuse things, though, *recuit* is sometimes called *mató* in Barcelona. In any case, both can be made either from cow's or goat's milk (the former being far more common), with *recuit* also sometimes employing the milk of sheep, and both taste very much alike—creamy, mild, and very slightly sour. Neither is salted. Traditionally, *mató* is made with whole milk (unlike ricotta, which is made with whey), and is set with what the Catalans call *herba-col*—derived from the blossoms of the cardoon (*Cynara cardunculus*)—instead of rennet. I suspect that modern-day commercial *mató* is manufactured without the benefit of this herb, though—and I suspect that any homemade pot cheese or ricotta-style cheese made with rennet would be a reasonable substitute. Otherwise, store-bought ricotta or pot cheese (unsalted) may be used.

TO SERVE 4 (AS DESSERT)

1 pound unsalted ricotta or pot cheese, homemade if possible

Cream (optional)
½ cup honey, preferably Spanish or Provençal
½ cup walnuts, roasted and coarsely chopped (optional)

Fluff up the cheese with a fork. Then divide it into 4 equal parts, and mold each portion into a flattened dome shape on each of 4 plates, or pack each portion into small terra-cotta pots, *cassoles*, or other similar vessels. (If the cheese is storebought and too dry, it may be thinned with a few drops of cream.)

Drizzle honey over the top of each serving, dividing it evenly, then sprinkle with the walnuts if desired.

Note: Mató is also very good, and very Catalan, topped with high-quality fruit preserves—especially cherry or strawberry.

Pa amb Formatge de Cabrot Torrat

(WARM GOAT CHEESE ON TOAST)

Warm goat cheese may well have become something of a cliché of nouvelle and "new American" cuisine, but this way of eating it has been around for centuries in the Roussillon.

TO SERVE 4 (AS DESSERT OR APPETIZER)

12–16 slices baguette-style French bread, cut ½–¾-inch thick

*12–16 slices (½-inch thick) round or
log-shaped goat cheese, about
2–2½ inches in diameter (for
instance, Montrachet without
ashes or Chenel or Kendall
California chèvre)*
Olive oil
Black pepper

Toast bread normally on one side only under a broiler or salamander; then remove and set aside.

Dip each slice of cheese in oil; then place it on the untoasted side of each slice of bread. Season with freshly ground black pepper, and return to the broiler or salamander, heating until warm. (Do not allow the cheese to brown.)

Camembert Fregit amb Confitura de Tomàquet

(FRIED CAMEMBERT WITH TOMATO PRESERVES)

The only thing really Catalan about this dish is the fact that it is served at the very good (and offbeat) Barcelona restaurant called La Odisea. Its vague sweet-and-sour flavor makes it a harmonious finish to a Catalan meal, in any case.

TO SERVE 4 (AS DESSERT)

*1½ pounds ripe tomatoes, peeled,
seeded, and coarsely chopped (not
grated), with juice reserved*
2 tablespoons lemon juice
1½ cups sugar
*1 whole 8–10-ounce ripe Camembert,
at room temperature*
Flour
1 egg, beaten
Bread crumbs
Olive oil

Cook the tomatoes, tomato juice, and lemon juice together until the mixture begins to boil; then lower the heat, and simmer, uncovered, for about 20 minutes, stirring occasionally.

Stir in the sugar, then cook over medium heat, continuing to stir, until the mixture is thick. Set it aside to cool.

Dip the whole Camembert in flour, then in beaten egg, then in breadcrumbs.

Fill a deep pan with at least 1 inch of oil (or use a deep-fryer), and heat the oil to 375°.

Fry the Camembert quickly until golden-brown on both sides, turning once if necessary; then drain on paper towels, cut into 4 or 8 wedges, and serve immediately with room-temperature tomato preserves.

See Also:

Flaó (Ibizenco Mint and Cream Cheese Tart), page 251

Gató de Formatge (Majorcan-Style Cheesecake), page 251

BEGUDES
(DRINKS)

Catalonia is a great place to drink, not only for all its good wine and *cava* ("champagne"), but also for the cocktails (*combinats* in Catalan), punches, and the like served in its profusion of cafés and bars. There are so many of the latter in Barcelona, in fact, and they are so important to the life of the city, that the popular local artist and designer Mariscal has proposed the charming theory that the city's very name is in fact a concatenation of the Catalan words *bar* (which means just what it does in English), *cel* ("sky," as in the bright blue one that so often frames the city), and *ona* ("wave," in honor of the Mediterranean, onto which Barcelona so casually gives)—these being what he considers the city's most attractive and definitive attributes. (The more common theory, it might be noted, though one disputed by etymologists, is that Barcelona's name has something to do with the Carthaginian leader Hamilcar Barca, who once ruled this portion of the Catalan coastline.)

One popular genre of drinking place, especially in Barcelona but increasingly in other cities in the region as well, is the *xampanería* or champagne bar, dedicated to the consumption of Catalan *methode champenoise* sparkling wines, usually with cocktails, snack foods, and desserts available too. For more serious drinking, Barcelonans visit places like El Dry Martini Bar (which offers a "martini of the day"), the Ideal Scotch (whose array of single malt whiskies is truly astonishing), Giardinetto Notte, L'Ascensor, Ricos y Bellas ("Rich Men and Beautiful Women"), the casually elegant Dos Torres, and the perfect little Boadas (see page 269)—all of them places, I can assure you, where the art of cocktail making is not dead.

There is a more down-to-earth kind of drinking done in Catalonia and vicinity, too—what might almost be called *folk* drinking, the drinking of real people, the everyday traditions of alcohol consumption not done for show or chicness. Instead of dry martinis and single-malt scotch, that means things like the *beguda de pobre* or "poor man's drink" I found a recipe for in one old volume—1 dozen orange peels, the juice of 3 oranges, 2 liters of anisette, and 1 pound of sugar, steeped in a pot for 24 days in the attic. It also means drinks like the Cuban-inspired *Cremat* of the Costa Brava, its far simpler counterpart the *Carajillo,* and the precocktail-era *combinat* known as the *Barreja*—recipes for all of which follow.

Cremat

(COSTA BRAVA RUM AND COFFEE PUNCH)

If you're lucky, some day you will have *Cremat* on the Costa Brava, preferably on a balmy night sitting a few feet from the sand on the crowded summertime terrace of the bar called Les Voltes in Calalella de Palafrugell. There, surrounded by the flower of Catalan youth (and that, it sometimes seems, of every other country in Europe), with perhaps just a few old local men off in the corner playing cards (the town is famous for its gaming prowess), you will have brought to you and your friends a large terra-cotta bowl illuminated with a graceful blue flame.

You will sit and watch the flame as it undulates and flickers, and you will stir the liquid in the bowl from time to time with a shallow ladle provided for the purpose. When the flame dies out, the alcohol burned off—the drink's name *means* "burnt"—you will apportion it out amongst the waiting cups, then, with your companions, lift it to your lips. And at just that moment, if you are *very* lucky, a handful of old-timers sitting in front of the house just up the road will pick up their guitars, start strumming softly, and begin to sing a *habanera*—one of the romantic, nostalgic, lilting ballads their fathers or grandfathers brought back from Cuba almost a century ago: "La Bella Lola," "La Gaviota," "La Caña Dulce," "La Reina del Placer." . . .

And if all this someday happens, you will quite possibly be convinced, at least for the moment, as I certainly was myself, that *Cremat* is the most delicious, wondrous drink you've ever tasted.

If, on the other hand, you happen to be sitting on an apartment balcony in New York City with the sound of screaming traffic in the distance, or in a rec room in Chicago with the Beastie Boys on the stereo, or in a backyard in Los Angeles with the neighbors' babies wailing at you from three sides, well . . . The stuff still tastes pretty good.

TO SERVE 4–6

1 cup Spanish brandy, warmed
1½ cups medium-bodied rum (for instance, Mount Gay Eclipse or Bacardi Añejo), warmed
3 tablespoons superfine sugar
2 sticks cinnamon
Peel of 1 lemon
4 cups strong black coffee, hot

Mix all the ingredients except the coffee together in a cassola (not one that has been used for cooking dishes in olive oil, since the oil will have permeated it and will affect the taste of the *Cremat*) or other *flameproof* (this is very important!) bowl or pot. Then carefully ignite the mixture. (It will flare up.)

Let the mixture burn, stirring occasionally (or continually, if you have the patience) until the alcohol has burned off sufficiently for the flame to die out.

Very slowly add the coffee, stirring well. Serve at once.

Note: For a more alcoholic *Cremat*, start adding the coffee before the flames have gone out completely, allowing the coffee itself to extinguish them.

El Carajillo

(CATALAN SPIKED COFFEE)

In Italy they call this drink *caffè corretto*, "corrected coffee"—the thing that was wrong with it in the first place having been its sorry lack of alcoholic strength. In Catalonia, the same thing is sometimes known in fancy venues as *café perfumat* ("scented coffee") or *café amb gotes* ("coffee with drops"), but in real life it bears a Castilian name, *El Carajillo*—a diminuative, as it happens, of *carajo*, a slang term for the male organ.

A *Carajillo* is simply a cup of strong black coffee with a shot of brandy or anisette added. I apologize for even presenting it as a recipe—but it is, after all, perhaps the single most popular alcoholic beverage, not counting beer and wine, in all the region, and as such demands inclusion here.

TO MAKE 1 SERVING

1 tablespoon (or more, or less, to
  taste) good-quality Spanish brandy
  or cognac, or dry anisette (see
  note)
1 demitasse cup of strong black coffee
Sugar (optional)

Add the brandy or anisette to the coffee, and stir well. Add sugar if desired.

Note: The best anisette to use is the Spanish variety, two of the best-known brands of which, Chinchón and Anís del Mono (the latter from Badalona in Catalonia), are widely available in the United States. Both companies make dry and sweet varieties; the former is recommended, but the latter (or any other sweet anisette, like the Marie Brizard brand) may be substituted—though this will of course alter the character of the drink somewhat.

La Barreja

(CATALONIA'S OWN COCKTAIL)

"The *barreja*," writes Garrotxan chef Domènec Moli, "is a brutal blow of the whip, strong, which stays the appetite and brings the whole body to life. . . . [It] isn't a drink for folks who eat white bread and store-bought chicken. . . . It is the first 'cocktail' indigenous to our own territory . . . a drink which defines a whole race."

After this buildup, you may perhaps be disappointed to learn how simple a thing the *Barreja* is. The word literally means "mixture" or "combination" (and also, in another context, "struggle" or "melee"—a sobering thought), and is traditionally an autumnal and hibernal mountain specialty. Irving Davis, in *A Catalan Cookery Book*, notes that it is best drunk from a *porró* (see page 289) while eating figs, and that in wintertime, when there are no figs, chocolate may be substituted.

TO MAKE 1 SERVING

2 ounces Spanish Moscato wine,
  well-chilled (see note)
1 ounce dry anisette, well-chilled (see
  note this page, left column)

Pour Moscato into a 4–6-ounce tumbler or wine glass, then add anisette, and stir once. The *Barreja* should not be served with ice, but both Moscato and anisette should be refrigerated before use.

Note: Robert brand Moscato from Sitges in Catalonia may occasionally be found in this country; in a sense, it is too good on its own to be used in a *Barreja*, but it does make a delicious one. Cheaper Spanish Moscatels are sporadi-

268

cally available around the country, too. If they are unavailable, a young Moscatel de Sétubal from Portugal may be substituted. The closest California equivalent is Beaulieu Vineyards' Muscat de Frontignan. Needless to say, avoid any muscatel with a screw top.

Alícia

Enough of "folk drinking." At least one sophisticated cocktail recipe is needed here, I think. When I spent a rather delirious week, in the spring of 1986, shepherding seven young American chefs and journalists around Barcelona in an attempt to introduce them to the pleasures of Catalan cuisine, our days were invariably framed by visits to two establishments—Boadas, a tiny, stylish bar just off the Ramblas on the Carrer Taller, where we would take a pre-luncheon aperitif, and Dos Torres, a beautiful mansion-turned-drinking-club on the Via Augusta, where we would usually find ourselves after dinner (which in Barcelona means around 2 A.M.).

Boadas is triangular in shape and paneled in dark lacquered wood, with a shiny brass rail on the bar itself; the walls are covered with scenes of elegant Barcelona bar life of the 1920s, with remembrances of the late proprietor's original establishment (in Havana, Cuba), and with sketches and photographs of the late Sr. Boadas himself—and, behind the bar, a small illuminated marquee advertises the *cocktail del día*, the "cocktail of the day." On our first collective visit to Boadas, that cocktail was the sidecar, a quintessentially 1920s tipple said to have been invented by a rich American in Paris during the First World War, who always traveled to his favorite watering hole (Harry's Bar, according to some sources) in the sidecar of a motorcycle. The drink was wildly popular in all the best European capitals (and among the American Smart Set) between the two World Wars, and, for whatever reasons, enjoyed another surge of popularity in Spain in the 1960s—and is still probably made more often, and better, in Spain than in any other nation.

In any case, some foolhardy member of our party decided that a sidecar would be Just The Thing, ordered one, and pronounced it delicious. It immediately became the official cocktail of our week-long tour—all the more so when we discovered, that evening, that Dos Torres also made a splendid version. Not everybody was convinced, though, and those of our number who didn't quite feel up to all those 1920s cocktails usually ordered a glass of *cava* in its place. (Boadas pours the particularly good Mascaró brand.)

On our last day together in Barcelona, in the haze of camaraderie that had by then developed among us, it was inevitable, I suppose, that the two factions—and specifically the two drinks—should somehow join together. This was accomplished at Boadas—on the amateur side of the bar, I hasten to add—by the simple if symbolic expedient of topping off a sidecar with a splash of *cava*. It was great—a sort of Catalan relation to the French 75. I dubbed it the Alícia, in honor of one noted member of our party.

TO MAKE 1 SERVING

2 ounces cognac or armagnac (do not use Spanish or California brandy, which make the drink too heavy)

½ ounce freshly squeezed lemon juice

¼ ounce Cointreau

Splash of sparkling wine, preferably cava (though champagne or good-quality California or Italian sparkling wine may be used)

1½-inch strip of lemon peel, 3–4 inches long

Shake the cognac or armagnac, lemon juice, and Cointreau together thoroughly in a cocktail shaker; then pour into a highball glass or large wine glass over 3 or 4 ice cubes.

Add a splash of sparkling wine (or more if desired) and garnish the rim of glass with lemon peel.

MISCEL·LÀNIA
«A MISCELLANY»

A handful of my favorite Catalan recipes just didn't seem to fit neatly into any of the preceding chapters. Thus, this miscellany . . .

Oliaigua amb Tomàtics

(OLIVE OIL SOUP WITH TOMATOES)

Oliaigua—the name literally means "oil and water"—is one of the simplest of all soups in Catalan cuisine. It is a specialty of Minorca and a dish that, according to Pedro Ballester in his classic book on Minorcan cooking, *De re cibaria*, "warms the stomach in the winter, cools it in the summer, and refreshes the tired body all year long." The simplest form of this simplest of soups literally includes nothing more than olive oil, water, garlic, parsley, and salt. The version presented here, given to me by Antonio Borrás of the Rocamar restaurant in Maó, adds onions, green peppers, and tomatoes (*tomàtics* in the Minorcan dialect).

"It's sort of a hot *gazpacho*," Borrás says— though, in fact, *oliaigua* (as Ballester's remarks suggest) can be eaten cold as well. "In the old days," Borrás told me one day, "we ate *oliaigua* with fresh peeled figs in the morning, taking a spoonful of soup with our right hand and a fig with our left. Then we'd have the same soup again for dinner, but with some strong, old, salty cheese and some cold grapes. *Oliaigua* should always be made the day before it is to be served, and the cassola in which we make it is never washed, only wiped out, and is used for this one dish exclusively." A less perfect *oliaigua* may of course be made in a conventional (and conventionally washed) soup pot.

TO SERVE 4–6 (AS APPETIZER)

2 onions, coarsely chopped
1 green bell pepper, seeded and coarsely chopped
3 cloves garlic, minced
Mild extra-virgin olive oil
4 tomatoes, peeled, seeded, and coarsely chopped (not grated)
2 sprigs parsley, minced
Salt
4–6 very thin slices French or Italian bread, lightly toasted

In a cassola or soup pot, sauté the onions, bell pepper, and garlic in about ½ inch of oil,

271

cooking over a low heat for about 15 minutes, stirring occasionally.

Add the tomatoes, parsley, and 2 cups hot water, then salt to taste. Simmer 15 minutes longer; then raise the heat, and cook until almost ready to boil. (Do not allow to boil.)

Place 1 slice of bread on the bottom of each of 4–6 soup plates, then ladle the hot soup over it.

Note: If you are serving the soup cold, use only a small amount of oil in the first step, and omit the bread.

Consomé de Pomes "Golden"

(GOLDEN DELICIOUS APPLE CONSOMMÉ)

The provincial capital of Lleida, once one of the most formidable citadels in Catalonia and today one of its most important industrial centers, has a reputation for being liberal-minded and imaginative—open to experimentation and change. Joan Lacorte is the assistant director of the fine Tarragona-based wine firm De Muller (see page 290) and lives in Tarragona itself, but his grandparents had a farm near Lleida, and he likes to tell this story as an illustration of the *lleidatà* approach to life:

"My grandparents grew cotton, but one day my grandfather decided that he wanted to pull out all the cotton and plant apple and pear trees instead. The local governmental agricultural advisers told him that that wouldn't work, because there wasn't enough iron in his soil. When he heard that, he promptly went to

a local factory and bought up all their iron shavings, then went home and plowed them into the soil." The punch line is obvious: "I don't know whether the agricultural adviser was wrong to begin with, or if the iron shavings worked—but the fruit my grandparents grew was the biggest and most delicious of the whole region."

I'm not sure what variety of apple trees Lacorte's forebears planted, but they might very well have been Golden Delicious. This species, hardy and productive and at least moderately true to the second half of its name, is today found in great quantity in orchards all over the *països catalans*. It is not always appreciated, it must be said. For instance, French Catalan food specialist Eliane Thibaut-Comelade, who has written a whole book on the apples of the Roussillon, claims that she never eats Goldens, far preferring her region's traditional *reinette du Conflent*—but the Golden Delicious is a fact of fruit life in Catalonia and vicinity, and more than one Catalan chef has created a recipe or two for it. This one comes from the one-star El Molí de la Nora in Vilanova de la Barca, just northeast of Lleida.

TO SERVE 4 (AS APPETIZER)

½ chicken
1½ pounds beef bones
1 onion
7 Golden Delicious apples, 6 halved and 1 left whole
Salt

Place the chicken, bones, and onion in a large soup pot with about 1 gallon water, then bring to a boil.

Skim the water, add the apple halves, lower the heat, and simmer, uncovered, until the liquid is reduced by half.

Drain and reserve the consommé. Discard the apple halves, beef bones, and the onion. Allow the chicken to cool; then remove the skin from the breast, and julienne the meat. Set aside the remaining chicken for another use (for instance, "*Pius Nonos*," page 72).

Return the consommé to the heat, and simmer. Salt to taste.

Meanwhile, peel and core the remaining apple, then cut it into ½-inch cubes. Divide the chicken and apple cubes evenly between 4 soup cups or bowls, then fill with hot consommé.

Note: This soup may also be served cold. If you are serving it cold, cook the apple cubes for 2–3 minutes in hot consommé, then remove them with a slotted spoon and set aside. Allow consommé to cool before placing it in the refrigerator. The consommé will gel when it is cold. To liquefy, beat well with a wire whisk just before pouring over the chicken and apple cubes.

Tumbet

(MAJORCAN VEGETABLE CASSEROLE)

"*Tumbet* is a dish that depends above all upon the quality of the raw materials," Majorcan journalist Pablo Llull warned me one afternoon in his office in Palma. "You can't do it with inferior products." The dish—which is simply an arrangement of sliced potatoes, eggplant, and bell peppers, first fried and then layered in a cassola and baked in fresh tomato sauce—is almost exclusively a summer dish in Majorca for just this reason. Majorcans can't conceive of making it with ingredients that are not at their best.

"You must understand how serious we are about our vegetables," Llull continued. "To give you an example, I have a friend who was going to build himself a new house a few years ago. He estimated that construction would take eight months. But the first thing he did, before beginning on the house, was to clear a garden and plant tomatoes. He was thinking like a true old-fashioned Majorcan."

Then there's the matter of eggplant: "Majorcan eggplant," Llull assured me, "is the best in the world, period. This is not just my opinion. This is an indisputable fact. Like [Andalusia's famous and extraordinary] Jabugo ham, it is unique. And the same is true of our potatoes. . . ."

To experience good summertime *Tumbet* for myself, Llull sent me driving off through the mountains north of Palma one July afternoon to the town of Valldemossa (where Chopin and George Sand spent the summer of 1838–39, to the subsequent and continuing delight of the local tourism industry), to have lunch at the Hostal Can Mario. Here, after a bowl of saffron-scented shellfish soup with rice, I had my first *Tumbet*—served as a side dish, as is usual, to some grilled baby lamb chops. Frankly, I found the potatoes rather mealy—but the eggplant was exquisite, and the dish as a whole was very good. The recipe below is my approximation, with apologies for the inevitable use of non-Majorcan products, of Can Mario's *Tumbet*.

TO SERVE 4 (AS SIDE DISH)

4 large Japanese eggplants or 2 small regular eggplants, cut into ½–¾-inch slices (see note page 275)
Salt
4 cloves garlic, minced
Olive oil
6 tomatoes, seeded and grated (see page 7) or peeled, seeded, and chopped
1 sprig fresh marjoram or oregano, minced, or ¼ teaspoon dried
2 large potatoes, unpeeled, cut into ½-inch slices (see note page 275)
4 bell peppers, preferably 2 red and 2 green, seeded and cut into ¼–½-inch slices

Spread the eggplant slices on several thicknesses of paper towel, salt well, and weight them with a heavy plate or baking dish for 1 hour; then pat the slices dry with paper towels, brushing off excess salt.

Meanwhile, sauté the garlic briefly in a small amount of oil, then add the tomatoes and

Bledes amb Panses i Pinyons

(SWISS CHARD WITH RAISINS AND PINE NUTS)

This is a version of the garnish used for *Bacallà a la Manresana* (see page 82)—itself an easy and unusual vegetable dish, particularly good, I think, with poultry.

TO SERVE 4 (AS SIDE DISH)

2 pounds Swiss chard, washed
thoroughly and with thick stems
removed, coarsely chopped (see
note)
2 cloves garlic, peeled and crushed but
not chopped
Olive oil
⅓ cup raisins, plumped in warm
water for 10 minutes
⅓ cup pine nuts, lightly toasted
Salt and white pepper

Blanch the chard in boiling water for 10–15 seconds; then immediately drain, and press the water out. Set aside.

In a cassola or large skillet, sauté the garlic cloves in a small amount of oil until golden but not browned. Remove and discard the garlic (or save for another use).

Sauté the raisins and pine nuts briefly in the garlic oil; then stir in chard, and salt and pepper to taste, and sauté for about 3 minutes on low heat, stirring constantly.

marjoram, and cook, covered, over low heat for 20–30 minutes. Salt to taste.

At the same time, sauté the potato slices slowly in batches in about ¼-inch of oil until golden-brown, removing and draining on paper towels as done. Then arrange the slices on the bottom of a lightly oiled cassola or baking dish.

Preheat oven to 350°.

Sauté the eggplant slices slowly in the same oil used for potatoes, adding more if necessary, until golden-brown. Remove them, drain, and arrange on top of potato slices.

Repeat the process with the bell pepper slices.

Pour the tomato sauce over the vegetables; then bake for about 15 minutes.

Let the *Tumbet* stand off heat for 5–10 minutes before serving, or allow it to cool to room temperature if desired.

Note: Try to choose eggplants and potatoes of approximately the same diameter.

Note: Though Swiss chard is preferable, this recipe works well with spinach, kale, and dandelion greens too.

Patates amb Allioli

(SCALLOPED POTATOES WITH *ALLIOLI*)

This dish combines two of my favorite foodstuffs, garlic and potatoes, with a simplicity and directness that I find almost luxurious. *Patates amb Allioli* go particularly well with grilled or roasted meats (see *Xai Rostit amb 12 Cabeçes d'All*, page 279, for instance).

TO SERVE 4 (AS SIDE DISH)

*4 large potatoes, peeled and cut into
¹⁄₂–³⁄₄-inch slices
Olive oil
1 recipe* Allioli Autèntic *(see page 30)
    or* Allioli amb Ous *(see page 31)
Salt*

Preheat the oven to 350°.

Parboil the potatoes in salted water for about 10 minutes; then drain and partially cool.

Place a layer of potatoes, slightly overlapping, in a lightly oiled baking dish; then spread with a thin layer of *allioli*. Repeat the process, finishing with a layer of potatoes, until potatoes are used up (there should be no more than 4 layers in all), and ¹⁄₃–¹⁄₂ cup *allioli* remains.

Bake for 30–40 minutes or until the potatoes are done.

Spread the remaining *allioli* on top of the potatoes, and brown lightly under a broiler or salamander. Salt to taste.

Note: I prefer to use *Allioli amb Ous* for this recipe, because it puffs up nicely when browned.

Conill Farcit amb Allioli de Poma i Mel

(STUFFED RABBIT WITH APPLE AND HONEY *ALLIOLI*)

There is a tradition in Spain that the nation's ancient name, Hispania (and thus its modern name as well), derives from a Punic (Phoenician) word variously rendered as *i-se-phamin* or *i-saphan-im*, meaning island or coast of the rabbits. Some scholars dispute this supposed derivation, but no scholar, to the best of my knowledge, disputes the fact that Spain has had a healthy rabbit population for at least 2,000 years. (The great Roman poet Catullus, in the first century B.C., once wrote venomously of *"cuniculosa Celtiberia"*—which I suppose might be loosely translated as "rabbity Spain.")

I've had slightly different interpretations of this rather elaborate and thoroughly delicious rabbit dish at two different Barcelona restaurants specializing in contemporary Catalan cuisine—Montse Guillén and La Odisea. This recipe is based on the latter's version.

TO SERVE 4 (AS MAIN COURSE)

*1 large rabbit (3–4 pounds), whole
4 ounces* pancetta *(see note page 149)
    or thick-cut bacon, minced
4 ounces lean ground pork
4 ounces* botifarra *sausage (see page 147)
Salt and pepper
2 onions, chopped
6 cloves garlic, minced
1 bay leaf*

*1 sprig fresh thyme, minced, or ⅓
  teaspoon dried*
Olive oil
2½ cups good red wine
1 recipe Allioli amb Fruta *(see page
  32), made with apples*
*2 tablespoons honey (preferably
  Spanish or Provençal)*

Wash rabbit thoroughly, pat dry, and remove the liver and kidneys and set aside.

Detach the front and hind legs of rabbit, and bone; cut the meat into small cubes.

Preheat the oven to 475°.

Put the *pancetta*, pork, sausage, and rabbit liver and kidneys through the coarse blade of a meat grinder, or process in a food processor until just mixed together. Work the cubed rabbit meat into the mixture; then salt and pepper to taste. (If desired, fry a small amount of the mixture, and taste to test the seasonings; then correct if necessary.)

Mix the onions, garlic, bay leaf, and thyme with about 4 tablespoons of the oil in a shallow roasting pan.

Rub the rabbit carcass inside and out with olive oil; then stuff the cavity with the meat mixture.

Roast the rabbit, breast side up, for about 20 minutes in the roasting pan with onions, etc. from step 5; then pour red wine over it, and turn rabbit over. Continue roasting until juices in the stuffing run clear (about 45–55 minutes).

Remove the rabbit from the oven, and keep warm.

Meanwhile, stir the honey into the *allioli*, mix well, and set it aside.

Pass the drippings from the roasting pan through a food mill or sieve (first removing and discarding the bay leaf); then reduce in a saucepan to about 1½ cups, and degrease.

To serve, slice the rabbit crosswise into 4 thick pieces, cover with sauce, and serve with *allioli* on the side.

Vedella amb Peres

(ROAST VEAL LOIN WITH PEARS)

His calling card read simply "Ramon Cabau Gausch, Agricultor"—farmer. Cabau was indeed a farmer, raising flowers, mushrooms, salad greens, fava beans and peas, and other crops on his handsome *finca* in Canet de Mar, just northeast of Barcelona—but he was far more than that, too: He was a licensed pharmacist; he held a law degree; and he was the founder (in 1962) and longtime proprietor of Agut d'Avignon in Barcelona—one of the most important and influential restaurants in modern Spain.

Cabau was in a sense the Alice Waters or Wolfgang Puck of contemporary Catalan cuisine—a champion of simplicity, a fanatic for first-rate raw materials, a redefiner of his field. Though he was a restaurateur and not a chef, he *understood* food deeply and intuitively, from the time it was produced until the time it was set down on the table—and, with Agut d'Avignon, he both reanimated the Barcelona restaurant scene and set new standards for professional cooking in Catalonia as a whole.

Cabau was a trim, good-looking man, dapper, a bit of a dandy, with bright eyes and a superb mustache. He nearly always wore a bow tie and a hat—usually a jaunty straw boater in the summertime and a plumed Tyrolean affair in winter. Alice Waters herself, who met and cooked for Cabau in Barcelona in 1986, thought he resembled a character out of her beloved Pagnol—unquenchably warm, vital, definitively Mediterranean. Locals called him "a Barcelona myth" and "a poet of the ovens."

In 1984, however, despite his great popularity and success, he decided to sell his restaurant—for personal reasons, it was said—and retire to his farm, to become a full-time *agricultor.* This at least assured him continued contact with an institution that was perhaps even more important to him than Agut d'Avignon had been—La Boqueria, the beautiful and richly stocked principal Barcelona food market (see page 295). Cabau was the king of La Boqueria. Everybody there knew and loved him, and his arrival in the mornings—striding down the aisles, tipping his hat and calling out greetings right and left—always seemed to kick the already bustling market into higher gear. (He told me once how pleased it had made him, the first time he entered the place as a competitor—a fellow vegetable seller and no longer an important wholesale customer—to find that everybody still hailed him with the same enthusiasm and affection.) La Boqueria was his life, Cabau liked to say; he felt as if he had been born there.

He also died there. On the morning of March 31, 1987, he arrived at the market at his usual hour, sold some produce, handed out flowers to friends, and then, before anyone realized what he was doing, drank the contents of a plastic glass into which he had dissolved a large tablet of what turned out to be potassium cyanide. One of the stallkeepers to whom he had been particularly close—Llorenç Petras, who sells wild mushrooms and snails at the

back of the building—heard him speak his last words: "I think this will be quicker." He could smell the strong bitter-almond odor of the poison on Cabau's breath, Petras later recalled.

Cabau's suicide shocked everyone who knew him. It was known that he had been depressed, but nobody had realized how seriously. He had been full of new plans, in fact—a TV series on Catalan gastronomy, a course of classes at a local hotel school, maybe even another restaurant. . . .

Cabau visited La Boqueria one last time. On the morning of his funeral, the hearse bearing his body paused at the portals of the market. Thousands of people, from within La Boqueria and without, crowded around the vehicle, covering it with wreaths reading "*A l'Amic Ramon,*" "To Friend Ramon." Then they applauded thunderously—"as if," one newspaper account suggested, "saluting a flawless performance in a popular opera."

Cabau sent me this recipe a few weeks before he died.

TO SERVE 6 (AS MAIN COURSE)

One 3–pound boneless veal loin
Olive oil
Lard
1 stalk celery, minced
1 onion, minced
1 leek (white part only), minced
2 carrots, shredded
3 tomatoes, coarsely chopped
1½ cups strong veal or beef stock
1 bay leaf
Salt and pepper
½ cup vi ranci (see note page 57) or dry sherry

½ cup cognac

*4 Winter Nellis or other
    small-to-medium-sized,
    firm-fleshed pears, each cut into 6
    pieces lengthwise, and seeded*

Preheat the oven to 425°.

Rub the veal loin generously with olive oil and quickly brown in a cassola or Dutch oven generously greased with lard. Remove the meat and set aside.

Sauté the celery, onion, leek, carrots, and tomatoes in the same cassola, adding more oil if necessary, until wilted. Return the veal to the cassola.

Roast uncovered for 45 minutes or until meat thermometer registers 170°. (It may be necessary to baste the meat several times during cooking with the pan juices.) Make sure the vegetables do not burn.

Remove the cassola from the oven, but do not turn oven off. Remove the veal, scraping off any vegetables that might adhere to it, and set aside. There should be about 1 to 1½ cups of liquid in the cassola.

Remove the vegetables from the cassola and pass through a food mill or sieve. Over medium heat, deglaze the cassola with the veal stock, *vi ranci*, and cognac. Stir in the puréed vegetables. Add the bay leaf and reduce liquid by about ⅓ to ½ depending on the thickness of the sauce desired. Salt and pepper to taste.

Return the veal to the cassola, covering well with the sauce. Roast for 5 more minutes, then add pears and roast for an additional 10–15 minutes or until the pears are soft.

Remove the veal from the cassola and allow to rest a few minutes. Thinly slice the meat, arrange on the plate alternating the pear slices with the meat, then nap with the sauce.

Xai Rostit amb 12 Cabeçes d'All

(ROAST LAMB WITH 12 HEADS OF GARLIC)

Vampires need not apply. This, as its very name proclaims, is a dish for serious garlic-lovers only. Of course, all that roasting softens and sweetens all that garlic considerably, but still. . . .

This recipe is a slight modification of one given to me by Ramon Parellada, proprietor of the delightful Barcelona restaurant called Senyor Parellada (and, incidentally, son of the owner of the acclaimed Fonda d'Europa in the industrial capital of Granollers, northeast of Barcelona, and grandson of the one-time proprietor of the legendary Set Portes or Siete Puertas in Barcelona itself).

Parellada, obviously not one to pussyfoot around in matters culinary, serves this dish with *Patates amb Allioli* (see page 276)—just to make sure nobody goes home without enough garlic.

TO SERVE 6–8

3–4 pounds lamb shoulder or
  butterflied lamb leg, cut into 6–8
  pieces of equal size (have the
  butcher cut the meat)
3 tablespoons lard
Olive oil
12 heads garlic, 6–8 (depending on
  number of servings) left whole,
  and the remainder separated into
  cloves and peeled
1½–2 cups vi ranci *(see note page 57)*
  or dry sherry

Preheat the oven to 425°.

Sauté the lamb pieces, 1 or 2 at a time, in lard and olive oil until well-browned.

Place the lamb pieces in a lightly oiled roasting pan or dish (preferably earthenware), large enough to hold the lamb and garlic heads and capable of being tightly covered. Sprinkle the peeled garlic cloves around the lamb; then add the garlic heads to the pan.

Roast the lamb and garlic uncovered for 20 minutes; then pour 1½ cups *vi ranci* over both, cover roasting pan, lower heat to 350°, and continue roasting for about 1½ hours. Check pan once to see if more liquid is needed, and if so add additional *vi ranci*.

Serve each piece of lamb with 1 head of garlic and a scattering of garlic cloves, and moisten the lamb and garlic with pan juices.

Note: Like most meat in the *països catalans*, this lamb should be very well done. If you prefer rarer lamb, shorten the roasting time accordingly. To eat the garlic heads, separate them into cloves with your knife and fork, then gently squeeze each clove with the flat of the knife to extrude the garlic purée.

LLEGENDS I CURIOSITATS
«LEGENDS AND CURIOSITIES»

Like all cuisines, that of the *països catalans* has its eccentricities—unlikely ingredients and extravagant combinations and dishes bigger than life, stranger than fiction. The *espardenya*, to begin with, is a foodstuff unique, to the best of my knowledge, to coastal Catalonia. Literally, an *espardenya* in Catalan is a hemp-soled canvas shoe—an espadrille (or what in Castilian is called an *alpargata*). The word has other meanings in slang or regional dialect, though. In and around Valencia, for instance, an *espardenya* can be something badly done, a screw-up; it can also be a *lapsus linguae*, a slip of the tongue, especially one involving the involuntary inclusion, in writing or speech, of a word in a foreign language. By extension of this latter meaning, the word has also come to be applied to a minor Valencian dish—a sort of *all-i-pebre* (see page 141) including chicken as well as the traditional eel. In Barcelona, on the other hand, as at the tiny Café Armengol on the Ramblas, an *espardenya* is sometimes a kind of oversized sandwich of grilled sausage, ham, and/or cheese on Catalan tomato bread.

On the Costa Brava, though (and today in Barcelona and perhaps a bit beyond), an *espardenya* is a kind of seafood—a holothurian or sea slug (*Stichopus regalis*, I think), to be precise. This *espardenya* is a bottom-dwelling creature, and thus is taken (accidentally, in fishermen's nets) mostly in rough weather; it is said to be inedible save for the fingerlike "filets" cut out of its back as soon as it is caught (the meat is apparently extremely perishable and must be immediately immersed in cold water, out of the sun), but these filets are today considered a great delicacy in some circles. They appear, in fact, to be the most expensive single variety of seafood on the coast, pound for pound—costing more even than crayfish or rock lobster. In China and elsewhere in Asia, of course, sea slugs or sea cucumbers are highly prized gastronomically as well—but *espardenyes* bear almost no resemblance, in color, texture, or taste, to what is eaten in those areas. The filets are small, about 2 or 3 inches in length and ½ inch or so in diameter, and are white or off-white in color and deeply striated—more like a bundle of tendons bunched together than a solid piece of flesh. (I've been told that the *espardenya* is so named because it lies flat and shoelike on the sea's floor—an explanation which would seem to be borne out by the fact that its French name is *sandale de mer*, "sandal of the sea." On the other hand, its striations resemble mightily the pattern on the soles of espadrilles.)

Espardenyes—which are usually eaten fried or in tomato sauce—are rather chewy, but not very gelatinous (as their Asian counterparts most certainly are), and have a unique flavor, very pronounced, rather earthy, a little bit like scallops and a little bit like monkfish but not a lot like anything else at all. They are, I suppose, an acquired taste—but one that I personally found very easy to acquire. I highly recommend them to the seafood-loving visitor to Catalonia (and if you don't love seafood, incidentally, perhaps Catalonia isn't where you ought to be in the first place).

I have *not* acquired a taste for *rates d'aigua* or *rat-bufos*—at least not yet; truth to tell, I've never even eaten them. These, as you might have guessed, are water rats. In earlier times, in the rice-growing region of the Delta de l'Ebre, such rodents were traditionally cooked with rice as a wintertime treat. They supposedly fed only on grape pomace and on rice itself, and are said to have tasted not at all unpleasant. In hard times, workers in the rice fields reportedly were served rice merely flavored with rat; the boss got the meat itself. According to Manuel Pagès, director of the Raïmat winery, who told me about *rates d'aigua amb arròs* in the first place, it is still possible to sample this curious specialty, in season, in the Delta de l'Ebre—if you know whom to ask. He has never tasted it himself, he says, and he and I have made a date to try it at some future time—perhaps not for many years. Meanwhile, I have been unable to find a recipe for the dish. I did find one, though, for a Majorcan *frito de ratas* (the name is Castilian), offered by Luís Ripoll in his *Cocina de las Baleares*—not water rats with rice but field rats from the marshes near the island's northern coast, stewed with garlic, leeks, tomatoes, and sweet peppers (and eaten, according to local advice, Ripoll says,

with abundant quantities of good red wine).

The principal of equal time demands, I suppose, that I also mention the recipe for *menjar de gat rostit*—a dish of roasted cat— given by Mestre Robert in his classic 1520-vintage *Libre del coch*. The cat was skinned and cleaned, and its head discarded. (If you eat the brains of a cat, Robert warns, you will go crazy.) Next, the carcass was wrapped in a cloth and buried for twenty-four hours, then disinterred and roasted on a spit with garlic and oil—and thrashed when partially cooked with "some green branches" (herbs?). This process, Robert assured his readers, would yield *"una vianda singular,"* "a singular dish." Indeed.

Frankly, I don't think I'd go out of my way to try roast cat, even in the interests of research. I did, however, make three separate (if ultimately unsuccessful) trips in one year up winding mountain roads into the fastness of Andorra in search of the fabled local specialty called *arròs amb esquirol*, rice with squirrel. Though it eventually became apparent that I wasn't going to get to taste it (the Andorran government having lately outlawed the hunting and sale of squirrels for gastronomic purposes), I was at least able to learn a bit about the history of the dish—thanks to Jordi Marquet, who owns the superb wineshop that bears his name in the Andorran town of Les Escaldes, and who knows a great deal about the local cuisine (as well as that, incidentally, of France and Spain).

Though the most common home-style dish in Andorra had long been a local version of *Escudella i Carn d'Olla* (see page 232) known as *vianda barrejada* (literally "mixed food"), Marquet explained, on special occasions the main course would usually be based on rice (a pricy import in the old days). In principal, this would be cooked with salt cod (another import), or with pork confit, rabbit, or *isard* (chamois, a goatlike mountain antelope much favored as food in the Pyrénées). But Andorra was a poor, isolated country until forty or fifty years ago (the first road from Spain wasn't built until 1913, remember, and the first one from France not until 1931), and salt cod or meat (even local game) weren't always available to everyone. At some point, Marquet continued, Andorrans discovered that squirrel, a very common animal in the region, actually tasted rather good—"a bit gamy, but not too much so, with somehow the flavor of the forest." There was very little meat on the average squirrel, of course, but because what there was had plenty of character, it seemed like an ideal thing to mix with rice. A kind of squirrel paella was created, according to Marquet, with onions, bacon, peas, and saffron. Though it is now forbidden to kill squirrels for food, he concluded, "it's rather certain that hunters out by themselves still do so, and still make this dish." Maybe next time, then. (It might be noted, incidentally, that Eliane Thibaut-Comelade, in the first volume of her *La Cuisine catalane*, offers a recipe for *civet d'écureuil du Capcir*, squirrel *civet* cooked in red wine and its own blood in the style of the Capcir region of the French Catalan Pyrénées. "Personally," Comelade adds rather primly, "I consider this recipe barbarous; I would never eat a squirrel.")

Tord or thrush (which the French call *grive*) is a highly regarded game bird in the *països catalans*—above all in the Empordà and the Balearics—and is essential to the great, legendary Majorcan wintertime specialty called *cassola mallorquina*. This isn't an easy dish to find these days outside of traditional households on the island, but local journalist Pablo Llull, who was my first guide to matters culinary on Majorca, arranged an expedition in its pursuit one cold, dark January evening, to the little town of Campos, southeast of Palma. There, at the modest, home-style Es Pla del Campos restaurant, I watched an authentic *cassola* being made to order for our party of four—the wild rabbit skinned and cut up, the chicken chopped into pieces, a brace of pigeons quartered, some pork sliced into strips, some little white meatballs of pork and breadcrumbs rolled deftly into smoothness, the wild mushrooms (*rovellons* or *Lactarius sanguifluus*, here called *esclat-sangs*, "blood bursts") wiped clean, and above all the *tords* (at least six or eight of them per person) stripped bare and readied for the pot—and then the whole lot stewed in water and their own juices in an immense aluminum kettle with potatoes, bits of *botifarra* sausage, oregano, and parsley.

This *cassola* doesn't need an opening act. It is traditionally served as the only dish of the evening; instead of an appetizer and a main course, one takes two complete helpings of the thing itself—and more if one is able. (This being serious eating country, of course, the meal doesn't stop there. The traditional conclusion to a *cassola* feast is a dessert of *bunyols de vent, bunyols* "of the wind"—*profiterole*-like fried pastries filled with honey or pastry cream and dusted with sugar.)

The *cassola mallorquina*, as might be imagined, is a challenging, surprising, grandly complicated concoction—and the *tords*, by their very nature (their tiny size, their large proportion of bones to meat, and thus their utter imperviousness to knife and fork), demand something of a primal, feral, approach—a hands-on attack. This is not a dainty dish. It is, however, a memorable one, profound in flavor (imagine a greatly reduced stock made from all those aforementioned ingredients, which is basically what the *cassola* liquid is), and almost darkly delicious. "The *cassola mallorquina*," says Majorcan winemaker Jaime Mesquida, who was one of our number that evening in Campos, "is the most interesting experience of old seasonal Majorcan peasant cooking you can find—a real symphony of a dish, with a rustic conception but an extraordinary *souplesse*."

The same things might very well be said of the still more legendary (and even less likely) specialty of the Empordà called *es niu*, "the nest." *Es niu* (*es* is the local form of the definite article *el*, as *sa* is the local equivalent of *la* in the Empordà—forms also used in the Balearics, where they were taken by Empordanese soldiers in the thirteenth century) is said to have been invented by the region's *tapers* or cork makers. The *comarques* of the Alt and Baix Empordà and neighboring Girona are the center of Spain's (and hence, I would imagine, the world's) cork industry, and before the cork manufacturing process became largely automated, workers in the trade were famous for

making good money and keeping short hours—and for being serious cooks and eaters. (It is also said that the average cork-making crew consisted of seven men—six to cut corks and a seventh to read the newspapers aloud all day so that the others wouldn't get bored.) On Monday, the *tapers* traditionally ate particularly well, because they had often spent the weekend hunting or fishing—bringing back bagsful of the forementioned *tords* or of *coloms* (doves), *colomins* (baby pigeons), and/or *guatlles* (quail). These birds became one of the definitive ingredients of the cork makers' greatest dish, and are responsible for its name (birds, that is, belonging in a nest).

Another essential part of *es niu*—and a much more elusive one, even in the Empordà itself—is *tripa de bacallà,* dried and salted cod innards. These are said to have been an invention of local fishermen on long voyages in the nineteenth century and, like *espardenyes,* were long considered a kind of junk food—to be eaten on board because they were unsalable on shore. Also like *espardenyes, tripa de bacallà* is today an expensive delicacy, costing as mush as $15 or $20 a pound. A third important part of *es niu* is *peixopalo* or stockfish, a close relative of *bacallà*—cod dried but not salt-cured. *Sèpia* (cuttlefish), little pork meatballs and/or sausages, potatoes, and a dark *sofregit* of onions are the other usual ingredients of the dish, with rabbit and/or eggs sometimes added as well. (Some recipes also call for a stock made with pig's feet to be stirred in as thickening.) *Allioli* is always served on the side, and spooned generously onto each plate—with real aficionados of the dish making a little impromptu purée of *allioli,* potatoes, and sauce and spreading it around their helpings.

Es niu takes about five hours to cook—one to make the *sofregit* and four to let the other ingredients stew together. The darkness of the onions and the ink of the cuttlefish combine to give the dish a chocolate-black color. The sauce grows dense. The meat and fowl and fish (and tripe of fish) seem to melt into one another, until it is by no means always possible to tell where one starts and the other leaves off. It is an intense, mysterious dish—more so even than the *cassola mallorquina*—with medieval overtones and a baroque sensibility. It is a *Mar i Muntanya* gone mad.

I think it's quite wonderful, at least as I met it at the Cypsele restaurant in Palafrugell (where the proprietor's mother comes in on Sundays in game season to make it). A poet of the Palafrugell region, Josep Martí Clara, who signs himself "Bepes," has even written an ode to the dish. And Manuel Vázquez Montalbán gets completely carried away in considering it, calling it "brown, aggressive, sweet . . . not an exquisite dish but rather a rotund one, like Catalan sexual acts and acts of political affirmation (the storming of the Bastille, the assault on the Winter Palace . . .)" Garrotxan chef Domènec Moli, on the other hand, simply calls it "one of the cheapest, most terrifying, and most incredible dishes in all of our cuisine." Personally, I can't think of another one that even comes close.

PART FIVE: WINES OF THE PAÏSOS CATALANS

Wine is the lifeblood of Catalan cuisine, its animating principle, inseparable from it. It has flowed copiously with food, *as* food, in the *països catalans* at least since the Romans hit the beaches in the third century B.C., and probably longer. One local proverb goes so far as to warn, *"Menjar sense vi, menjar mesquí"*—which might be ungrammatically but not at all inaccurately translated as "Eat wineless, eat lousy."

Traditionally, Catalan wine has been simple stuff, sometimes rough and harsh as rocky soil, sometimes light as water, drawn from barrels as required and drunk communally from a *porró*—a glass pitcher shaped like the lower half of an hourglass, but with an elongated neck curving backward and a needle-nose spout extending from its base. (As with the *bota* or wine bag found elsewhere in Spain, the *porró* is held high in the air with its spout angled toward the open mouth; it takes a bit of practice to get the stream of wine directed properly, and timidity in the attempt is guaranteed to dampen one's veneer.)

Beyond such everyday plonk, though, there has been serious winemaking in the re-gion for at least a century, too—quite a bit of it in the last ten or fifteen years, in fact—and today the *porró* is slowly but unmistakably being nudged to the back of the table by bottles, standing tall, of good local wine made both from such noble grapes as chardonnay, cabernet sauvignon, and syrah (this last in the Roussillon), and from lesser indigenous varieties that turn out to be capable of a lot more than has been asked of them in the past—principally, in Catalonia itself at any rate, parellada, xarel-lo, and macabeo for white wines and carinenya (carignan), garnatxa (grenache), monastrell, and ull de llebre (tempranillo) for reds.

This isn't the place for a lengthy description and analysis of the many wines of the *països catalans*, but what follows is a brief listing of recommended labels from the region, with special attention paid to those available or soon to be available in the United States. Names in boldface are those of *denominación de origen* (geographical appellation) or location. The letter code is as follows: (a) aperitif wine; (d) dessert wine; (r) red wine; (ro) rosé wine; (w) white wine.

CATALONIA

Alella: Marqués de Alella (w).
Empordà-Costa Brava: Cavas del Ampurdán Blanc Pescador (w); Gran Recosind (r); Oliveda Garnatxa de la Bota del Racó (d); Corinosa Garnatxa de l'Empordà Reserva (d).
Penedès (*cava* or *méthode champenoise* sparkling wine): Codorníu Blanc de Blanc, Brut Noir, Gran Codorníu, and Brut Classico; Raïmat Brut Grapa; Freixenet Cordon Negro, Brut Nature, and Brut Barocco; Segura Viudas Reserva Heredad; Castellblanch Brut Zero and Gran Cremant; Cavas Hill Brut de Brut; Juvé y Camps Reserva de la Familia; Mont-Marçal Brut Tradición and Brut Gran Reserva; Marqués de Monistrol Brut Nature; Lembey Brut; Nadal Brut; Gramona Celler Batlle; Torello Brut and Brut Nature; Llopart Reserva; Mascaró Brut.
Penedès (table wines): Masia Bach Viña Extrísima Reserva (r) and Extrísimo Gran Reserva (d); Parnàs Xaloc Blanc (w); Torres Viña Sol (w), Gran Viña Sol Reserva Etiqueta Verde (w), De Casta (r), Sangre de Toro (r), Gran Sangre de Toro (r), Gran Coronas (r), and Gran Coronas Etiqueta Negra (r); Jean Leon Chardonnay (w) and Cabernet (r); Cavas Hill Gran Toc (r) and Castell de Foc (ro); Juvé y Camps Ermita d'Espiells (w); Mont-Marçal Cabernet Sauvignon (r); Quinter & Ventosa Montgros (w); Josep Ferrer Mateu Viña Laranda "Bodegas del Foix" (r); Freixedas & Pomés Tinto 5° Año (r); Valldosera Blanc Argent (w); Josep Maris Torres i Blanco Mas Rabassa (w).
Tarragona: De Muller Garnacha Solera 1926 (d), Priorato Dulce Extra Rancio Solera 1918 (d), and Dom Juan Fort Extra Rancio Solera 1865 (a/d).
Priorat: Cartoixa Scala Dei Reserva (r).
Sitges: Bodegas Robert Moscatel (d), Malvasía (d), and Malvasía Reserva (d).

VALENCIA

Valencia: C. Augusto Eglí Alto Turia (w).
Alicante: Salvador Poveda Fondillon (d).

BALEARIC ISLANDS

Majorca: Jaime Mesquida Cabernet Sauvignon (r), Vinya Esther Rosat (ro), and Xenoy Generoso Dulce (d); Jose L. Ferrer Binisalem Auténtico Tinto (r); Viños Oliver Mont Ferrutx (r).
Ibiza: Can del Mulo Alghibiza (w), Tinto del Mulo (r), and Pep Daifa (*cava*).

ROUSSILLON

(Most producers make wines from several appellations.) Château de Jau Côtes-du-Roussillon (r), Muscat de Rivesaltes (d), and Ban-

sillon (r), Muscat de Rivesaltes (d), and Rivesaltes Tres Vieux "Cuvée Aîme Cazes" (d); Domaine de Mas Blanc (Dr. Parcé) Cuvée Les Piloumes Collioure (r), Cosprons Levant Collioure (r), Mas Blanc "Dry" Banyuls (a), and Banyuls Rimage (a/d); Vignerons Catalans Taïchat Côtes-du-Roussillon Blanc (w), Côtes-du-Roussillon Rosé (ro), Côtes-du-Roussillon Rouge Guittard-Rodor (r), and Côtes-du-Roussillon Caramany "Cuvée Caveau de Presbytère" (r); Mas Chichet Cuvée Spéciale Cabernet.

BRANDY, ETC.

Among the good alcohols distilled in the *països catalans* are these: an *estomacal* or *digéstif* called Bonet, from the Costa Brava town of Sant Feliu de Guixols; a whole line of excellent liqueurs and Alsatian-style *eaux-de-vie* made by Joaquim Vich under the Gerunda label in Girona; *marc* or grape-pomace brandy in the style of France's *marc de champagne* made by Segura Viudas and several other *cava* producers in the Penedès; a line of dry, sophisticated brandies from Torres, also in the Penedès; three brandies from the Penedès *cava* producer Mascaró—the cheapest of which, Marivaux, is particularly good; Suau brandy from Pont d'Inca, Majorca; and the old-fashioned French *apéritif* called Byrrh (pronounced "beer"), from the town of Thuir, southwest of Perpignan, in the Roussillon.

yuls (d); Templers Banyuls Perlé (a), Cuvée Amiral François Vilarem Banyuls (d), Ancestral Banyuls (d), Mas de la Serra "Demi-Sec" Banyuls (d), Cuvée Viviane le Roy "Dry" Banyuls (a), Castell des Templers Grand Vin des Hospices de Banyuls (d), and Aphrodis Muscat de Rivesaltes (d); Cazes Frères Côtes-du-Rous-

APPENDICES

APPENDIX 1—LA BOQUERIA

Saturday morning at La Boqueria: You fight your way past the crowds that inevitably mill around the main entrance—the accordion player and the seller of lottery tickets, the workmen leaning on their carts, the tiny white-haired women adjusting their heroic bundles before heading for the bus stop, the loiterers and coffee drinkers and sidewalk philosophers. Inside, the smells and colors and human hubble-bubble of the place immediately engulf you, dwarf you.

If it is springtime, your first visual impression will probably be one of fire-bright intensity—endless arrays of strawberries, oranges, blood oranges, tomatoes, and red peppers, almost blinding in their luminescence. In fall, the hues are more like those of an enchanted forest—the browns and earthy yellows of wild mushrooms, the eerie purple or lime green florets of local broccoli, the scarlet-green of chard, the iridescence of the wings of game birds hung beak down on racks. Winter grows deeper into browns and grays, summer into light greens and slightly faded reds.

In any season, with appropriate variation, the character of the air here changes every few feet—the damp spiciness of just-picked lettuce or the grassy scent of cabbage near the produce stalls giving way to the thick smell of blood and smoke that haunts the sausage shops, the woody aroma of freshly roasted hazelnuts and almonds at the dried fruit stands yielding to the briny pungency exuding from the marble tables full of salt cod, anchovies, and salted herring.

What never changes is the density of the crowds here, and the speed and sense of purpose with which they move—buying, selling, bargaining, resisting, giving in, hurrying from one stall to the next. Shopping at La Boqueria can be a sensual experience of the highest order, if you want to look at it (and sniff at it) that way; but it is also serious business—because, after all, the whole point of shopping here in the first place is that there's serious eating to be done.

To know a city's food, first learn its markets. (If that's not an ancient culinary aphorism, it ought to be.) And to know Catalan cuisine, first visit La Boqueria—the big downtown covered market that is the single most important source of food, both retail and wholesale, in Barcelona.

Markets in general tell us a lot about the gastronomy of the place they serve, of course. They reveal to us what foods are most favored locally, to begin with, and in what variety they are available; they show us plainly what's in season and what's at its best; in countries whose language we don't understand, they offer an illustrated crash course in the names of raw materials unknown to tourist dictionaries and menu translators—unfamiliar kinds of fish, for instance, or unlikely animal parts. Beyond all that, though, markets tend to be microcosms of the communities they serve. They immerse us instantly and vividly into the local mainstream, showing us not just what the people of a city eat (and, incidentally, how much they're willing to pay for it), but also how they dress and talk and act in their unguarded, busy moments. Markets sell food; but they give away the real spirit of a place. That's why I like to go to markets in cities I don't know—and why I've rarely spent a day in Barcelona without stopping at La Boqueria at least once.

La Boqueria is the largest of six main covered markets in the city. *Boqueria* is an old Catalan word for butcher shop or abattoir, and the name has been applied to the location since the first meat markets were installed there centuries ago. The market's real name is the Mercat de Sant Josep (Mercado de San José in Castilian)—but a Barcelonan would no sooner call it that than a New Yorker would refer to Sixth Avenue as Avenue of the Americas. La Boqueria is an impressive building—a cavernous ironwork structure, not unlike some turn-of-the-century French train stations in design. (It was itself begun in 1836, with the metal roof added around 1870.) It is set back from the Rambla de Sant Josep, on the west side of the street, between the carrer del Carme and the carrer Petxina, in such a way that the unobservant passerby could almost miss it. Once you turn between the two buildings that frame and partially conceal its gaping entrance, though, La Boqueria will draw you in quickly and far.

There are said to be about 500 individual merchants permanently ensconced in La Boqueria. Some of the best and most representative of these are clustered around the entrance, at the beginning of the main aisle: Soley (stall No. 509–510) and Pons (No. 512–513) for fresh fruit and vegetables of all kinds; Pons Vidal (No. 471–475) for dried fruits and nuts; J. Colomines (No. 477–478) for exotic vegetables and herbs; an unnamed stall next door to Colomines (No. 481–482) for the best seasonal local produce, and so on. A bit to the right are Bar Pinocho (see page 297) and the aforementioned A. Rossel olive stand (see page 115). Straight ahead, deep into the market, though, are all *kinds* of wonderments, examples of almost any foodstuff you'll find on Barcelona tables.

A fresh food market is of limited practical use to the casual visitor, I realize; apart from some fruit, or maybe some nuts or cheese or olives, there's not a great deal that the hotel-bound out-of-towner can easily utilize here. But just to see, smell, *sense* the food at La Boqueria—just to get some sort of abstract feel for it by being around it in its native state for an hour or two—will teach you a lot about the cooking of this rich and fascinating region, and will help bring Catalan cuisine alive for you.

APPENDIX 2—RESTAURANTS OF THE PAÏSOS CATALANS

What follows is by no means a comprehensive restaurant guide to Catalonia and the other *països catalans*, but rather a highly arbitrary selection of my own favorite eating places in these regions. I have listed only establishments serving Catalan cuisine (sometimes in regional variation) in whole or in part, incidentally, whether traditional or contemporary or some combination of the two—and as a consequence I have omitted some of the area's best restaurants, simply because they're of little interest to the diner with a hankering for victuals of the Catalan persuasion. The *Guide Michelin, Guía del viajero,* or *Gourmetour Guía gastronómica y turística* will fill you in on places I've left out.

BARCELONA

Antigua Casa Solé (also called *Can Solé*), San Carlos 4, tel. (93) 319.50.12. In portside Barceloneta. Busy and informal. Very fresh seafood simply cooked.

Bar Pinocho, #66-67, La Boqueria market (see page 295), no telephone. Ten stools at a funky counter in the middle of the market, with food good enough for white tablecloths. Catalan specialties, fresh market supplies.

Casa Costa, Baluarte 124, tel. (93) 319.50.28. Another seafood place in Barceloneta. Nice people, nice view from the top floor, good paella Barcelona-style.

Casa Isidro, Les Flors 12, tel. (93) 241.11.39. Popular celebrity spot. Trattorialike, with French and Catalan dishes. Consistent high quality (and a great selection of armagnac).

Chicoa, Aribau 71, tel. (93) 253.11.23. Traditional Catalan food of the highest quality. Try the *bacallà* assortment.

La Dida, Roger de Flor 230, tel. (93) 207.20.-04. Catalan dishes in an updated "continental" style. Cabbage stuffed with *brandada de bacallà* (see page 85) and goose liver sautéed with sweet Extrísimo Gran Reserva dessert wine are musts.

Eldorado Petit, Dolors Monserdà 51, tel. (93) 204.51.53. Arguably the best in town. French dishes, Catalan ones, and successful marriages of the two. Great fish and shellfish. Low-key attractive and chic.

Florian, Bertrand i Serra 20, tel. (93) 212.46.-27. Imaginative contemporary Catalan cooking of the highest order, with French and Italian accents. Famous *escabetxos* (see pages 176–178); specializes in wild mushroom dishes.

El Gran Cafè, Avinyó 9, tel. (93) 318.79.86. Pleasant, informal (authentic) turn-of-the-century decor. Catalan bistro food, with live piano music at night.

Jaume de Provença, Provença 88, tel. (93) 230.00.29. Modern Catalan dishes with plenty of other European influences in Scandinavian-cool decor. Appetizers are particularly good.

La Odisea, Copons 7, tel. (93) 302.36.92. Highly creative cuisine, Catalan-French in inspiration, by a colorful poet-chef. Marinated fish salad and stuffed rabbit (see page 276) are standouts.

L'Olivé, Muntaner 171, tel. (93) 230.90.27. Handsome casual decor and well-made traditional Catalan specialties.

Passadís del Pep, Plaça Palau 2, tel. (93) 310.-10.21. Tiny, hard to find, and always jam-packed with *tot* Barcelona. Home-style cooking with lots of fresh seafood. Regulars never bother with a menu, just taking what comes.

Els Perols de l'Empordà, Villaroel 88, tel. (93) 323.10.33. Homey husband-and-wife-run place producing straightforward food in the style of the Empordà region, but with surprising finesse. The black rice (see page 65) and simple oven-roasted fish might be the best in Barcelona.

Petit París, París 196, tel. (93) 218.26.78. Imaginative cooking with a solid Catalan base, in a small, clubby-looking restaurant. *Bacallà* a specialty.

El Raïm, Pescadería 6, tel. (93) 319.29.98. Small "legendary" place (lots of literary lights have dined here), kitchen-table informal, with good home-style Catalan specialties.

Reno, Tuset 27, tel. (93) 200.91.29. A Barcelona classic. Impeccable French, Spanish, and Catalan dishes in old-fashioned upscale surroundings. The best smoked salmon and the best *canalons* in town.

Senyor Parellada, Argentería 27, tel. (93) 315.-40.10. Good-looking, trendy place serving traditional Catalan dishes and sensible modern-day variations thereon.

Siete Puertas (also called *Set Portes*), passeig d'Isabel II 14, tel. (93) 319.30.33. The La Coupole of Barcelona, big, bright, and noisy, with a large menu of dishes ranging from the acceptable to the very good. Well-made rice dishes (including paella).

Via Veneto, Ganduxer 10 i 12, tel. (93) 200.-72.44. Another class act in the Reno category. Overblown imitation art nouveau decor (in black leather, yet!) but subtle, highly professional food, much of it genuinely Catalan—including wonderful stuffed pig's feet (see page 153) and sausage and white beans raised to an art form.

COSTA BRAVA AND VICINITY

Figueres: *Hotel Ampurdán*, carretera N-11, tel. (972) 50.05.62. Birthplace of the new Catalan cuisine. Highly accomplished kitchen serving traditional French, Spanish, and Catalan fare plus innovations galore. Well-run dining room. Plain decor but all the important amenities.

Llagostera: *Els Tinars,* carretera de Santa Cristina, tel. (972) 83.06.26. Big, bright place, reminiscent of a roadside trattoria outside Rome, serving solid Catalan food—especially dishes of the Empordà (black rice, *mar i muntanya,* etc.).

Palafrugell: *Cypsele,* Ancha 22, tel. (972) 30.01.92. Home-style local specialties, dependably good. The legendary *es niu* (see page 284) is available here—by special order and for large parties only.

Pals: *Sa Punta,* Platja de Pals, tel. (972) 63.-64.10. Elegant versions of traditional Catalan specialties in a good-looking upstairs dining room. Fried baby fish, black *fideus* (see page 201), and *bisbalenc* pastry are musts.

Peretallada: *Can Bonay,* Plaça Espanya 4, tel. (972) 63.40.34. Duck with turnips, pig's feet with snails, roasted pork jowls, and other no-nonsense local fare, all very authentic and very good. Highly informal.

Platja d'Aro: *Big Rock / Carles Camós,* Barri de Fenals 5, Urbanització Mas Nou, tel. (972) 81.80.12. One of the region's best. A classy restaurant and five-room inn set in an old Catalan hilltop mansion. *Fideus rossejats* (see page 197), salt cod purées, great fresh fish roasted with potatoes, and other culinary glories of the region.

Riudellots de la Selva: *Hostal La Pequeña,* carretera N-11, tel. (972) 47.-71.32. Superb *canalons,* a good selection of local sausages (including sweet *botifarra,* not to be missed), perfect potato

omelets, and other basic home cooking of the highest order. A real find.

Sant Feliu de Guixols: *Eldorado Petit,* Rambla Vidal 23, tel. (972) 32.18.18. The original of the great Barcelona restaurant of the same name. More casual and smaller, but more or less the same menu, and food of exactly the same impressive quality.

Tamariú: *Hostal Vora la Mar,* tel. (972) 30.-05.53. Simple fisherman-style dishes (suquet, grilled spiny lobster, a version of paella, etc.) on the edge of the sand in a small resort town.

THE PYRÉNÉES

Artiés: *Casa Irene* (also called *Hostal Valartiés*), Major 4, tel. (973) 64.09.00. Near the French border in the Vall d'Aran and serving French specialties with some local flavors and occasional local dishes included. One of Catalonia's finest.

Bagergue: *Casa Perú,* Sant Antoní, tel. (973) 64.34.87. One of the best *borda* (barn) restaurants in the Vall d'Aran. Neat and homey. A few dishes only, including great *Pa amb Tomàquet* and potato omelets (see pages 189 and 122 respectively).

Balaguer: *Cal Morell,* passeig Estació 18, tel. (973) 44.80.09. Simple, hearty Lleida-style dishes. Snails a specialty.

Garós: *Et Restillé,* Plaça Carrera 2, tel. (973) 64.15.39. Another excellent *borda* restaurant. Grilled *botifarra,* grilled trout, and *olla aranese* (a hearty soup) are highly recommended.

Martinet: *Boix,* carretera Lleida-Puigcerdà, tel. (973) 51.50.50. Sophisticated Catalan-based cooking in a quiet mountain hideaway hotel. Great soups, wonderful rare duck breast with Pyrenean honey sauce.

La Seu d'Urgell: *El Castell,* carretera C-1313, tel. (973) 35.07.04. Sophisticated French, Spanish, and Catalan food in a Relais et Châteaux motel. Game dishes in season, good mountain cheeses, formidable wine list (full of old Riojas, etc.).

Vielha: *Can Turnay,* Plaça Major (Escunyau), tel. (973) 64.02.92. *Olla aranese, civet* of wild boar, and other specialties of the Vall d'Aran in a comfortable, casual, ski-lodge atmosphere.

ELSEWHERE IN CATALONIA

Arenys de Mar: *Hispania,* carretera Reial 54, tel. (93) 791.04.57. One of Catalonia's best, a short drive from Barcelona. Many Catalan classics, superbly made.

Cambrils: *Ca'n Gatell,* passeig Miramar 27, tel. (977) 36.01.06. *Romesco de peix, fideus a banda,* and other specialties, mostly seafood, of the Tarragona region.

Casa Gatell, passeig Miramar 26, tel. (977) 36.00.57. More great seafood dishes in an extremely civilized dining room. Standouts include clams with red *fideus* (see page 200) and tuna Cambrils-style (see page 133).

Eugenia, Consolat de Mar 80, tel. (977) 36.01.68. Elegant seafood restaurant. Lobster paella is a specialty. (This and the two Gatell establishments are owned by different branches of the same family.)

Lleida: *Forn de Nastasi,* Salmerón 10, tel. (973) 23.45.10. Typical dishes of the Lleida region (roasted meats, *fricandó* with wild mushrooms, etc.), plus some modern touches. Lots of complimentary extras.

Molins de Rei: *Esteve,* avinguda Barcelona 23–25, tel. (93) 668.10.02. Unglamorous surroundings but terrific Catalan cuisine—*canalons,* pig's foot flan (see page 155), grilled fish with garlic and parsley, *estofat* of beef, etc. Near Barcelona.

Salomo: *El Celler,* Joan Maragall 10, tel. (977) 62.90.10. Authentic *calçotada* (see page 167)—in winter only—and other old-style country dishes of the Tarragona region. Open by advance reservation and to large groups only.

Tarragona: *Sol Ric,* via Augusta 227, tel. (977) 23.20.32. The city's best. Urban-rustic, with a large menu. *Romesco de Peix* (see page 223) and other Tarragonese specialties, plus dishes from other parts of Catalonia.

Vilafranca del Penedès: *Casa Juan,* Plaça de l'Estació 8, tel. (93) 890.31.71. Simple, well-made Catalan food—omelets, roasted goat, baked fish, partridge in vinegar sauce, etc. Plenty of good wines of the region.

THE VALENCIA REGION

Alcoy: *Venta del Pilar,* carretera a Valencia, tel. (965) 59.23.25. One of the region's most famous restaurants. Skilled kitchen, producing both regional and international specialties. Salt cod and red pepper salad, stuffed peppers, various traditional soups and stews.

Benisano: *Levante,* carretera de Valencia a Adamuz, tel. (96) 278.07.21. Real Valencian-style paella (without seafood) and a few appetizers, period, in basic surroundings.

Valencia: *El Plat,* Conde Altea 41, tel. (96) 334.96.38. Authentic Valencian cuisine, including a different paella every day, plus several versions of *all-i-pebre,* including an unusual one made with lamb.

La Riva, Mar 27, tel. (96) 331.71.72. Folkloric decor, pleasant staff, and a small menu of unabashedly homey regional dishes—lentils and sausage, chicken with garlic, several *paelles* and other forms of rice, etc. Local wines.

THE BALEARIC ISLANDS

Majorca

Calviá: *C'ana Cucó,* autopista a Palma Nova, tel. (971) 67.00.83. Elementary Majorcan specialties—pork-stuffed apples, *frit* (sautéed lamb's offal with red peppers and potatoes), veal *estofat,* and such.

Campos: *Es Pla,* Petra 5, tel. (971) 65.11.10. Small oral menu. About the closest thing to Majorcan home-cooking you'll find in a public place. *Cassola mallorquina* (see page 283) by special order in winter.

Inca: *Celler C'an Amer,* Miguel Duran 39, tel. (971) 50.12.61. Traditional Majorcan food (fish soups, roast suckling pig, *sopas mallorquinas*) and homemade desserts, including excellent and unusual ice creams. Restaurant occupies an impressive old wine cellar filled with huge antique barrels.

Palma de Mallorca: *Es Reco d'en Xesc,* Paseo Maritimo 17, tel. (971) 45.40.20. "Scalded soup," *escaldums de pavo* (which is more or less Majorcan turkey pot pie), excellent simply cooked fish dishes, and other Majorcan basics—mostly from family recipes.

Honoris, carretera Vieja de Buñola 76, tel. (971) 28.83.32. Beautiful *auberge*-style restaurant incongruously located in an industrial park on the outskirts of town. International menu with some Majorcan dishes (vegetable *puding,* Majorcan-style baked fish, etc.), very well-prepared.

Rififi, avinguda de Joan Miró 186, tel. (971) 40.20.35. First-rate local seafood of all kinds.

Xoriguer, Fábrica 60, tel. (971) 28.-83.32. "Market" cuisine, with international, mainland Spanish, and Majorcan dishes.

Minorca

Fornells: *Es Pla,* pasaje d'Es Pla, tel. (971)

37.51.55. Informal but good-looking port-side restaurant in a little fishing village. Famous for lobster *caldereta,* stuffed egg-plant, and other Minorcan specialties.

Maó: *Pilar,* Cardona i Orfila 61, tel. (971) 36.68.17. In the middle of town, but small and cottagelike. Soups, eggplant dishes, and rabbit, all typical of the island, are particularly good.

Rocamar, Fonduco 32, tel. (971) 36.-56.01. The island's best. Second-story restaurant with good view of Maó harbor serving international, mainland Spanish, and Minorcan dishes. Local *escupinya* clams, fish-stuffed eggplant (see page 50), and Minorcan-style baked fish highly recommended.

Es Mercadal: *Ca N'Aguedet,* Lepanto 23, tel. (971) 37.53.91. Friendly, extremely pleasant place with good local cooking. Stuffed vegetables and roast suckling pig are excellent.

Ibiza

San Rafael: *Grill San Rafael,* carretera San Antonio, tel. (971) 30.63.78. Spanish and Catalan food, with a few local specialties.

Cases-de-Pène: *Château de Jau,* tel. 68.-54.51.67. A winery, not a restaurant, but serving a single prix-fixe lunch most of the year (call ahead to make sure) on a pretty outdoor patio. Always the same menu, French Catalan in style, including tomato bread with ham and *botifarra-*like sausage grilled over vine cuttings, plus the château's excellent and varied wines.

Vivès: *Hostalet de Vivès,* rue de la Mairie, tel. 68.83.05.52. Rustic, farmhouselike restaurant. Great local *charcuterie* (including memorable pâté; see page 148), snails, grilled rabbit with *allioli,* meatballs with green olives, etc.

ANDORRA

Andorra la Vella: *Celler d'en Toni,* Verge del Pilar 4, tel. (9738) 218.43. Trout Andorra-style, *civet* of *isard* (mountain antelope), and other authentic Andorran dishes in warm surroundings.

THE ROUSSILLON

Banyuls-sur-Mer: *Le Sardinal,* place Paul-Reig, tel. 68.88.30.07. French Catalan cuisine and innovations of the chef. Collioure anchovies, fresh fish, and *pintada a la catalana* (see page 74) are highlights.

ALGHERO

La Lepanto, via Carlo Alberto 135, tel. (079) 97.91.59. The city's best, and most Catalan. A large Italian and non-Algherese Sardinian menu, but also six or eight Algherese/Catalan specialties a day (cuttlefish with potatoes, spaghetti with pressed tuna roe, etc.). The lobster salad called *gliagosta a la catarana* ("spiny lobster Catalan-style"), however, is an invention of the house, unknown to Catalan tradition.

Note: If you are dialing telephone numbers in Spain or Andorra from outside those countries, omit the 9 in the area code (but use it within Spain or Andorra). Similarly, if you are dialing Alghero from outside Italy, omit the 0 in the area code. In France, under the new phone system introduced in 1986, dial all eight digits of each number whether in France or elsewhere.

APPENDIX 3—SOURCES FOR SPANISH PRODUCTS

Most large American cities now have at least a handful of markets carrying Spanish or Hispanic products. Some, like Los Angeles, San Diego, Houston, Dallas, Miami, and New York, are positively rich with them. Such markets are good sources for salt cod, Spanish-style rice and white beans, anchovies, olive oil, canned or glass-packed *piquillo*-style sweet peppers, and other foodstuffs called for in the preceding recipes—and sometimes also for Spanish-style (though American-made) sausages and for unusual cuts of meat (calf's head, etc.). Stores offering particularly good selections of Spanish and Spanish-style items include the following:

Atlanta: *Diaz Market,* 106 Sixth Street NE, Atlanta, Georgia 30308, tel. (404) 872-0928.

Chicago: *Supermercado Gutierrez,* 1628 West Montrose Avenue, Chicago, Illinois 60613; tel. (312) 271-7741.

Houston: *Fiesta Mart,* 5600 Mykawa Road, Houston, Texas 77037, tel. (713) 644-1611.

Los Angeles: *Grand Central Market,* 317 South Broadway, Los Angeles, California 90013. (Various shops and stands, with various phone numbers.)

Miami: *Ayestaran Supermarket,* 701 SW 27th Avenue, Miami, Florida 33135, tel. (305) 642-3539.

New York: The best source for Spanish products in New York, Casa Moneo on West 14th Street, closed recently. There is a possibility that it might reopen in another location so it might be worth a call to directory assistance. Otherwise, certain items are available at The Kitchen Food Shop, The International Grocery, and La Marqueta, all in Manhattan, and the Ines Grocery in Mineola, Long Island. Lake Success Liquors in Lake Success has an extensive selection of Spanish wines, including Catalan.

Newark: *Estrela da Beira,* 194–196 Ferry Street, Newark, New Jersey 07105, tel. (201) 344-2605.

San Francisco: *Casa Lucas Market,* 2934 24th Street, San Francisco, California 94110, tel. (415) 826-4334.

Some of the above will accept mail orders and ship products throughout the United States. Other useful mail order sources include these:

Corti Bros., 5770 Freeport Boulevard, Sacramento, California 95822, tel. (916) 391-0300. Catalan olive oil and anchovies,

Spanish-style white beans, salt cod, Spanish wines (including hard-to-find *vi ranci*) and cheeses, etc.

Dean & DeLuca, 110 Greene Street, Suite 304, New York, New York 10012, tel. (212) 431-1691 or (800) 221-7714. Dried peppers, glass-packed *piquillo* peppers, wild mushrooms, olive oils, etc.

La Española, 2020 Lomita Boulevard, Building No. 7, Lomita, California 90717, tel. (213) 539-0455. Spanish-style sausages, including *botifarra* (order their *butifarrita* for *botifarra* recipes in this book), *botifarra negra* (order *morcilla con cebolla*), and *sobrassada (sobreasada)*. Also, salt cod, turrons, olive oil, etc.

Williams-Sonoma, P.O. Box 7456, San Francisco, California 94120-7456, tel. (415) 421-4242. Catalan olive oil, paella pans, *cassoles* (including small ones for *crema catalana*), etc.

APPENDIX 4—A BRIEF PRONUNCIATION GUIDE

As noted earlier, Catalan is not particularly difficult to pronounce. It's certainly a good deal easier for the English-speaker to manage than Castilian, I think—and many words in Catalan sound exactly (or almost exactly) as they would in our own tongue. Nonetheless, there are some tricky areas: The *x,* for instance, is often pronounced as *ch* or *sh*—as in the *xef* who cooks the meal you wash down with your *xampany* (*ny* representing the same sound the French get from *gn* or *gne*). The double *l* is not the simple *y* of American Spanish, but the palatized *l* of Castilian—rather like the lli in "scallion." A dot or dash between two *l*'s—*l-l* or *l·l*—gives them a conventional double *l* sound, as in English; a *t before* two *l*'s—*tll*— keeps the palatized sound, but lengthens it, with the *t* itself usually silent, though faintly sounded in some regions.

It isn't my intention to offer a complete Catalan pronunciation guide here; for that, I refer you to Joan Gili's *Catalan Grammar* (see bibliography) or some other scholarly Catalan language text. The following pronunciation hints, given in rather crude phonetics of my own device, are meant as the roughest guidelines only—so that if you cook some dish from this volume for company and someone asks what it is called, you'll be able to reply with a modicum of confidence. I have chosen only words appearing in the names of dishes, incidentally, and only those whose approximate pronunciations aren't already obvious.

albergínies (ahl-bear*jee*-nee-ez), eggplant (plural)

all (*ahl*-yuh, pronounced in as close to one syllable as possible), garlic

allioli (ahl-*yo*-li), sauce of olive oil and garlic

amb (um), with

ametlles (ah-*mell*-yez), almonds

anxoves (ahn-*cho*-vez or ahn-*cho*-bez), anchovies

bacallà (bah-cal-*ya*), salt cod

beixamel (*besh*-a-mel), béchamel sauce

bou (*boe*-u), beef

bledes (*bled*-ez), Swiss chard

caça (*cah*-sha), wild game

calçotada (cahl-so-*ta*-da), grilled green onions with spicy sauce

ciureny (see-u-*renge*), cepes (wild mushrooms)

conill (cun-*eel*-yuh, with the last two syllables pronounced as much like one as possible), rabbit

coques (coe-*kez*), flat pastries, Catalan "pizzas" (plural)

cotzes (*coat*-zez), mussels (Algherese word)

dolçes (*duhl*-sez), sweets (plural)

escabetx (ess-ca-*betch*), cooked and pickled or marinated fish or fowl

escalivada (ess-cahl-ee-*va*-da or ess-cahl-ee-*ba*-da), Catalan roasted vegetables (sweet peppers, eggplant, etc.)

escudella (ess-ku-*dell*-ya), soup or stew; also bowl

esqueixada (ess-kee-*shawd*-ah), literally "shredded"; a shredded salt cod salad

farcellets (farce-uhl-*yetz*), literally "bundles" or "bolts" (as of cloth); cabbage dumplings or rolled meat

fetge (*fedge*-uh, pronounced in as close to one syllable as possible), liver (usually calf's liver unless otherwise specified)

figues (*fi*-guz), figs

formatge (for-*mahdge*-uh, with the last two syllables pronounced as much like one as possible), cheese

fruites (fru-*eet*-ez, with the first two syllables pronounced as much like one as possible), fruits

guatlles (*gwall*-yez), quail (plural)

llagosta (luh-yah-*ghos*-ta, with the first two syllables pronounced as much like one as possible), spiny lobster

llagostins (luh-yah-ghos-*teens*, with the first two syllables pronounced as much like one as possible), prawns

llaminadures (luh-yawm-een-a-*du*-rez, with the first two syllables pronounced as much like one as possible), pastries and desserts, sweets

llauna (luh-*yow*-na, with the first two syllables pronounced as much like one as possible), literally "tin"; a kind of baking dish

llenties (luh-yen-*tee*-ez, with the first two syllables pronounced as much like one as possible), lentils

llobaro (luh-yo-*bar*-oh, with the first two syllables pronounced as much like one as possible), sea bass

llom (luh-*yohm*, pronounced in as close to one syllable as possible), literally "loin"; usually loin of pork

lluç (luh-*youss*, pronounced in as close to one syllable as possible), hake

maduixa (ma-*dweesh*-ah), strawberry

mandonguilles (man-don-*gweel*-yez), meatballs or quenelles

Manxego (mahn-*chay*-go), a variety of cheese from the La Mancha region

mongetes (muhn-*jet*-ez), white beans

neules (ne-*yool*-ez, with the first two syllables pronounced as much like one as possible), Catalan rolled cookies

oilaigua (o-lee-*eye*-gwa), Minorcan olive oil soup

olives (*o*-lee-vez), olives

olla (*ohl*-ya), pot or kettle; stew or soup made in a pot

ous (*o*-us), eggs (plural)

paella (pa-*ail*-ya), Valencian rice specialty

pagès (pa-*jess*), farmer or peasant

panellets (pa-nuhl-*yets*), Catalan marzipan cookies

peix (pesh), fish

peus (*pay*-oos), feet

platillo (pla-*teel*-yo), class of dish from the Empordà region

pollastre (puhl-*yahss*-tray), chicken

rotllo (*roll*-yo), roll

saltejat (sahl-tuh-*zhot*), sautéed

samfaina (sam-fie-*ee*-na), Catalan mixed vegetables

seques (*sek*-ez), dried (feminine plural)

tall (tahl-yuh, pronounced in as close to one syllable as possible), literally "edge" or "cut"; steak

tomàquet (toe-*ma*-ket), tomato

vedella (vuh-*del*-ya or buh-*del*-ya), veal

xai (shy), lamb

xató (sha-*toe*), a variety of salad

xocolata (shock-o-*la*-ta), chocolate

APPENDIX 5—RECIPES ACCORDING TO CATEGORY

SAUCES AND CONDIMENTS

Allioli amb Fruita (*Allioli* with Fruit), 32
Allioli amb Ous (*Allioli* with Eggs), 31
Allioli Autèntic (Authentic *Allioli*), 30
Allioli Negat (Drowned *Allioli*), 32
Maionesa (Mayonnaise), 34
Mussolina d'All (Garlic Mousseline), 33
Picada (Catalan "Roux"), 40
Romesco I (Tarragona-Style *Romesco* [Spicy Nut] Sauce), 224
Romesco II (Josep María Morell's *Romesco* [Spicy Tomato] Sauce), 225
Salsa per Calçots (*Calçot* [Grilled Green Onion] Sauce), 168
Samfaina (Catalan Mixed Vegetables), 42
Sofregit (Catalan Sauce Base), 38

APPETIZERS

Albergínies d'Anfós (Eggplant "Sandwiches" with Grouper Mousse), 50
Albergínies Farcides amb Anxoves (Stuffed Eggplants with Anchovies), 48

Anxoves Fregides (Deep-Fried Anchovies), 59
Bolets a la Graella (Grilled Wild Mushrooms), 91
Brandada amb Carxofes (Salt Cod Purée with Artichokes), 86
Brandada de Bacallà (Salt Cod Purée), 85
Bunyols de Bacallà (Salt Cod Fritters), 85
Bunyols de Ciurenys (Cepe Fritters), 90
Calamars Saltejats amb All i Julivert (Squid Sautéed with Garlic and Parsley), 138
La Calçotada (Grilled Green Onions with Spicy Sauce), 167
Calçots Fregits (Deep-Fried *Calçots* [Green Onions]), 169
Canalons a la Barcelonesa (Barcelona-Style *Canalons*), 204
Canalons d'Anec (*Canalons* with Ground Duck), 205
Canalons de Peix al Cabrales (*Canalons* with Fish Mousse in Blue Cheese Sauce), 206
Cargolada (Grilled Snails), 99
Cargols de la Padrina Mercé (Godmother Mercedes's Roasted Snails), 103
Cargols Estil Porreres (Snails Porreres-Style), 100
Cassola d'Albergínies (Eggplant "Omelet" with Raisins and Pine Nuts), 52
Cebas Farcides (Meat-Stuffed Onions), 184
Cigrons amb Mussolina d'All (Chick-Peas with Garlic Mousseline), 108

SOUPS

Caldereta de Llagosta (Minorcan Spiny Lobster Soup), 218

Consomé de Pomes "Golden" (Golden Delicious Apple Consommé), 272

Crema de Faves (Cream of Fava Soup), 107

Escudella i Carn d'Olla (Catalan Soup with Boiled Meats and Vegetables, in Two Courses), 232

Oliaigua amb Tomàtics (Olive Oil Soup with Tomatoes), 271

Sarsuela (Seafood "Operetta"), 221

Sopa de Bolets (Catalan Mushroom Soup), 89

Sopa de Fredolics (*Fredolic* [Wild Mushroom] Soup), 90

Suquet (Catalan Fish and Potato Soup), 219

SALADS

Amanida Catalana (Catalan Salad), 160

Amanida de Bacallà (Salt Cod Salad), 174

Amanida de Faves amb Menta (Fava Salad with Fresh Mint), 106

Amanida de Llenties (Lentil Salad), 108

Amanida de Mongets i Bacallà Empordà (Empordà-Style Black-Eyed Pea and Salt Cod Salad), 110

Amanida Valenciana (Valencian Salad), 162

Esqueixada (Shredded Salt Cod Salad), 172

Esqueixada de Lluç amb Caviar (Marinated Hake Salad with Caviar), 174

Esqueixada de Pollastre (Shredded Chicken Salad), 175

Esqueixada Estil Llorenç Torrado (Llorenç Torrado's Shredded Salt Cod Salad), 173

Trempó (Majorcan Salad), 163

Xató (Salt Cod and Tuna Salad with *Romesco* [Spicy Nut Sauce] Dressing), 163

EGG AND VEGETABLE DISHES

Albergínies Farcides amb Anxoves (Stuffed Eggplant with Anchovies), 48

Bledes amb Panses i Pinyons (Swiss Chard with Raisins and Pine Nuts), 275

Bolets a la Graella (Grilled Wild Mushrooms), 91

Bunyols de Ciurenys (Cepe Fritters), 90

Cassola d'Albergínies (Eggplant "Omelet" with Raisins and Pine Nuts), 52

Escalivada (Catalan Roasted Vegetables), 170

Estofat de Quaresma (Catalan Vegetable Stew), 236

Flam d'Albergínies (Eggplant Flan), 51

Ous Remenat amb Bolets, Tofones, i Manxego (Scrambled Eggs with Wild Mushrooms, Truffles, and Manchego Cheese), 124

Patates a la Catalana (Catalan-Style Stuffed Potatoes), 185

Patates amb Allioli (Scalloped Potatoes with *Allioli*), 276

Patates amb Rabassoles (Potatoes with Morels), 92

Samfaina (Catalan Mixed Vegetables), 42

Truita de Pagès (Farmer's Omelet), 123

POULTRY, GAME, AND RABBIT
(MAIN DISHES ONLY)

MEAT
(MAIN DISHES ONLY)

PASTRIES AND DESSERTS

BEVERAGES

BIBLIOGRAPHY

In the following partial bibliography, double last names joined by hyphen or conjunction are alphabetized according to the first of the two names (i.e., Newnham-Davis under *N* and Torrents i Olivella under *T*); those not so joined appear under the latter of the two (i.e., Abrinas Vidal under *V*). When an author is listed under more than one form of his or her name, however, all listings appear under whichever form comes first alphabetically. Official government publications are listed alphabetically under the author's name when given, otherwise alphabetically under the title, interspersed with authors' listings. The latter form is also followed for anonymous works.

Most of the foreign-language sources cited here are in Catalan, Castilian (Spanish), or French. These are indicated as follows: (C) for Catalan, (S) for Castilian, and (F) for French. Other languages are identified by name when necessary. Books with no indication of language are of course in English. I have marked works on which I have relied particularly heavily with an asterisk (*).

1. COOKBOOKS, WINE BOOKS, HISTORY AND BACKGROUND.

Adserà i Martorell, Antoni, *El Romesco.* Tarragona: Llibreria Adserà, 1983 (C).

*Agulló, Ferran, *Llibre de la cuina catalana.* 6th ed. Barcelona: Editorial Alta Fulla, 1985 (C). (This is an augmented facsimile of the 1933 2nd ed., Llibreria Puig i Alfonso, Barcelona.)

Alziator, Francesco, *Il Folklore sardo.* Bologna: Edizioni La Zattera, 1957 (Italian).

*Ballester, Pedro, *De re cibaria.* 4th ed. Barcelona: Editorial Sintes, 1979 (S/C).

*Bettónica, Luís, *Cocina regional española.* Barcelona: Ediciones Hymsa, and Milan: Arnoldo Mondadori Editore, 1981 (S). (This book is also available in an English translation as *The Feast of Spain.* New York: A&W Pub., Inc., 1982.)

Bettónica, Luís, Manuel Ibañez i Escofat, and Josep Valls i Grau, *Un Home de Cadaqués, Portbou i Figueres.* Girona: No publisher given, 1986 (C/S).

Bullich, Josep, *Hàbits gastronòmics dels catalans.* 2nd ed. Barcelona: D.E.A.P.P., 1985 (C).

Callizo, Gloria Rossi, *La Cuina catalana.* Barcelona: Edicions Cap Roig, 1986 (C).

Camo, Louis, et al., *Les Vins du Roussillon.* Paris: Éditions Montalba, 1980 (F).

Casas, Carmen, *Barcelona a la carta.* Barcelona: Editorial Laia, 1981 (S).

——— *Barcelona en 50 menús.* Barcelona: Ediciones Juan Granica, 1983 (S).

——— *Comer en Catalunya.* Madrid: Ediciones Penthalon, 1980 (S).

Casas, Carmen, and Guillermina Boyata, *Catalunya en 50 menús.* Barcelona: Ediciones Juan Granica, 1983 (S).

Casas, Penelope, *The Foods & Wines of Spain.* New York: Knopf, 1982.

Catalogo de embutidos y jamones curados de España. Madrid: Ministerio de Agricultura, Pesca y Alimentación, 1983 (S).

Cinc mil refranys catalans i frases fetes, populars. Barcelona: Biblioteca Popular Catalana Vell i Nou/Editorial Millà, 1985 (C).

Ciurana, Jaume, *Els Vins catalans.* Barcelona: Departament d'Agricultura, Ramaderia i Pesca/Generalitat de Catalunya, 1980 (C).

Ciurana, Jaume, and Llorenç Torrado, *Els Olis de Catalunya i la seva cuina.* Barcelona: Departament d'Agricultura, Ramaderia i Pesca/Generalitat de Catalunya, 1981 (C).

Collier, Basil, *Catalan France.* London: J. M. Dent & Sons, 1939.

Comarques de Catalunya. Barcelona: Departament de Comerç i Turisme/Generalitat de Catalunya, 1984 (C).

Congres Catala de la Cuina, 1ᵉʳ, 1981–1982. Barcelona: Departament de Comerç i Turisme/Generalitat de Catalunya, 1984 (C).

Corrall, Caty Juan de, *Cocina balear/Las Cuatro estaciones.* Palma de Mallorca: Caja de Baleares ''Sa Nostra,'' 1985 (S).

La Cuina de l'Empordanet/Recull de receptes, 2.ª Mostra Gastronomica de Costa Brava Centre. Barcelona: L'Edició d'Antalbe, 1985 (C).

Cunill de Bosch, Joseph, *La Cuyna catalana.* Barcelona: Llibreria de Francesch Puig, 1907 (C).

La Cuynera catalana. 2nd ed. Barcelona: Editorial Alta Fulla, 1982 (C). (This is a facsimile of the original 1851 edition, Torras, Barcelona.)

Davidson, Alan, *Mediterranean Seafood.* 3rd ed. London: Penguin Books, 1981.

Davis, Irving, *A Catalan Cookery Book/A Collection of Impossible Recipes.* Edited by Patience Gray. Paris: privately published in an edition of 165 copies, 1969.

Domènech, Ignasi, *Àpats.* 3rd ed. Barcelona: Editorial Laia, 1979 (C).

——— *Llaminadures.* Barcelona: Pequeña Biblioteca Calamus Scriptorius, 1980 (C). (This is a facsimile of the original 1929 edition, Tipografia Bonet, Barcelona.)

——— La Teca. 14th ed. Barcelona: Edicions Marc 90, 1984 (C).

Eiximenis, Francesc, *Com usar be de beure e menjar.* Edited by Jorge J. E. Garcia. Barcelona: Classics Curial, 1983 (C). (This consists of selections from *Lo Crestià,* 1384.)

*Espinàs, Josep M., *Del rebost i de la taula.* Barcelona: Editorial Pòrtic, 1975 (C).

Fàbrega, Jaume, *La Cuina gironina*. Barcelona: Graffiti Edicions/Editorial Laia, 1985 (C).

Johnson, Hugh, *The World Atlas of Wine*. 3rd ed. New York: Simon & Schuster, 1985.

Lassus, P. L., *Cocina de cuaresma*. Barcelona: Francisco Puig, 1904 (S).

Libre de Sent Soví/Receptari de cuina. Edited by Rudolf Grewe. Barcelona: Editorial Barcino, 1979 (C). (This is the definitive modern edition of a manuscript written c. 1324.)

Lladonosa, Josep, *La Cuina que torna*. 3rd ed. Barcelona: Editorial Laia, 1982 (C).

Lladonosa i Giro, Josep, *La Cuina medieval catalana*. Barcelona: Editorial Laia, 1984 (C).

*Luján, Nèstor, *El Menjar*. Barcelona: Dopesa 2, 1979 (C).

*Luján, Nèstor and Tin, *La Cocina moderna en Cataluña*. Madrid: Espasa-Calpe, 1985 (S/C).

March, Lourdes, *El Libro de la paella y de los arroces*. Madrid: Alianza Editorial, 1985 (S).

*Millo, Llorenç, *La Taula i la cuina*. Valencia: Diputaciò Provencial de Valencia, 1984 (C).

*Moli, Domènec, *A la recerca d'una cuina garrotxina*. Olot: no publisher given, 1982 (C).

*Montalbán, Manuel Vázquez, *L'Art del menjar in Catalunya*. 2nd ed. Barcelona: Edicions 62, 1984 (C).

Morell i Bitria, Josep María, *Els Fogons de Lleida*. Lérida: Dilagro, 1984 (C).

Newnham-Davis, Lieut.-Col., and Algernon Bastard, *The Gourmet's Guide to Europe*. London: Grant Richards, Ltd., 1903.

Nicolau, M. del Carme, *Cuina Catalana*. Barcelona: Llibres Guia Arimany, 1977 (C). (This work is also available in an English translation by Anna Lankester as *Catalan Cooking*. Barcelona: Editorial Miguel Arimany, 1972.)

Olot, Fra Sever d', *Llibre de l'art de quynar*. Perelada: Edicions de la Biblioteca del Palau de Perelada, 1982 (C). (This is the first printed edition of a manuscript written in 1787.)

Ortíz, José Guardiola, *Gastronomía Alicantina*. Alicante: Sucesor de Such, Serra y Compania, 1959 (S).

Palau i Ferrer, Pere C., *Les Plantes medicinals baleariques*. 3rd ed. Palma de Mallorca: Editorial Moll, 1983 (C).

Pascual, Ramon, *El Llibre dels bolets*. Barcelona: Pol-len Edicions, 1982 (C).

Penya, D. Pere d'Alcàntara (?), *La Cuyna mallorquina*. Palma de Mallorca: Palma Edicions, 1982 (C). (This is a facsimile of the 1886 edition, Bartomeu Reus, Felanitx.)

Pla, Josep, *Aigua de mar*. 3rd ed. Barcelona: Edicions Destino, 1982 (C).

———— *Alguns grans cuiners de l'Empordà*. Barcelona: Llibres a Mà, 1984 (C).

———— *De l'Empordanet a Barcelona*. 2nd ed. Barcelona: Edicions Destino, 1981 (C). (This book was originally published in 1942.)

Pla, Josep and F. Català Roca (photographer), *El Que hem menjat*. Barcelona: Edicions Destino, 1981 (C). (This book was originally published in 1971, without photographs.)

Platillos de l'Empordà. 2nd ed. Girona: Chaîne des Rotisseurs/Batllia, 1979 (C).

Pomés, Leopold, *Teoria i práctica del pa amb tomàquet*. Barcelona: Tusquets Editors, 1985 (C/S/French/English).

Read, Jan, *The Catalans*. London & Boston: Faber & Faber, 1978.

—— *The Simon & Schuster Pocket Guide to Spanish Wines*. New York: Simon & Schuster, 1983.

—— *The Wines of Spain*. London: Faber & Faber, 1982.

*Ripoll, Luís, *Cocina de las Baleares*. 3rd ed. Palma de Mallorca: Luís Ripoll, 1984 (S).

—— *Libro de cocina menorquina*. Palma de Mallorca: Luís Ripoll, 1983 (S).

*Robert, Mestre, *Libre del coch*. Edited by Veronika Leimgruber. 2nd ed. Barcelona: Biblioteca Torres Amat/Curial Edicions Catalanes, 1982 (C). (This is the definitive modern edition of a book first published in Barcelona, c. 1520; the author is also sometimes known as Robert or Rupert de Nola.)

Romero, Luís, *Libro de las tabernas de España*. Barcelona: Editorial AHR, 1956 (S).

Rondissoni, Josep, *Classes de cuina popular/Curs de 1924–1925*. Barcelona: Institut de Cultura i Biblioteca Popular de la Dona, no date (1925?) (C).

—— *Classes de cuina/Curs de 1927–1928*. Barcelona: Institut de Cultura i Biblioteca Popular de la Dona, no date (1928?) (C).

Salvia, Marta, *Art de ben menjar/Llibre català de cuina*. Revised by J. Cabané. Barcelona: Tipografía Emporium, no date (c. 1930) (C).

Serra, Josep, *Manual del cuiner*. Barcelona, no publisher given, 1914 (C).

Serrano, Vincenç, *Manual del boletaire català*. Barcelona: Editorial Barcino, 1959 (C).

Thibaut-Comelade, Eliane, *La Cuina medieval a l'abast*. Barcelona: Edicions de la Magrana, 1986 (C).

*—— *La Cuisine catalane*. Tome I. Malakoff: Éditions J. Lanore, 1984 (F).

*—— *La Cuisine catalane*. Tome II. *Països valencians/Baléars*. 3rd ed. Malakoff: Éditions J. Lanore, 1984 (F).

—— *La Pomme du Conflent et d'ailleurs*. Villefranche-de-Conflent Syndicate Intercommunal de la Vallée de la Rotja, 1984 (F).

Thibaut-Comelade, Eliane, and Pierre Torrés, *Gastronomie et vins du Roussillon*. Perpignan: Crédit Agricole des Pyrénées-Orientales, 1982 (F).

Torrado, Llorenç, *Els Embotits a Catalunya*. Barcelona: Federatió Catalana d'Indústries de la Carn/Departament d'Agricultura, Ramaderia i Pesca/Generalitat de Catalunya, 1985 (C).

Torres, Marimar, *The Spanish Table: The Cuisines and Wines of Spain*. Garden City, N.Y.: Doubleday & Co., 1986.

Trueta, J., *The Spirit of Catalonia*. London: Oxford University Press, 1946.

*Vidal, Coloma Abrinas, *Cocina selecta mallorquina*. 15th ed. Palma de Mallorca: no publisher given, 1982 (S).

Watt, Bernice K., and Annabel L. Merrill, *Composition of Foods*. Agriculture Handbook No. 8, 2nd ed. Washington, D.C.: Government Printing Office, 1975.

Wolfert, Paula, *The Cooking of South-West France*. Garden City, N.Y.: The Dial Press/Doubleday & Co., 1983.

2. REFERENCE WORKS AND GUIDEBOOKS

Alcover, Mn. Antoni Maria, *Diccionari català-valencià-balear.* Edited by Francesc de B. Moll with Manuel Sanchis Guarner. 10 volumes. Palma de Mallorca: no publisher given, 1977.

Campa, Maria del Carmen, Maria Teresa Campa, Jep Montoya, and Andres Ané, *Ûn Libret dera Val d'Aran.* Barcelona: no publisher given, 1983 (Aranese).

Colomer, Jordi, *Nou diccionari anglès-català/català-anglès.* Barcelona: Editorial Pòrtic, 1983 (C/English).

Fabra, Pompeu, *Diccionari general de la llengua catalana.* 20th ed. Barcelona: Edhasa, 1985 (C).

Gili, Joan, *Catalan Grammar.* 4th ed. Oxford: Dolphin Book Co., 1974.

Oliva, Salvador, and Angela Buxton, *Diccionari anglès-català.* 2nd ed. Barcelona: Enciclopedia Catalana, 1985. (C/English).

——— *Diccionari català-anglès.* Barcelona: Enciclopedia Catalana, 1986 (C/English).

Recull de restaurants, fondes i cases de menjars. Barcelona: Departament de Comerç i Turisme/Departament d'Agricultura, Ramaderia i Pesca/Generalitat de Catalunya, 1982 (C).

3. ARTICLES AND PAPERS

*Grewe, Rudolf, "Catalan Cuisine, in an Historical Perspective," in Alan Davidson, ed., *National and Regional Styles of Cookery/Oxford Symposium 1981.* London: Prospect Books, 1981.

Perry, Charles, "Buran: 1100 Years in the Life of a Dish," *The Journal of Gastronomy,* Vol. 1 (Summer 1984).

——— "The Oldest Mediterranean Noodle: A Cautionary Tale," *Petits Propos Culinaires* 9 (October 1981).

——— "Puff Paste is Spanish," *Petits Propos Culinaires* 17 (June 1984).

INDEX

INDEX

ABOUT THE AUTHOR

Colman Andrews, the editor of *Saveur* magazine, is one of America's most distinguished writers on food. In addition to *Catalan Cuisine,* he has also written *Everything on the Table* and *Flavors of the Riviera.* One of the fifty inaugural members of the James Beard Foundation's Who's Who of Food and Beverage in America, he was awarded the M.F.K. Fisher Distinguished Writing Award by the Beard Foundation in 1998 and the Bert Greene Award for magazine food journalism by the International Association of Culinary Professionals in 1996. Formerly a columnist for the *Los Angeles Times* and *Los Angeles Magazine,* he has also written for *Metropolitan Home, Travel & Leisure, Food & Wine,* and *Bon Appétit,* among other publications. He lives in Old Greenwich, Connecticut.